Readers' Advisory Service
in North American Public
Libraries, 1870–2005

Readers' Advisory Service in North American Public Libraries, 1870–2005

A History and Critical Analysis

Juris Dilevko and Candice F.C. Magowan

McFarland & Company, Inc., Publishers
Jefferson, North Carolina, and London

Juris Dilevko and coauthor Lisa Gottlieb are the authors of
*Reading and the Reference Librarian: The Importance to
Library Service of Staff Reading Habits* (McFarland, 2004)

LIBRARY OF CONGRESS CATALOGUING-IN-PUBLICATION DATA

Dilevko, Juris.
   Readers' advisory service in North American public libraries,
1870–2005 : a history and critical analysis / Juris Dilevko and
Candice F.C. Magowan.
      p.   cm.
   Includes bibliographical references and index.

   ISBN-13: 978-0-7864-2925-7
   (softcover : 50# alkaline paper) ∞

   1. Readers' advisory services—United States.   2. Readers' advisory
services—Canada.   I. Magowan, Candice F.C.   II. Title.
Z711.55.D55   2007
025.5'4097—dc22   2006037124

British Library cataloguing data are available

On the cover: School librarian and assistant, Woodrow Wilson High School,
Washington, D.C., 1943 (Library of Congress); background and student ©
2007 Photospin

Manufactured in the United States of America

McFarland & Company, Inc., Publishers
   Box 611, Jefferson, North Carolina 28640
      www.mcfarlandpub.com

Table of Contents

Preface and Acknowledgments

This is not a conventional history of adult readers' advisory service in North America that recounts the accepted version of its evolution. Instead, it is a critical history of readers' advisory philosophy based on our interpretation and analysis of published sources. Many public librarians will no doubt object to our interpretation of the historical arc of readers' advisory service. We nevertheless offer what we hope will be a thought-provoking and unique perspective of what the *Dictionary for Library and Information Science* defines as a set of services provided to adult library patrons "by an experienced public services librarian" who "recommends specific titles and/or authors, based on knowledge of the patron's past reading preferences, and [who] may also compile lists of recommended titles and serve as liaison to other adult education agencies in the community."[1]

We have necessarily drawn heavily upon the accounts of previous writers who have explored the history of various periods of readers' advisory service and adult education efforts in North American public libraries. Especially valuable for our purposes were Esther Jane Carrier, *Fiction in Public Libraries, 1876–1900*; Stephen Karetzky, *Reading Research and Librarianship: A History and Analysis*; Robert Ellis Lee, *Continuing Education for Adults through the American Public Library, 1833–1964*; and Margaret E. Monroe's *Library Adult Education: The Biography of an Idea*. Our thinking process about readers' advisory began by reading these authors and then referring to the footnotes and endnotes for the sources that they relied on. Our book could not have been written without these works, nor could it have been written without all the other books, articles, and documents mentioned in our endnotes and bibliography. We are very much indebted to all the authors that we cite. We recognize, however, that these authors would likely not agree with the general argument of our book.

We also acknowledge the following individuals for their help. Joe Cox, Director and Metadata & Borrower Services Librarian, Inforum, Faculty of Information Studies, University of Toronto, allowed Juris Dilevko to have a microfilm reader in his office for an extended period during the latter part of 2005. He also gave Juris Dilevko extended access to rare materials typically kept in storage or special-collections areas. Adam Lauder and Patrick Mooney reminded Juris Dilevko of the importance of Guy Debord's *Society of the Spectacle* for understanding the late 20th-century emphasis on entertainment in public libraries. This they did through their essays submitted for the course "Readers' Advisory: Reference Work and Resources" taught by Juris Dilevko at the Faculty of Information Studies, University of Toronto, during the Winter 2005 term.

Above all, we would like to acknowledge 69 students in two iterations of that same course in Summer 2004 as well as Winter 2005. These students allowed two of their graded assignments to be used for Case Study 1 of chapter 6 of this book. Additional details about these assignments are contained in Appendix A. Each participating student was given a print credit of $5 for each assignment that he or she allowed to be used for the purposes of Case Study 1 in chapter 6. Students were given a choice as to whether they wished to be acknowledged by name. The following students indicated that they wished to be acknowledged publicly for their contribution of both assignments: Jennifer Burns; Antonia Castro; Christine Dalgetty; Amy Fenton; Amanda French; Rachelle Gooden; Naseem Hrab; Krista Jensen; Monique Koevoets; Susan Lai; Anuska Lawrence; Alexia Loumankis; Athanasios Maragos; Eric McDonald; Mindy Myers; Annie Ng; Jennifer Peters-lise; Cameron Ray; Jennifer Schmitt; Anne Simms; Jessica Waintman; and Colleen Williamson. We thank them again. Our book would have been immeasurably poorer without their collective and individual contributions.

Funds to cover the payments for print credits were drawn from the University of Toronto Faculty Association (UTFA) annual allowance provided to each faculty member, as negotiated in annual contracts between the University of Toronto and UTFA. We thank Susan A. Brown, Finance and Personnel Officer, Faculty of Information Studies, University of Toronto, for allowing Juris Dilevko to use a part of his allotted UTFA allowances in the fiscal years 2003–2004 and 2004–2005 for the above-mentioned purpose. We also thank Joe Cox for ensuring that each student received the appropriate amount of print credits. Any royalties that may accrue from sales of this book are being donated to the Toronto Humane Society for the Safety and Protection of Animals.

Chapter 1

Staking Out the Territory
of Readers' Advisory Service

Starting in the early 1980s, readers' advisory became a much-discussed topic in North American public libraries. By 2005, almost every public library in the United States and Canada offered some form of readers' advisory service. Words such as renaissance, resurgence, and revival—indicators that readers' advisory had been of crucial importance for public librarianship in the past, but more recently had fallen on hard times—were used to describe the explosion of interest in readers' advisory between 1980 and 2005. An important catalyst for the promotion and growth of readers' advisory in public libraries in the late 1980s, 1990s, and 2000s was the Adult Reading Round Table (ARRT).[1] Founded by a group of Chicago-area public librarians in 1984, ARRT sponsored local readers' advisory workshops, seminars, and genre-study groups, stimulating other public librarians to implement readers' advisory service at their home institutions as word of ARRT's efforts reached a national stage.[2]

By the early 2000s, numerous libraries subscribed to NoveList and/or What Do I Read Next?—electronic databases that, in addition to containing synopses and reviews of recent fiction, delivered suggestions about future reading material to patrons based on customizable searches. The web sites of many public libraries featured readers' advisory sections, which often contained long lists of fiction and nonfiction titles in various genres and about various topics. Some public libraries offered live chat-based readers' advisory and e-mail "reading recommendation services."[3] "Fiction_L," an electronic mailing list for "all aspects of reader's advisory for children, young adults and adults, including non-fiction materials," was labeled in 2005 as "[t]he most important web-based resource for readers' advisory"—a far cry from its origins in 1995 as a "treasure hunt[]" activity for "those elusive patron requests for a five-year-old suspense novel, set in the wilds of Montana, with a red cover."[4] Librarians recommended genre-specific online book groups, such as 4_Mystery_Addicts (4MA), as "extraordinary" sources of readers' advisory information for "avid readers" because these clubs engaged in "regularly scheduled and impromptu sharing of reading lists and ad hoc reviews, forming a worldwide network of friends in the process."[5] Taking note of the growing interest in fiction spurred by the resurgence of readers' advisory, the Online Computer Library Center (OCLC) began to offer FictionFinder, described as a "prototype [system] for fiction in WorldCat."[6] Based on the Functional Requirements for Bibliographic Records (FRBR) data model, FictionFinder extracted "elements that are potentially useful in finding and selecting a work of fiction, such as summaries, genre terms, and subject headings" from bibliographic entries. It then filtered, indexed, and displayed them in visually appealing catalog records so that librarians and readers could search by genre, setting, imaginary place, fictitious characters, and other categories.

An avalanche of readers' advisory print resources also inundated librarians and patrons. By late 2005, the *Genreflecting Advisory Series*, which provided annotated lists of reading suggestions in popular fictional genres such as romance and horror for different age groups, featured more than 15 titles, including *Blood, Bedlam, Bullets, and Badguys: A Reader's Guide to Adventure/Suspense Fiction*; *Make Mine a Mystery: A Reader's Guide to Mystery and Detective Fiction*; *Strictly Science Fiction: A Guide to Reading Interests*; and *Christian Fiction: A Guide to the Genre*.[7] *The Real Story: A Guide to Nonfiction Reading Interests*, which included nonfiction genres such as True Adventure, Travel, True Crime, Environmental Writing, Memoirs and Autobiographies, Relationships, and Making Sense, was added to the series in 2006.[8] Its flagship title, *Genreflecting: A Guide to Reading Interests in Genre Fiction*, reached six editions by early 2006. The first edition, written in 1982 by Betty Rosenberg, contained 254 pages and positioned genre fiction as the central arena in which readers' advisory work was conducted.[9] The third edition, published in 1991, had 345 pages; it initiated the gradual transfer of the *Genreflecting* enterprise to Diana Tixier Herald.[10] The fifth edition, published in 2000, was 553 pages, and the sixth edition, published in early 2006, had 559 pages.[11] The spectacular increase in page counts alone was a testimony to the widespread legitimization of genre fiction and entertainment-oriented reading in the late 20th and early 21st centuries.

Not to be outdone, the American Library Association (ALA) published multiple editions of Joyce G. Saricks and Nancy Brown's *Readers' Advisory Service in the Public Library* and, in 2001, Saricks's *The Readers' Advisory Guide to Genre Fiction*.[12] Again, page counts of the three editions of *Readers' Advisory Service in the Public Library* published up to and including 2005 revealed a phenomenal growth of interest in readers' advisory work. While the first edition in 1989 had 84 pages, the second edition in 1997 almost doubled to 160 pages. The third edition in 2005 reached 211 pages. The *ALA Readers' Advisory Series* included titles such as *The Horror Readers' Advisory: The Librarian's Guide to Vampires, Killer Tomatoes, and Haunted Houses* and *The Romance Readers' Advisory: The Librarian's Guide to Love in the Stacks*.[13]

Edited collections offering practical essays about how libraries could improve their readers' advisory service also mushroomed. In the 1990s, *Developing Readers' Advisory Services: Concepts and Commitments*, edited by Kathleen de la Peña McCook and Gary O. Rolstad, was followed by *Guiding the Reader to the Next Book*, edited by Kenneth D. Shearer.[14] In the 2000s, *The Readers' Advisor's Companion* and *Nonfiction Readers' Advisory*, both of which were either edited or co-edited by Robert Burgin, appeared.[15] Nancy Pearl became a celebrity on the strength of *Book Lust* and *More Book Lust*, two books that listed her favorite fiction and nonfiction on a wide array of topics.[16] In addition, there was an outpouring of articles and columns in professional library journals dissecting every aspect of readers' advisory and encouraging all public librarians to institute it. Beginning with its winter 2000 issue, *Reference & User Services Quarterly* published a readers' advisory column edited by Mary K. Chelton.[17] Other than Juris Dilevko and Keren Dali's 2003 article that identified shortcomings in the way that NoveList provided intellectual access to translated fiction, there was little critical analysis about post–1980 readers' advisory.[18] It is no exaggeration to say that readers' advisory was a major phenomenon in public libraries during 1980–2005.

The concept of readers' advisory has a vibrant history that can be traced back to the beginnings of the public-library movement in North America. But throughout the late 1990s and early 2000s, that history was viewed through a self-satisfied and triumphalist lens such that the ubiquity and success of post–1980 "New-Style" readers' advisory was presented as proof of its virtue and the correctness of its philosophical underpinnings. This book has two purposes. First, we outline major developments in the evolution of readers' advisory service for adults in North American public libraries from their origins circa 1870 to circa 2005. What debates shaped and accompanied readers' advisory throughout its history? How did it assume its present form? These questions are discussed in chapter 2 from a broad ideological perspective. Chapter 3 examines the period 1870–1916, while chapter 4 describes developments between 1917 and 1962. Chapter 5 covers 1963–2005, with emphasis on the post–1980 period. Chapter 6 contains case studies about the NoveList database and Pearl's *Book Lust* series. Chapter 7 offers recommendations for the future.

We argue that post–1980 readers' advisory has lost its way. It focused less on the meaningful educational and cultural rationale with which it was associated in its earlier phases than on a mindset in which the reading of books, no matter their intrinsic quality, is construed as good and where discretionary reading becomes commodified and disposable entertainment, as manifested principally in genre fiction and genre nonfiction (genre titles), bestsellers, celebrity-authored books, and prize-winning titles. This philosophy was an outgrowth of the 1960s' "Give 'Em What They Want" movement,[19] which employed the rhetoric of 1960s' New Left cultural dissent to entrench demand-driven collection development and readers' advisory service that disproportionately benefited economically advantaged users, providing them with commodified and entertainment-oriented products. Originally associated with the Baltimore County (Maryland) Public Library system, the "Give 'Em What They Want" philosophy claimed that "[a] book of outstanding quality is not worth its price if no one will read it," paid attention "to the books mentioned on yesterday's *Donahue Show*," and bought multiple copies of bestsellers.[20] We suggest that post–1980 readers' advisory was an unwitting promoter of unfettered capitalism despite the fact that its practitioners liked to see themselves as stalwart defenders of a 1960s' New Left counterculture ethos based on a radical interrogation of existing social structures. If readers' advisory in North American public libraries is to be a real force in community life in the 2000s and beyond, we recommend that it re-assume the mantle of meaningful education with which it was invested in its pre–1963 period.

The Rise of Market Censorship

There was a tangled skein of reasons for the proliferation of genre titles, bestsellers, celebrity-authored books, and prize-winning titles in North American public libraries starting in the 1960s—a proliferation that reached flood-like proportions in the late 1990s and early 2000s. As the phenomenon of 1960s' New Left dissent swept across the political and social landscape, many public librarians wanted to imbricate themselves and their institutions in the groundswell of countercultural rhetoric and ideas, thus proving their relevance to changing times. Allegiance to forms of popular culture became synonymous with social dissent. Opening the public library to popular culture implied opening it to everyone who—and everything that—had been previously excluded. Popular culture became a metonym for a user-centered public library that constantly strove to satisfy customer demands, gauging those demands through questionnaires whose collective responses were quickly implemented so as to make the library even more user-friendly and responsive. And so between 1963 and 2005, genre titles, bestsellers, celebrity-authored books, and prize-winning titles became the mainstay of public-library collections, functioning as proxies for "Give 'Em What They Want" popular culture. They were deemed worthy simply because popular culture was positioned as a necessary alternative to what was perceived as 1950s' conformism. Patrons metamorphosed into consumers, and consumers, as anyone who has taken a single business course knows all too well, are unabashed kings and queens whose slightest wish is to be met, preferably yesterday.

This is not to say that genre titles had not been present in public libraries before the 1960s. As Hans Robert Jauss notes, epics and romances are some of the oldest forms of literature,[21] and public libraries typically carried these genres, as well as mysteries and westerns.[22] Neither is this to say that bestsellers, celebrity-authored books, and prize-winning titles were not present in public libraries before the 1960s.[23] As Christine Pawley documented in *Reading on the Middle Border*, a study of the reading practices of residents of Osage, Iowa, 19 out of the top 21 circulated library books between 1890 and 1895 were fiction, and only 8 of those 19 fiction titles were listed in the ALA "model library," which Pawley called a "rough indicator of acceptance by cultural authorities."[24] What changed was the sheer quantity of popular and ephemeral fiction and nonfiction titles that found a ready welcome there. What also changed was the extended promotion and valorization that these books received through the actions of readers' advisors. Most importantly, public libraries were faced with inordinate pressures generated by the marketing efforts of publishing conglomerates because an entertainment-obsessed public demanded that the cultural products of this marketing onslaught be made available in tax-supported public libraries.

Many readers' advisors succumbed to these pressures, transforming helplessness into a virtue by formulating what they thought to be a dutiful theory of responsiveness in which customer demand was accorded the highest priority. One example was *The Responsive Public Library: How to Develop and Market a Winning Collection*, a popular handbook by Sharon L. Baker and Karen L. Wallace that was published in its second edition in 2002.[25] We discuss this book further in chapter 2. Others saw the flood of genre titles and bestsellers as a challenging opportunity that, if correctly framed, had many benefits for readers. Saricks and Brown developed the theory of appeal elements, which we analyze in chapter 5. In a series of articles in the 1990s that culminated in *Reading Matters* in 2005,[26] Catherine Sheldrick Ross extended Janice A. Radway's insights from *Reading the Romance: Women, Patriarchy, and Popular Literature*. Based on reader-response theory, Radway's book argued that active audiences engaged in a process of personal meaning-making from the torrent of entertainment-based cultural products that was part of their daily lives.[27] For Radway, Ross, and Saricks and Brown, there was inherent value in genre titles and bestsellers. The result was a public library where readers' advisors promulgated an ethos driven by seemingly harmless-sounding watchwords such as pleasure reading or recreational reading. But it was also an ethos that was based on reacting to the dictates of the powerful structural forces undergirding entertainment-oriented cultural production in general and book publishing in particular. We discuss Radway further in chapter 2 and Ross in chapter 5.

As Pierre Bourdieu explained in *An Invitation to Reflexive Sociology*, social microcosms such as professions may be considered as contested fields, where individuals and groups that possess various "species of capital"—especially social, cultural, economic, and symbolic capital—compete and struggle to define and shape the structure of the field on their specific terms.[28] The profession of public librarianship, and more specifically the profession of readers' advisor, is no exception. For readers' advisors, the struggle centers around the question of which type of cultural production (i.e., books) will be privileged within the library and, by extension, which books will be suggested to patrons. Readers' advisors therefore must understand the dynamics of the literary field, which is "the site of the antagonistic coexistence of two modes of production and circulation obeying inverse logics."[29] The choices that readers' advisors make with regard to the books they suggest to patrons therefore position them in relation to the stakes at play in the literary field. These choices are also instrumental in defining the field of readers' advisory.

Readers' advisory is an important field, since it plays a crucial role in mediating between the production capacities of the publishing industry and potential readers. And even though it is ancillary and tangential to the literary field, readers' advisory is all the more important because it is so far down the rung of "institutional filters" through which "cultural productions must pass ... prior to reaching a 'public.'"[30] Because readers' advisors are often the penultimate filter between publishers and readers, they potentially affect "the geography of reading" in any given community.[31] Will readers' advisors be content to pass down (to library patrons) what has already been institutionally filtered down to them (as librarians) through multiple layers, in effect replicating the existing power relationships inherent in upstream institutional filters? Or will readers' advisors decide to step outside the institutional matrix and act as necessary counterweights to powerful institutional forces by making reading suggestions that go against prevailing commercial trends?

Competing Definitions

According to Bourdieu in *The Rules of Art: Genesis and Structure of the Literary Field*, at one end of the cultural-production spectrum "there is the 'economic' logic of the literary and artistic industries which, since they make the trade in cultural goods just another trade, confer priority on distribution, on immediate and temporary success, measured for example by the print run, and which are content to adjust themselves to the pre-existing demand of a clientèle."[32] This is the "commercial pole" of the literary field, consisting of "heteronomous" publishers that produce "industrial literature."[33] A publishing entity approaches this pole "the more directly or completely the products it offers on the market respond to a *pre-existing demand*, and in *pre-established forms*."[34] These entities have "a *short production cycle*, aiming to minimize risks by an advance adjustment to predictable demand and benefiting from commercial networks and procedures for marketing (advertising, public relations, etc.) designed to ensure the accelerated return of profits by a rapid circulation of products which are fated to rapid obsolescence."[35] For heteronomous publishers and writers, along with the public that reads these writers, "success is in itself a guarantee of value."[36] At the other end of the spectrum, there is "the anti-'economic' economy of pure art," which is based on "the obligatory recognition of the values of disinterestedness and on the denegation ... of 'economic' profit (in the short term)."[37] Emphasizing "the accumulation of symbolic capital," this type of literary production—which has "no market in the present," accepts a large degree of risk, and is avant-garde or "autonomous"—may generate profits "under certain conditions and in the long term."[38] At that point, it becomes part of "the classics," defined as "lasting bestsellers which owe to the education system their consecration, hence their extended and durable market."[39]

Most, if not all, publishing ventures fall somewhere between these "two extremes," never attaining "either total and cynical subordination to demand or absolute independence from the market and its exigencies."[40] One way to situate them on the spectrum is to examine "the share they give to risky, long-term investments and to sure, short-term investments and, by the same token, according to the proportion among their authors of writers for the long term and writers for the short term, the latter including journalists who extend their ordinary activity by 'topical' writings, 'personalities' who offer their 'testimony' in essays or autobiographical accounts and professional writers who bow to the canons of a tested aesthetic ('prize-winning' literature, successful novels, etc.)."[41] But one of the greatest dangers to the entire literary field is that heteronomous producers are systematically encroaching upon the purview of autonomous producers through various strategies, exercising an ever-tighter grip not only "over the instruments of circulation," but also "of consecration."[42]

As a result, "industrial literature" is stronger than ever, since "the logic of commercial production tends more and more to assert itself over avant-garde production (notably, in the case of literature, through the constraints of the book market)."[43]

Middle-brow culture can be understood as the quintessential example of this "blurring of boundaries"[44] because it works very hard to provide "accessible versions" (or "outward signs") of legitimate or autonomous culture.[45] Middle-brow culture, which is "the product[s] of a productive system dominated by the quest for investment profitability," is "characterized by tried and proven techniques and an oscillation between plagiarism and parody most often linked with either indifference or conservatism" because of the need to reach "the widest possible public."[46] This should not be surprising, since it is "most often the culmination of transactions and compromises among ... various categories of agents" who successfully use "their specific competencies to guarantee a wide variety of cultural interests" and "reactivat[e] the self-censorship engendered by the vast industrial and bureaucratic organizations of cultural production through invocation of the 'average spectator.'"[47]

The results of these processes are "film 'adaptations' of classic drama and literature"[48] or books that "grip[] you within the first three pages" and are "easily read by the widest possible public,"[49] a public that has been falsely convinced, through various strategies engaged in by the producers of middle-brow art, that a specific middle-brow art product is really an example of high art. The public therefore becomes complicit in the imposture, since it "has most interest in taking the copy for the original, like the purchasers of 'seconds,' 'rejects,' cut-price or second-hand goods, who need to convince themselves that 'it's cheaper and creates the same effect.'"[50] In sum, items of middle-brow culture become "fetishized commodities" insofar as the public has little knowledge of the vast subterranean apparatus of "social relations" that has produced them.[51]

Strategies to Create Demand

By instruments of circulation and consecration, Bourdieu meant increasingly pervasive strategies that publishing houses used "to catch the attention of journalists who will make [an item of cultural production] exist by speaking about it."[52] Alain Roy summarized these strategies as "the tacit and tactical alliance between cultural industries, the discourse of publicity, sponsoring agencies, and the mass media."[53] As Joe Moran observed in *Star Authors: Literary Celebrity in America*, because book publishing is an integral part of vast entertainment conglomerates that also own movie and music production and distribution companies; newspapers and magazines; television, cable, and radio stations; and online services, multiple "opportunities" are created for book publishers "to decide which authors are noticed and read by consumers."[54] Engaging in "cross-subsidization between different strata of the same company," corporations manufactured "synergy in the area of book publicity" so that "the largest possible readership for a small number of books" was created.[55] Books published by one division of an entertainment conglomerate turned into movies or television shows produced by another division of the same conglomerate, which were then promoted by its magazines, television news and talk shows, and web ventures. In "Stacked," the Fox television show "revolving around a ditzy character played by Pamela Anderson who works in a bookstore, the books on display are from HarperCollins," not surprising since the Fox television network and HarperCollins Publishers were both units of News Corporation.[56]

In an inventive twist on cross-subsidization, the presidents of ABC Daytime, part of the ABC television network, and Hyperion, a publisher of general-interest fiction and non-fiction, both divisions of the Walt Disney Company, developed a plan that the president of Hyperion described as "the synergy answer to quantum physics."[57] Scriptwriters of the ABC Daytime show "One Life to Live," seen by "about 3 million viewers a day," created a storyline in which one of the main characters, Marcie Walsh, a resident of the fictional town of Llanview, "decided to write a mystery novel."[58] At the same time as "One Life to Live" engaged in a year-long buildup in which the show's plot centered on Walsh's struggles to complete her novel and "a climax with a pretend on-air book party" after it was "accepted," Michael Malone, one of the scriptwriters for "One Life to Live" and a published mystery writer, actually wrote Walsh's novel. The resulting book, *The Killing Club*, reached both the *New York Times* and *Wall Street Journal* bestseller lists. With about "150,000 copies in print," *The Killing Club* benefited from built-in publicity on "One Life to Live."[59] And with sequels and movie spin-offs on the horizon for "author" Marcie Walsh, her book was a cautionary example of the power wielded by profit-oriented publishers to influence reading choices.

Synergy was not the only technique that corporate publishers used to manufacture "buzz." Multi-dimensional promotional campaigns consisted of some combination of the following: word-of-mouth opinions, as spread by influential people to whom publishers sent advance copies of a book in the hope that they would become "big mouths" who vaunted the merits of the book within their spheres[60]; extensive advertising in newspapers and magazines; promotional book tours in which the author was positioned "as commodity" in "a weirdly dehumanizing experience"[61]; pre-arranged authorial interviews in print and electronic media, which invariably turned into puff pieces; the appearance of almost-simultaneous reviews in numerous national and local publications, a coordinated effort that was dependant on the number of free copies publishers could afford to send to reviewers; and "jacket photos of writers looking as sexy as possible, be they men à la mode de Sebastian Junger, adventure journalist extraordinaire, or brainy men looking sultry, or brainy women showing lots of skin."[62] Publishers complemented these techniques with strategies to "place" their books as advantageously as possible, all the while taking great pains to conceal the artificiality of the placement. The idea of "product placement" assumed numerous forms, ranging from "lifestyle" placement (where specific books were associated with products and services that were known to appeal to targeted demographic groups) to "product integration" (a promotional tactic whereby the name of a product was interwoven into films, television shows, video games, and books "not as an obvious ad, but as a distinct part of the story."[63] Often, these strategies imperceptibly blended and merged as publishers worked to "brand" individual books, authors, series, and even imprints.

Noticing that Tom's of Maine enjoyed "a 14 percent rise in toothpaste sales" after contracting with American Historic Inns (AHI) to place 1.8 million natural toothpaste tubes in hundreds of inns, Little, Brown and Company contracted with AHI to promote Anita Shreve's 2005 novel *A Wedding in December*.[64] AHI subsequently placed Shreve's novel in many of the same inns in which it had previously placed toothpaste, orange juice, and headache remedies.[65] Hoping that "a reader drawn into the book while tarrying over a stack of blueberry pancakes will subsequently drill into Ms. Shreve's backlist," Little, Brown not only created artificial demand for a book through a "seamless integration opportunity,"[66] but effectively admitted that a book was nothing more than a disposable commodity with a short-shelf life, just like toothpaste or orange juice.[67]

So-called "cooperative advertising agreements" were another example of placements. Here, publishers made payments to chain bookstores and electronic retailers for preferential placement of titles in stores or web sites, just as manufacturers of household products paid supermarkets "to put their boxes of cereal or detergent in eye-catching spots."[68] Publishers gave bookstores "a certain percentage of a publisher's net sales, usually 3 percent to

5 percent annually" in return for book displays near checkouts, end-of-aisle displays, tall and visible racks called "stepladders," or face-out displays on shelves.[69] Alternatively, they paid "between $10,000 and $20,000 per book" for "front-of-store promotional tables for only a few weeks or a month."[70] In the electronic realm, Amazon in 1999 offered an "E-merchandising" program for book publishers that, for fees up to $12,500, included "a wide variety of features such as ... E-mail alerts to customers about not-yet-published books or placement in the 'What We're Reading' slots of category pages for cooking or mysteries and thrillers." For example, Simon & Schuster, the publisher of Stephen King's Bag of Bones, paid $10,000 for a "Tier 1 premium package" that included "an author profile, feature coverage in the 'Destined for Greatness' category and announcements on [Amazon's] home page touting the book's on-sale date."[71] Stung by criticism about its e-merchandising plan, in the early 2000s Amazon revised its "paid placements" policy, offering publishers the "Buy X, Get Y" (BXGY) program, defined as "paid merchandising placements that increase the visibility of your product on Amazon.com by pairing it with another product and having it featured in the 'Best Value' section of each product's detail page."[72] Publishers whose annual retail sales with Amazon were less than $1 million were sent a list of bestsellers with which their books could be paired. They could then "pay $750 per month to be linked with one of Amazon's bestselling authors, sometimes pairing for multiple months and rotating among several bestsellers."[73] By making "promotion budgets even more lopsided in favor of the Stephen Kings and Danielle Steels of the book world," co-operative advertising agreements caused "a reverse Robin Hood effect" as they "further concentrate money and attention on the books that need it least," giving "new authors or less prominent books ... little advertising or display help."[74] Even in the case of Amazon's BXGY program, which was designed to help relatively small publishers, a publisher's financial resources dictated a book's popularity and sales. Selling books based on their intrinsic quality and cultural value was nothing more than a quaint notion.

Other publishers turned "to the film and television industries" for marketing inspiration, using "street teams," defined as "groups of young people armed with posters dispatched to talk up [a] book at events like concerts," and extensive web campaigns, which consisted of official promotional sites, blogs, "unofficial" web sites based on characters and entities present in the book in question, and the initiation of discussions in relevant online forums known to be frequented by individuals in the book's target demographic.[75] Still other publishers implemented "direct-to-consumer marketing" to build brand loyalty through tools such as "AuthorTracker, which lets readers sign up for e-mail updates when an author's next book is released," and "First Look, which provides early copies to some readers and solicits their reactions to aspects of the books, including the cover art."[76] According to Jane Friedman, president and chief executive of HarperCollins Publishers, the goal of this promotional activity was to hasten the day "when a reader in a bookstore will reach for a HarperCollins novel the way some parents of young children now reach for a Disney film in a video store—a result of faith in the producer rather than the specific content."[77] As some writers discovered, proposals for books that "don't articulate the message of the brand" were rejected, with publishers pointing to "market segmentation models" as proof of what customers did, and did not, want in a brand.[78]

Branding was also the primary impetus behind the rise of "book packagers" in the mold of 17th Street Productions (SSP).[79] In 2000, SSP was sold to Alloy Inc., described as a "web-focused marketing company that hosts a teen website ... and mails 40 million catalogs per year."[80] The merger resulted in a new company called Alloy Entertainment. Through its web site that discusses style, fashion, and entertainment, Alloy sells clothes, accessories, and books to teenage girls.[81] In the process, Alloy created a multi-million-name database with "a total reach of 10 million individuals per month" in 2000.[82] Site visitors registered to join the Alloy community, received a catalog, and subscribed to the free e-zine, which allowed them to "[t]ake the newest quizzes, enter the sweetest contests, read big time celeb interviews, and surf around for cool sales in the shop, plus much, much more."[83] Quizzes, supplemented by focus groups and message board postings, were a key component of Alloy's strategy, allowing it to develop a rich portrait of the evolving concerns and lifestyles of its target audience.[84] Based on the derived information, Alloy "create[d] plotlines and characters" for book series such as "Gossip Girl," "A-List," "Clique," "The Sisterhood of the Traveling Pants," "Au Pairs," and "Private"; "recruited writers who were told to follow ... directions closely"[85]; entered into partnerships with publishers such as Little, Brown and Company, Delacorte Press (an imprint of Random House), and Simon Pulse (an imprint of Simon & Schuster)[86]; sold the books on its web site; and "leverage[d] book-based content" into film and television properties.[87] Alloy's "assembly-line production" book packages were so successful that the *New York Times* children's paperback bestseller list for April 30, 2006, ranked books created by Alloy at No. 1, 5, and 9.[88]

But, as Naomi Wolf, author of *The Beauty Myth*, observed, "Gossip Girl," "A-List," and "Clique," each of which sold over a million copies by early 2006, depicted "a value system in which meanness rules, parents check out, conformity is everything and stressed-out adult values are presumed to be meaningful to teenagers," not to mention numerous sex scenes, one of which takes place "in a Bergdorf's dressing room."[89] It was a world in which "the rich are right and good simply by virtue of their wealth. Seventh graders have Palm Pilots, red Coach clutches, Visas and cellphones in Prada messenger bags. Success and failure are entirely signaled by material possessions—specifically, by brands."[90] Contrasting "Gossip Girl," "A-List," and "Clique" with "[t]he great reads of adolescence[, which] have classically been critiques of the corrupt or banal adult world," Wolf concluded that "[i]t's sad if the point of reading for many girls now is no longer to take the adult world apart but to squeeze into it all the more compliantly. Sex and shopping take their places on a barren stage, as though, even for teenagers, these are the only dramas left."[91]

Branding became such a powerful force that books were developed as promotional vehicles for other products, which became "supporting characters or even the stars [of a book] rather than mere scenery."[92] In 2001, the British author Fay Weldon, perhaps most famous for *The Life and Loves of a She Devil* (1983), wrote *The Bulgari Connection*, a novel commissioned by the Italian jeweler, which contained "34 mentions of Bulgari and about 15 other rhapsodies of jewelry, which in the context of the novel directly refer back to the jeweler."[93] Originally printed in a limited edition for Bulgari "to distribute at a party," the novel was also published by HarperCollins in Britain and Atlantic Monthly Press in the United States.[94] An executive at HarperCollins termed the connection between "a publishing house and a commissioned book ... 'fantastic' and that 'it gives me a lot of ideas.'"[95] The arrangement certainly gave ideas to the Ford Motor Company, whose British division contracted with Carole Matthews, who "writes books and short stories in the genre known as chick lit," to include references to the Fiesta, "a small and sporty car sold in Europe," in her novels *The Sweetest Taboo* and *With or Without You*.[96] As a Ford spokesperson observed, the sponsorship arrangement was directed to 28- to 35-year old career women, who "needed to [be made] aware that Fiesta is around and if you're a sassy young woman, it's a car you might consider buying."[97] To comply with her contract, Matthews changed all existing references to Volkswagen Beetles and Peugeots in her books to Fiestas.[98]

With the success of the Bulgari and Ford campaigns as models, HarperCollins developed a business plan to seek out "corporate collaborations" on a wide scale, including "sports and entertainment entities and packaged good companies."[99] Thus was born the children's book *Cashmere as You Can*, sponsored by Saks Fifth Avenue, which "follows the misadventures of Wawa Hohhot and her family of Mongolian cashmere goats who just happen to live on the roof of Saks's Midtown Manhattan store."[100] Unlike *The Cheerios Counting Book* with its "obvious corporate tie-ins," *Cashmere as You Can* had "no clear disclosure of Saks's involvement" despite the fact that it was part of Saks's chain-wide "promotion for a certain expensive fabric."[101] Distributed nationally in 2006 "as if it were any other children's picture book," *Cashmere as You Can* was also pitched to movie and television executives as the potential basis of a show "on the antics of the Hohhot goat family."[102] Similar business arrangements soon followed. In 2006, Running Press, a member of the Perseus Books Group, entered into "an unusual marketing partnership" with "consumer products giant" Procter & Gamble (P&G) to promote Sean Stewart and Jordan Weisman's *Cathy's Book: If Found Call (650) 266-8233* on Beinggirl.com, a web site administered by P&G and "directed at adolescent girls that has games, advice on handling puberty and, ... makeup tips."[103] Not surprisingly, *Cathy's Book* contained numerous references to Cover Girl makeup, a P&G product. Brokered by Creative Artists Agency, the marketing arrangement allowed the president and chief executive of Perseus to say that "[w]hat we are selling here to the customer or the reader is an experience that transcends the book itself.... The relationships with Beinggirl.com and Cover Girl are enriching that experience."[104]

One of the most revealing examples of branding was the licensing agreement between Harlequin Romance novels and NASCAR to publish novels that had "plotlines centering on NASCAR and will bear the NASCAR brand on their covers."[105] As NASCAR worked to attract a female audience in the early 2000s, it entered into licensing agreements with Track Couture, a manufacturer of women's clothing, as well as producers of "vegetables, fruit, bacon, sausage and barbecue sauce."[106] The partnership with Harlequin was a natural next step. It resulted in the publication of *In the Groove* by Pamela Britton, the first of a projected 22 titles in 2006 and 2007.[107] With over 200,000 copies shipped by early 2006, *In the Groove* described the adventures of Sarah Tingle, a former kindergarten teacher who ends up "driving the motor coach for racing star Lance Cooper." Although Sarah has no knowledge of NASCAR nor her famous employer, it is only a matter of time before "she turns hot as race fuel" in Cooper's presence,[108] a plot twist that Harlequin and NASCAR reified by launching a contest in which Carl Edwards, one of NASCAR's most famous and telegenic drivers, took the winner out on a date.[109]

A more subtle, though no less powerful, type of branding was instituted by the Starbucks coffee chain.[110] After initial success with becoming "a tastemaker" in music by "promoting artists like Coldplay and Bob Dylan and introducing the group Antigone Rising and the singer-songwriter Sonya Kitchell," Starbucks "selectively link[ed] [its] brand with certain kinds of movies and books in the belief that Starbucks customers trust the company, in essence, to choose their entertainment for them."[111] Howard D. Schultz, the company's chairman, was blunt about what Starbucks wanted to achieve. Not only was the company "aiming to extend the reach of its brand," but it was also trying to "enhanc[e] the experience of being in Starbucks stores."[112] "It's more than just coffee," he observed, "it's human connection.... In terms of content, the linkage is tied to that aspiration. We want to add texture to the brand, and value to the experience."[113] Starbucks-sponsored books thus became ambient "texture"—subsidiary background material that would "add" value to the consumer act of drinking Starbucks coffee. As such, they were no less promotional vehicles for products than *Cathy's Book*, *Cashmere as You Can*, *In the Groove*, or *The Bulgari Connection*.

Authors too started to think of themselves as brands, openly speaking about the need to view writing "in the way you would look at any business."[114] Janet Evanovich, author of the popular Stephanie Plum and Metro Girl series mysteries, admitted that, in writing and marketing her books, "her strategy is little different than it might be for selling toothpaste." "When you're trying to expand your business," she observed, "it's about real estate in stores."[115] Incorporating herself as Evanovich Inc., she embarked upon a host of "marketing machinations" to expand her brand, including an outsourced "online store that sells hats, mugs and other paraphernalia."[116] Evanovich was not shy in asserting that writing books was simply churning out product to well-defined specifications: "You have to look at it in the way you would look at any business. You have to have honesty to the product. You have to meet consumer expectations. You give them value for their money and give them a product that they need."[117] As Faith Popcorn observed, "we are a culture that is branding everything, and the branding will become part of the culture before people become sophisticated enough to recognize it."[118] It will soon be commonplace, she continued, for authors to "look at this branding as a new art form, and it wouldn't be considered sleazy at all—it will be taking the branding and propelling it through literature."[119]

Little wonder that books were sold as commodities in grocery chains and mass-merchandise stores like Wegmans, Kroger, Albertsons, Wal-Mart, and Costco. Managers used "the techniques that move large amounts of Velveeta and Count Chocula and appl[ied] them to Nora Roberts and John Grisham" such that "[e]ye-catching displays of new hardcovers are sprinkled throughout the stores, encouraging impulse purchases."[120] As grocery chains urged store managers to compete with one another "to build the best displays of bestsellers" and as publishers offered prizes to managers "for the best display and the most books sold," supermarkets saw no real difference between books and their other products. As both an indication of the commodification of books and as a metaphor for the fate of reading in the early 21st century, it was hard to surpass the comment of Heather Pawlowski, a vice president for general merchandise at Wegmans: "So much of what Wegmans talks to its customers about is freshness. That includes freshness within the reading category."[121]

Strategies such as synergy, product placement, branding, and assembly-line production "put[] citizens on extended intellectual vacation"[122] by favoring what Ulrich Beck termed "organized irresponsibility."[123] Thinking that they are making a choice when that choice has already been made for them, library patrons consume, desire to consume, or receive suggestions to consume those books that have been consecrated by the promotional reach of the entertainment industry. No less than other manufacturers, publishers created consumer demand after "figuring out what they can convince consumers they need."[124] As Rachel Donadio pointed out, publishers frequently decided which books to publish by assessing the degree to which the book was promotable: "The more promotion and advertising a book has, the more copies a buyer is comfortable ordering. Often, the more copies a publisher prints, the more seriously a store will take the title, and consider it for a well-trafficked front table, where the publisher will pay co-op advertising fees for its placement. The better the placement, the greater chance a reader might stumble upon the book."[125] Thus, readers' advisors who made suggestions to patrons that they consume industrialized literature or middle-brow books manufactured and promoted by corporate publishers were complicit in legitimizing the entertainment-oriented framework denounced by Bourdieu.

Lulling Readers to Sleep

The methods mentioned above were only some of the more visible and concrete ways in which the economic power of commercial cultural producers was manifested. There were others, deeply embedded in the woof and weft of a publishing system "designed to ensure the accelerated return of profits by a rapid circulation of products which are fated to rapid obsolescence."[126] As independent publishing houses became divisions of entertainment conglomerates in the 1990s in a process of "accelerating corporatization," these new divisions were asked to generate profit margins "in the range of 12–15 percent, three to four times what publishing houses have made in the past."[127] In *The Business of Books*, André Schiffrin discussed how each book produced by the publishing division of a corporate entity was expected to be profitable. No longer would it be possible, as it had been in the past for independent publishers, to support a large number of slow-selling serious fiction and nonfiction books by publishing one or two bestsellers per year. To ensure maximum profitability, Schiffrin explained how "decisions on what to publish are made not by editors but by so-called publishing boards, where the financial and marketing staff play a pivotal role [such that] [i]f a book does not look as if it will sell a certain number—and that number increases every year (it's about 20,000 in many of the larger houses today)—then the publishing board decides that the company cannot afford to take it on."[128] Schiffrin also detailed how editors were held accountable, through sales quotas, for the titles that they chose to publish. If an editor did not meet a pre-determined quota, his or her employment prospects suffered. The entire process could be summarized as "market censorship."[129]

As publishers worked to sell as many copies of a book as possible, they created a pantheon of literary celebrities. It was a "star system"[130] that produced "assembly-line fiction" sold by numerous "hypesters," defined by John W. Aldridge in *Talents and Technicians* as "merchants operating a vast corporate enterprise engaged in the mass manufacture and promotion of books; merchants, furthermore, who wish to be free as possible from, and would like to deny the existence of, the quality controls that serious criticism might impose on their products."[131] As George Garrett noted, "the great corruption ... of the last half of the century has been the attempt on the part of the publishers to create (by fiat as much as fact) its own gallery of stars and master artists."[132] Because certain authors were given "an unfair advantage ... in the quest for public recognition," consumer demand was "stabilized and standardized through the 'name recognition' of certain prominent figures"[133] who followed "fashionable"[134] trends prevalent in "formal academic instruction in creative writing."[135] The result was "standardized and safe" writing that was marketed to produce literary celebrities, which in turn stoked consumer demand.[136]

The creation of literary stars by various media was therefore a deliberate strategy to bring about "the continuing integration of literary production into the entertainment industry, making authors and books part of the cultural pervasiveness of celebrity as a market mechanism of monopoly capitalism."[137] And once literary celebrities were created, the mere mention of their names served as "a promotional booster in itself."[138] Stardom "becomes wholly self-fulfilling," generating for stars a disproportionate share of "visibility" within the field to the detriment of all others.[139] In the end, "what finally counts in the fraternity system of values is not the quality of the work produced but the continued existence and promotion of writers."[140] As Leo Baudry observed, the "frenzy of renown"[141] created "a public rhetoric of individualism" whose goal was to "offset[] an increasingly pervasive web of institutional and corporate relations."[142] Andrew Wernick simply called it "promotional culture."[143] For Bourdieu, promotional culture consisted of "the 'charismatic' ideology," where the "more consecrated" an author or creator of a work is "personally," the "more strongly he consecrates the work" itself—all for the benefit of "the cultural businessman" who put the work on the market.[144] Authors who were chosen as the beneficiaries of "promotional culture" thus dominated bestseller lists, further consecrating their reputations and concentrating book sales in what Donadio labeled a "top-heavy pattern."[145] In 2005, for example, "almost half of all sales in the literary fiction category came from the top 20 best-selling books," with the three top sellers being Mark Haddon's *The Curious Incident of the Dog in the Night-Time* (640,000 copies); Arthur Golden's *Memoirs of a Geisha* (560,000 copies); and Edward P. Jones's *The Known World* (274,000 copies).[146] Confronted with the immense deployment of economic resources whose purpose was the manufacture of celebrity, consumers were duped about the value of individual cultural items, whether books, music, or art. Yearning somehow to partake of culture, the average consumer "bows, just in case, to everything which looks as if might be culture," not realizing that he or she has been fooled into craving and revering pale imitations of true art and literature.[147]

Another way in which late 20th- and early 21st-century society engaged in "value production" and "star production" was through "the dominant apparatus" of prizes and awards, which functioned as entertainment-based "spectacular distractions that conformed with the 'new is hot, old is not' temporality of all fashion-dominated fields."[148] In *The Economy of Prestige: Prizes, Awards, and the Circulation of Value*, James F. English demonstrated how prizes work as a "cultural practice" that arbitrarily created and assigned prestige.[149] And even though "the likelihood of a major American book award going to a [top-10 list] bestseller has diminished over the past half-century,"[150] the astronomical proliferation of literary prizes and awards in the 20th century (just under 100 awards per 1,000 new titles published in the United States in 2000)[151] meant that prizes played an important part in "the intensification of the winner-take-all character of the symbolic economy in arts and entertainment," especially because "strenuous efforts" were made "to leverage prizes ... in the marketplace—and even to position the prize as a sort of brand deserving of consumer loyalty."[152] As an instance of symbolic capital, the prize was inscribed within the logic of competitive sports and "a formidable institutional system of credentializing."[153] Prize frenzy meant that the prize "above all else ... defines the artist" as well as cultural worth.[154] Only winning counted, as is made clear by "[t]he striking change in the language of cultural obituaries," which devolved "on the model of athletics" into "mere skeletal catalogs of victories and podium finishes."[155] An intense competition for supremacy developed among prizes, which increased not only their entertainment value, but also their "economic value, as potentially predictive data concerning [future] industry trends."[156] Prizes became part of an "awards industry" intent on publicity and "taste management."[157]

It is not hard to see "taste management" as a kind of social control, all the more so because the awards industry is "highly dependant on networks of professional association and obligation, on friendship and the exchange of favors: on 'social capital' in lieu of money," with the result that "the power to judge is not as firmly in the hands of judges as one might be led to believe."[158] Structural factors typically drove groups of judges toward "consensus and compromise, toward safe, obvious, and expected choices."[159] The "machinery" of judging was "always geared to produce a winner, and a winner that falls within a certain range" because cultural administrators, caught in a competitive economic and entertainment universe, took numerous steps to ensure that they did not lose control of the process of consecration.[160] They excluded contentious or maverick judges; increased the number of judges to drown idiosyncratic views; and instituted bureaucratic constraints such as cumbersome eligibility criteria, complicated nomination requirements, and the secretive process of "prejudging," which winnowed the range of works from which the final judges chose.[161] Over time, prizes tended "to drift toward the center of their respective fields."[162] As a large number of prizes "accrue[d] to a handful of big winners," the star system was further entrenched.[163] The prize became "an agent in the cultural economy, producing and circulating value according to its own interests—that is, according to what is good for the prize and for prizes in general."[164] And as the cultural economy globalized in the 2000s, the new "global market for cultural prestige impose[d] its increasingly transnational system of values," following "the same logic of intensifying devotion to the blockbuster/superstar model, and find[ing] value in minor forms only to the degree that they may be repackaged or recontextualized for mainstream consumption."[165] As a final testament to the power of prizes, sponsors and committees welcomed denunciations of their prizes because criticism "keeps the prize a focus of attention, increasing its journalistic capital, *and* speeds its accumulation of symbolic capital, or cultural prestige."[166]

The ethos of prizes and "taste management" also facilitated the growth of related phenomena such as "One Book Reading Promotion Projects," book tournaments, and celebrity book clubs. These initiatives had at least two common points: the selection of a single book deemed worthy by one individual or a group of individuals and an extensive campaign to bring that single book to the attention of a broader community in the hope that many others would read it. Marketed as fun and engaging ways to entice people to read books and converse about the issues therein contained, these prize-like programs legitimized the philosophical underpinnings of what Robert H. Frank and Philip J. Cook called the "winner-take-all-society,"[167] directing readers to books that, in most cases, had already received their fair share of promotion and publicity in other venues and that were, with a few notable exceptions,[168] safe, obvious, and "within a certain range," as English remarked about prize-winning titles.[169] For every one book selected, thousands of others were symbolically relegated to "also-ran" status, effectively deemed not worthy of attention. Consider "The First Annual TMN Tournament of Books," sponsored by The Morning News (TMN), "a daily online magazine," and Powells.com, an online bookstore.[170] Set up "exactly like an N.C.A.A. basketball tournament, with ladders, seeds, and head-to-head contests," the TMN tournament included 16 books, with top seeds going "to books that were much hyped before or after publication" and lower seeds "to books that appeared on many best-of-lists." Most of the books were well known, and an online bookseller was a prominent sponsor. And even though the organizers recognized the arbitrariness of their contest, the intersection of the logic of prestige and commercial interests described by English was very much on display.

Ultimately, the many "One Book Reading Promotion Projects," which originated in 1998 with the "If All of Seattle Reads the Same Book" program[171] and was replicated by hundreds of public libraries across the United States and Canada,[172] and Oprah Winfrey's Book Club[173] partook of the same prize-winning sensibility.[174] In both cases, the solitary and contemplative act of reading was transformed into a fashionable, competitive, and public spectacle—something to boast about to one's neighbors and friends. Although commenting specifically about Oprah's books choices, Gavin McNett identified a number of salient points that also apply to "One Book" programs.[175] The choices, McNett wrote, were designed "to play on base sentiment, to reaffirm popular wisdom, to tell readers what they expect to hear and to help them learn what they already know." Much like "any sort of middlebrow dry-good or specialty food on the shelves at Target or Starbucks," the choices were carefully selected "to express their readers' ... tastes, and to reinforce what they think is right and wrong in the world." And because the books came "with an easy issue and a correct opinion already attached," they did not require "much greatness of soul or much hard thinking." Moreover, the nature of the choices implied that the act of reading literature consisted of getting through a book quickly for the sake of being able to say that it had been completed. There was little recognition that the real purpose of reading is to admit that it "makes you feel not bigger, but incalculably smaller, because you're forced to realize that there are entire worlds—locked up in distorted bits and fragments—in more books than you'll ever have time to open," that the act of reading literature "takes a long time," is "hard," and cannot be reduced to a scheduled event, as one more responsibility to be juggled in a frenzied world.

The Changing Nature of Bookstores

As corporate publishers worked hard to create demand for industrial literature and increasingly compromised middle-brow literature, profound changes in the landscape of North American bookstores ensured that the "taste management" strategies described above were enacted and reinforced at thousands of standardized locations. As Laura J. Miller summarized in *Reluctant Capitalists: Bookselling and the Culture of Consumption*, bookselling moved from being "a Genteel Industry" marked throughout much of the period 1900–1980 by "a small number of independent shopkeepers, department stores, and drugstores thinly scattered across the country" to a position where, at "the beginning of the twenty-first century," it was controlled by retail chains such as Barnes & Noble, the Borders Group, and Books-A-Million.[176] As these giant retailers expanded, they assumed an ever-increasing share of total dollar sales in all bookstores, thus driving many "well known" independent bookstores out of business.[177] Because these chains in their early manifestations were owned "by firms whose primary business was not in books" and because they were later organized "as public corporations," questions were raised about "whether they were accountable to the traditions of book culture or to investors' demands for profitability."[178]

While the owners and managers of chain bookstores claimed that they democratized reading by giving it "a populist image" that no longer made it the exclusive preserve of "cultural elites,"[179] the chains' overriding belief in the principle of "consumer sovereignty" and their perception of themselves as "[c]onduit[s] for [c]onsumer satisfaction" meant that they placed themselves within "prevailing cultural models of consumption" that emphasized "selection, convenience, good service, and low prices."[180] Because consumers really did not care much "about [the] power relations" and "politics" of the book publishing industry and felt that shopping should provide "personal satisfaction and entertainment" in a way that was "not constrained by the judgments of others,"[181] book chains relinquished the "educative" and "intellectual advisor" functions of former generations of booksellers.[182] They devoted themselves to providing friendly service, the hallmark of which was "the encouragement of reading in general, not the ability to convert readers to an appreciation of the 'best' books."[183] While chain bookstore employees remained "knowledgeable," this word was defined more in terms of knowing their "own store's stock" or being able to "identify the specific book or author a customer is referring to" rather than being knowledgeable about the contents and intellectual and cultural contexts of the books themselves.[184] And when they did assume "cultural leadership," this role took the form of "widening the choices given to consumers" rather than "teaching readers to distinguish between absolute standards of good and bad."[185]

As chain book retailers embarked on initiatives that were meant to highlight their "service orientation" and "democratic impulse,"[186] they conveniently forgot that "book readers do not occupy a marketing vacuum" and downplayed the importance of "the actual organization of the industry that ends up making a large number of books generally unavailable and therefore almost impossible to choose."[187] There were more books than ever at the beginning of the 21st century, but the ways in which bookstores chose them for their stock and then displayed them on their shelves meant that, by the time a customer walked into a store, real choice was a contingent notion. For chains, the "rationalization" of selection practices involved relying on centralized purchasing that was "computer-guided."[188] Although positioned as a boon to consumers because they ensured availability of popular titles, technology-driven rationalization processes led to a uniformity of selection that often made "tomorrow's bookstore look like yesterday's store—only more so" because they mechanically assigned great weight to factors such as "past sales of the author's previous works, the current popularity of the book's genre, the publishers' promotional budget and plans, whether the author will be touring or making any media appearances, ... the ease of ordering and receiving from the book's suppliers."[189] And while chain bookstores did buy small-press books and "more esoteric titles," these often served as "wallpaper," contributing "to the desired ambiance but ... not actively pushed or expected to sell well."[190]

Another aspect of rationalization was automated inventory control systems. Because these systems were able "to track sales so precisely," the average shelf life of non-selling books was shortened, thus enforcing homogeneous selection even more.[191] As Donadio observed, "[i]n a market dominated by the big chain stores, if a novel doesn't sell a healthy number of copies in the first two weeks after its publication, its chances of getting longer-term momentum are slim."[192] Low sales for an author's current book also detrimentally affected the size of orders for any future books by that author: inventory control systems thus fed seamlessly into next year's selection decisions. These systems also compiled consumer purchasing profiles, which gave birth to the field of "database or relationship marketing," where consumers received "personalized" recommendations for future purchases.[193] But because the recommendations were based "on analyses of prior sales to the user" or "derived from books purchased by other customers with similar buying histories," they collectively tended "to replace idiosyncratic bookseller passion with a dispassionate polling of the like-minded, and to increase sales of those books already in the public eye."[194]

Just as chain bookstores rationalized their inventories, they also standardized the look and feel of their individual stores, ultimately "[m]ass-[p]roducing" in the 1990s a feeling of "Homeyness" that belied the fact that mainstream books were deliberately positioned to achieve maximum sales,[195] with prime locations (such as point-of-purchase displays and end-caps) paid for by corporate publishers who were often advised by Sessalee Hensley, an influential book buyer for Barnes & Noble "to change a book jacket" in order to make the book more promotable or worthy of "an attention-grabbing front table."[196] "Homeyness" entailed the transformation of the chain superstore into a "community center" with "elaborate events," "high-profile charitable efforts," and "an inviting atmosphere that facilitates social interaction"—a place where customers could "relax over a cappuccino or a meeting space for a reading group."[197] The idea of community center thus metamorphosed into entertainment center, with books becoming the "building blocks of entertaining experiences."[198] One example of this was Indigo Books, Canada's largest chain bookstore, which in 2004 expanded "its assortment of 'lifestyle' merchandise" to include items such as jewelry, aromatic candles, and body creams.[199] As Indigo aimed to become "the world's first cultural department store," books were reduced to "approximately 60 per cent" of its total offerings, down from about "80 or 85 per cent." News reports summarized the views of Heather Reisman, Indigo's chief executive officer, as follows: "when yoga books became popular, Indigo began stocking yoga mats. When sales of British cooking star Nigella Lawson's books took off, the retailer added her branded cookware." While consumers accepted the rhetoric of community, they failed to understand that the idea of community was being redefined: it was no longer something "whose essence is public and cooperative," but something that was "reconceptualized as an alienable experience, produced by private organizations, and sold to individual consumers."[200]

Books were now "an entertainment medium" and bookstores were "an entertainment institution" that "reinforced the equation of shopping with leisure, fun, and diversion."[201] Books became "good 'wallpaper' for a setting in which other entertainments occur," providing "an agreeable atmosphere" such that "the mere presence of books is sufficient to create the desired experience" and where "the actual contents of them become less relevant."[202]

Standing up for Independent Readers

To survive in this new landscape, independent bookstores often had little choice but to follow, however reluctantly, the "lead" taken by chain bookstores in making reading an act of public entertainment instead of an act of serious, purposeful, and private contemplation that was frequently non-conformist.[203] Many North American public libraries also followed the entertainment orientation found in chain bookstores, equally convinced that they had no choice but to do so. But did they really have no choice?

Instead of conforming to the dictates of Bourdieu's heteronomous cultural producers, readers' advisors in public libraries could see themselves as part of a vanguard of intellectuals "committed to defending the autonomy of the universes of cultural production ... (and hence of evaluation and consecration)."[204] True consecration of a cultural item can only happen through a long process of ageing in which "intrinsic artistic value" is adjudicated by "the educational system."[205] As Bourdieu pointed out, this autonomy is increasingly threatened by the "greater interpenetration between the world of art and the world of money," where "new forms of sponsorship ... [and] new alliances [are] being established between ... economic enterprises ... and cultural producers," where "the empire of the economy" has countless ways of consecrating as art diverse forms of industrialized literature and middle-brow culture.[206] In this environment, readers' advisors could take cognizance of the numerous tentacles of "the empire of the economy" so as not to make public libraries subject to the immense structural power of an intertwined media, entertainment, and cultural establishment. They could then become involved in supporting autonomous cultural producers so that these producers could, without having to worry about economic or bureaucratic forces, produce works of art that in the long term could become "universal" icons and classics whose "intrinsic artistic value" is adjudicated by "the educational system" after a suitable ageing process.[207] Otherwise, the literary field will be redefined completely in favor of corporate publishers and chain bookstores, becoming a site where "all forms of social stranglehold—that of the market, of fashion, of the state, of politics, of journalism—are imported into the field of cultural production."[208]

Why would readers' advisors want to embark upon a project where they would become a counterweight to the socio-cultural hegemony of corporate publishers and chain bookstores? Simply because these publishers and chains are already so powerful, and already possess so many methods of influencing reading tastes. Put another way, if public librarians and readers' advisors collect, and suggest that library patrons read, the wide range of genre titles and bestsellers manufactured by corporate publishers and easily available at chain bookstores, then they abdicate their responsibility to provide patrons with a meaningful education based on serious and purposeful reading of important and valuable books, which at one time had been the central function of North American public libraries.

In this scenario, public libraries become the equivalents of chain bookstores, reproducing and reinforcing an economic logic that overwhelmingly benefits powerful corporate publishers for whom the "success" of their products "is in itself a guarantee of value."[209] The fact that many North American public libraries were being designed or redesigned in the early 21st century to emulate chain bookstores was all the more disconcerting,[210] since emulation on the level of design symbolically implied an embrace of the economic logic governing chain bookstores. As indicated above, this was a logic that was heavily dependant on chains' participation in an institutional matrix in which they entered into "cooperative advertising agreements" with corporate publishers to preferentially position certain books or recommended alterations in book jackets, all in the interests of increasing sales. In an era where book production rose dramatically and where judicious book selection therefore assumed the utmost importance, the profitability of bookstores more than ever depended "on the distribution of a limited number of titles to an extremely large number of people."[211] But the financial benefits accruing to chain bookstores from "steer[ing] readers to a circum-scribed number of titles"[212] made it difficult to "conceive of culture as an instrument of freedom presupposing freedom, as a *modus operandi* allowing the permanent supersession ... of the desolate, cultured 'thing.'"[213] In a situation where approximately 78 percent of the books read in the United States were purchased from stores and only 19 percent "were bor-rowed from a public, school, or employer library,"[214] why would public libraries want to con-tribute to further enforcing "the empire of the economy" present in bookstores? Instead, they should see themselves as real alternatives to the prevailing entertainment ethos impli-cating publishers and bookstores. Readers' advisors should be especially interested in being strong supporters of Bourdieu's ageing process insofar as it alone contributes to meaning-ful education that is not subject to the compromised values and standards associated with the entertainment industry and corporate publishers.

If the act of becoming advocates of popular culture had been in the 1960s a way for public librarians to assert their independence of and distaste for the social and political val-ues then prevalent in North America, by the late 1990s and early 2000s popular culture had been co-opted by the same economic and structural forces that public librarians and others had rebelled against in the 1960s. That readers' advisors expended much energy rationalizing their support for industrialized and middle-brow cultural products in the name of entertainment-based pleasure reading was a sad, yet telling, irony. After all, Bourdieu, whom the *New York Times* referred to as a champion of "antiestablishment causes" and as someone who described himself as "to the left of the left,"[215] was both an outspoken oppo-nent of the "cultural fast food" (genre fiction, bestsellers, celebrity-authored books, and prize-winning titles) that readers' advisors took to be the foundation of their work and a strong supporter of autonomous art (which alone can produce enduring classics).

We hope that our book will provide useful historical information and context about the evolution of readers' advisory service. We also hope that it will raise controversial issues that public librarians might want to ponder, especially those working in small and mid-sized libraries in North America, which constitute the majority of public libraries.[216] Because these libraries have small collections and small annual budgets for collection development, in our view it is difficult for them to rationalize purchasing—and therefore having on hand to serve as the basis for readers' advisory suggestions—the kind of ephemeral fiction and nonfiction discussed in this chapter if they want to retain any meaningful educational func-tion in their communities. Those public libraries that do decide to buy large amounts of genre titles, bestsellers, celebrity-authored books, and prize-winning titles run the risk of becoming little more than venues offering commodified and disposable entertainment prod-ucts, no different from chain bookstores or retailers like Wegmans, Albertsons, Kroger, and Wal-Mart, which sell books in the belief that newness and freshness are the only attributes that matter. In the final analysis, the choice is between serious and purposeful reading that leads to meaningful education, on the one hand, and entertainment and fun—edutain-ment—masquerading as education, on the other.

In the museum world, the increased reliance on edutainment to attract customers is controversial.[217] As public libraries increasingly stock their shelves with genre titles, best-sellers, celebrity-authored books, and prize-winning titles, they too are moving toward full-scale participation in edutainment. The stakes are high, because at the same time that readers' advisors focus on entertainment-oriented pleasure reading, they overlook in-depth knowledge. Edward Rothstein's description of the Abraham Lincoln Presidential Museum (ALPM) in Springfield, Illinois, is a good analogy for the processes at work in readers' advisory in the late 20th and early 21st centuries.[218] Officially opened in 2005, ALPM boasted of being an "experience museum" that, in the words of Richard Norton Smith, its executive director, will stop at nothing "to get people in." ALPM's goal "is not to fully explain all of the issues that confronted Lincoln but to inspire in the visitor a deep sense of personal connection and empathy with the man." ALPM was tailor-made to achieve Smith's desires. There were "fiberglass and silicone figures inhabiting lifelike dioramas"; there were sound effects such as "whispered insults like those hurled at President Lincoln by editorialists and cartoonists"; and there was video, "including a mock television studio in which the news-caster Tim Russert reports on the election of 1860, complete with campaign commercials." And while some of these scenes were "eerily lifelike" insofar as they "were created using photographs and computer modeling, to simulate the characters' appearances at different ages," they were not historically accurate.

Rothstein noted how "[t]he words of the insults hurled at Lincoln and the arguments by his opponents are almost all paraphrased or invented." Similarly," [t]he soundtrack of the assassination of Lincoln omitted John Wilkes Booth's declaration from the stage after the murder—"Sic semper tyrannis," Virginia's motto, meaning "thus always to tyrants"—because there was concern about whether it would be understood." This simplification made it impossible "to appreciate the glorious rhetoric and pungent argument of Lincoln him-self, ... [to] understand Lincoln's ideas about slavery, or why the Emancipation Proclama-tion affected only the Confederacy and not the four slave-holding border states that remained in the Union." Finally, there was no mention of debates about Lincoln's sexuality, nor about "the shifting nature of his religious beliefs," nor about "his view of civil liberties." Instead, Lincoln "remains an icon: the Suffering Servant of the Union, a martyr for the cause of equality." Any and all "[c]omplications are shunted aside for a series of psychodramas" as "the political becomes personal, represented not by argument but by shouted insults and condensed formulas, as if the sound bites of 2005 really resembled the political debates of the early 1860's." Of course, it was all entertaining, as it was meant to be. But something was lost: complexity; historical depth and perspective; and intellectual challenge. In the name of entertainment and edutainment, knowledge and the possibility of meaningful edu-cation vanished.[219]

Chapter 2

Positioning Readers' Advisory Service Ideologically

Much insight into how readers' advisory was positioned at the beginning of the 21st century can be gained by analyzing the introductory chapter of the third edition of Saricks's *Readers' Advisory Service in the Public Library*, as well as Bill Crowley's "A History of Readers' Advisory Service in the Public Library."[1] Saricks began with the following definition: "Readers' advisory service ... is a patron-centered library service for adult leisure readers. A successful readers' advisory service is one in which knowledgeable, nonjudgmental staff help fiction and nonfiction readers with their leisure-reading needs."[2] There is real demand for such service: a Harris poll in 2003 showed that "reading remains the favorite leisure activity for Americans."[3] But Saricks also noted that the traditional alphabetical organization of fiction books is a "daunting" challenge and "a major barrier" for "patrons who walk into the library in the mood for light, quick, escapist books" or who want to find a book similar to one that they previously enjoyed.[4] In this context, "[t]he readers' advisor provides th[e] vital link between the library's leisure-reading materials and readers."[5] Readers' advisors therefore "strive to be knowledgeable about fiction and nonfiction—particularly that which is popular in their libraries."[6]

It is no exaggeration to say that there is a clear emphasis on the leisure and recreational aspects of reading popular books, many of which can be categorized as "light, quick, escapist." Moreover, post–1980 readers' advisory differs from previous models, which were "didactic," had "pedagogical origins," and were interested in "elevating the masses" by "mov[ing] readers toward classic works[] ... [and] outlin[ing] a plan of reading that would be educational, not recreational."[7] For Saricks, these past models were problematic.

> Saddled with this worthy but formidable goal of providing materials for adult continuing education and expected to fulfill almost a tutorial role with patrons, readers' advisors who subscribed to this philosophy found that the work involved in providing this service eventually became too burdensome. Librarians were unable to meet the demands for so many individually prepared and extensive reading lists. Out of necessity, the lists became more standardized, and some of the individual contact [with patrons] was lost.[8]

We quote extensively from Saricks's overview because her discussion crystallizes many of the issues surrounding post–1980 readers' advisory. It is interesting to follow the logic of her argument. First, she admits that there was large-scale demand for education-based readers' advisory in the past. Many people wanted individualized and comprehensive reading lists, the creation of which took much time and energy, since librarians had to possess not only in-depth insight about patrons and their unique circumstances, but also extensive knowledge of the contents of any recommended books so as to be able to make the best possible match between books and patrons. Yet the creation of personalized lists—as well as the tutorial aspect of the work—was "too burdensome," and so librarians resorted to preparing standardized lists in order not to become "saddled" with educational responsibilities that, although "worthy," were too "formidable." But this led to less personal contact with patrons, and so librarians reformulated readers' advisory so that personal contact could be achieved without undue burden to themselves and without an underlying educational component—a component that was thought to be too didactic, too pedagogical, too hierarchical. Post–1980 readers' advisory thus became an opportunity to converse with patrons about "light, quick, escapist" books—popular and ephemeral fiction and nonfiction for entertainment, pleasure, and recreation—because such conversations were not "too burdensome."

Post–1980 readers' advisors effectively gave up work that was "too burdensome" in favor of work that was less burdensome, justifying the transformation by demonizing serious and purposeful reading and by pointing out that a large proportion of the demand in public libraries was for popular fiction and nonfiction. It was a superb sleight-of-hand that allowed them to congratulate themselves for being non-judgmentally democratic, neutral, and professional: "Readers' advisors in the 1920s and 1930s saw themselves as educators; they *knew* what was good for readers and led them in specific directions. Readers' advisors today see themselves as *links* between readers and books, just as reference librarians are the connection between users and informational materials."[9] Here, Saricks construes readers' advisors who are knowledgeable educators in negative terms, while praising readers' advisors who are linking connectors as positive role models. But it was a sleight-of-hand that neglected those numerous patrons who wanted "individually prepared and extensive reading lists." By not differentiating between and among books of unequal intellectual weight and worth, it was a strategy that privileged "light, quick, escapist" books through a rhetorical stigmatization of books that were their opposites: classic, thought-provoking, and universally true. At the very least, it placed "light, quick, escapist" books on the same level as more valuable literary classics.

If Saricks was content to vaunt the entertainment, leisure, pleasure, and recreational aspects of reading popular fiction and nonfiction, Crowley understood that, in an era where public organizations were called upon to prove their value in measurable terms, an additional rationale besides pleasure and recreation should be used to justify popular fiction and nonfiction—as well as readers' advisory in which popular fiction and nonfiction assumed a key role—in public libraries. Explaining that readers' advisory meant discussing with readers books that tell "a story," including, of course, fiction, but also "biography, history, or even a cookbook or gardening book with a strong narrative content,"[10] he formally defined it as "an organized program promoting both fiction and nonfiction discretionary reading for the dual purposes of satisfying reader needs and advancing a culture's goal of a literate population."[11] He continued: "Even when perceived as a recreational activity, effective RA [readers' advisory] is inevitably in the service of an educational end."[12]

But how was this "educational end" to be defined? For Crowley, the "educational rationale for recreational reading" was succinctly stated in the *Strategic Plan 2000-2010* of the Evanston (Illinois) Public Library (EPL). The plan reads in part: "We believe that reading is to the mind what exercise is to the body. People who don't read regularly and often are in great danger of not having the intellectual or emotional resources they need to deal with assignments at school or work, the challenges of everyday life, personal problems, and the huge challenge of giving meaning to their lives. In that sense reading for pleasure is a sur-vival skill."[13] Other than brief references to assignments for school or work, this definition of education is a highly diluted and informal one that concentrates on inner-directed devel-opment: giving meaning to one's life; gaining emotional resources; and resolving personal problems. In fact, it seems very much like edutainment. There is nary a word about read-ing as a serious and purposeful endeavor undertaken to gain detailed knowledge and under-standing of historical, political, social, cultural, and economic forces external to oneself. This was the kind of knowledge associated with now-outmoded phrases such as "the clas-sics," "great books" or "great ideas," "standard texts," or "liberal education," in the sense accorded those phrases by Mortimer J. Adler in *How to Read a Book: The Art of Getting a Lib-eral Education* or *A Second Look in the Rearview Mirror* and Allan Bloom in *The Closing of the American Mind*.[14] As Adler summarized, the works that comprise the foundation of a great-books education meet three criteria: "contemporary significance," defined as "relevance to the problems and issues of the twentieth century"; "infinite rereadability" or repeated "stu-diability"; and "relevance ... to a very large number of great ideas and great issues that have occupied the minds of thinking individuals for the last twenty-five centuries."[15] These are the books that have undergone Bourdieu's ageing process and have turned into enduring classics that are the foundation of a liberal education.

Until the middle 1960s, education defined in these terms was the animating spirit of the North American educational system. We may glimpse what that education comprised by looking at the syllabi of Great Books Programs or Core Curricula Programs at the hand-ful of colleges and universities in the United States and Canada that had these programs in the early 2000s.[16] Jane Austen, Willa Cather, René Descartes, George Eliot, Cervantes, Dante, John Locke, John Milton, Flannery O'Connor, Sophocles, Spinoza, and Virgil, among others, appear frequently on these syllabi. The benefits of reading great books are legion. According to the Great Books Program of East Carolina University,

> There are fundamental works in every discipline that have shaped the modern world. Great books are to be found not only in literature and philosophy, but in the sciences, social sciences and all branches of learning. Modern critics may disagree about what constitutes a 'great' book, but the fundamental mysteries of nature and especially of human nature remain. Homer's *Iliad* will be a great book so long as a single person wrestles with what it means to have a divine soul trapped in a human body, so long as the needs of the many impose upon the happiness of the one, and so long as there is interest in what is meant by 'civilization.'[17]

At Thomas Aquinas College, the Great Books Curriculum is introduced as follows: "These works—whether philosophy or science, history or drama—describe things as they really are. They reveal the reality at the core of human experience, a reality that—regardless of time or place—does not change. A person hungry for wisdom can return to these books over and over again without exhausting their meaning. These are the books that have the power to shape human events and to change lives."[18] Reading these works is above all a meaningful educational endeavor with significant cultural, political, and social purpose. People read to become cognizant of the "fundamental works in every discipline that have shaped the mod-ern world" or "the national psyche" of their countries. And, as Adler noted, there was lit-tle, if any, unanimity on any topic in the great books. They contained "a wide variety of divergence of views or opinions, among which there is likely to be some truth but much more error."[19] Readers could "think for themselves" and "make up their own minds on every topic under consideration."[20]

But as the definition of post–1980 readers' advisory outlined by Saricks and Crowley gained strength, it replaced readers' advisory that was associated with serious and purposeful reading that led to meaningful education. Readers' advisory was eviscerated of its educational rationale in the name of "Give 'Em What They Want" entertainment, pleasure, and recreation—concepts that, in a neat socio-cultural twist that functioned as an appropriate sign of the times, were accorded an educational pedigree and legitimized as edutainment. The impetus for this transformation can be traced back to 1960s' New Left cultural dissent. In the library context, this meant making greater efforts to collect a wide range of alternative materials. For some librarians, the collection of alternative materials revolved around the newspapers, magazines, newsletters, oral histories, and other fact-based documents of marginalized groups, both past and present, so that their underrepresented voices would have historical resonance within a given community. This was a valuable undertaking. For many other librarians, opening the library to alternative materials was equated with championing entertainment-oriented recreational reading in the form of formula-based genre titles, bestsellers, celebrity-authored books, and prize-winning titles. Concepts such as "important and influential," "the best," "enduring literature," and "the canon" were discarded as undemocratic, elitist, and hegemonic. If public libraries were to become more open and less stuffy, librarians had to "Give 'Em What They Want" because all books were equally worthy. As a result, patrons need not feel guilty about their reading tastes. After all, it was all about them and their attempts to create personal meaning. Delivering readers' advisory service by stressing "light, quick, escapist" books also entrenched librarians' sense of themselves as neutral, non-judgmental professionals who had users' best interests at heart. It appeared to be a win-win situation.

There are, however, lingering questions. It is telling that Crowley chose to highlight Evanston, Illinois, a wealthy university town whose public school district—along with the school districts of Princeton, New Jersey; Eugene, Oregon; Shaker Heights, Ohio; and others—is part of the Minority Student Achievement Network, an alliance of communities that has "a large number of superachieving students and a smaller but persistent number of low-income, nonwhite stragglers."[21] Evanston—home to world-renowned Northwestern University; where the average single-family home is valued at $290,800; where the median family income is $78,886; and where 39 percent of families have incomes above $100,000—is also home to Evanston Township High School (ETHS), which, along with Princeton High School in Princeton, New Jersey, and other schools in wealthy districts, was not certified as making "Adequate Yearly Progress" (AYP) in 2004 under the No Child Left Behind Act of 2001 (NCLB).[22] Why? Although 89.3 percent and 89.6 percent of white students at ETHS met or exceeded standards in reading and mathematics, respectively, only 29.6 percent and 25.9 percent of ETHS black students (and 30.9 percent and 34.5 percent of ETHS Hispanic students) met or exceeded reading and mathematics standards, respectively. Moreover, economically disadvantaged students met reading and mathematics requirements at a rate of 23.2 percent and 20.5 percent, respectively.[23] Because NCLB required that 40 percent of certain subgroups exceed a state's targets in mathematics and reading assessments, ETHS did not receive AYP certification for 2004. Racial achievement gaps at the high-school level exist in towns like Evanston and Princeton. Often, these gaps led to "a tone of defensiveness, even smugness" among school leaders who point to the overall success rates of their institutions, but they were nevertheless real: products of the many historic and economic "contradictions" present in these towns.[24]

Against this background of persistent inequality, the emphasis placed by Crowley on the value of pleasure and recreational reading at the EPL is incongruous. Certainly, the EPL is not ETHS—and the EPL cannot be held directly accountable for the failure of ETHS to receive AYP certification in 2004—but it is intriguing to speculate about the unintended effect of the pleasure and recreational ethos woven through the EPL's strategic plan. An emphasis on pleasure and recreational reading may serve the interests of the wealthy white inhabitants of Evanston who want popular fiction and nonfiction that is "light, quick, escapist" and that may help them cope with "the huge challenge of giving meaning to their lives," but it may not be providing meaningful education for its young non-white and low-income residents. EPL's emphasis on pleasure and recreation may fall within the ambit of the phrase "the soft bigotry of low expectations," first used by George W. Bush in 2000.[25] As public librarians appropriated the rhetoric of 1960s' New Left dissent to justify and valorize the presence of large amounts of popular culture products in their institutions, they neglected their responsibility to provide meaningful educational opportunities for less-advantaged populations, justifying that neglect by convenient recourse to the "Give 'Em What They Want" slogan, which structurally favored the entertainment, pleasure, and personal meaning-making needs of economically advantaged patrons.

Contrast the Evanston situation with the life story of Dr. Condoleezza Rice, a professor of Political Science and Provost at Stanford University in the 1980s and 1990s and a former National Security Advisor and Secretary of State in the early and middle 2000s. Growing up in the racial cauldron of 1950s–1960s' Birmingham, Alabama, Rice was capable of hitting a softball "as far as any boy, a student who devoured the great books 'as casual reading,' a ballet dancer and a pianist whose music 'filled our streets.'"[26] The comparison is instructive: on the one hand, a library ethos in Evanston where pleasure reading of "light, quick, escapist" books is promoted against the backdrop of consistently poor results on state achievement tests on the part of minority high school students; on the other, a successful African-American woman who, despite growing up in a Deep South devoid of civil rights, became steeped in the great-books and cultural tradition of western civilization.

There is ample documentation that the percentage of adults in the United States who have proficient levels of prose literacy, defined as "reading lengthy, complex, abstract prose texts as well as synthesizing information and making complex inferences," is low. Only 15 percent of adults between 40–49 years of age were proficient in 2003 (down from 23 percent in 1992); only 18 percent of adults between 25–39 years of age were proficient in 2003 (down from 20 percent in 1992); and only 31 percent of adults who graduated from college or university were proficient in 2003 (down from 40 percent in 1992).[27] Assessing these results, a government official remarked that "[w]e're seeing substantial declines in reading for pleasure, and it's showing up in our literacy levels."[28] The implication was that pleasure reading was something to be encouraged, not the least because it would lead to higher prose literacy levels. The official was probably referring to the much-analyzed 2004 report *Reading at Risk: A Survey of Literary Reading in America*, issued by the National Endowment for the Arts, which showed that only 46.7 percent of adult Americans read literature in 2002, a drop of 10.2 percentage points in 20 years, which translates into a 14 percent rate of decline. "Literature reading is fading as a meaningful activity, especially among younger people," the report observed, noting that declines of literary reading were to be found in all age groups, all educational levels, both sexes, and among whites, African-Americans, and Hispanics.[29]

Was there another explanation for low rates of literary reading and subsequent low prose literacy levels? It may well be that many adults were bored with, and found little value in, the entertainment-oriented industrial literature produced by corporate publishers and promoted by public libraries, colleges, and universities as relevant popular culture. It might be that they were frustrated with the "conscious decision taken by our intellectual elites to regard the monuments of Western literature and culture as nothing more than political-window dressing, designed to conceal the oppressive realities of pre-revolutionary power structures"[30] and their concomitant decision to hail "light, quick, escapist" books as valuable items that contributed to personal freedom. Perhaps adults expected schools and public libraries to provide them not with opportunities for entertainment and pleasure euphemized as edutainment, but with meaningful education that leads them to explore through serious and purposeful reading significant cultural, ethical, historical, moral, political, and social issues that, in turn, would allow them to gain insight into "the reality at the core of human experience, a reality that— regardless of time or place—does not change."[31] In short, they may be yearning for meaningful education based on serious and purposeful reading of classic literature.

Ideology and Post–1980 Readers' Advisory

Many post–1980 readers' advisors took great satisfaction in indicting the apparent elitism, Puritanism, and censorious tendencies of those who look askance at genre titles, bestsellers, celebrity-authored books, and prize-winning titles. Arguing that patrons should be encouraged to read what they like, they invoked Herbert J. Gans, who wrote that, insofar as "popular culture reflects and expresses the aesthetic and other wants of many people," all individuals "have a right to the culture they prefer, regardless of whether it is high or popular."[32] They also quoted Rosenberg's "First Law of Reading," which enjoined readers to "Never apologize for your reading tastes."[33] Reveling in their passion for books, they talked about their "blissfully squandered reading life" spent among genre titles,[34] or boasted about being "addicted" and "promiscuous" "readaholic[s]."[35]

But as Joseph Epstein pointed out, "[p]eople who openly declare themselves passionate readers are ... usually chiefly stating their own virtue, and hence superiority, and hence, though they are unaware of it, snobbery." While claiming to "adore reading," they also "reveal that much of what they read is schlock, and of a fairly low order even for schlock."[36] The underlying assumption behind the glorification of "book lust" was the notion that "reading is, per se, good," that reading, like broccoli or sound dental hygiene, is intrinsically good for you" because "[w]hen you are reading, after all, you are, ipso facto, not raping or pillaging."[37] Individuals who make these assumptions, Epstein concluded, failed to take a more complex approach—one where "everything depends upon what is being read and the degree of perspicacity brought to the task."[38] The "reading is, per se, good" principle was an integral part of a "personality-oriented" and solipsistic popular culture that, as David Brooks remarked, had difficulty accepting that serious "culture is good for your character, and that a respectable person should spend time absorbing the best that has been thought and said." This was an idea that can be traced to "Ralph Waldo Emerson and the belief that how one spends one's leisure time is intensely important" such that "[t]ime spent with consequential art uplifts character, and time spent with dross debases it." Conversely, popular culture saw nothing wrong with an approach that Brooks characterized as "Less Rembrandt, more Me. Fewer theologians, more dietitians." This approach results in adult readers who, despite being educated at college and universities, had "less interest" in Rimbuad, Faulkner, or Hemingway "than readers 40 years ago."[39] Many of the books published in *The Library of America* series, Oxford University Press's *The World's Classics* series, *Penguin Classics*, or *Everyman's Classics* series were consequently neglected.

Because post–1980 readers' advisors made a point of valorizing the value of *any* reading, they contributed to the "Less Rembrandt, more Me" ethic, helping to justify popular culture and entrench an entertainment-obsessed environment where readers felt "less of a need to go outside themselves to absorb works of art as a means of self-improvement" and where they were "more interested in exploring and being true to the precious flower of their own individual selves."[40] As Michiko Kakutani remarked, "navel gazing" was part of "our culture's enshrinement of subjectivity—'moi' as a modus operandi for processing the world."[41] Brooks and Kakutani drew much of their inspiration from Christopher Lasch's *The Culture of Narcissism*, which outlined the way in which North Americans in the 1960s and 1970s created a culture of self-absorption in which everything revolved around the self.[42] In this culture, people had "no interest in external events except as they throw back a reflection of [their] own image," which was one reason why the "mechanical reproduction of culture" and "the proliferation of visual and audial images" had strong appeal.[43] Validated by the constant emphasis of mass media on celebrities, which "intensif[ied] narcissistic dreams of fame and glory,"[44] and contributing to the rise of an educational system that focused on giving students the resources to understand themselves rather than the external world, the culture of narcissism sanctioned entertainment-oriented reading whose primary purpose was personal meaning-making. The value of serious and purposeful reading to gain significant cultural, historical, and political knowledge was downplayed; the value of reading as an activity associated with narcissistic entertainment and pleasure was highlighted.

For some post–1980 readers' advisors, there were structural advantages in becoming advocates of popular culture and an entertainment-oriented mindset. They could claim that their libraries adhered to the precepts of the Project for Public Spaces (PPP) initiative and the "civic library" movement, both of which viewed public libraries as "evolving into multidimensional public spaces" and "community front porch[es]" that functioned as "attraction[s]" and "instrument[s] for civic and social life."[45] Rhetorically aligned with PPP was the "responsive" library movement, whose manifesto was Baker and Wallace's *The Responsive Public Library: How to Develop and Market a Winning Collection*, a second edition of which was published in 2002.[46] Using the rubric "societal-marketing orientation"[47] to describe their approach, they referred to books as "products" and "product lines,"[48] advocated "identifying and expanding product lines so that sufficient quantities exist to meet the needs of regular users,"[49] and recommended that libraries consider emulating "[p]rofit-making organizations [who] regularly review the vitality of their products, withdrawing them when demand dissipates."[50] Despite a series of half-hearted caveats to avoid practices that will "significantly impair collection depth over time,"[51] they outlined an approach that was a sophisticated version of the demand-based philosophy implemented by the Baltimore County (Maryland) Public Library (BCPL) in the 1960s, a central part of which consisted of buying multiple copies of bestsellers after taking into consideration "the amount of money the publisher commits to advertising the work, and the extent of planned promotion on major radio and television talk shows."[52]

Employing the heady rhetoric of "core markets," "market segmentation," "standard life cycle" of products, "product analysis," and "stock turnover rate,"[53] Baker and Wallace wanted librarians to think of themselves as retail managers whose stores only carried products that moved off the shelves.[54] Typically, those books were heavily promoted genre titles, bestsellers, celebrity-authored books, and prize-winning titles—all of which could be subjected to formula-based purchasing decisions. A revealing example of their beliefs occurred when they praised the Wiggin Memorial Library (WML), a small public library in Stratham, New Hampshire. After adopting the "best aspects" of the BCPL collection-development approach, WML doubled its annual circulation and "increased tax support by 70 percent over a five-year period."[55] What public library wouldn't want to say as much? And so WML's strategy, based on BCPL principles, was entrenched as a model worthy of replication. But the titles that a theoretical readers' advisor in one of Baker and Wallace's "responsive" public libraries could suggest to a patron were limited, since their "responsive" collections were mostly confined to genre titles, bestsellers, celebrity-authored books, and prize-winning titles.

While demand-driven collections increased circulation statistics and made the public library "a place for community," an "attraction," and "a community front porch," the reliance on "products" to create that community testified to how market forces had appropriated the concept of community. Positioning itself as a gentrified destination venue stocked with the latest products designed for personal meaning-making, the public library gained customers, but lost its vitality as an educational force dedicated to the pursuit of serious and purposeful reading that promoted independent thought "removed from the pressures and enticements of the commercial world."[56] Rationalizing demand-driven public libraries by arguing that "the public library is based on democratic principles which leave to the individual the right to respond to, and interact with, the world through whichever symbol systems are appropriate to personal and social needs, as determined by the individual,"[57] post–1980 readers' advisors saw themselves in the tradition of 1960s' counterculture librarians. But as Judith McPheron noted, these librarians forgot that, in trying to reform public libraries by including popular culture items, they contributed to "the rampant anti-intellectualism of American life"[58] and the development of what Susan Sontag called "a culture where intelligence is denied relevance altogether, in a search for radical innocence."[59]

While genre titles and bestsellers may be popular, that popularity had a price. Consider Scarlett Thomas's article "The Great Chick Lit Conspiracy," which described the plight of Rosie, who reads "a lot of chick lit," but "throws the books away afterwards." Why? "It's embarrassing.... You just feel ashamed of yourself after you've read something like that." Quoting Dr. Stacy Gillis, described as "an expert in gender and popular fiction from Exeter University," Thomas pointed out how "chick lit is not feminist, but backlash [since] [i]t serves to reinforce traditional categories of sex and gender divisions while appearing to do the opposite."[60] Consider also Amy Johnson Frykholm's *Rapture Culture*, which described how Betty reads the evangelical novels of the *Left Behind* series: "I couldn't read them fast enough. It was like a chocolate bar that is put in front of you ... and you just keep eating ... you know what I mean? And you can't, you can't ... I was just devouring them. I was really hungry."[61] The impulses animating these readers are problematic. They clearly want the type of novels they devour, but they also recognize on some level their unhealthy effects. And so the issue of what kind of readers' advisory public libraries should offer is part of a larger question about the purpose of public libraries. It is also about how post–1980 readers' advisory constructed itself as an ideological response to certain socio-cultural and socio-political forces, and how, as a result, it became an ideological construct in its own right.

Educational Foundations of the Public Library

As Jesse H. Shera explained in *Foundations of the Public Library*, the central purpose of the public library was education, conceptualized in terms of serious and purposeful reading that was a continuation of formal school-based instruction. During the 1820s, New Hampshire embarked on an ambitious scheme to found a state university. Towns contributed to a Literary Fund, but when it became apparent that a state university was not to be, the collected monies were returned to the contributing towns, with the proviso that "the said share or proportion of said fund, so paid over, shall be applied by the respective towns to the support and maintenance of common free schools, or to other purposes of education ... in such manner and at such time as said towns may order."[62] In 1833, the residents of Peterborough, New Hampshire, decided to apply their portion of the returned funds to the establishment of a free public library, using as their legal basis the "or to other purposes of education" clause. This marked the beginning of the educational rationale for North American public libraries. As Sidney Ditzion wrote in *Arsenals of a Democratic Culture*, "the public library was historically an agency of adult education" whereby "[e]ducational gaps were to be filled in, errors to be corrected; [and] the level of the collective culture was to be raised immeasurably," often by recourse to "the pedagogical principle of graded reading" in which individuals who initially read "simple popular books" would eventually "graduate to the more solid forms of reading."[63]

In the early 1850s, during debates about the founding of the Boston Public Library (BPL), the public library was described by George Ticknor as an entity that would become "the crowning glory of our public schools"[64] insofar as it "would put the finishing hand to that system of public education that lies at the basis of the prosperity of Boston."[65] Ticknor, one of the founders and trustees of BPL (1852–1866), had been Harvard College's first professor of Modern Languages and Literature and the author of the three-volume *History of Spanish Literature* (1849).[66] When the BPL trustees submitted a report to City Council in 1852 "on the objects to be attained by the establishment of a public library," they stated that the public library would "carry[] on the great work" begun by "the school and even the college and the university."[67] The public library was "the next natural step to be taken for the intellectual advancement of th[e] whole community" and as "the means of completing our system of public education" so that individuals would be encouraged in "the acquisition of the knowledge required to complete a preparation for active life or to perform its duties."[68] Just as public schools were worthy of taxpayer support because they were an investment in the future, so too were public libraries.

The educational purpose of public libraries was reiterated in 1875 by the examining committee of the BPL. After castigating a "vast range of ephemeral literature" that, because of its "exciting and fascinating nature" attracted "multitudes" of readers, the committee noted that "[n]otwithstanding many popular notions to the contrary, it is no part of the duty of a municipality to raise taxes for the amusement of the people, unless the amusement is tolerably clearly seen to be conducive to higher ends of good citizenship, like the encouragement of patriotism, the promotion of the public health, or the undermining of immorality; and the sole relation of a town Library to the general interest is as a supplement to the school system; as an instrumentality of higher instruction to all classes of people."[69] While the public library should admit "certain works of imagination of pure moral tendency, which have proved their vitality by living at least a year or two, it is quite another thing to assume that the town library is to be made a rival agency to the book club, the weekly paper, the news stand, and the railroad depot, for disseminating what are properly enough called 'the novels of the day.'"[70] When public funds were in question, great care must be exercised in the purchase of materials. Otherwise, public libraries lose sight of their essential purpose and become rental libraries, well known as "purveyors of entertainment" that dealt in large quantities of bestsellers.[71] A difference existed between meaningful educational purposes, in which government had a vested interest, and entertainment, which was a personal matter.

The ALA motto, adopted in 1879, was an attempt to resolve some of the issues raised by the BPL examining committee and others: "The Best Reading for the Largest Number at the Least Cost."[72] Yet, while the phrases "for the largest number" and "at the least cost" suggested an economic calculus favorable to popular fiction, the phrase "the best reading," by virtue of its lead position, signified a continuing focus on literary standards and cultural excellence. In 1893, when the ALA published the catalog of its 5,000-volume "model library," only 15 percent of the titles were fiction. Nonfiction titles dominated, with 14 percent classified as history and 12 percent as biography.[73] In 1893, the ALA also ordered its publishing section to compile a list of "questionable novels" and circulate it privately to librarians, who would then use it as a guide for what not to purchase and what to remove from their shelves.[74]

Despite the growing emphasis on popular and sensational fiction in public libraries during the 1900s and 1910s, influential voices within librarianship, including the directors of the Buffalo and St. Louis Public Libraries, maintained that public libraries and schools were "parts of one and the same great organic institution," that libraries should be considered "people's universit[ies]."[75] As will be discussed in chapter 4, the association of public libraries with educational imperatives became even stronger between 1920 and the early 1960s. An important impetus for librarians' renewed faith in educational ideals was the Library War Service Program (LWSP), in which over 700 librarians "provid[ed] personal guidance to readers" in libraries attached to 36 military training camps after the United States entered World War I in 1917.[76] The LWSP produced "an energizing effect on the profession as a whole" as librarians realized that "the educational commitment of the public library was still a valid one and needed to be revitalized."[77] In 1924, William S. Learned's *The American Public Library and the Diffusion of Knowledge* called for public libraries to become "community intelligence service[s]" or "adult intelligence center[s]" staffed by "an intelligence personnel" who possessed the knowledge of college and university teachers.[78] Because of their in-depth subject expertise, public librarians would be leaders in "preparing and presenting important material to students for the purpose of arousing their progressive interest" about various subjects.[79]

Alvin S. Johnson was even more adamant than Learned that public libraries should devote themselves to adult education. In *The Public Library—A People's University* (1938), he noted that libraries began to downplay their educational role "around the turn of the century" when "[c]overage, an extensive conception, rather than education, an intensive one, came to be an accepted criterion of successful library activity."[80] He lamented that libraries were held hostage by a public who "wanted second-rate or third-rate fiction," which "had to be supplied, and promptly, while everybody was talking about a book and wanted to get it read."[81] Supplying popular fiction increased circulation statistics, but using circulation statistics to justify the library's existence was self-defeating. Only by "the explicitness and effectiveness of its adult educational activities" could the public library hope to secure its future.[82] As Esther Jane Carrier summarized, "[t]he extent to which librarians thought the library should limit its activities to the furtherance of its educational objectives generally determined their attitude toward how much and what kind of fiction should be included in library book collections."[83]

The legacy of the LWSP—as well as the cluster of ideas animating Learned's and Johnson's books—spurred public libraries toward a sustained involvement with adult education in the 1920s and 1930s. Among the many adult-education initiatives were the formation of the ALA's Commission on the Library and Adult Education, the launch of the journal *Adult Education and the Library*, and the *Reading with a Purpose* series. The most visible manifestation of the adult-education movement was the growth of formal readers' advisory service. By 1935, 63 readers' advisors worked in 44 public libraries "of varying sizes and types," enthusiastically creating annotated reading lists and courses for thousands of individuals.[84] The educational imperative of public libraries continued in the 1940s and 1950s: librarians offered individual readers' guidance; guided group discussion programs such as Great Books, Great Issues, and American Heritage; and the *Reading for an Age of Change* series, a direct descendant of the *Reading with a Purpose* series.

A final echo of the LWSP legacy of adult education sounded in the early and middle 1970s under the rubric of the Adult Independent Learning project (AIL), in which about 15 libraries participated.[85] Jose Orlando Toro, director of AIL, envisioned that public libraries would be "convert[ed]" from their "comfortable role of responding to people's requests to the more dynamic role of true community learning centers, and would substitute a planned learning experience for what for many adults is largely a 'happening.'"[86] Readers' advisors who would plan courses of study and select appropriate materials for learners were a key part of the AIL plan. In the face of often vitriolic criticism, Toro's concept foundered. By 1975, he lamented that "the public library's own educational mission" was being left in abeyance as it tried to fulfill its learning function "in an informal setting, lacking purpose and direction."[87] In the context of the times, Toro's use of the word "happening" had fraught undertones, suggesting that public libraries had devolved into informal entertainment-oriented venues, where, according to the definition of "happening," "people get together just to be together, usually involving music."[88]

Demonizing Education

With no pun intended, what happened? Starting in 1963, there was a fundamental change in the way that the relationship between public libraries and education was construed—a change encapsulated in Toro's use of the word "happening" to describe the direction that public libraries took. When Toro spoke of "convert[ing]" public libraries away from "happenings" to venues where adults could experience "planned learning experiences" in the company of readers' advisors, he not only recognized that libraries had changed into places of entertainment "where people get together just to be together," but also expressed a desire that they return to their educational heritage. His was a lost battle. D. W. Davies summarized this change: "Librarians who look upon libraries as centers for social services and entertainment do not necessarily believe that books and culture are out of place in libraries. They simply believe that reading and uplift are incidental to the library's main purpose."[89]

The view that the North American public library should function primarily as a "happening" or entertainment center was thus legitimated in the middle 1960s. Davies invoked the existence of diverse entertainment options at 19th-century British lyceums, mechanics' institutes, and settlement houses in an attempt to historically situate and justify the North American public library as an entertainment center. Certainly, these British antecedents had games and social events, but they were primarily concerned with improving the lot of their members by providing access to rigorous self-education activities through reading. If British mechanics' institutes were anything like the early Canadian Mechanics' Institutes in Halifax or Québec, their libraries contained books about botany, geology, medicine, natural history, philosophy, law, and ethics; histories of Arabia, England, China, Spain and Portugal, Scandinavia, and Russia; biographies of Sir Isaac Newton, Benjamin Franklin, and Thomas Jefferson; Greek, Latin, German, and Italian grammars; English-Latin and English-Spanish dictionaries; and volumes by Aeschylus, Herodotus, Homer, Horace, Euripides, Fielding, Josephus, Livy, Locke, Milton, Plutarch, Pope, Scott, Shakespeare, Tacitus, and Thucydides.[90] These libraries testified to the meaningful educational purpose behind mechanics' institutes.

When Davies positioned entertainment-based public libraries in the 1960s and 1970s as the natural heirs of 19th-century mechanics' institutes, it was a shrewd strategic move, but it was also a move that cast a dubious comparative light on the entertainment activities that supposedly were the direct descendants of the legacy of mechanics' institutes. Consider the following representative cases, all of which Davies takes from accounts published between 1969 and 1972: the Oak Park branch of the Sacramento Public Library, where "chess, checkers, pick-up sticks, puzzles, word games, spirograph, and coloring books" were the "biggest attractions"; the Young Adult Project libraries in northern California, which offered "chess, scrabble, and table-tennis, and two or three guitars for those who desire to play them"; the Model Cities Library (Albuquerque, New Mexico), which had "games, toys, and pets"; the Inglewood (California) Public Library, which scheduled "judo and karate demonstrations in its branches"; the Union Street Branch Library in La Grange, Georgia, which "circulates lawn mowers and rotary tillers"; and the North Las Vegas (Nevada) Public library, which "offered a free auto mechanics workshop, a kite-making clinic, a legal rights of young adults class, instruction in making art from junk, yoga classes, and natural childbirth classes."[91] Davies also praised the appearance of "rap rooms" in public libraries, which enlivened the atmosphere: "a group of boys took over the reading room for an informal discussion of the merits and demerits of professional football teams and individual players[,] [but] [fa]vored topics for the more formal panel discussions are peace, sex, and drug abuse."[92] If some public libraries during the 1960s and 1970s embarked upon programs of social good works (i.e., bookmobile librarians in the poverty-stricken Arkansas River valley who "offered practical advice" on domestic questions),[93] this impetus quickly dissipated under assorted administrative and financial pressures, leaving behind libraries that were predominantly entertainment centers based on popular culture. Forgetting that true radical change was only possible through rigorous education and wide-ranging exposure to classic and enduring books, librarians became enthralled by the idea that an emphasis on popular culture would allow them to assert their independence from what they took to be ossified patterns of thought in the library world and to display their progressive credentials. Caught up in the spirit of Bob Dylan's 1963 *The Times They Are A-Changin,'* public librarians eagerly divested themselves of what they considered to be the albatross of meaningful education and focused instead on entertainment, pleasure, and recreation. In many ways, it was change for the sake of change— an ethos exemplified in the late 1970s by the founding of a tool library in Berkeley, California.[94]

    Philosophically, the change was at least partly due to the work of Michael H. Harris about the origins of North American public libraries. Two of Harris's most influential articles were "The Purpose of the American Public Library: A Revisionist Interpretation of History" and "Everett, Ticknor and the Common Man: The Fear of Societal Instability as the Motivation for the Founding of the Boston Public Library."[95] To a lesser extent, it was also due to Dee Garrison's 1979 book *Apostles of Culture: The Public Librarian and American Society, 1876–1920,* which was based on her 1973 dissertation.[96] Both Harris and Garrison argued against "the progressive interpretation" of library history, an interpretation in which the public library, established by "liberal, idealistic, middle-class leaders ... as the counterpart to the public school in bringing educational and economic opportunity to the common people," was regarded as "one aspect of the general movement for social reform and moral uplift in the late nineteenth century."[97] Instead, Garrison explained that the public library was conceived "as a means of arresting lower-class alienation from traditional culture" by "ruling elites" who, fearing "egalitarianism and upheaval from below," wished "to perpetuate their power by disseminating their own cultural values."[98] Acting as a "social stabilizer," the public library was "a direct rival to the saloon," helped "to prevent crime and social rebellion," and "blunt[ed] the impact of the class consciousness which was growing in proportion to the rate of immigration, the number of strikes, and the intensity of economic distress."[99]

Harris made similar arguments, describing how the public library was established as a "conservator of order" and "stabilizing agent in society"[100] by individuals who exhibited personality traits such as "Conventionalism"; "Authoritarian Aggression"; "Superstition and Stereotypy"; "Power and Toughness"; "Projectivity," defined as the "[d]isposition to believe that wild and dangerous things go on in the world"; and "Elitism."[101] In mortal fear of "immoderate and irrational behaviour" and the "social instability" resulting from "the bustling, burgeoning growth of the Nation" marked by an influx of immigrants, library founders "came to view formal, organized, and publicly supported educational institutions as the best means of securing the Republic against the winds of destructive change."[102] Education was thus a tool of oppression, helping "to Americanize" destructive elements by "render[ing] them temperate, moderate, and controllable, and thereby reduc[ing] the violence and urban strife that threatened the stability of American society."[103] Public libraries contributed to educating the masses by luring unsuspecting "hares" through the "carrot" of popular fiction.[104] Once safely inside, librarians performed the bait-and-switch tactic, improving unsuspecting patrons' reading tastes by supplying them with the "best books," which in turn would make them "more inclined to be conservative, patriotic, devout, and respectful of property."[105] The disdain with which early librarians greeted popular culture was therefore an index of their continuing "authoritarian and elitist stance," which was "encouraged ... by the philanthropy of hundreds of wealthy Americans, and most notably, of Andrew Carnegie."[106] These wealthy individuals "considered the library a wise investment in order, stability, and sound economic growth."[107] Harris disparagingly quoted Carnegie, for whom the knowledge gleaned from libraries will "make men not violent revolutionists, but cautious evolutionists; not destroyers, but careful improvers."[108]

The revisionist histories of Harris and Garrison depicted public libraries as elitist institutions founded and supported by imperious, paternal zealots dedicated to preserving social stability through cultural authoritarianism and a conservative value system as embodied in serious and enduring books. Any efforts undertaken by public librarians "to reach the disadvantaged, the poor, the unserved" were doomed to failure, since "the man on the street" intuitively recognized that the public library "was designed to control him and not to liberate him."[109] The unstated implication was clear. If "the man on the street" was to view public libraries as liberating institutions, popular culture must find a welcoming home there. Moreover, popular culture should be considered inherently valuable, not a mere conduit to materials falling under the rubric "great books." Following this theory, public libraries must be reinvigorated by a re-orientation toward entertainment, pleasure, and recreation.

As a recapitulation of the general outlook with which the 1960s' generation viewed its predecessors and existing institutions, the theories of Harris and Garrison were consistent. As Richard Harwell and Roger Michener pointed out in response to Harris' work, it partook of what Edward Shils calls "the tradition of anti-institutionalism" as well as the "tradition of antitraditionalism."[110] As defined by Shils, anti-institutionalism regards institutions "as restraints on spontaneous expression[,] ... inhibitors of the development of 'genuine individuality,' ... [and] repressive instruments of authority, which are thought to represent the 'dead hand of the past.'"[111] More importantly, as Francis Miksa indicated in 1982, Harris's and Garrison's theories were misguided. Harris's beliefs, premised on an "unspoken notion of correct library purpose as something approximating a populist, Jacksonian vision of the public library or as a reflection of the social concerns that came out of the 1960s,"[112] represented "at best a narrowly conceived, conspiratorial view of the American public library movement."[113] Similarly, Garrison's writings could be understood "against the backdrop of the more recent past when highly critical and at times seriously pessimistic evaluations of American social and cultural institutions and traditions have more often than not served as evidence of the drive to forge a new understanding of human rights in the modern world."[114] And, as Harwell and Michener stated, Harris's work discounted the fact that founders of the public-library movement, imbued with the ideas swirling around *The Federalist Papers*, based their actions on "the essence of liberalism of the Enlightenment as expressed in the American democratic order,"[115] which in turn was based on the principles of "republican morality" and "civic virtue," where good citizens would "transcend self-interest in [their] devotion to the common good."[116]

Despite these criticisms, Harris's and Garrison's views had a lasting effect in the library world, all the more so because they were part of the wave of ideas sweeping through the 1960s and 1970s, when social and political upheaval left no segment of society untouched. Librarianship was no exception. On a symbolic level, the work of Harris and Garrison was part of what James Piereson identified as the chain of events leading to the entrenchment of the "left university":[117] an institution driven "by radical preoccupations with cultural change,"[118] where students and teachers "view our history as a tale of oppression,"[119] where students "learn[] a great deal about racial and gender identity, but little about the intellectual foundations of their civilization."[120] For many public librarians, participating in social change meant bringing popular culture into the library. It also meant liberating themselves from what they thought to be the antiquated, musty, and oppressive models of public librarianship described by Harris and Garrison. As they embraced social change, they were aided by both theory and events.

Valorizing Popular Culture

As Davies pointed out, library professionals were greatly affected by the Marshall McLuhan-inspired idea that "Everything is information," which was used to construct the argument that, "since libraries are traditionally interested in information, the modern social library is interested in everything."[121] But the importance of McLuhan's idea for librarians can only be understood against the background of what came to be known as "the social and political uprising of the 1960s ... against the consensus and the culture of civility that reinforced it."[122] Drawing on the work of David Reisman, E. Digby Baltzell, and others, Mark Hamilton Lytle suggested that the root cause of generational unrest and dissent was "the unwillingness or inability of the WASP establishment 'to share or improve its upper-class traditions by absorbing talented and distinguished members of minority groups into its privileged ranks.'"[123] Members of "[t]he American social elite," which was comprised of "patrician Protestants who held positions of political and institutional power and 'set the style in arts and letters, in the universities, in sports, and in the more popular culture, which governs the values and aspirations of the masses,'" abdicated their leadership responsibilities by "promot[ing] their own interests rather than advancing a national agenda."[124] Because the elite was "inadequately inclusive to address the aspirations of a more socially diverse population" and because "African Americans, Latinos, gays, political dissenters, and women ... found the paths into the elite blocked," these groups began to challenge the prerogatives of elites to continue to exercise authority or arbitrate moral, institutional, or political issues.[125] Elites, however, associated dissent "not with traditional American perfectionism or egalitarianism, but with Communism" as well as "[t]he popular culture of teenaged America[,]" which was most exuberantly manifested in the "subversive world" of comic books, "the rock revolution," and "teen flicks."[126] According to Alan Nadel, they tried to delimit this exuberance through "containment narratives," where the idea of containment not only "equated containment of communism with containment of atomic secrets, of sexual license, of gender roles, of nuclear energy, and of artistic expression," but also lauded "[t]he virtue of conformity," whether "to some idea of religion, to 'middle-class' values, [or] to distinct gender roles and rigid courtship rituals."[127]

The championing of non-elite popular culture was therefore a political act. The New Left saw support for popular culture as shorthand for good judgment, intelligence, sensitivity, and decency because it implied real commitment to democratic principles. It was, moreover, part of the movement in North American university literature departments to expand the canon so that the object under study was no longer literature *per se*, but texts or discourses. Many scholars claimed that the narrowness of the existing canon, which consisted of the great-books tradition, "engendered cultural oppression" by "creating a sense of inferiority, immobilizing activity, and promoting acquiescence."[128] As Louis Kampf put it, "force-feeding people on a rich diet of Western masterpieces will only make them more sick."[129] For "emotional and intellectual liberation" to occur, literature must be placed "within a living context close to daily life and removed from its sacrosanct place in the great tradition."[130] The concept of value became an empty husk, no longer "an intrinsic property," but rather "derived from certain groups in specific situations in which particular criteria served given purposes."[131] As "the serious academic study of diverse cultural discourses, as opposed to the study of only elite or canonical literature" was legitimized, "a popular romance might have more value, aesthetic and otherwise, than a Shakespearean text."[132]

All culture—just like all information—was good. This idea was formalized by Gans in the early 1970s. Based on his concept of "taste cultures and publics," Gans argued "against the idea that only cultural experts know what is good for people and for society" and for greater "cultural pluralism" and "cultural democracy."[133] He defined taste cultures as "aggregates of similar values and usually but not always similar content."[134] Taste publics were "aggregates of people with usually but not always similar values making similar choices from the available offerings of culture."[135] There were many taste cultures (the five main ones were "high culture, upper-middle culture, lower-middle culture, low culture, ... quasi-folk low culture," but there was also youth culture, black culture, and a variety of ethnic cultures), and taste publics often engaged in "cultural straddling," which meant that cultural categories were fluid and evolving.[136] All cultural manifestations should be treated as having equal value because "the major source of differentiation between taste cultures and publics is socioeconomic level or *class*," defined in terms of "income, occupation, and education."[137] Still, Gans admitted that "[i]f one compared the taste cultures alone, without taking into account the taste publics who choose them, it would be fair to say that the higher cultures are better or at least more comprehensive and more informative than the lower ones."[138] But since taste publics must be taken into account, "the evaluation of any item of cultural content must be related to the aesthetic standards and background characteristics of the relevant public," which meant that "to the extent that all taste cultures reflect the characteristics and standards of their publics, they are equal in value."[139] Because egalitarian societies should respect individual differences, let alone individual cultural tastes, any critique of popular culture was "an attack by one element in society against another: by the cultured against the uncultured, the educated against the uneducated, the sophisticated against the unsophisticated, the more affluent against the less affluent, and the cultural experts against the laity."[140]

Moreover, popular culture empowered the people who like it because they actively created diverse meanings from it for diverse purposes. As John Fiske explained in *Understanding Popular Culture*, active audiences "transform the cultural commodity into a cultural resource, pluralize the meanings and pleasures it offers, evade or resist its disciplinary efforts, fracture its homogeneity and coherence, [and] raid or poach upon its terrain."[141] Popular culture became "a process of struggle, of struggle over the meanings of social experience, of one's personhood and its relations to the social order and of the texts and commodities of that order."[142] Because it was "progressive, not revolutionary,"[143] it challenged the existing "power bloc" because it was "one of the sites where th[e] struggle for and against a culture of the powerful is engaged."[144] It enabled people "under the appropriate social conditions ... to act, particularly at the micropolitical level, and by such action to increase their socio-cultural space, to effect a (micro)redistribution of power in their favor."[145] Or, as Clifford Geertz remarked, all manifestations of culture are multiple "webs of significance"[146] from which "frames of meaning" can be derived about how individuals "enact their lives."[147] By extrapolation, the act of belonging to any cultural system (e.g., grunge culture, science fiction culture, or the culture of romance readers) was a forceful act of personal "meaning-making" by any individual who choose to belong to that system.[148] Reception analysis and reader-response criticism were cognate phenomena. Reception analysis, defined as "the study of audience interpretations," was responsible for intensifying "our interest in the ways in which people actively and creatively make their own meanings and create their own culture, rather than passively absorb pre-given meanings imposed upon them."[149] Reader-response criticism, which "tended toward a politics of liberal pluralism," did much the same thing as reception analysis, "envisag[ing] the reader's activity as instrumental to the understanding of the literary text ... and conceiv[ing] the reader's activity as identical with the text so that this activity became the source of concern and value."[150]

These theories and events allowed public librarians to build an aura of legitimacy around popular culture: it was worthwhile *per se* and from a socio-political perspective. Many librarians used popular culture as a tool to foment rebellion in the library world against what they considered to be outmoded ideas and practices. According to Wayne A. Wiegand, these outmoded ideas and practices included: a pre-occupation with useful knowledge and information that would meet the needs of an "influential combination of 'serious' readers, community leaders, and students of adult education"; the circumstance that "the vast majority of postwar library literature and library research continued to address issues of library expertise and institutional management"; the perpetuation of "a sophisticated and involved system ... to profile 'quality' work" that had the effect of creating "a consensus" on a classificatory (and exclusionary) hierarchy of all works; and "the principle of 'neutrality' most often advocated by veteran librarians [as] an excuse *not* to address inequities in library practice caused by racism, sexism, and homophobia, a rationale *not* to confront a government bent on conducting an unjust war in southeast Asia, and a mechanism to give the Library Bill of Rights a strict construction that rendered it ineffective in the fight to include alternative perspectives in library collections."[151]

Rejecting this cluster of interlocking ideas, librarians who supported popular culture looked favorably upon the idea of "culture as practice" or "culture as agency," which "addressed questions of how people use the multiple cultural forms available to them to validate their existences and make sense of their worlds."[152] The value of popular culture resided not just in genre titles, comic books, pop art, radio, and television.[153] Its value also lay in a series of political and symbolic meanings of which its concrete manifestations were only the visible tip. The inclusion of popular culture in public libraries therefore provided an answer to individuals such as Don Roberts who, in his article "Listen, Miss, Mrs., Mr. Librarian," complained that librarians "continue to run the vestiges of a defunct Western humanism and post–Renaissance classicism (typified in a way by the Caldecott/Newberry

Awards and our book selection mystiques) on the hapless, cynical library dropout taxpayers and their children."[154] At the same time that hierarchical judgments about a book's value were to be avoided, the needs of serious readers or those interested in adult education were to be downplayed. Instead, an entertainment- and pleasure-oriented ethos centered on popular culture designed to entice "dropouts" fed up with "defunct Western humanism and post–Renaissance classicism" became the new order of the day.

Public librarians engaged in what Gans called "subcultural programming," defined as "a policy based on the concept of aesthetic relationism and the common sense notion of cultural pluralism: to provide cultural content to express and satisfy the specific standards of every taste public."[155] By giving the same value to popular culture as high culture, both of these cultures (and their publics) would be equalized—something that would contribute to the dissolution of elite prerogatives and symbolically lead to a more egalitarian society. But when librarians stated that popular culture had inherent worth, they effectively denied that the taste publics gravitating toward popular culture had the ability to reach high culture. They accepted that these taste publics would be perpetually defined by the world of popular culture, with little or no access to high culture. Ironically, the exclusion of lower-order taste publics from elite cultural realms was metaphorically akin to the exclusion of diverse minority populations from socio-political spheres that had occasioned 1960s' New Left dissent in the first place.

If popular culture functioned as a symbolic vehicle toward greater equality, it was often forgotten that equality could also be achieved by another method that Gans presented as an option, but rejected: upward "cultural mobility."[156] It was a method that public librarians supportive of popular culture also rejected. Gans defined culture mobility as follows: "American society should pursue policies that would maximize educational and other opportunities for all so as to permit everyone to choose from higher taste cultures."[157] But because those opportunities were not available, "it would be wrong to expect a society with a median education level of twelve years to choose only from taste cultures requiring a college education, or for that matter, to support through public policies the welfare of the higher cultures at the expense of the lower ones."[158] For public librarians in favor of popular culture, Gans's statement constituted yet another irony because the public library was founded as an educational institution whose mission was serious and purposeful reading and learning about important social, cultural, and historical issues. By filling their libraries with popular culture materials that did not meet the criteria for serious and purposeful reading and relying on popular culture to haphazardly provide informal learning opportunities focused on individual meaning-making, public librarians contributed to the very lack of meaningful educational achievement that Gans decried and that prevented patrons from achieving a higher level of taste culture. Toro's comment about the public library's lack of purpose and its participation in a "happenings" mindset had much truth behind it.

Convinced that 1960s' New Left dissent was the only viable way to effect reform, many librarians dismissed other solutions to the ambient social malaise. As the titles of books such as John A. Andrew III's *The Other Side of the Sixties: Young Americans for Freedom and the Rise of Conservative Politics* and Godfrey Hodgson's *The World Turned Right Side Up: A History of the Conservative Ascendancy in America* indicated, the New Left was not the only movement critical of existing social structures.[159] If the New Left was more adept at capturing the attention of the public and successfully delineating a liberal consensus that was influential in establishing the type of thinking encapsulated by the terms popular culture and "the left university," the New Right also had a rich set of ideas that addressed social exclusion. As summarized by Lytle, a movement called traditionalism, or new conservatism, "railed against the rootlessness of modern mass society"[160] as embodied in what Bernard Iddings Bell called the "complacent, vulgar, mindless, homogenized, comfort-seeking, nouveau riche culture of the common man."[161]

Drawing upon Richard Weaver's 1948 book *Ideas Have Consequences*, traditionalists in the 1950s and 1960s traced the decline of Western culture to the loss of "transcendental values,"[162] to the circumstance that "a fascination with what Henry Luce called 'The American Century' had seduced Americans to ignore or forget the great traditions, the moral and religious foundations, on which their success rested."[163] As Hodgson explains, traditionalists derived comfort from the philosophy of Edmund Burke, who argued that society should be based on an organic model—"a partnership not only between those who are living but between those who are living, those who are dead, and those who are to be born."[164] This implied allegiance to core ideas, enduring literature, and a profound appreciation of the contribution of philosophies and religions to the quest for "a transcendent moral order," which was the only means by which "the spiritual crisis in society" could be addressed.[165] To be sure, there were philosophical divisions among New Right supporters, just as there were philosophical differences among New Left supporters.[166] But, taken as whole, the New Right had a constellation of beliefs that sharply differentiated it from the New Left. And, no matter our political allegiances, the constellation of beliefs advocated by the New Right was as capable of addressing "the aspirations of a more socially diverse population" as the constellation of New Left beliefs. If public librarians had wished to help disadvantaged minority groups to achieve social, economic, and political success, they could have done so by reiterating the public library's traditional goal of meaningful education through serious and purposeful reading. They could have chosen to emphasize educational opportunities that lead to "cultural mobility," as defined by Gans, and the social and economic mobility that is often an adjunct of cultural mobility, as personified by Dr. Condoleezza Rice.

The Politics of Genre Titles

In many public libraries, genre titles were important representatives of entertainment-oriented popular culture. For readers' advisors, their faith in the value of genre titles and other forms of popular culture was given scholarly support in 1984 by Janice A. Radway's *Reading the Romance: Women, Patriarchy, and Popular Literature*.[167] Presenting an extended case study about the ways in which a group of midwestern American women used romance genre fiction in their daily lives, Radway summarized and elaborated upon more than a decade's worth of arguments about popular culture. Despite the fact that "contemporary romance publishing is guided by [an] entrepreneurial vision of the book as an endlessly replicable commodity,"[168] romances offer their readers the opportunity "to resist, alter, and reappropriate" many of the "ideologically conservative" formulas of romance fiction "in order to better their lives."[169] Readers form an "interpretive community" engaged in an "active process" of reading.[170] Radway's idea that "active individuals and their creative, constructive activities" appropriate "the mass-produced art of our culture"[171] for their own purposes became one in a series of seductive justifications for the concerted focus in public libraries on entertainment-based pleasure reading. It was simply not true that "commodified objects exert such pressure and influence on their consumers that they have no power as individuals to resist or alter the ways in which those objects mean or can be used."[172]

It was easy to overlook that Radway's analysis did not rest on "a particular reader's concretizations of particular texts" nor on "readers' explicit statements about ... what they understand the story to say," but rather on a "composite-reader approach" based on her own "interpretation of twenty 'ideal' romances" through the prism of "a structural analysis of their shared plot."[173] It was also easy to overlook that Radway admitted that it was just as likely that romance fiction was "an active agent in the maintenance of the ideological status quo because it reconciles women to patriarchal society and reintegrates them with its institutions" in a way that "leaves unchallenged the male right to the public spheres of work, politics, and power ... even as it serves as a locus of protest against some of [the] emotional consequences" of that "institutionalized ... patriarchal control."[174] But her conclusion read more like an apologia for romance fiction (and all genre titles) than a strong defense of it. Stating that "the ideological power of contemporary cultural forms is enormous, indeed sometimes even frightening," she claimed that "[i]nterstices still exist within the social fabric where opposition is carried on."[175]

But, as Meaghan Morris and Ien Ang observed, the problem with audience ethnographies like Radway's was that "[t]here is a romanticizing and romanticist tendency ... that emphasizes (symbolic) resistance," which "can all too easily lead to an apologetic '*yes, but ...*' discourse that downplays the realities of oppression in favour of the representation of a rosy world 'where there's always a way to redemption.'"[176] It is no great discovery to say that audiences actively engage with texts, "but it would be utterly out of perspective to cheerfully equate 'active' with 'powerful,' in the sense of 'taking control' at an enduring, structural or institutional level."[177] Partaking in popular culture by reading genre titles may be personally empowering, but "we must not lose sight of the *marginality* of this power."[178] Genre titles become soporifics that allow readers to feel good about not taking the time and energy to read timeless (and difficult) books and think about timeless (and difficult) ideas that are the basis for real change. By emphasizing how entertainment-oriented genre titles contributed to personal meaning-making, public librarians positioned themselves in the 1960s' "happening" sensibility, at the antipodes of serious and purposeful reading, meaningful education, and real change.

Given these criticisms, it was ironic that post–1980 readers' advisors spent little time discussing how publishers, especially corporate publishers with large advertising budgets, artificially created the demand for the entertainment-oriented bestsellers and formula-based genre titles that readers' advisors stated that their patrons want and that became the core of post–1980 readers' advisory work. Readers' advisors therefore run the risk of becoming little more than publishers' representatives or clerks in chain bookstores, not only helping to generate readership (and hence future sales) for entertainment conglomerates whose overall interest lies in publishing profitable books, but also creating an atmosphere where these books are accorded legitimacy and respect. They run the risk of becoming supporters of and apologists for Bourdieu's heteronomous cultural producers, who consider cultural items as commodities.

Far from being elitist or censorious, Epstein and Brooks were harsh critics of entertainment-driven cultural commodification and market censorship, where the power of market forces determines the nature of what gets published, what is advertised, and what is demanded by a public constantly in search of pleasure and entertainment. Guy Debord used the phrase "society of the spectacle" to describe the effects of cultural commodification. While a spectacle claims to be "something enormously positive, indisputable and inaccessible," in reality it "says nothing more than 'that which appears is good, that which is good appears' [and] [t]he attitude which it demands in principle is passive acceptance which in fact it already obtained by its manner of appearing without reply, by its monopoly of appearance."[179] Debord's "society of the spectacle" drives out the possibility of intellectually challenging alternative choices. The "society of the spectacle" effectively privileges genre titles, bestsellers, celebrity-authored books, and prize-winning titles—popular culture items that are disposable commodities, to be consumed voraciously, narcissistically, and unthinkingly as one waits for the next spectacle to arrive.

According to Nick Chiles, a good illustration of this occurred in the early 2000s in the field of African-American literature when "ghetto fiction" and "street lit" monopolized an ever-increasing percentage of shelf space devoted to African-American Literature in chain bookstores.[180] Mainstream publishers offered authors such as Dewitt Gilmore multi-book contracts for sums "in the low six figures" to turn out books with titles like *Push, Topless,* and *Platinum Dolls* that were "saturated with sex, violence, gangsters and drug dealers," as well as "crude language and ghetto slang."[181] Other titles included *Hustlin' Backwards, Legit Baller, A Hustler's Wife,* and *Chocolate Flava*—what Chiles describes as "pornography for black women."[182] Although immensely popular, that popularity diminished the legitimacy and influence of serious African-American literature, whose authors found it difficult "to compete with ... purveyors of crassness" and who felt "defeated, disrespected and troubled about ... [their] little subsection of this carnivorous, unforgiving [publishing] industry."[183] Literature as a whole suffers, since it will be difficult to explain "to the next generation of writers and readers ... why they have so little to read of import and value produced in the early 21st century, why their founts of inspiration are so parched."[184]

Failing to recognize that recommending culturally and historically important fiction and nonfiction by well-respected authors was the kind of meaningful educational activity that public libraries were originally established to perform, post–1980 readers' advisors—with their emphasis on recommending books that were not necessarily worthwhile or good, but which, because they had appeared and because they were being demanded, must therefore be supplied—perpetuated and enabled market censorship. It was easy to recommend recent arrivals, genre titles, bestsellers, celebrity-authored books, and prize-winning titles, thus indulging patrons' desires for formulaic and ephemeral fiction and nonfiction in the name of giving them what they want. It was much harder, and more subversive, to suggest fiction and nonfiction books that had enduring cultural, historical, and social value and that addressed universal questions and issues. As Epstein explained, "Read Balzac and the belief in, say, reining in corporate greed through political reform becomes a joke; read Dickens and you'll know that no social class has any monopoly on noble behavior; read Henry James and you'll find the midlife crisis and other pop psychological constructs don't even qualify as stupid; read Dreiser and you'll be aware that the pleasures of power are rarely trumped by the advertised desire to do good."[185]

In *Vamps & Tramps*, Camilla Paglia urged students at Harvard University to take back their campus from professors and administrators who erected a "slick career system that has made deception, pretension, and manipulation business-as-usual in the humanities since the Seventies."[186] For her, this system was something whose intellectual foundations were based on "an amateurish mishmash of this and that," which called itself "cultural studies."[187] It was a system promulgated by "an amoral coterie"[188] of interconnected "conference crowd"[189] sycophants who espoused "hostility to the 'canon' of great European writers and artists"[190] and by "very pampered fat cats who have never stood on principle at any point in their careers"[191] yet make a huge show of "speaking of the campus as a 'community,' which, faculty soon discovered, was governed by invisible codes of acceptable speech, opinions, and behavior."[192] How were Harvard students to take back their campus and, by extension, gain access to meaningful education "organized around vigorous intellectual inquiry, not therapy or creature comforts"?[193] The answer was simple: students should "make the library [their] teacher." But it was a library whose core consisted of serious and purposeful literature. Only in this way could they accomplish the important task of "[r]ediscover[ing] the now neglected works of the great scholars of the last 150 years."[194] Only through concerted study of the library's reference collection could they "master chronology and etymology."[195] Only in this way could they avoid becoming what Allan Bloom called "homogenized persons" whose "[f]reedom had been restricted ... by the impoverishment of alternatives" resulting from a 1960s-inspired "egalitarian self-satisfaction that wiped out the elements of the university curriculum that did not flatter our peculiar passions or tastes of the moment."[196]

Paglia's advice for Harvard students is relevant for readers' advisors. Like universities, public libraries had once been places of meaningful education based on serious and purposeful reading, where the great ideas contained in enduring books were at the heart of learning. With the penetration of popular culture into public libraries, they went the way of post–1960s' universities, focusing on entertainment- and pleasure-based consumption that Brooks characterized as "Less Rembrandt, more Me." Library patrons developed the false sense that they were learning something by reading genre titles, bestsellers, celebrity-authored books, and prize-winning titles. They were supported in their beliefs by readers' advisors who, following Radway and other cultural theorists, had become convinced that entertainment-based pleasure reading was a worthy undertaking. While readers' advisors thought they were being user-friendly and responsive, they were actually shortchanging their patrons, making public libraries into institutions organized around "therapy" and "creature comforts" instead of venues for meaningful education, the precursor of real social and cultural accomplishment.

Writing in *The Foundations of Education for Librarianship*, Shera observed that Lowell Martin's article "The American Public Library as a Social Institution," originally published in 1937, was the key statement for any librarian interested in making the public library a relevant institution implicated in ameliorative social change.[197] It is interesting to look at Martin's article, especially in light of the way in which popular culture was positioned in the late 20th-century and early 21st-century public library as an agent of social change. Calling the public library one of society's "social elevators," Martin noted that it should have two goals.[198] First, "it transmits the social heritage and inculcates the values and experiences of the past into the group, with a unifying effect." Second, "it enables the individual to appraise present trends and future values, enhances the quality of his personal life, and provides a means for climbing the social ladder."[199] One of the villains in Harris's revisionist account of North American library history, Andrew Carnegie, also linked the public library with social mobility. As Michael Lorenzen pointed out, "Carnegie believed that the public library was an efficient and rational way that allowed those who were most able and motivated to educate themselves and allowed them then to attain high status positions regardless of their background," thus allowing "the meritocratic nature of America to work."[200] As Peter Mickelson stated, the public library was understood by Carnegie as a democratic American response to "European countries dominated by monarchs or elite ruling classes" because "[w]ithin its walls as within the American republic there were to be no artificial restrictions, no ranks, no privileges, no classes."[201] Since the public library, unlike colleges and universities, was and remains accessible to all, gaining a meaningful education that could lead to social mobility was a matter of individual will and personal responsibility. Individuals seriously committed to improving themselves and society could do so by reading "solid literature,"[202] defined as "the kinds of materials that would encourage the working-men and youthful entrepreneurs to advance and would inform the citizen about his world ... and works that would give all users a chance to achieve spiritual edification."[203]

As Carnegie explained in his autobiography, he attributed his success to the J. Anderson

Library of Allegheny City, Pennsylvania, where he and other young working men in the 1850s educated themselves. Anderson's library had initially been open only to "working boys," but after Carnegie, then "a messenger boy for a local telegraph company,"[204] wrote a letter to the *Pittsburgh Dispatch* asking him to open his library to "messenger boys, clerks, and others, who did not work with their hands," Carnegie's life changed: "the windows were opened in the walls of my dungeon through which the light of knowledge streamed in."[205] He continued:

> Every day's toil and even the long hours of night service were lightened by the book which I carried about with me and read in the intervals that could be snatched from duty. And the future was made bright by the thought that when Saturday came a new volume could be obtained. In this way I became familiar with Macaulay's essays and his history, and with Bancroft's "History of the United States," which I studied with more care than any other book I had then read. Lamb's essays were my special delight … ¶ … Books which it would have been impossible for me to obtain elsewhere were, by [Anderson's] wise generosity, placed within my reach; and to him I owe a taste for literature which I would not exchange for all the millions that were ever amassed by man. Life would be quite intolerable without it. Nothing contributed so much to keep my companions and myself clear of low fellowship and bad habits as the beneficence of the good Colonel.[206]

From this perspective, Carnegie was more of a populist egalitarian than librarians care to admit. By positioning themselves as entertainment- and pleasure-based environments stressing popular culture, public libraries turn their backs on upward social and cultural mobility, contributing to the perpetuation of the class barriers that they were established to help break down. For Martin and Carnegie, social change was not something that could be accomplished by making the public library a locus of entertainment-based popular culture in all its myriad forms. Rather, it was a locus of opportunity that rested on the firm foundation of meaningful education, which began with serious and purposeful reading of enduring books.

Recent Histories of Readers' Advisory Service

Five other accounts of the history of readers' advisory were published between 2000 and the early months of 2006: Crowley's book chapter, which was condensed and slightly reworked in a subsequent article[207]; Brendan Luyt's article "Regulating Readers: The Social Origins of the Readers' Advisor in the United States"[208]; Saricks's introductory account from her handbook[209]; Melanie A. Kimball's chapter in the sixth edition of *Genreflecting*[210]; and Ross's brief section entitled "Advising Readers" in *Reading Matters*.[211] Except for Luyt, they all presented readers' advisory in a linear fashion, as something that achieved its most realized expression between 1980 and 2005 after a series of fitful starts, stops, and reversals in previous decades. Like Saricks, Kimball juxtaposed the dark pre–1920 "early years" of readers' advisory, where librarians were concerned about providing "wholesome enlightenment," with the "Renaissance" of post–1980 readers' advisory, which was characterized by "a complete overhaul" of previous conceptions.[212] Her use of the word "overhaul" spoke volumes, implying that pre–1980 readers' advisory was something that was broken, rusty, and obsolete. Crowley's cursory treatment of pre–1920 readers' advisory was even more disturbing, since he insisted that all one needs to know about it was contained in the words of F. B. Perkins of the BPL, who argued in 1876 that it was "unreasonable" for patrons to "plague the librarian by trying to make him pick out books."[213] As will be apparent in chapter 3, nothing could be further from the truth: readers' advisory had a strong and rich tradition starting around 1870, a tradition that included the BPL.

Particularly dismaying was the fact that Crowley's characterization of pre–1920s' readers' advisory was accepted at face value by others. Ross based her indictment of pre–1920s' readers' advisory as a benighted phase that could best be described with the words "Don't ask, don't tell" on Crowley's anecdote about Perkins.[214] She then contrasted the "Don't ask, don't tell" phase with the more ebullient "New-Style" readers' advisory, whose avowed goal was "[p]utting the reader in the driver's seat."[215] And although Crowley suggested that "[e]ven the best among us have much to learn from our predecessors in the ongoing effort to adapt readers advisory thinking, philosophy, and service to the constantly changing educational, informational, and recreational needs of current readers and generations of readers yet to come,"[216] it is clear that, for him as well as for Kimball, Ross, and Saricks, readers' advisory underwent steady improvement and progress away from generally outmoded principles to an activity worthy of strong administrative support because it put "the reader in the driver's seat." Crowley, Kimball, Ross, and Saricks erected the "Give 'Em What They Want" approach into a philosophy of readers' advisory, forgetting that "pleasure" and "recreation" were often synonyms for convenient popular entertainment that facilitated the creation of a narcissistic "society of the spectacle" and the maximization of corporate profits. In this world, meaningful education became an afterthought.

For Luyt, who examined the readers' advisory movement in the 1920s and 1930s from a Marxist perspective, its rise was part of what T. J. Jackson Lears identified as the "therapeutic ethos," defined as "a concept that centered the well-being of the individual in the exuberant living of life, in contrast to Victorian ideals of frugality and conservation of energy."[217] Books, especially classic literature, were promoted as important components of "life-enhancing activities" for "[p]eople yearning to realize their full potential."[218] Readers' advisors thus helped "to construct a new mode of regulation" by imposing serious and purposeful reading on library patrons.[219] In this way, their leisure time could be transformed into productive work that would lead to a reversal of the "worsening of relations between capital and labor" during the Great Depression.[220] Readers' advisors participated in a "society-wide project" that exerted cultural control over individuals,[221] helped to establish a "technocratic social order" emphasizing "respect and obedience to experts,"[222] and installed a system of discipline that resulted in "a routinized form of living that made the most of [workers'] energy and channeled it in constructive ways."[223] Luyt's thesis was scornful of readers and their individual aspirations for intellectual growth. Deriding the impetus to self-improvement through education, Luyt neglected to mention that, for many individuals, reading was a political act connected with personal emancipation and development through exposure to a world of historical and cultural accomplishment in the form of enduring literature. Because literary classics were typically perceived as the preserve of socially and economically advantaged classes, the reading of classics by the less-advantaged majority was seen as a significant revolutionary act with ameliorative social and economic outcomes.

There are numerous examples of this. In *Reading Lolita in Tehran: A Memoir in Books*, Azar Nafisi recounts how Persian and American classics such as *A Thousand and One Nights*, Austen's *Pride and Prejudice*, Gustave Flaubert's *Madame Bovary*, F. Scott Fitzgerald's *The Great Gatsby*, Henry James's *Daisy Miller* and *Washington Square*, and Vladimir Nabokov's *Lolita* helped her and her students understand the complex historical and political forces buffeting contemporary Iran. One of the most eloquent comments in *Reading Lolita* about the value of literary classics for the "less fortunate" comes when Nafisi is momentarily beset with doubts about her choice of James's novel *Washington Square* for a university literature class. "In these revolutionary times," Nafisi says to Razieh, one of her poverty-stricken students who has been forced "to steal books and sneak into movie houses" throughout her life, "it's hardly surprising that students wouldn't care much about the trials and tribulations of a plain, rich American girl [Catherine Sloper, the heroine of *Washington Square*] at the end of the nineteenth century." Razieh, however, begs to differ, "vehemently" objecting that "[i]n these revolutionary times ... they care even more. I don't know why people who are better off always think that those less fortunate than themselves don't want to have the good things—that they don't want to listen to good music, eat good food or read Henry James."[224]

Perceptively identifying the condescension of the "better off" toward the "less fortunate," Razieh implied that, because the "better off" have convinced themselves that the "less fortunate" do not wish to read seemingly difficult and obscure authors such as Henry James, they have also convinced themselves that the "less fortunate" want to read insignificant authors, listen to bad music, and eat atrocious food, with the result that the "better off" feel that they should provide the "less fortunate" with large amounts of said insignificant authors, bad music, and atrocious food. In fact, the opposite was true: only literary classics can fill voids and bring readers to a lasting awareness of beauty. In this regard, Razieh drew an interesting contrast. Having "borrowed" and "cherished" books such as *Gone with the Wind* and *Rebecca* from "houses where my mother worked," she finally discovers the world of Henry James during her university years. Her amazement knows no bounds: "But James— he is so different from any other writer I have ever read. I think I am in love."[225]

Another example comes from Jonathan Rose's *The Intellectual Life of the British Working Classes*.[226] Rose describes how T.A. Jackson, a "proletarian philosopher"[227] who was a leading Marxist in Great Britain in the early 1900s, educated himself through "a conservative canon" of 100 classics of world literature compiled by Sir John Lubbock.[228] The list included "Aristotle's *Ethics*, *The Koran*, Xenophon's *Memorabilia*, [and] *The Nibelungenlied*."[229] Jackson, Rose writes, "owed his intellectual gifts largely to Sir John Lubbock" because "reading through nearly all of those one hundred books set in motion an intellectual odyssey that eventually brought [him] to Marxism, though Marx was certainly not on the list."[230] Jackson recalls how "reading translations of Greek and Roman classic authors ... started me off upon an intensive study of English poetry and, thereafter upon a similar study of Romance and Saga literature," which eventually led to the histories of Thomas Macaulay, who "as much as anybody ... gave me a push-off on the road from the conventional conception of history as a superficial chronicle-narrative to the wider philosophical conception of history as an all-embracing world-process as understood by Marx."[231] Although Lubbock's list consisted of classics, it was "conservative only in the sense that it included no living authors." For Jackson and other readers, the list was "profoundly radical," an inspiration "to range far beyond" its original parameters.[232] It was the essential starting point for a meaningful education.

Elizabeth McHenry's *Forgotten Readers: Recovering the Lost History of African American Literary Societies* is equally relevant.[233] She recounts how African-American literary societies were formed in large urban areas in the United States starting in the mid–19th century as "a direct response to community leaders' understanding that education was essential to improving the status and condition of the nation's African Americans, free and enslaved."[234] And to help their members become educated, many of these societies adopted "courses of study" that emphasized "classical texts," the reading of which, as one member of the Philadelphia Colored Reading Society put it, was the best way to "discipline the mind itself, to strengthen and enlarge its powers, to form habits of close and accurate thinking, and to acquire a facility of classifying and arranging, analyzing and comparing our ideas on different subjects."[235] Members of the Boston Literary and Historical Association (BLHA), founded in 1901 as a "self-conscious attack on the prestige and [accommodationist] racial policies of Booker T. Washington,"[236] were frequently reminded to read and "know something about the really great literature of Homer, Virgil, Dante, Shakespeare[,] and don't slight the really great works for the latest publication."[237] George W. Forbes—an African-American graduate of Amherst College who worked at the BPL and, along with William Monroe Trotter, was one of the cofounders and coeditors of the "militant" *Boston Guardian*—vaunted the merits of Milton, Spenser, Aeschylus, Emerson, Dryden, Pope, Browning, Pindar, and Sappho.[238] Trotter, one of the guiding figures behind BLHA, was adamant that "Negroes must by encouraged to seek and succeed in the highest forms of liberal arts education [because] from this sort of education came the capacity for strong intellectual and political leadership."[239] Social, economic, and political advancement was closely associated with a liberal arts education premised on literary classics, knowledge of which could also serve "as a prelude to the establishment and maturation of an African American literary tradition."[240] As McHenry observes, the fact that African-Americans did not have a "political voice" in American society meant that the "literary activities of free blacks" in literary societies took on "an aspect of resistance."[241] The cultivation of "a literary background" through literary classics and the subsequent development of a "dreaded eloquence" became "a necessity" that would allow African-Americans "to interact in a larger American society where they needed to defend themselves against the condemnation and ridicule they regularly confronted."[242]

This was especially true for African-American women's literary societies, where reading and the study of literature were "integral to the challenge ... against the negative stereotypes assigned to them and the hostile environments in which they lived."[243] And even though "texts by African American and women authors" were read, works of a "classical nature" by Carlyle, Milton, Ruskin, Shakespeare, and Tennyson predominated.[244] Some societies, including two in Denver, Colorado, organized "their reading around historical time periods or significant events" because they believed that "something about ... history and the texts that documented it ... was authentic, real; to study it was to tap into the aura and prestige with which it was associated."[245] Again and again women were urged, in the columns of *Woman's Era*, a newspaper founded in 1894 in Boston and "devoted to the interests of Women's Clubs, Leagues, and Societies throughout the country,"[246] to read "the best novels and romances, authors like Sir Walter Scott, George Eliot, Thackeray, Dickens and Hawthorne ... [and] with great care *study* the masters of the art of literature, authors like Milton, Dante, Shakespeare, Bacon, Goëthe, Cervantes, Schiller, and others."[247] *Woman's Era* columnist Medora Gould urged readers to be highly selective: "It is not only necessary to know what to read, but it is also necessary to know what not to read."[248] Gould saw some diversionary value in "light reading"—"a few light novels wisely interposed between serious study" could "break the current of habitual thought"—but, as McHenry noted, Gould "clearly articulates the importance of intellectual rigor and the danger of excessive light reading."[249] Another *Woman's Era* columnist, Leslie Wilmot, recommended applying Emerson's selection criteria, a three-part injunction to read only "famed books" published at least one year previously and that an individual reader actually liked.[250] McHenry concluded that the African-American women's club movement had a "measurable impact" both "on the development of literary activism" and "in the experiences of individual clubwomen who credit the transformation of their lives to their work as members of black women's clubs."[251]

The ways in which Crowley, Kimball, Ross, and Saricks, on the one hand, and Luyt, on the other, approached readers' advisory were two sides of the same coin. While Crowley, Kimball, Ross, and Saricks praised "New-Style" readers' advisory that focused on pleasure and recreational reading, Luyt derided the emphasis on serious and purposeful reading that was the hallmark of readers' advisory in the 1920s and 1930s. The cumulative effect was that "New-Style" readers' advisory, with its focus on entertainment, pleasure, and recreation as inspired by Gans's theory of popular culture and Rosenberg's "First Law of Reading," was viewed as an improvement on older readers' advisory models that stressed adult education. "New-Style" readers' advisors typically operated within the ideational framework that serious and purposeful reading to gain meaningful education should be downplayed. Instead, pleasure and recreational reading from the world of popular culture should be privileged because it contributes to personal meaning-making and can also be educational. Edutainment became legitimized.

Here was the crux of the matter. The definition of education became so diluted that just about anything qualified as educational, including personal meaning-making. It was therefore easy for post–1980 readers' advisors to accept the principle that entertainment-oriented pleasure reading qualified as educational. The mindset embodied in the phrase "Less Rembrandt, more Me. Fewer theologians, more dietitians" was accorded validity and respectability. Neil Postman, in the foreword to *Amusing Ourselves to Death*, an indictment of television published in 1985, observed that Aldous Huxley's *Brave New World* was a much more prescient vision of the way in which people would be oppressed than George Orwell's *1984*. The greatest danger to truth—as well as to "autonomy, maturity and history"—lay in the advent of "trivial culture," where individuals, "preoccupied with some equivalent of the feelies, the orgy porgy, and the centrifugal bumblepuppy," would be "drowned in a sea of irrelevance" and "controlled by inflicting pleasure."[252] Post–1980 readers' advisory, with its focus on entertainment and pleasure, has eerie parallels with the Postman's world of "trivial culture."

Reading does matter, but it also matters what is read. Otherwise, there is the risk of drowning "in a sea of irrelevance" as the self-absorbed reader, urged to read for entertainment and pleasure, ends up immersed in "some equivalent" of the "centrifugal bumblepuppy." To perform readers' advisory in a conscientious, intelligent, and creative manner that goes beyond the superficial and mechanical level of suggesting recent arrivals, genre titles, bestsellers, celebrity-authored books, and prize-winning titles, readers' advisors must spend long hours immersing themselves in the contents of fiction and nonfiction books with an eye to determining which items are worthy of being recommended to patrons so that they receive the best possible return on their investment of time and energy. Invariably, these are classics that provide historical, political, economic, and cultural knowledge.

Redeeming Library History

The emphasis on entertainment, pleasure, and recreation in the work of post–1980 readers' advisors was philosophically part of an attempt to reformulate the public library as a destination attraction and a community center for social interaction. By participating in a movement to make the public library more responsive to perceived community needs through a "Give 'Em What They Want" approach, "New-Style" readers' advisors saw themselves as the descendents of 1960s' counterculture librarians. Building on Gans's writings about the importance of popular culture; taking support from reader-response theories about active readers who, like Radway's romance readers, create personal meaning and significance from the various strands of popular culture with which they come in contact; receptive to the historical revisionism of Harris and Garrison; situating themselves in opposition to "a definition of information that was largely driven by emerging technologies"[253]; and rebelling against "more than a decade of delving into seemingly more high-powered subjects, such as automation, planning, and grantsmanship,"[254] post–1980 readers' advisors undertook a project that de-emphasized the public library's potential as a place for meaningful education and concomitantly enabled "the suburbanization of the mind."[255]

Post–1980 readers' advisors did not want to see themselves as the heirs of Harris's and Garrison's conservative and authoritarian elites. They became reticent about asserting that public libraries should provide meaningful educational opportunities for patrons, since the concept of meaningful education had been shown by Harris and Garrison to be associated with personality traits and ideals they rejected. Eschewing an orientation toward literary classics and the rigorous educational standards that reading and study of the classics implied, "New-Style" readers' advisors emphasized that public libraries were responsive "Give 'Em What They Want" institutions devoted to entertainment, pleasure, and recreation. They no longer performed the bait-and-switch tactic, convinced that the "carrot" was the entire meal. In so doing, they hoped to redeem—if not exorcize—the history of the origins of North American public libraries as recounted by Harris and Garrison. If, in the past, the public library had been a cloistered place that, in the name of a conservative authoritarianism interested in preserving social order, encouraged "serious, independent thought" and meaningful education; and the kind of "critical, dialectical, skeptical, desimplifying"[256] intellectual activity that was possible through exposure to classic literature, then now the public library must focus on popular fiction in the name of a pro-active response to anticipated user demands, personal meaning-making, and edutainment.

But this thinking shortchanged the many thousands of patrons who—like Razieh, T.A. Jackson, and members of African-American literary societies—believed that reading of literary classics was economically, politically, psychologically, and socially liberating. As Razieh poignantly remarked: "I don't know why people who are better off always think that those less fortunate than themselves don't want to have the good things."[257] Stephen Akey expressed a similar view in "McLibraries."[258] Because "[t]rash fiction, celebrity biographies, and diet fad books increasingly constitute the core collections of many of our public libraries," the serious reader is abandoned.[259] "Walk into any branch of the Queens Public Library and try to find a copy of, say, George Orwell's *Homage to Catalonia* or *The Portable Nietzsche*. More and more such books, if they're to be had at all, must be obtained through the time-consuming and restrictive process of interlibrary loan."[260] Striving to distance themselves from the elitist-authoritarian librarians described by Harris and Garrison, post–1980 readers' advisors became the sort of elitist-authoritarian described by Jerry Spiegler. Spiegler explained that the "Give 'Em What They Want" philosophy minimized "the potential of public libraries" because librarians, traveling "the expeditious route of popular demand," turned into "elitist-authoritarians" who gave "the relatively small group of regular, middle-class library users all the popular fiction they desire."[261] But, he continued, this also meant "ignoring the immigrants, school dropouts, ex-offenders, functional illiterates, and other 'undesirable non-users' who are then denied the means to a self-education."[262]

In our view, the period 1980–2005 was not the golden age of readers' advisory. Rather, these years marked a frustratingly sad, though inevitable, surrender by readers' advisors to market-based processes of entertainment-oriented cultural commodification that were inseparable from demand-driven service models. Post–1980 readers' advisors asserted that their focus on entertainment-oriented popular culture was an enlightened, open, and progressive "culture as practice" response to elitist or conservative notions of cultural authority and an obsolete conception of "culture as text."[263] But as McPheron—writing about

1960s' counterculture librarians, but in words that also apply to post–1980 readers' advisors—noted, "in attempting to 'open up' the library, they do not adequately comprehend the larger forces that work to dominate and keep things closed."[264] Their incomprehension "add[s] to, rather than decreas[es], the controlling power of the social, political, and economic status quo."[265]

At the same time that post–1980 readers' advisors privileged popular culture "in the name of community responsiveness,"[266] they also "court the frenzy of commercialism with an almost religious zeal,"[267] thus contributing to "the rampant anti-intellectualism of American life."[268] They fail to understand that public libraries should be "maintained, as far removed as possible from the mainstream of activities"[269] if a better social order is to arise, since that better social order is wholly dependent on fostering "the development of serious, independent thought."[270] Because many items typically associated with popular culture are "little more than distorted images of the dominant culture, and are easily absorbed into the Madison Avenue ethic," public libraries that fill their shelves with "pulp 'romances' ... or counter-culture 'alternatives' ... [and] where one looks in vain for, say, the collected Freud or Marx" do little to build the "intellectual independence" necessary to transform society.[271]

Challenges and Dilemmas of Readers' Advisory

Our view of readers' advisory might be seen by some to be contrarian. Just as we do not agree with Crowley, Kimball, Luyt, Ross, or Saricks, there will be many who do not agree with us. So be it. It has long been accepted that a single version of the history of anything does not exist. Instead, there are "competing realities" and any number of completed "mosaics" assembled from "discrete tiles of information" or "jigsaw pieces."[272] If our way of arranging the tiles or jigsaw piece about readers' advisory in North American public libraries proves nettlesome, it may nonetheless serve as a starting point for a searching examination about the current state and future direction of readers' advisory in a media-saturated and entertainment-based landscape that privileges an endless consumption of popular cultural commodities by extolling and maximizing their tenuous positive characteristics.

The issues swirling around readers' advisory are numerous. The kind of readers' advisory service that each librarian chooses to offer—or feels compelled to offer—speaks to the vision of librarianship that is dominant at a specific public library or is present in a librarian's mind, or a commingling of the two. And so, while each readers' advisory transaction is a discrete event given form and substance by the proximate factors impinging upon it, at a theoretical level it can be constructed as a staging ground for a debate between competing models of public librarianship. On the one hand, the public library as an institution whose central mission is meaningful education through serious and purposeful reading, a library that reaffirms a long-standing faith in the ability of enduring classics, cultural excellence, and intellectual standards to raise the level of national, community, and personal achievement and promote comprehensive understanding of social, historical, and political forces. On the other, the public library as a social institution catering to mass-market entertainment and pleasure in the name of narcissistic edutainment: "Less Rembrandt, more Me. Fewer theologians, more dietitians."

There are shades of grey in this stark dichotomy. Many public libraries try to be both educational and entertainment-oriented social venues. After all, few public librarians want to disavow completely the educational heritage of the public library even as they orient their institutions toward entertainment and recreation. Tensions between the "library as a meaningful educational institution" and the "library as entertainment-oriented social institution" exist, and it these tensions that give piquancy to the history of readers' advisory, especially because many public librarians in the late 20th and early 21st centuries asserted the validity of edutainment because it contributes to personal meaning-making.

There is another tension that overlays the previously described one: a multi-level tension between service to a patron qua individual and service to a patron who, through mechanical processes, is slotted into pre-defined categories based on past actions, beliefs, and choices, and is subsequently dealt with on the basis of those actions, beliefs, and choices. The former service takes much time and energy; the latter streamlined service does not. The former service demands that readers' advisors possess in-depth knowledge of patrons; it also demands that they possess in-depth knowledge of the contents and cultural value of numerous fiction and nonfiction books that could possibly suit the unique circumstances of patrons such that patrons walk away with a book that provides them with an opportunity for sustained reflection and a meaningful educational experience. The latter streamlined service relies on mechanical statements: "if you liked author-genre-title *xyz*, you might also like author-genre-title *fgh*"; "people who liked author-genre-title *xyz* might also like author-genre-title *fgh*"; "if you liked character-mood-theme element *pqr*, you might also like character-mood-theme element *abc*"; or "people who liked character-mood-theme element *pqr* might also like character-mood-theme element *abc*."

In busy public libraries, mechanical service is preferred, chiefly due to its cost effectiveness. Often, the level of service to be provided is addressed in institutional policy statements. Administrators make it clear that, since the public library must serve as many members of the public as possible, it is neither fair nor feasible to devote scarce human resources to time-intensive and in-depth readers' advisory, where only a handful of patrons can be served each day. Conversely, a more streamlined readers' advisory approach means that dozens of additional patrons can be processed. One of the criticisms of 1920s-1930s' readers' advisory, which was the cornerstone of the library adult-education movement, was that it reached relatively few people because each transaction required an initial in-depth interview and extensive follow-up by readers' advisors as they researched and prepared reading courses. Yet streamlined service often devolves into ecological fallacy, where generalizations about aggregated data (e.g., a group or class of people) are put forward to explain smaller units of data (e.g., individual cases), with the result that the reality of the individual case is misunderstood. Readers' advisors who fail to account for the nuances of the individual during each transaction risk basing their suggestions on inadequately grounded generalizations that may not be relevant to that individual, with the result that the match between the suggestion(s) offered by the readers' advisor and the person on whose behalf the suggestion is given becomes, at best, approximate.

What should be the balance between the public library's responsibility for meaningful education and its desire to be viewed as a social space in which the governing watchwords are entertainment, pleasure, and recreation masquerading as edutainment? How do readers' advisors juggle traditional educational imperatives in a public-service atmosphere that equates success with ever-increasing circulation statistics, which are often possible only through concentration on entertainment-oriented genre titles, bestsellers, celebrity-authored books, and prize-winning titles, which, in turn, are not meaningfully educational? Should readers' advisors work intensively with a patron in a time-consuming process that is not readily quantifiable in performance measurements favored by administrators, but that often results in reading suggestions that go beyond popular culture toward books that have meaningful cultural, educational, and social value? Should readers' advisors possess in-depth knowledge about literary classics built up over years of study? Or should they focus on serving the greatest number of people possible by categorizing patrons into groups based on a set of characteristics or a history of prior choices, and then giving members of those groups what others in their group wanted or selected, typically items of popular culture? The push and pull between the differing visions of readers' advisory service contained in these questions is a microcosm of the challenges, pressures, and dilemmas faced by public librarianship throughout its history.

Chapter 3

The Formative Years:
Philosophical Debates
and Lively Tensions

There are many ways to divide the history of readers' advisory into chronological periods. Crowley makes a fourfold division: 1876–1920 ("inventing" readers' advisory); 1920–1940 ("privileging nonfiction" readers' advisory); 1940–1984 (readers' advisory "'lost' in Adult Services"); and 1984–2005 ("reviving" readers' advisory).[1] This division reflects his belief that the resurgence of readers' advisory in the 1980s was a phoenix-like rebirth that ushered in a golden age. We disagree. As noted in chapter 2, we do not share Crowley's interpretation that readers' advisory achieved its fullest expression in the post–1980 era. For this and other reasons, our chronological division does not follow his. We divide the history of North American readers' advisory service into three broad periods: ca. 1870–1916; 1917–1962; and 1963–2005. The years 1917–1962 can be further subdivided into pre–World War II and post–World War II segments. Similarly, the years 1963–2005 can best be understood in terms of a gradual build-up to what we call a post–1980 period whose basic framework was defined by the publication of Rosenberg's *Genreflecting* in 1982 and the founding of ARRT in 1984. Both events set the stage for Saricks's multiple editions of *Readers' Advisory Service in the Public Library* and librarians' growing fascination with automated readers' advisory, as represented by the NoveList database and its descendants.

We refer to the period ca. 1870–1916 as "the formative years." This was a time when the concept of readers' advisory was new and hence the theater of crucial philosophical debates and lively tensions about its meaning. We refer to the period 1917–1962 as "the commitment to systematic adult education," when intensive attention to patron reading needs was combined with a strong commitment to meaningful education through serious and purposeful reading. Unlike Crowley, we do not believe that readers' advisory was "lost" in the years immediately following World War II and during the 1950s. Gaining strength from its significant achievements in the 1920s and 1930s, readers' advisory continued its adult-education orientation in the 1940s and 1950s through programs such as Great Books, Great Issues, and American Heritage. We label the period 1963–2005 "the devolution into entertainment." Here, the emphasis in public libraries on popular culture resulted in the application of the "Give 'Em What They Want" approach, first practiced by Charlie Robinson and Jean-Barry Molz at the Baltimore County Public Library in the 1960s, to readers' advisory. As the 1960s gave way to the 1980s and then to the 2000s, this approach was increasingly legitimized through recourse to theories about personal meaning-making. By the beginning of 2006, readers' advisory was construed in terms of commodified entertainment.

Just as Crowley's fourfold division was inspired by his linear view of the evolution of readers' advisory toward an ever-improved service-delivery model, our threefold division reflects the view that, after a necessary debate about definitions in its early period, readers' advisory reached and maintained a high level of accomplishment during 1917–1962 only to see that accomplishment eroded in the post–1963 period by a series of practices that vitiated its fundamental educational premises. This is not to say, however, that the two last periods were monolithic in their approaches, since they too were marked by competing philosophies and visions of what ideal readers' advisory should be.

The Origins of Readers' Advisory

As Crowley noted, it is a difficult and "frustrating, almost arbitrary exercise" to assign a precise date for the origins of readers' advisory, since precision "can founder on such basic issues as the absence of common definitions [of] ... a public library or ... readers advisory."[2] But it is probably safe to say that the guiding philosophy of readers' advisory in its early period was described by Samuel S. Green, Justin Winsor, and Charles A. Cutter. Frederick M. Crunden, William E. Foster, and Adolph L. Peck also made significant contributions. It was a period when many public libraries operated under a closed-stack system, where "the point of initial contact between reader and book was the delivery desk, a long, straight, uninterrupted counter designed to isolate the public from the library's treasures," where "readers approached to hand in their request slips, retreated while the page [or clerk] disappeared into the book storage area, and approached again a few minutes later to receive delivery of the books requested."[3] Here patrons charged out books. Some came with a specific request; others came only with the vaguest of requests, often just asking for "a nice book." There was necessarily conversation, or at least some obligatory interaction, among clerks, librarians, and patrons before patrons held a book in their hands. It was within the general parameters of these conversations that readers' advisory was born. The thinking went as follows: why not use these "natural" moments at the delivery or circulation desk to elevate patrons' reading tastes? And since many public libraries in the United States in the late 19th century allowed a patron to charge out only one book at a time, the choice of that single book became a contested site for important issues.

We begin by looking at Green's 1876 article "Personal Relations between Librarians and Readers," which discussed the procedures he implemented at the Free Public Library of Worcester, Massachusetts, starting in 1871–1872.[4] Green advocated "[p]ersonal intercourse and relations between librarians and readers"[5] such that all patrons are immediately placed "on a home footing" upon entering the library.[6] He also distinguished between two library functions: reference service and readers' advisory. Patrons used libraries either "for purposes of investigation"[7] or "to select stories,"[8] and so it was natural that different staff members would offer two kinds of personal assistance to two kinds of patrons.[9] Patrons looking for information "for purposes of investigation" were to be helped by a librarian who was "to mingle freely,"[10] greet investigators "with something of the cordiality displayed by an old-time inn-keeper," and "show a persistency in supplying their wants similar to that manifested by a successful clerk in effecting a sale."[11] Conversely, readers' advisory was performed at a fixed location—the circulation department—by a library assistant, usually a woman. Green's description of the attributes that readers' advisors should possess and the way in which they should go about their tasks is worth quoting in full.

Place in the circulating department one of the most accomplished persons in the corps of your assistants—some cultivated woman, for instance, who heartily enjoys works of the imagination, but whose taste is educated. She must be a person of pleasant manners, and while of proper dignity, ready to unbend, and of social disposition. It is well if there is a vein of philanthropy in her composition. Instruct this assistant to consult with every person who asks for help in selecting books. This should not be her whole work; for work of this kind is best done when it has the appearance of being performed incidentally. Let the assistant, then, have some regular work, but such employment as she can at once lay aside when her aid is asked for in picking out books to read. I am confident that in some such way as this a great influence can be exerted in the direction of causing good books to be used. The person placed in charge of this work must have tact, and be careful not to attempt too much. If an applicant would cease to consult her unless she gives him a sensational novel, I would have her give him such a book. Only let her aim at providing every person who applies for aid with the best book he is willing to read.[12]

Many of the characteristics of readers' advisory as it is conducted in the 21st century are present in Green's 1876 formulation. First, readers' advisory makes up only part, albeit an important part, of a designated employee's job description. Other more regular work is done by this employee while she awaits queries. Second, readers' advisors must have many special qualities—accomplishment, education, cultivation, sociability, enthusiasm, and tact— that make them sensitive to the unique reading needs of patrons. Third, while the primary goal is to recommend "good books," readers' advisors understand that it is just as important to ensure that a patron keeps returning to the library, and so a plausible alternative to "good books" is "the best book [the patron] is willing to read," even if that means a "sensational novel." Green was adamant that "[t]here must be some sensational books in a public library" because "neither citizens nor city government will support a library generously that does not contain the books they and their families want."[13] In fact, "[a] large portion of the community will get no education unless they receive it in the form of imaginative literature."[14] However, public libraries should not indiscriminately stock everything: the supply of books represented by the novels of "Mrs. Southworth and Mrs. Stephens" should be kept "as low as will be tolerated by the supporters of the library."[15]

Winsor, Superintendent of the Boston Public Library (1868–1877) and subsequently Librarian of Harvard University, took up many of the same themes as Green, but put new emphasis on librarians' duty to elevate reading tastes and thus fulfil the educational mandate of the public library. In 1876 in "Reading in Popular Libraries," he wrote that librarians must recognize that "A spurns as trash what elevates B, who looks down on the highest reading C is capable of, and so on till you get down to the mere jingle that amuses a half idiot, who is happy because he can understand something above the caterwauling of the roofs."[16] But, he was quick to add, this recognition does not mean that "however we [as librarians] take things, we must leave them as we find them."[17] That is to say, librarians "do not do their whole duty unless they strive to elevate the taste of their readers, and this they can do, not by refusing to put within their reach the books which the masses of readers want, but by inducing a habit of frequenting the library, by giving readers such books as they ask for and then helping them in the choice of books, conducting them, say from the ordinary society novel to the historical novel, and then to the proofs and illustrations of the events or periods commemorated in the more readable of the historians."[18] And because Winsor was convinced that "[m]ultitudes of readers need only to be put in this path to follow it,"[19] the librarian's role as an advisor and guide was crucial if readers are to be "helpfully advanced."[20] Here was a concise statement of a central aspect of early readers' advisory: helping to elevate the tastes of readers on a continual basis.

But how was such help to be provided? Winsor suggested that "records of circulation" should be "kept in a way to be a guidance rather than an obstacle to the librarian."[21] Since principal contact between patrons and librarians occurred at the delivery desk, a librarian who looked at a patron's circulation record could see the kinds of fiction books that the patron had already borrowed and, based on that knowledge, could recommend nonfiction books that might also appeal to the patron. Thus patrons "can be made to glide into what is commonly called instructive reading quite as early as it is good for them."[22] Winsor recognized that readers' advisory work depended on a librarian's knowledge of patrons' prior reading interests. If circulation records were suitably organized, they could serve as valuable artifacts that could help orient librarians about patrons' reading histories. Armed with this background knowledge, librarians could then offer informed suggestions for future reading that would intellectually advance patrons.

But Winsor also knew that, before effective readers' advisory could occur, patrons needed to be convinced to make return visits. Librarians were therefore as much publicists for and promoters of the library as discriminating guides to appropriate reading material. The key to ensuring repeat visits lay in overcoming "several interfering influences," the chief of which was that "[m]ost of the frequenters of a popular library drop off when you have begun to have the most effect upon them, because they have attained an age when business first begins to engross their attention, and they confine their reading to a newspaper on week days and to a chance number of a periodical on Sundays."[23] There was a clear relationship between repeat visits and "better reading." If older patrons could be induced to continue to use the library, both they and the library would benefit. While patrons would be "helpfully advanced" in their reading, the library could prove that its users were not just "crav[ing] pastime only" by pointing to the high number of "better reading" materials borrowed by older patrons.[24] After all, young people, who "find all the instructive reading they ought to have in their school books," come to the library mainly for "story books," which "swell[s] the issue of fiction," but also "prevent[s] the statistics of that better reading into which you have allured the older ones, from telling as they should in the average."[25]

Why was Winsor concerned about circulation averages? First, he realized that these averages did not provide an accurate picture of the library's utility, since they did not give proper weight to "better reading." Second, he realized that circulation statistics were often examined by local authorities who wanted to ensure that the town or city was receiving a good return for the money allocated to the public library; that is, they wanted to ensure that the library was primarily being used for meaningful educational purposes, which they equated with circulation of "better reading." If the library consistently reported high circulation statistics for popular or sensational fiction and low circulation statistics for "better reading," thus skewing the average toward popular fiction, this might be taken as an indication that the library was mainly being used for purposes other than meaningful education. And if the library was not being used for meaningful educational purposes to the extent that municipal leaders thought proper, questions might be raised about its ongoing usefulness and adequate funding levels might be jeopardized.

The role of the public librarian therefore took on an additional layer of complexity in Winsor's mind. Because their salaries were subsidized by public monies, librarians had a social responsibility to ensure that educational and cultural progress was being made by patrons—progress that could be measured by circulation statistics that reflected "better reading." Consequently, readers' advisory was at the heart of the public-library mission. The goal of librarians was to educate patrons, which could be done by elevating their reading tastes, which was dependent on librarians' wise and judicious guidance in patrons' choice of books, which would go a long way toward ensuring repeat visits to the library, which would mean further elevation of reading tastes, which would be documented in circulation statistics that took into account "better reading," which would bear witness to the meaningful educational progress that the public library was established to provide. Librarians who were not readers' advisors were not doing their jobs properly. While circulation statistics that showed only large amounts of popular fiction being borrowed were technically accurate, they were also a sign of librarians' failure to convince patrons to delve into better reading material and to make return visits to the library—two interrelated elements that were, in Winsor's opinion, at the center of readers' advisory work.

Judging by his 1879 article "On Aimless Reading and Its Correction," Foster, the Librarian at the Providence (Rhode Island) Public Library, had many of the same views as Winsor.[26] There were two kinds of reading: "aimless and purposeless reading" that "requires no effort, but simply a yielding to indolent inclination" and its opposite, purposeful reading that requires substantial intellectual effort.[27] And while individuals can to some degree be held responsible for their aimless reading, their propensity to read aimlessly is really the fault of parents, teachers, and librarians because they have failed to instill "quickened perceptions, habits of close observation, and an intimate and active interest in the concerns of life" in readers.[28] Everyone suffers as a result. Readers are rarely exposed to "some of the best books," and on those few occasions when good books do come to their attention, they "fail[] to appreciate the contents of [them]" because they peruse them "listlessly" at best.[29] Society as a whole also suffers, since good books are left unread on library shelves, not giving value for the funds expended to purchase them. But readers' advisors can change patrons' inclinations and increase the collective benefit to be derived from the many "excellent books" held by any given public library.

One of the primary ways to do so, Foster believed, was through the creation of lists or bulletins on various topics. While bulletins are typically published at regular intervals (i.e., quarterly, monthly, daily), lists are more ad hoc. Foster insisted that lists or bulletins cannot just be long enumerations of library holdings. Rather, they must be copiously annotated, with "suggestive notes, illustrations, and references" so that readers are guided to related materials.[30] This is particularly important in the realm of fiction, where the accompanying annotations should "link[] each story with the historical event it illustrates," thus becoming "a strong incentive" to "parallel historical reading."[31] As an example of the positive effects of annotated lists, Foster identified the "History, Biography, and Travel catalogue of the Boston Public Library," observing that, in the years after its publication, use of books in these categories "more than quadrupled," while fiction use dropped "from 74 per cent of the whole to only 69 [per cent]."[32] Green was also a strong proponent of lists. While praising librarians who issue "once or twice a year lists of the more desirable of the recent additions, and scatter these about the library rooms, and distribute them among readers," he believed that these lists would possess much "added value" were they to contain "notes ... printed under the titles, calling attention to attractive features in the books."[33]

Lists or bulletins based on current events were also useful. "Thus if the invasion of Afghanistan be a matter of public interest at one time, the bulletin contains a comprehensive list of works on that country. Similarly, when the interest of the public is turned largely in the direction of pottery and porcelain, the bulletin reveals minutely the resources of the library in this department of art."[34] But no matter the topic, emphasis must be placed on appending to each mentioned title "brief notes, original or borrowed, [which] giv[e] an indication of the character of some of the books." Compiling lists for current-events topics also provides an invaluable opportunity to highlight books "not published in the immediate present."[35] Librarians who believe that only the most recent titles are worthwhile are doing patrons a disservice, since "few of the subjects which successively in the course of a year command public attention do not have important light thrown on them" by books that have been in the public library for a long time.[36] The task of readers' advisors is to "take the trouble to bring these works to the attention of ... readers while their interest is still lively."[37] In so doing, neglected yet worthy books are requested by patrons. The key point here is the phrase "take the trouble to," because it takes much time and trouble to create lists with meaningful educational content. But the payoff can be immense: "A reader has frequently been started, by so slight a thing as a list of references to the historical basis of a play at that time on the stage, on a course of reading which, step by step, has led him much further than he originally intended."[38]

Crunden, Librarian of the St. Louis Public Library (SLPL) from 1877 to 1909, went one step further when developing "special lists on subjects of popular interest."[39] In 1885, he asked eminent local experts to prepare six lists, each of which "consisted of a few preparatory remarks as to methods of study, followed by a list of the best books on the topic treated."[40] Thus, about 40 years before the ALA's *Reading with a Purpose* series, St. Louis residents enjoyed reading courses on Buddhism; French History; The Renaissance; Travel; Music; and Children, their Training and Management.[41] The French History course was prepared by Marshall S. Snow, Professor of History at Washington University, while the Buddhism reading course was compiled by another well-loved teacher, William M. Bryant.[42]

Lists were not the only way that readers' advisors could guide patrons toward "better reading." Foster recommended establishing a "notes and queries" area. Here, in an early version of electronic discussion lists, "[q]uestions of suggestive interest are ... proposed by some one reader, and answered by any other one who may be able to do so," thus "frequently open[ing] attractive and profitable fields of research."[43] In the first of a series of "Reports on Aids and Guides" (RoAG) delivered on a semi-regular basis at ALA conferences in the 1880s and 1890s, Green described how the Free Public Library of Worcester and various societies co-operated to hold lectures and classes in library facilities so that these lectures could be made more instructive using "costly illustrated works" owned by libraries.[44] Classes sponsored by art societies, churches, and women's clubs held illustrated lectures about Eastern Antiquities, Roman Architecture, and English Geography.[45] In the second RoAG, Foster suggested that librarians give lectures about selected topics so as to give "an impetus to reading on specific subjects."[46] Displays were also useful tools in the arsenal of readers' advisors. According to Minerva A. Sanders, the librarian at the Pawtucket (Rhode Island) Public Library, a prominently displayed table of 100–150 nonfiction books about a variety of subjects resulted in much increased circulation in those subject areas.[47] Although lists, bulletins, reading courses, lectures, and displays were effective methods for aiding patrons, by the time that Crunden delivered his RoAG in 1886, which summarized the results of a questionnaire that he had sent out to American public libraries about the range of practices they had adopted to help readers, 53 out of 108 libraries felt that "[a]mong the most acceptable and effective methods" for helping patrons find the best books for their needs was "personal help."[48]

Adding Complexity to Readers' advisory Service

If Green and Winsor described the underlying philosophy of readers' advisory, Cutter, the developer of "a system of alphanumeric author marks ... to permit the arrangement of items of the same classification, alphabetically by author's last name," formulated the term advisor in 1889.[49] Like Green and Winsor before him, Cutter understood readers' advisory as something that was deeply imbedded within the educational mandate of the public library. He reiterated Green's point that the job could not be done by just anyone because, in addition to extensive knowledge about books, it called for knowledge of human nature. And, again like Green and Winsor, Cutter envisioned readers' advisory being performed at the circulation desk by an educated and caring assistant or clerk. At least one of the on-duty staff members should possess the skills necessary to perform readers' advisory: "Let no one imagine ... that this attendant—whom in library matters we might call the Adviser or Suggester—will have an easy time, or that a successful adviser can be found everywhere."[50] Cutter noted that the advisor is someone whose "qualification is tact, tact, tact—first, last, and all the time, quite as much as book knowledge."[51] In addition, the advisor needed "enthusiasm and unfailing patience."[52]

But before the advisor can assume his or her central role at the public library, Cutter explained that the mentality of library administrators and the public must change. He minced no words: "library committees, and the public that is behind library committees, [must] wake up to the perception that in this supplementary public school which we call [the] public library, it is their duty to provide teachers as well as text-books."[53] Cutter pictured knowledgeable circulation attendants as teachers, not just "animated machines, with no higher ambition than to pass over the counter 300 volumes an hour."[54] Cutter therefore believed that the creation of a readers' advisory position by a public library testified to the seriousness with which that library approached its educational responsibility. As the title of his article indicated, the presence of a readers' advisor was an example of "Common Sense in Libraries."[55]

Yet it was not as simple as waving a wand and decreeing the creation of a readers' advisor. Other mentalities in the library world must also change if the readers' advisor was to be effective. If civic leaders in Boston were interested in breaking down overall circulation statistics so that some insight into the statistics for "better reading" could be obtained, politicians in many other cities were content to equate high total circulation statistics with excellent library service. For Cutter, this latter practice should cease. The readers' advisor will not increase circulation statistics; rather, he or she will positively affect the quality of books read by patrons. Statistics "will not indicate that good fiction is read where bad fiction was read before; they do not indicate if the novels taken are read with a purpose or not, with the mind open or shut, if they are devoured at the rate of one a day, or as by the young people's society I knew of where *Romola* was gone through one winter and the *Tale of Two Cities* another."[56] Second, the library must firmly commit itself to a policy of "having a plentiful supply of good reading, *all interesting,* and a scanty supply of reading that is not so good."[57] This policy, in turn, must be based on the recognition that the most popular and sensational novels—Cutter cites the ubiquitous presence in library catalogs of novels by the notorious Mrs. Southworth—can easily be replaced, initially, by "some other story-tellers who have greater merits, who can tell as interesting stories better, and with a better moral, and *next* ... in part [by] some higher class of reading that shall give more information and exercise the mind more."[58] Successful readers' advisory thus depends on wise collection-development policies and a willingness to overlook stagnant or decreasing circulation statistics. Otherwise, readers' advisory cannot fulfil its bright promise, part of which lies in giving credence to the words of "Sir John Herschel ... [who] regard[ed] 'the novel in its best form as one of the most powerful engines of civilization,' or prompt[ed] the Bishop of Ripon's glowing eulogy on the usefulness of fiction."[59]

Readers' advisors should therefore encourage patrons to embark on what Crunden called a "process of self-culture."[60] As he explained in 1891 in "The Most Popular Books," those most likely to benefit from that process are patrons "whose taste is in [a] nebulous condition," who vaguely ask for "something good to read."[61] Here was the perfect opportunity for librarians to "educate the public" because they could question patrons about their reading habits.

> If his mental pabulum is furnished by books of a very low class, the librarian recommends something not quite so low. If the applicant confesses a fondness for Mrs. Southworth, she is given one of Mrs. Holmes' novels, but if she has already risen to the height of Mrs. Holmes, an attempt is made to still further elevate her taste and one of Roe's moral tales is handed out. This plan is followed persistently, and if the individual is not discouraged in her ambition to read "something good" the librarian will soon have her reading Dickens and Thackeray, and perhaps Hawthorne or Howells. But when she gets to this point she will probably choose her own reading and allow the librarian to devote his attention to later applicants who have just begun the process of self-culture.[62]

The "process of self-culture" was a gradual one and marked with pitfalls, since it depended on whether or not the patron felt "discouraged in her ambition." Crunden likely would not have disagreed that librarians, in their capacities as readers' advisors, needed to understand patrons on an individual basis so as to circumvent their discouragement and keep their ambitions alive.

In a 1901 article called "Should Libraries Buy Only the Best Books or the Best Books that People Will Read?" Cutter addressed the often fraught relationship between patron and readers' advisor, defining the "tact" and "unfailing patience" that readers' advisors should possess in terms of the work done by the clergy.[63] Starting from the premise that each patron has "the natural inclination to better one's self," Cutter stated that this inclination "must be gently and unobtrusively assisted."[64] For him, readers' advisory was a ministry.

> Here, as in all *pastoral* work, success comes from sympathy. He can best minister to another's wants who can put himself into another's place, enter into his mind, and so feel those wants himself. As the librarian will do injustice to the scholar unless he has himself felt the sacred thirst for knowledge; as he will not, indeed, cannot supply the demand for the beautiful unless he has himself felt the artistic thrill, so he will fail in properly providing for many of his people unless he remembers the gradual opening of his own mind or is able by imagination to recreate his forgotten states of ignorance and inability.[65]

All patrons are not the same, and so suggestions or recommendations must be calibrated to fit diverse needs, abilities, and personalities. Many readers' advisors fail in their tasks because they do not understand this, with the result that "many most excellent persons do not really enter into the state of mind of those who are at a stage of culture or mental ability or aesthetic taste which they [themselves] have passed beyond."[66] Readers' advisors must therefore differentiate between what people do read from what people will read, given a little encouragement. Cutter provides the following example.

> A man came to our library repeatedly and asked for Mrs. Southworth's novels. We had only two or three, and when none of them was in he would go away without taking anything. The attendant tried to get him to borrow something a little better, but without success. Then she recommended some of the same sort, Mrs. Mary J. Holmes and the like; but he would have none of them. "Why don't you get some of Mrs. Southworth's?" he burst out; "they're splendid!" Those novels were just suited to his capacity, "the best he would read," "the best" for him. And we shall give them to him. We are even getting more of them at his request. But I do not yet despair of introducing at least a little variety into his diet.[67]

No wonder that readers' advisors need tact and patience. They must know exactly the right moment when a patron is open to having "a little variety" introduced "into his diet," and when he or she wants another novel by Mrs. Southworth. As Cutter stated, "[p]eople improve," and "[t]hey are not always averse to, in fact they often desire—the young usually desire—to read what is a little above them, if it is not too unintelligible, and if it is not forced upon them."[68] The issue of forcing is a key one, since it implies that readers' advisors should have some insight into a patron's personality and character so as not to force something unwillingly on him or her. And this flexibility in approach—on some occasions enticing someone to read at a level higher than Mrs. Southworth, at other times indulging the patron's predilection for Mrs. Southworth—could only be achieved if library collections were flexible. That is, they must have books for each grade of reader, because "[t]he mere presence of the books-just-beyond-them in the library is sure to lead some [patrons] ... sometimes to attempt these and so to move up to a little higher plane. And the library is sure to have the books that are just a little better than any of its readers if it proceeds on the principle of getting what suits each grade, which, of course, will be a little above those that suit each lower grade."[69] A public library should therefore resemble a "Gothic cathedral" rather than a "Grecian temple[], made by rule, all just alike wherever they are, perfect in form, suited to one limited use." And a good librarian should select books "as Shakespeare wrote his plays, the highest poetry, the deepest tragedy side by side with the comic and the vulgar," avoiding the "succès d'estime" model that can be seen in "the regularity, balance of parts, dignity of expression, of the French classic drama."[70]

In addition to tact, readers' advisors who want to bring about "improvement in the quality of reading" among their patrons must "gain the confidence of those they wish to guide," according to Peck in his 1897 article "What May a Librarian Do to Influence the Reading of a Community?"[71] Speaking specifically about the way in which librarians can advise children in a way that is free "from prejudice and cant," Peck, who was the Librarian of the Gloversville (New York) Public Library, offered a solution that could easily be applied to adult readers.[72] When working with a child who likes the Horatio Alger books: "Ask yourself, 'What does he like in the Alger books?' The answer is simply that he likes to read about real boys and their successes. It is success and wealth that attract him, and he dreams that his career may be similar."[73] Or it may be that the child likes to read about schoolboys or adventures in general. Regardless, once the key thematic element(s) that causes patrons to like a book have been identified, astute readers' advisors can then recommend other "better" books containing the identified thematic element(s). If a patron liked the themes of success and wealth in Alger, librarians can suggest "[t]he Trowbridge, the Kellogg, and the Kaler books."[74] If it was, instead, the theme of adventure, then "Ballantyne and some of the earlier Reid books, the Henty books, or ... Du Chaillu" might be recommended."[75] If the patron wants other stories about schoolboys, "you may not at first succeed in getting him to read *Tom Brown*, but give him some other books about schools and schoolboys."[76] Not all patrons who like Alger will gravitate to the same handful of other authors. Each patron has specific reasons for liking a book, and it is these reasons, once identified, that will permit readers' advisors to make nuanced suggestions from a wide range of choices.

For readers' advisors to succeed in this endeavor, they must have broad-based knowledge of the numerous themes contained in numerous books. Readers have expectations about what they want, and it is only by meeting those expectations—that is, by suggesting a book that the patron will actually like—that "the first step toward gaining [the patron's] confidence" can be taken.[77] And although Peck leaves unsaid the obvious corollary, it is clearly present: if the readers' advisor fails to meet the patron's expectations by recommending a book that the patron does not like, there is little hope that confidence between librarian and patron can be established. A readers' advisor who has limited knowledge about books has scant hope of making nuanced and precise suggestions that give a patron a sense of confidence. Simply put, this type of readers' advisor does not have as many options from which to choose when making his or her suggestions as does a readers' advisor who has read broadly and thus can easily connect a patron's favorite themes with other better books that also contain those themes. Knowing only that a patron likes Alger is not sufficient for making astute recommendations, Peck believed. Readers' advisors must also know the precise reason why Alger is liked so as to be able to recommend Kellogg instead of Henty or Ballantyne to a patron interested in the theme of wealth and success, even though Henty and Ballantyne are also popular among fans of Alger.

Creating bonds of confidence between readers' advisors and patrons is difficult because it presupposes a vast amount of knowledge on the part of readers' advisors. But if librarians want patrons to gravitate to "better reading," bonds of confidence are vital. As Foster observed in "Methods of Securing the Interest of a Community," the focus should be on serving "individual readers" with "individual methods," not on "general and indefinite" assistance.[78] Even in large and busy public libraries concrete steps should be taken so that "[t]he librarian almost mechanically learns 'to pigeon-hole' in his mind the peculiar tastes and lines of reading of single readers, and, when the occasion presents itself, can bring to their notice books and articles which they are glad to obtain."[79] Good practice even demands that librarians "drop a postal [note or card]" to patrons about some newly received item that may be of interest to them because "[t]he more the conducting of a library can be made an individual matter, bringing particular books to the notice of particular readers, the more effective it becomes."[80]

Beyond the personal qualities that librarians acting as readers' advisors must possess when interacting with patrons, they should also be willing to go outside the library to encourage, and improve the quality of, reading among members of the community at large. Public librarians, argued Peck, should especially want to "take an active interest in all societies that are formed for mutual improvement by study and research."[81] Here the key point is the word active. Librarians, especially those working in small institutions, cannot afford to wait until representatives of debating clubs and reading circles come to them with requests for books, which the library may or may not own. They "must influenc[e] the topic or program committee to compile their programs at the library, and thus instead of asking afterward for what the library has not, make use of the books which the library has, no matter how few."[82] Beatrice Winser, Assistant Librarian at the Free Public Library of Newark (New Jersey), had much the same idea in 1903, urging librarians to "make it part of [their] business to prepare programs for clubs and societies" by having "on file outlines of all sorts of topics" from which "various program committees" could then "make selections."[83] In this way librarians become engaged in their communities, creating goodwill and appreciation for the library's collection. Foster's vision of the public library as the hub of a community's intellectual life was thus largely dependent on the abilities of librarians to convince diverse groups of people that the library could provide them with meaningful educational opportunities.

> Here is a machine-shop with its hundred or more workmen, many of whom are anxious to study some mechanical work. The library has such works, and is glad to supply them. Here again is a society of natural history, whose members are systematically studying some department of natural science. To them, also, the library willingly offers its resources in that department. With no less willingness it offers its co-operation to those who are following a course of public lectures on

some topic of political science or of art, to a college class studying topically some epoch of history or period of literature; or to a public-school teacher, with a class in geography; or a parent desiring some suitable reading for a child.[84]

Once this realization takes hold, librarians will have a reservoir of trust and confidence to draw on. They might not feel compelled to seek popularity by succumbing to the unabated public demand for "infus[ing] 'new blood' into the library by frequent and regular purchase of the latest [fiction] publications."[85] Each library must have a certain amount of popular fiction, Foster admits, but overemphasis on fiction detracts from the library's educational purpose. Librarians who gain public support for the library by positioning it as a place to borrow popular fiction are building their edifice on quicksand. Stocking the library with the newest titles may secure ephemeral "popularity," but it will not secure "gratitude," which can only be gained when patrons feel that "they have been personally aided and improved through [the] agency" of the library.[86] And it is the public's gratitude that would be the single most important factor in leveraging moral and financial support for the library's future growth. Librarians must therefore forgo the easy temptation of being popular and concentrate on the more arduous task of developing the basis for gratitude by "improving" as many members of the public as possible.

There was no limit to community outreach. Peck discussed how librarians could offer to help local booksellers by giving them access to trade journals used by the library in book selection or by informing them of the imminent publication of good books. In this way, librarians ensured that local residents who never set foot in libraries still felt their influence.[87] In Gloversville, New York, "the quiet elevating influence of the library" was partly responsible for private citizens buying "five complete sets of Duruy's histories of Rome and Greece; ... over 200 sets of cyclopædias; excellent editions of Ruskin, Hugo, Dumas, Scott; also de luxe editions of the Riverside classics, and a large number of valuable illustrated books on art and books of reference."[88] Such successes were possible only when librarians were "wide awake to their possibilities, and sympathizing with the reader and with the community." It was not enough to "sit still in [one's] chair and allow the public simply to help themselves."[89]

Adding Innovative Ideas

Once the basic principles of readers' advisory had been established, the range of ideas that public librarians developed over the last quarter of the 19th century and the first years of the 20th century in an attempt to lead patrons toward serious and purposeful reading was nothing short of impressive. For Foster, writing in 1879 in "The School and the Library: Their Mutual Relation," the work of readers' advisors comprised elements of what, in the vocabulary of the early 21st century, might be called information literacy.[90] Teachers and librarians working together should develop a series of ad hoc exercises and programs ensuring that young people in "primary school, high school, or college" are "led to continue their systematic reading after leaving school."[91] One example of "mutual action" was a program to familiarize pupils with reference books, which are not treated as repositories of facts that are to be consulted only rarely, but as a habitual means of supplementing the knowledge gained from other books.[92] Reference books, Foster said, ensure that "the pupil forms the habit of following up his reading of a work of history or travel with an atlas on which he may trace the routes, and gain a definite picture in his own mind. In reading a scientific work, let him turn to the cyclopædias for an explanation of some process or term with which he is unacquainted, and, in reading any work, let him consult the English dictionary for the meaning and derivation of unfamiliar words."[93] And precisely because reference books were so important, librarians should, like teachers, "work aloud" when students ask for advice and instruction in their use: "Set to work *with* him; show him your method of 'chasing down' a subject; teach him how to use dictionaries, indexes, and tables of contents ... [and] show him how to carry on investigations for himself."[94] Students will thus develop a life-long habit of treating reference books as necessary complements to any book that they may happen to read. Passive reading will turn into an active process of "intelligent observation and investigation."[95]

In the mid–1880s, Agnes Hill, Librarian of the Bridgeport (Connecticut) Public Library, emphasized the importance of involving key community members in readers' advisory work, perceptively identifying some of the factors that would later in the 20th century lead to gate-keeping theory.

> I find my greatest help in intelligent workingmen. Such men are educational centres, and their opinions are usually respected by their less-educated comrades. In every factory here there are a few such men, and we make it our business to know them. A work recommended to one of these, and approved of by him, will always have a large circulation among his friends. The best reading done in our library is by factory employees.[96]

James M. Hubbard had a somewhat similar idea in "How to Use a Public Library."[97] Because he felt that it would be highly irresponsible if patrons were left to their own devices—"We might as well turn out children into a school-house, fully furnished with books and apparatus, but with only a janitor to see that no injury is done to them"—he recommended that the entire community should become involved in readers' advisory.[98] Willing lay-experts would choose a subject area (e.g., United States History, Biography, etc.) in which they were particularly interested or had some degree of expertise and visit the library to see what it had in that area. They would then make themselves known to the librarian as being ready to aid patrons who requested help in their area of expertise. When a patron approached the librarian asking for help in choosing reading material connected with a subject area claimed by a lay-expert, the librarian would refer that patron to the lay-expert, who would "naturally endeavor to find out something of the character, circumstances, and abilities of the applicant before selecting the books best fitted in his or her opinion for him to read."[99] Patrons would thus be saved from "dissipating" their energies on less-than-valuable reading materials.[100]

Another early method of trying to encourage better reading was the two-book system, first proposed in 1894 by C. Knowles Bolton, Librarian of the Brookline (Massachusetts) Public Library.[101] Since many libraries only allowed patrons to check out a single book at a time, it was felt that allowing a patron to check out two books would "lead the borrower, who would otherwise read only fiction, to extend his reading into other classes of literature." [102] Also, there was nothing preventing "the reader of solid literature to add a novel to the work which he would otherwise take."[103] By 1898, 140 public libraries had adopted the system, with 91 of them doing so in the years 1895–1897.[104] In an analysis of the effect of the two-book system on the quality of circulation, E. A. Birge concluded that in libraries employing the system "the percentage of solid literature in the total circulation is from 3 per cent to 4 per cent greater than in libraries using the one-book system [with the result that] ... such libraries circulate from 15 per cent to 20 per cent more of solid literature than do the others."[105]

Compared with Bolton's plan, Ida Rosenberg's idea was simplicity itself, yet it worked just as well: the purchase of new and attractive editions of literary classics and their prominent display in well-trafficked areas of the Grand Rapids (Michigan) Public Library (GRPL).

Works by Austen, Hawthorne, and Dickens literally flew off the shelves. Rosenberg's idea was so successful that GRPL extended it to most of the books on John Lubbock's "great books" list, including works by Pascal, the Koran, and "150 books of dramatic literature ranging from Euripides to Ibsen and Maeterlinck."[106] The Springfield (Massachusetts) Public Library also made concerted attempts to display classic literature prominently. The results were beyond the wildest hopes of the librarian: the *Odyssey*, Dante's *Divine Comedy*, Plato's *Republic*, Goethe's *Faust*, Plutarch's *Lives*, and Thomas Carlyle's *Sartor Resartus* were just some of the classics that enjoyed astounding circulation rates.[107]

At the Pratt Institute School of Library Science at the turn of the 20th century, students and instructors worked to develop fiction classification schemes designed "to encourage the purposeful reading of fiction" and "for the sake of the reader who wants the best but knows not what it is."[108] As Josephine Adams Rathbone, a teacher at Pratt since 1893, explained, students in a "Fiction Seminar" class analyzed "border-land" fiction (popular fiction) in order to discover "the essential characteristics of the author; the kind of work, whether novels of incident, manners, etc.; influence of his work, wholesome, elevating, morbid or depressing; other writers he is nearest akin to; the kind of people to whom he would appeal, etc.; ... the qualities that attract readers, the use that could be made of these books, and the writers next higher in rank whose works might be substituted, and through whom the reader could be led to better things."[109] Rathbone's students constructed reading "ladders" for popular authors. Rhoda Broughton's *Joan* and *Nancy* led to novels by Jessie Fothergill, then to Mrs. Walford's novels, then to Walter Besant, then to Thomas Hardy's *The Woodlanders* and *Far from the Madding Crowd*, then to R. D. Blackmore's novels, then to Charlotte Brontë's *Jane Eyre* and *Shirley*, and finally to George Eliot's *Middlemarch* and *Mill on the Floss*. Rathbone's students also assigned genres to novels. Marie Corelli's *Sorrows of Satan* was categorized as a "psychological novel" that was at the bottom of a reading ladder leading to *Tale of Two Cities*, *Romola*, *The Scarlet Letter*, *Tess of the D'Urbervilles*, and *Les Miserables*. Based on a shelving scheme developed by a colleague, Rathbone recommended that "the rank of books" be designated "by covers of different colors." She was also a strong proponent of extensive subject headings for fiction in card catalogs, recommending that topics, narrative voice, plot complexity, and authorial perspective be indicated not only for historical fiction, but also "for novels dealing with social, religious, and other questions."[110] As an experiment at the Buffalo Public Library in the middle 1900s showed, Rathbone's graded fiction lists were successful in guiding readers to better quality fiction.[111]

Perhaps inspired by Rathbone's work, in 1909 William Alanson Borden, Librarian of the Young Men's Institute in New Haven, Connecticut, developed a fiction classification system to counteract the phenomenon whereby "two-week-old novels accumulate[d] waiting-lists of impatient patrons" but "better ones" forlornly and anxiously wait "to have the dust blown off their tops."[112] Attributing this to the "charted flood" of "newspaper reviews, publishers' advertisements, lists of the most popular books, or ... alleged literary conversations," Borden separated novels by type in an attempt not only to elevate reading tastes but also to avoid "compel[ling] the library to keep purchasing floods of second-rate books that were sure to become dead-stock in a short time."[113] "Group[ing] all the impossible stories together, and the short stories, and the detective stories, and the historical and descriptive novels," as well as "love stor[ies]," "character sketch[es]," "sea yarn[s]," and "army stor[ies]," he moved them into a separate alcove, thus differentiating them from "all the standard novels, those usually called for by author."[114] His results spoke for themselves: recent fiction was requested less often, with "four-sevenths of ... fiction circulation com[ing] from the classified shelves."[115]

In her 1896 article "The Librarian as Host," Maude R. Henderson suggested that public librarians arrange evening programs consisting of lectures by local experts about music, art, science, and the history of printing.[116] Potential audience members would be "urged to read upon the subject before and after the evening," a process helped by the distribution of lists specifying the resources of the library on the appropriate topic, as well as constant mention of those resources by the speakers. Of particular importance for readers' advisory was her idea that librarians should hold regular evenings where they, "assisted by others," would "give suggestions and information about books and reading, either for reading in general, or judicious help in any branch of study, poetry, history, economics, art, biography, or hints as to the direction of children's reading."[117] It is easy to imagine a fireside-chat atmosphere with the librarian as convivial host, especially since Henderson recommended that "special invitations ... be sent out to the different organized societies of working people, such as the retail clerks, labor unions, etc., who might not include themselves readily in a general published invitation."[118]

In time, public libraries would become the centers of intellectual life in their cities, as in the case of St. Louis, where the SLPL was the "chief resource" in supplying "classes and clubs organized for the study of various subjects" with reading material.[119] Women's clubs especially made substantial use of the library, undertaking guided lecture-based courses with recognized experts about Milton, Dante, Shelley, Emerson, Goethe, and Shakespeare, not to mention broad overview courses on "The Trend of Modern Thought in Fiction" and "Christian History."[120] Or it may lead to the kind of workingmen's reading and study circle established by Peck in the Gloversville Public Library.[121] Meeting weekly on Friday nights in Peck's office, the club studied "constitutional history of the U.S., civil government, monetary science, and ... practical economic questions, following in each case the syllabi published by the Extension Department of the University of the State of New York."[122] Sub-topics of "practical economic questions" included: "Capital, its source and function; Combination of capital, monopolies and trusts; The condition and claims of the working class; ... [and] Labor differences and their settlements."[123] Each club member led the discussion or contributed a paper on a weekly sub-topic, with Peck acting as secretary, "it being his duty to lay out the work, provide references to books and magazines, and to assist the leaders of the evening in preparing brief papers."[124] The club was a resounding success, with "[d]iscussions continu[ing] after adjournment in front of the library building and continu[ing] also in the different shops during the week."[125] In addition, "men who thought they could not find time to take up the study with the class would come to the library and ask for the books used by the class during the preceding week; and in this way men were brought into the library who would have never been interested in its work had it not been for the influence of this class."[126] In both St. Louis and Gloversville, public librarians assumed responsibility for developing serious and purposeful reading habits in patrons. The Gloversville example is especially instructive, since it shows that the ripple effects of serious and purposeful reading, once established among a core group, can spread throughout a town or city.

Yet there was always more to be done. In 1903, Alice B. Kroeger, in "The Encouragement of Serious Reading: Survey of the Field," noted that the Cincinnati Public Library (CinPL) had instituted a program "to prepare for individual students courses of reading" on topics requested by patrons.[127] Patrons filled out forms that asked for specific information: "If you wish to study the history of Germany, ask for a general history of Germany; if you wish information upon the Thirty Years' War, so state; if you want to know about the Siege of Nuremberg, put that down. The selection of books can be made only when the librarians know exactly what the reader is looking for."[128] Patrons were also asked to indicate the names of books already read on the requested topic and whether "this is a new line of reading for you."[129] For Kroeger, it was a shame that the CinPL was the only public library offering this service, and so she drew attention to an initiative by the Pratt Institute Library (PIL) that she believed other libraries could emulate. PIL advertised that it was willing to give "help in the forming of courses of reading in the subject of their occupation" to "young men or women engaged in any skilled manual labor or handicraft."[130] Perhaps inspired by Kroeger's comments, the Portland (Oregon) Public Library by 1914 not only had entered into partnerships with the University of Oregon, Pacific University, and Reed College to offer courses in "The new democracy," "Twentieth century problems," and "The Voter and the City of Portland," but also provided "lists of suggestive reading ... for the majority of the lectures" and offered to prepare individualized reading lists "on any subject that may interest" its patrons.[131] Only through initiatives that extended the work of CinPL and PIL, Kroeger felt, could public libraries reaffirm their leading position in educational endeavors—a position that, by the 1900s, was starting to be eroded.

Continuous Personal Improvement
Through Meaningful Education

Early readers' advisors considered themselves responsible for elevating, or at least trying to elevate, the intellectual life of their respective communities. Readers' advisory was crucial work that demanded much learning, insight, and care. It was not enough to know about books; the complexities and idiosyncrasies of human nature also entered into the picture. Early readers' advisory was therefore a vital public trust: adults would continue to improve themselves through meaningful education under the solicitous eye of readers' advisors whose duty it was to recommend serious and purposeful reading. Just as schools gave careful thought to their curricula, so public libraries must give careful thought to their book collections, since both institutions were part of the same educational continuum. Just as good teachers had to decide which path among many would lead to a desired educational goal, so too did public librarians as they advised readers about book choices. Differences of opinion existed about the best methods to provide meaningful education to patrons, but there was little dispute that it was the role of public libraries to do so. As Green remarked, it was their role to provide "rational entertainment" as they strove to elevate the reading tastes of their patrons to the highest possible level.[132]

It is in this context that we may understand William Kite, the director of the Friends' Free Library in Germantown, Pennsylvania. Kite did not permit fiction on the shelves of his institution from about 1870 to at least 1892, arguing that even classical novels should be excluded because "the world contains so much that is better."[133] Patrons did not need "exciting volumes" to entice them to read.[134] In fact, "[i]f unprofitable books are denied [patrons], they can be induced to accept better, and can be turned to useful reading by a little care on the part of the librarian."[135] For Kite, readers' advisory was a matter of transforming a desire for the "poor trash" of novels into a desire for nonfiction.[136]

Applications for novels of some character are of almost daily occurrence at our desk, but on learning they are not in the library the applicant is usually willing to be guided in the choice of a book. And here lies the secret of our management. We must be willing to take the guidance of such readers into our hands till a better taste is formed. I know this is a different thing from simply handing the book asked for and letting the responsibility of the case rest on the reader: that is easily done. But I have come to believe I can help form a character for good that might otherwise be led into evil, and have cheerfully accepted the position. Popular works on natural history I find a help in the desired direction, and I rely also much on travels for entering wedges, opening the way, frequently quite early, to history, science, and general literature. Many of our less educated applicants take at first to works of quite a juvenile character, from which we lead them to more solid reading as we can.[137]

It is easy to mock Kite's conception of readers' advisory. Yet he was convinced that, because librarians and teachers were "public officers," they had a vested "duty" to differentiate between literature that was "profitable" and literature that was "pernicious."[138] For all his surface paternalism, Kite was intensely interested in bringing about real intellectual development among his library's patrons. Even if most of Kite's contemporaries disagreed with him about the fiction question, his efforts spoke to an abiding conviction that all individuals, no matter their station in life, deserved a meaningful education.

Noah Porter, who saw much educational value in fiction, was just as concerned about the moral influence of books as Kite.[139] "Not only is it clear that fiction and poetry may exert a good influence," Porter wrote in 1881 in *Books and Reading*, "but it is equally obvious that they do in fact exert an influence that is both healthful and elevating" from the moral perspective,[140] since "imagination is an endowment from God ... [that] is ... one of the noblest human powers—the power which in some of its aspects is nearest to the divine, and as such is capable of the most exalted uses, and of an influence for good which cannot be computed."[141] But potential readers should be aware that there were different kinds of novels and equally different ways of reading them. On the bottom rung were "novels of incident."[142] Overmuch reading of these novels was to be avoided, since they were "a kind of intellectual opium eating, in its stimulant effects upon the phantasy and its stupifying and bewildering influence on the judgment."[143] They make the reader a "literary roué" and "intellectual voluptuary, with feeble judgment, a vague memory, and an incessant craving for some new excitement."[144] Somewhat higher up were "novel[s] of character."[145] But to reach novel reading's highest rung, the reader must not just read "novels of character," but learn "to study and analyze the characters which he finds in fiction; when they not only enlist his sympathies by assuming distinct and personal being, but [when] he can study them in their motives, trace out their springs and discover their leading traits, and illustrate them to his own judgment by examples from real life."[146] As a result, "wise reading of novels is fitted to enlarge our acquaintance with human nature" because it "often compels us to enter into the thoughts and feelings, and to share in the experiences of men and women most remote from our personal observation or our possible acquaintance."[147] It also instructs the reader in political and military history, "the domestic and social life of other countries, or grades of life in our own country to which few readers can have direct access,"[148] and "suggests elevated and quickening topics of conversation, [an] advantage [which] is not a trivial one, when we reflect that conversation too readily degenerates into gossiping personalities or unmeaning twaddle about the weather, or the last insignificant occurrence" of interest.[149]

Green, in his 1879 essay "Sensational Fiction in Public Libraries," assumed a middle position between Kite and Porter. "I take it for granted," he wrote, "that nearly all librarians and friends of education consider novel reading desirable when the selection of books read is judicious, and when the practice is indulged in only in moderation."[150] Still, librarians should always strive to "replace[] the poor stories in our libraries with good ones, and having ascertained that the quality of its imaginative literature is as high as it can be and yet retain readers, the next step to take is to lead the young away from an immoderate use of the best stories even, to books of other kinds."[151] By this he meant nonfiction. Yet his main goal was always to "raise the standard of books circulated,"[152] and in this goal the act of readers' advisory was both indispensable and multifaceted. For example, Green felt that librarians could accomplish "much good" by choosing "every morning from the books in the library ten or twenty volumes, one of which may be given by an assistant to any one who asks to have an interesting book picked out for him."[153] Better yet, public librarians should regularly "form classes" from among "the more studiously inclined, but not especially well-informed frequenters of a library."[154] These groups of patrons should then "be taken to the alcoves by the librarian, or others for conversation about the literature of different departments of knowledge."[155] Well-run public libraries, staffed by hard-working librarians who took their readers' advisory functions seriously, constantly strove in various ways to provide patrons with opportunities for meaningful education, which inevitably meant a decreasing emphasis on popular fiction.

Public libraries where popular fiction was in the ascendancy were not educational institutions in the true sense of the word. These libraries were more concerned with perpetuating their own existence than with any lofty ameliorative goals. Consider the arguments made by Beatrice Winser in her 1903 article "Encouragement of Serious Reading by Public Libraries,"[156] which criticized librarians for making the public library a repository of popular fiction. Librarians buy "at the very least, five to ten copies of the latest novel, costing $1 apiece," but rarely purchase "two copies of a book costing $3, on some technical or serious subject."[157] The reason is not so much because ephemeral novels are "in demand" or because librarians are "afraid of the criticism of the public that you are not giving them what they want," but because "after all, our fetish, circulation statistics, depends for its life upon the much-abused novel, without which we could not make so brave a showing in our annual reports."[158] She was no less withering with regard to library staffing priorities.

> Whom do we have at our delivery desk to aid the youth who wishes to devote spare evenings to the study of electricity, for instance? Would the average desk assistant be able to give him the best authority upon the subject or make him feel that she really knew the difference between a motor and a dynamo? ... Do I want every assistant to be a specialist upon one or more subjects? If that were possible, yes; but it is not impossible to get well-educated men and women for the work if you pay better salaries.[159]

Instead of paying high salaries to "expert catalogers," Winser urged librarians to convince library trustees to "infuse life into the most neglected department" of the library: the circulation desk.[160]

If we recall that Green, Winsor, and Cutter envisioned readers' advisory as something that occurred at the circulation desk, Winser's lament about the inadequacy of desk assistants is also a lament about the insouciance with which public libraries approached the intertwined questions of readers' advisory and their educational responsibilities. At a time when correspondence schools and Chautauquas were popular because "some one in whom the public has confidence assumes the authority of directing its studies," librarians were missing a golden opportunity to be "looked upon as leaders in the educational work they are supposed to be doing."[161] Winser's central point was that people did not trust public librarians as educational leaders. Instead, librarians were using the "give the people what they want" argument to put themselves in a favorable light. If they gave people the popular fiction people apparently craved, librarians could generate strong annual reports that showed rising circulation figures. They could also justify hiring low-paid and relatively uneducated desk assistants, since these assistants would only be answering questions about popular fiction. If the public kept coming to the library solely for popular fiction, it may be because librarians had abandoned the cause of meaningful education and were predominantly offering popular fiction, secure in the knowledge that popular fiction would ensure rising circulation statistics that would make their annual reports look "brave." By 1903, the act of advising readers, if it was occurring at all, was almost exclusively associated with popular and ephemeral fiction because the position of desk assistant was not sufficiently remunerated to attract well-educated men and women capable of directing patrons to "better reading" and opportunities for meaningful education.

Agnes Hill shared many of Winser's concerns.[162] Admonishing librarians to remember that "public libraries are established for the education and uplifting of the people," she urged her colleagues "to maintain a certain standard in literature and morals in spite of the mistakes we shall inevitably commit."[163] It was their duty to exert "personal courage to urge the exclusion of a book when you know that the library ten miles away has just put in twenty or thirty copies."[164] But these standards were difficult to uphold for two reasons. First, "the librarian runs some obvious risks in letting the circulation of his library fall below the average."[165] Second, the rise of what she labels "the 'ticket-office' ideal of librarianship" meant public libraries lacked "men and women of broad education whose duty should be to meet the public and give them intelligent help."[166] Instead, public libraries "have tried every possible mechanical device except librarianship by automatic figures," with the result that "we shall soon have to face the possibility of there being a singular contrast between our gorgeous American library buildings and the educational values for which they stand."[167] Like Winser, Hill made a strong connection between the increasing presence of popular fiction in public libraries and the rise of librarianship predicated on mechanical procedures and obsession with circulation statistics. In this new "ticket-office" ideal of librarianship, which consisted of "the mere mechanical handing out of books," there was little room for the "fitting of the right book to the right person,"[168] a precondition for meaningful education.

The Ascendancy of Popular Fiction

As the articles by Winser and Hill indicate, the tide had indeed turned on the question of popular fiction. As Robert Ellis Lee remarked in *Continuing Education for Adults*, "[w]hereas the librarians of the earlier period (1876–1897) discussed the desirability of including popular fiction in the library's collection, the librarians of this period (1898–1919) debated about *how much* popular fiction should be supplied."[169] In terms of the ALA motto, it was as if "The Best Reading" had disappeared, leaving only "the Largest Number at the Least Cost." It was a gradual change, as a rising crescendo of voices made various arguments about the need to transform public libraries into venues for popular fiction.

We discuss three of these voices: Tessa L. Kelso, Lindsay Swift, and Melvil Dewey. At first, writers who recommended that public libraries turn away from an educational agenda were conflicted. Kelso's 1893 "Some Economical Features of Public Libraries" is a good example.[170] She began by stating that the library's emphasis on serving "the needs of the student" was fundamentally useless because "to the student books are his working materials, and he seldom depends on the resources of a public library."[171] Labeling students as "this minority," Kelso, Librarian at the Los Angeles Public Library, suggested that the public would not fully accept psychological ownership of the library until it became committed "to add[ing] to the fast-diminishing store of human pleasure, to be a means of overcoming the intemperance of work."[172] In her view, the public library should function as a safety valve: by providing "trashy and flabby literature" that was "amusing," it safely channeled energy that had few other outlets.[173] But Kelso also wanted the public library to be "the direct power to cultivate and foster the intellectual and material advance of its community" by creating opportunities "for the development of appreciation and culture of a high order in the use of books."[174]

No one could say that Swift, an employee in the Catalogue Department of the Boston Public Library, was conflicted. Writing in 1899 in "Paternalism in Public Libraries," Swift offered a full-throttle indictment of the way in which public libraries determine and influence the reading of their patrons.[175] He chastened the heavy-handedness of "reading committees," who took upon themselves the task of determining the kinds of books to be allowed in public libraries, observing that these committees invariably consisted of women and those who had too much leisure.[176] Moreover, it is not "[r]obust men and women with steady nerves and wholesome natures" who wanted to direct the reading of others when it came to popular fiction; rather, it was "the feeble and incomplete [who] take the attitude of fastidious opposition, and speedily become morbid."[177] Another manifestation of paternal control was the "travelling library," where pre-selected books, packed in boxes or cases, were sent to smaller communities on a rotational basis. The practice may, at first glance, be "enchanting."[178] But on closer examination,

> it is taking the responsibility off the hands in which it belongs, and rendering the communities which accept such gratuity less efficient and less self-respecting. Somehow it appeals to me as a childish scheme to send these collections of books to people who haven't moral energy or intellectual hunger enough to bestir themselves in the matter.[179]

For Swift, the act of "choosing literary paths for other folks to tread" and the act of "turn[ing] our libraries into quasi-educational institutions" was nothing but "[p]aternal solicitude," which in turn was "a restrictive, almost an inhibitive, principle" that "opens a way to unlimited control."[180] After all, "[p]eople nowadays want their books *à la carte* and not *table a' hôte*."[181]

The fact that paternal solicitude was to a large degree carried out by women was an irony that was not lost on Swift, since he explicitly mentioned the preponderance of women on reading committees. For all intents and purposes, his paternal control was maternal control. What are we to make of this? First, he associated the public library's educational function with women, but then he disparaged this function along with those who engaged in it. Second, he associated popular fiction with robustness and independence—typically, though not exclusively, male characteristics. If Swift's article was any indication, popular fiction was being positioned as a healthy, vigorous, and efficient response to serious and purposeful reading that was meaningfully educational. Of course, to get such reading into the hands of patrons required a series of cumbersome procedures—the type of careful and considered selection procedures that occasionally led to mistakes and that therefore lent themselves to Swift's caricature of reading committees—but these procedures were meant to create a collection that would allow patrons to aspire to and partake of inherently valuable fiction and nonfiction that had meaningful cultural and educational purpose.

The gendered nature of Swift's categories is intriguing. Marking the educational imperatives of the public library as feminine and popular fiction (the antithesis of education) as masculine, Swift inverted the conventional wisdom that it was old-fashioned male scholar-librarians, with their emphasis on literary classics, who were preventing public libraries from reaching the widest possible public. Instead, for Swift, the fact that public libraries wanted to be educational institutions was the root cause of their halting growth, and he laid this responsibility squarely at the feet of women. Swift's logic was illuminating. If women wanted to participate in a (male) public-library world that was robust, dynamic, and independent, they had to leave behind their cumbersome reforming and educational inclinations through which they wanted to guide and improve the intellects, morals, and sensibilities of patrons. More broadly, they had to leave behind the social-reform movements of the post–Civil War era, which used the language of progressive Christianity to extend the values of virtuous domesticity into the public sphere. By welcoming popular fiction into public libraries, women could prove, according to Swift, that they were no longer "feeble and incomplete," a euphemistic way of saying maternal. When all was said and done, it was a searing indictment of the entire post–Civil War reform movement, of which the Woman's Christian Temperance Union (WCTU) was one of the most visible embodiments.

As Ruth Bordin demonstrated in *Woman and Temperance: The Quest for Power and Liberty, 1873–1900,* the WCTU may have started out as an one-dimensional movement committed to fighting the scourge of alcoholism, but it quickly evolved into a multi-dimensional organization whose guiding principle was that, because "an unjust society made alcohol an inevitable escape from poverty," "only fundamental changes in the environment would heal" that unjust and immoral society. Making extensive use of church networks, the WCTU became the pre-eminent women's organization of the 19th century, promoting "general prison reform, special facilities for women offenders, the eight-hour working day, model facilities for dependent and neglected children, the kindergarten movement, ... shelters for the care of the children of working mothers, social rooms ... for the urban poor, federal aid to education, mothers' education, vocational training for women, and a dozen other causes that they believed would improve the lot of the underprivileged, especially the urban poor."[182] As Allison M. Parker noted in *Purifying America,* the WCTU was divided into 19 departments, each of which was "devoted to achieving a specific social-reform goal, ranging from child-labor laws to international peace and from arbitration to social purity."[183] In some respects a forerunner of the settlement-house movement, the WCTU was an organization in which community well-being was sacrosanct. The private ideal of the happy, loving, religious, and peaceful home was to be exported to the public sphere so that as many "glaring social evils" as possible could be vanquished after suitable investigation, analysis, and educational initiatives.[184]

One of the WCTU's departments was the Department for the Suppression of Impure Literature.[185] Impure literature, which included "trashy" fiction as well as obscene literature,[186] was to be avoided not only because of its "destructive and addictive" nature, but also because "it created an unproductive dissatisfaction with ordinary experience without offering activist or progressive alternatives to life's problems."[187] Frances Willard, a long-serving president of the WCTU in the late 19th century, was convinced that, by reading romance and fantasy novels, individuals "turn [their] possibility of success in life to the certainty of failure."[188] Wanting to repudiate the "well-entrenched image of feminine passivity" and to assert "an experimental activist ethics," Willard "presented censorship as an act of political and personal empowerment," where women, no longer "passive recipients of 'unhealthful' novels," would become "the principal actors and writers, not simply the audience."[189] More specifically, the time spent reading romance novels could be put to much better use "on education" or in lobbying for an extension of voting and other rights for women.[190] As Willard bluntly observed, "You girls can begin reading now the class of literature which will teach you all about such things."[191] The WCTU saw itself as a progressive educational entity concerned for the welfare of all community members. Together with the National Congress of Mothers and the General Federation of Women's Clubs, it "represented relatively *uncontroversial* opinions at that time."[192] It did not look upon itself as censorious; instead, it was part of a progressive social, cultural, and economic movement.

When Swift criticized public libraries for attempting to direct the reading tastes of patrons toward better literature, he was also criticizing the WCTU's censorship activities. In effect, he was lashing out at the entire women-dominated social-reform movement as something that was constraining the free functioning of industrial society. In the context of public libraries, women who spoke in favor of popular fiction could thus prove that they were not restrictive and inhibitory censors hiding behind the rationale that public libraries were meant to be institutions for meaningful education. In so doing, they could show that they belonged to a male-inscribed robust world where the watchwords were independence, dynamism, and vigorous efficiency. Swift made his position clear in his concluding paragraph.

> We should not, like Martha of old, be cumbered about much serving; and there is no need of being so confoundedly serious about this whole library question. Among the printed directions to conductors on the Boston Elevated Railroad is the following injunction: "Try to make everyone who gets on your car feel perfectly at home." There is a good side to that suggestion and there is a ludicrous side. It is "up to us," as the boys say, not to miss the humor of our own situation.[193]

Swift implies that we can either be like Martha (a biblical reference to Luke 10: 38–42), weary with taking things "so confoundedly serious" and with "much serving." But, like public-library reading-committees or WCTU members, she became "ludicrous." Or we could emulate the rational efficiency of the male conductors of the Boston Elevated Railroad, whose main task was not making passengers "feel perfectly at home," but ensuring that the trains mechanically run on time so that each passenger could go about his or her own business in a time-obsessed industrial world with the least amount of fuss.

Dewey's "Advice to a Librarian," published in 1897, encapsulated librarianship's turn away from meaningful education and progressive cultural improvement through the reading of serious literature.[194] For Dewey, who laid the groundwork for the cataloging system that bears his name while in his early twenties at Amherst College in 1872 and opened the first library school in 1887 at Columbia College, librarianship was all about mechanical efficiency and technical organization. In *The Foundations of Education for Librarianship*, Shera characterized Dewey's approach as vocational because it was "almost exclusively concerned with acquainting the students thoroughly, and at first hand, with the actual tasks the practice of librarianship entailed."[195] As Shera explained, Dewey's influence was manifest throughout the curricula of early schools of library science at Columbia, Drexel, and the Armour Institute, where phrases such as "entirely practical," "main reliance must be on experience," "work assignments," "object teaching," and "the practical things of Library life" were used to describe the training that students received.[196] This often monomaniacal emphasis on efficiency and mechanical procedures went hand-in-hand with a profound distrust of intellectual accomplishment.[197]

Dewey was convinced that the job of a librarian was "more of an executive business affair than a literary one."[198] He urged future librarians to "[b]e more than content to be ignorant on many things." Ignorance was a blessing that would permit librarians to "[l]ook at your position as a high-grade business one, [such that you] look after the working details, have things go smoothly, know the whereabouts and classification of the books, and let people get their own meat or poison."[199] Librarians were to confine themselves to "get[ting] the confidence of as many readers as you can, grapple some of the most divergent minds with hooks of steel, and in finding out how little you know that is of any real value to anyone else, you will begin to be of some little value to yourself."[200] In fact, "it is in no sense your business to dictate to others as to what they may or may not, should or should not, read, and if you attempt to assume such responsibility you will make unnumbered enemies and take upon yourself a thankless and uncalled-for task."[201]

But, armed with scant knowledge based on scant reading, how were librarians to gain the confidence of patrons and "grapple" them "with hooks of steel"? Dewey does not say, but throughout his writings he "favored military analogies" in which librarianship was "recast along aggressively masculine lines"—that is, principles of order, efficiency, and technical prowess—in an obvious attempt to guard against "the perceived feminization of American culture."[202] And while librarianship was to become an activity "requiring conventionally male qualities,"[203] Dewey believed that "most of the men who will achieve [librarianship's new-found] greatness will be women."[204]

The rise of Dewey's mechanical efficiency movement within librarianship coincided with a sharp decline of the female-inscribed educational imperatives animating librarianship up to that point. Educational imperatives were conflated with what were described as inappropriate tendencies to direct and influence the reading tastes of patrons in better and more meaningful directions. Patrons in the future were to be left to their own devices. This philosophy was facilitated by the rise of open-stack access in many public libraries, which was presented as a highly efficient practice, saving much time and effort for library staff members who no longer had to perform all the duties associated with the closed-stack and delivery-desk model of circulating books. As the elongated delivery desk emblematic of closed stacks became a thing of the past, patrons were no longer compelled to speak to a staff member before making their initial choice of reading material. The opportunity for a "natural" readers' advisory moment had disappeared. Instead, vocationally trained librarians in the mold of Dewey would reassert control of the public sphere by implementing time-saving, efficient, and streamlined procedures for the common good. Dewey's "aggressively masculine" principles of mechanical efficiency—a harbinger of Frederick Winslow Taylor's 1911 *The Principles of Scientific Management* that extolled the virtues of time-and-motion studies so that workers would become machine-like in carrying out their tasks—slowly but surely became the accepted definition of professionalism in librarianship.[205] This reassertion of male power would not totally remove women from the public sphere (witness Dewey's statement that "most of the men who will achieve this greatness will be women"), but it would deprive them of their accumulated power to import domestic and moral virtues into the public realm by making them more like men. In the name of scientific management, it would also deprive them of the chance to influence people toward serious and purposeful reading that led to meaningful education and social change.

Many public librarians, given sanction by Dewey to be "ignorant," became practical-minded business managers. They organized, cataloged, and circulated materials in as efficient a manner as possible. But, as Abigail A. Van Slyck explained, Dewey's vision signified that "the library was transformed into an efficient machine for the distribution of books" that many compared to a factory.[206] Sitting at a centrally located charging desk from which she oversaw an open-shelving arrangement, the female librarian of the 1890s and 1900s was a somewhat "less prestigious" kind of "factory manager," occupying a position that was analogous to "a telephone operator, a typist, or a file clerk."[207] Her rote duties confined her to "a work station designed to minimize necessary movements [and where] she was surrounded by technologically advanced tools that defined and structured the work into a series of repetitive tasks."[208] And, like telephone operators and typists, librarians had their days and accomplishments "measured quantitatively, in the number of books discharged, in the number of cards filed, in the number of calls put through, in the number of pages typed."[209]

In this factory-like environment, it was a decided advantage for public librarians not to spend prolonged time with patrons discussing reading choices and making suggestions about the best possible reading materials. Patrons could simply choose among the vast array of popular fiction available on the shelves and present themselves to a librarian or desk clerk who, because he or she had likely been trained to follow Dewey's precepts about library science, did not care in the least what the patron had chosen as long as it had been cataloged properly and that it could be efficiently checked out. Or, as Winser stated, if a patron wanted to be guided about what to read, the librarian or desk clerk, not knowing much about anything, would likely point to the shelves containing multiple copies of recent popular fiction and leave the patron to fend for herself or himself.

By 1903, when Winser wrote "Encouragement of Serious Reading by Public Libraries," readers' advisory had almost vanished as public libraries gave disproportionate heed to a Dewey-influenced definition of library science where "expert catalogers," symbols of technical efficiency and mechanical organization, were in the ascendancy. If at one time the purpose of public libraries revolved around guiding patrons toward serious and purposeful reading material in the interests of meaningful education, by 1903 the act of nurturing serious reading habits in patrons was just one of many listed purposes for public libraries. In the eyes of some librarians, it was far down that list, well behind supplying the public with popular fiction and making the public library technically efficient. As such, it became decentered and devalued. It was no longer one of the core components of public librarianship, even though there were indications that patrons craved serious and purposeful reading material that could provide them with meaningful education.

The Library Hostess

In tracing the origins of readers' advisory, we touched upon some of the methods used by public librarians as they matched books with readers: Foster's overview of the value of annotated lists and bulletins; Crunden's decision to ask experts to produce reading courses; Hubbard's involvement of local citizens in the work of readers' advisory; Peck's and Winser's discussions of community outreach; and Green's suggestion about forming small groups for subject-specific overviews. We noted Cutter's emphasis on tact and patience, as well as Peck's insights about thematic appeal. We glanced at Rathbone's ideas for fiction classification and Hill's use of gatekeepers. These methods were in the service of an overarching philosophy of meaningful education based on serious and purposeful reading. And, while readers' advisory moved away from meaningful education in the post–1963 period to become, at best, edutainment or, at worst, entertainment, there was a striking continuity in the methods adopted by readers' advisors in both eras to serve different ends.

We now turn to one of the major ways in which readers' advisory was delivered in the pre–1917 era: the library hostess. This is a vexed issue, since the hostess position was not a static one, evolving to fit local circumstances and changing times. Sometimes the hostess was a host. Hostesses and hosts were typically associated with large public libraries, where task specialization was possible. In the case of small public libraries staffed by only one or two employees, these employees were by definition hostesses and hosts. As Almira L. Hayward indicated in 1892 in "The Training of a Librarian," the librarian should always remember that, no matter how "busy, annoyed, or 'out-of-sorts' she may be," she "is in the position of a hostess to all who cross the library threshold."[210] As in private homes, courtesy and hospitality were the essence of a warm and inviting welcome, much more so than "gilded furniture or sumptuous living."[211] And even if some hostesses in large public libraries were assistants or clerks, they exhibited characteristics of what Virginia E. Graeff, former Supervisor of Kindergartens in the Cleveland (Ohio) Public School System, termed "the gentle librarian": "[t]o the stranger, the passing inquirer, the gentle librarian does the honors of the library as a hostess and is always ready to 'lend a hand' in helping her to the desired book."[212]

As explained above, Green first traced the parameters of the hostess position in his 1876 article "Personal Relations between Librarians and Readers." In 1879, he returned to this question, advocating in "Sensational Fiction in Public Libraries" that every public library hire a person whom he called "a friend of the young."[213] It was this "friend" that young people could "consult freely when in want of assistance, and who, in addition to the power of gaining their confidence, has knowledge and tact enough to render them real aid in making selections."[214] Green's two formulations offer a good definition of the late 19th-century library hostess. By the middle of 1880, both his ideas had been implemented in the Lower Hall of the Boston Public Library (BPL) "with the happiest results," as he observed at the 1882 ALA conference in Cincinnati.[215] BPL was a large public library, and so it is perhaps natural that the position of library hostess and host found fertile ground there.

How did BPL decide to avail itself of a hostess and host to perform readers' advisory? The background should by now be familiar, since much of the impetus for the hostess/host was a lingering concern that patrons were primarily using public libraries to read popular fiction. In chapter 2, we discussed the views of the 1875 BPL Examining Committee on this point. For the committee, meaningful education was the central purpose of public libraries; all other considerations paled. Popular fiction was to be indulged only temporarily until more elevated tastes had developed. In 1878, another BPL Examining Committee compared the reading habits of Boston's citizens to the reading habits of a family. "A city is not unlike a family," wrote Warren H. Cudworth on behalf of the Committee, where "we see in the father's hands works containing the last results of science or the most recent speculations in philosophy, in the mother's hands some treatise on Æsthetics or Sociology, ... in the hands of the older children, poems, histories, works of invention, travel and discovery, or adventure, [and] ... in the hands of the little children ... fables, and fairy stories, with all sorts of grotesque and fantastic imaginations to stimulate the nascent power of thought and compel judgment and the understanding to take their places on the stage of action."[216] All this is as it should be because, according to the New Testament, "childish things" will eventually be "put away" in the due course of life as the cultural and intellectual tastes of individuals mature in step with their heightened responsibilities.[217]

To aid this maturation process, Mellen Chamberlain, BPL's then-chief Librarian, instituted a system in September 1879 whereby the catalog cards pertaining to the library's Lower Hall were transferred from the much larger Bates Hall and put under the care of Thomas H. Cummings or, "in his absence," Miss Mary A. Jenkins.[218] Two distinct catalogs were formed. Bates Hall continued as the Main Reading Room, housing books "of solid and permanent value" whose purpose was "to serve the higher requirements of the studious classes, or of investigators in special matters" and whose purchase was funded by the accumulated interest of donor trust funds.[219] The Lower Hall, focusing mostly on current fiction but also containing biography, travels, science, and history books, was designed "to meet the most ordinary demands of the people."[220] It, along with the Periodical Room, was funded entirely by "the money allowed by the City Council."[221] Both halls circulated books for home use, but the home-circulation figures for the Lower Hall were far greater.[222] Cummings was given the title of "Curator of Lower Hall Card Catalogue" and Jenkins, who in BPL's 1878 *Annual Report* was labeled an "Assistant," was promoted to the position of "Assistant Librarian."[223] In fact, the whole Lower Hall department was re-organized, and the number of employees pertaining to it fluctuated. In 1878, it had 17 employees during regular day service. In 1880, it had 19; by 1882, it was down to 16. More importantly, job descriptions changed dramatically. If in 1878, 10 of the employees were simply called "Assistants," in 1880 the title of "Assistant" had given way to more precise definitions. Caroline E. Porée became "Reading

Room Clerk"; Ellen E. Bresnahan became "Assistant in Reading Room." Starting in late 1881, Bresnahan was replaced as "Assistant in Reading Room" by Louisa Twickler.[224] Other employees likewise saw their job descriptions grow more specific: positions and titles now included the words "Delivery Desk," "Receiving Desk," "Registration," "Record of slips," and "Return of slips."[225]

These changes were meant to improve service in the Lower Hall by identifying a small core of employees who would be responsible for dealing with patrons who needed help in determining what to read. It was the central task of Cummings and Jenkins to "assist all comers in finding the books they desire, and, what is of more importance, to direct the attention of young and inexperienced readers to the best literature."[226] Edward Tiffany, Librarian of the Lower Hall, also participated in these endeavors.[227] By virtue of their new job descriptions that differentiated them from other Lower Hall employees, Porée, Bresnahan, and Twickler likely aided Cummings and Jenkins from time to time, since Jenkins principally dealt with "the younger visitors of the Hall."[228] Between December 1879 and April 1880, some "7,351 persons were assisted on special subjects; and of general readers, including readers of fiction, juvenile books and miscellanies, there were above 10,000."[229] In 128 working days, "the daily average of special readers assisted [was] 57, and of general readers, 84."[230] If the first year of the new readers' advisory service was a success, the second year saw even greater success. From May 1880 to the end of April 1881, 45,664 readers were helped: 16,939 were "readers of non-fiction" who were "assisted on special subjects"; another 8,000 were juveniles; and 20,725 were "general readers" who were accorded help with popular fiction.[231] During 1882–1883, a total of 57,614 people were helped. Of these, 24,002 asked questions about special subjects; the remainder were "general readers" and juveniles.[232]

What was the service like? One indication is given by an anonymous report from *The Boston Herald*, reprinted in *Library Journal* in 1881 under the title "Fiction at the Boston Public Library."[233] Here we are informed about the existence of "[t]he little woman who greets the boys and girls who frequent the Public Library so kindly, and to whom she is often in the place of father or mother to tell them what to read and how to read it."[234] Based on the 1881 *Annual Report*, this person was most likely Jenkins. Moreover, the article recounts in detail several examples of the "wise and efficient efforts" made by library assistants functioning as hostesses to ensure that "young persons may be led on from one book to another until they acquire a taste for good reading."[235] We may here envision Porée, Bresnahan, or Twickler as readers' advisory adjuncts to Jenkins. In one case, a young girl was first given *Under the Lilacs*, subsequently read Virginia Townshend's *Six in All* and Mrs. Whitney's *Boys of Chequassett*, and then quickly progressed to Miss Yonge's *Stories of English History*, as well as a natural history book called *Ocean Wonders*. In another case, a library hostess brought together four boys who shared a common interest in natural science and botany—an interest that led the boys to form a "scientific society" and hold meetings to which the library hostess occasionally came.[236] And, according to Tiffany, Jenkins worked with "a number of boys of the Brimmer and Eliot schools" by providing "regular weekly assistance and advice ... in connection with their studies in English and American history."[237]

But the bulk of readers' advisory service was directed toward adults. In what did this service consist? In 1882, Cummings explained that "our plan of direction embraced the pointing out not only of *what to read*, but also *how to read*."[238] His department was not so much concerned with the question of "how best can be diminished the number of fiction readers" but "how best can be formed habits of mental and moral culture whether with or without the aid of fiction."[239] To achieve these goals, he and other staff members "have sought to bring readers regularly, at fixed intervals, to the Library."

This ensures their perseverance besides giving us a chance to know them individually. From the personal relations thus established, we are better able to quicken their interest in good books and to stimulate their love for reading. With their perseverance assured and a taste for reading formed, or even in the process of formation, there is an absolute certainty ... of the attainment of a degree of culture, which persevering years in the use of catalogues or in indiscriminate reading will never give.[240]

Similar service was extended to the eight BPL branch libraries. Tiffany or Cummings visited the branches "two afternoons a week," and "the respective Branch librarians are to be instructed to give similar advice to readers to what is given in the Lower Hall."[241] As the 1882 *Annual Report* stated, "[n]othing is now left undone in the way of helping young and old, both to obtain suitable books and to work their way up to the best kinds of reading," with assistants always at the ready "to suggest books to boys and girls who did not know what books to call for, and to guide them in the selection when this was advisable."[242]

Cummings's approach to readers' advisory was an active one, incorporating Winsor's 1876 thoughts about the importance of repeat visits to the library if meaningful educational progress was to be achieved by patrons. One of the chief effects of these efforts was a reduction in the circulation of popular and ephemeral fiction. Cummings confidently asserted that there was "a decided advance in the reading of the Lower Hall, ... [f]or, not only has much of the useless reading of fiction dropped off during the past year, but even the quality of fiction now circulated has itself been much improved."[243] In 1878, 72 percent of the total books circulated from the Lower Hall were "fiction and juveniles."[244] By 1882, "fiction and juveniles" accounted for 64.23 percent of the total circulation, with small, but nevertheless noteworthy increases in the percentages of books borrowed in the categories of "History and Biography," "Travels and Voyages," "Science, arts, fine and useful, theology, law, medicine, professions," and "foreign languages." Cummings also believed that his department's advisory work was responsible for "a marked increase in the use of Bates Hall books" and for the "steady increase in the use of Lower Hall reference books."[245] And so if we are to anoint someone as the first library hostess/host and, by extension, one of the first readers' advisors, that honor could very well be bestowed equally upon Mary Jenkins and Thomas Cummings. Most of their tasks were probably carried out at the delivery desk, but, judging from *The Boston Herald* report, their job also involved moving away from its fixed location.

Philosophically, readers' advisor, hostess, and host were job titles that addressed the pressing need for society-wide diffusion of knowledge and the creation of an environment where patrons understood that socio-economic advancement was closely associated with meaningful education through the elevation of reading tastes. In this environment, every librarian was, or should aspire to be, a readers' advisor, welcoming patrons and offering them the best items in the library. After all, what host or hostess would want to be known as someone who steered patrons to third- or fourth-rate titles? Readers' advisors were quality filters in the same way that teachers were quality filters, shaping cultural tastes, advancing historical and political knowledge, and honing ethical and moral sensibilities. Because of their in-depth knowledge of the contents of books, their presence allowed public libraries to follow "[t]he argument of Milton, in his Areopagitica, against a censorship of books ... which might possibly be injurious, on the ground that it is not the intention of the Almighty to place us in a world from which all temptation is excluded."[246] Libraries should judiciously purchase novels by the likes of Rhoda Broughton and Edgar Fawcett, if only to permit readers' advisors to lead patrons eventually to *Jane Eyre*, *Adam Bede*, and *The Scarlet Letter*, as well as to "copies of the works of Fielding, Smollett, Swift, Richardson, and other classic authors of like character."[247] After all, "[s]ome of the most important lessons taught in the

Scriptures are in the form of fiction."[248] As the concept of readers' advisory became widespread, it was entirely natural that, as in the BPL's Lower Hall, the reading of popular and ephemeral fiction would decline and "the reading of books which may be said to be educational" would increase.[249]

Additional insight into the hostess position comes from the SLPL, the Public Library of the District of Columbia (PLDC), and the Multnomah County (Portland, Oregon) Public Library (MCPL). While the hostess position at the BPL was in the closed-stack and delivery-desk model of librarianship, the hostesses at SLPL, PLDC, and MCPL worked primarily in an open-stack access model. The SLPL hostess position was established by Crunden in 1894, and its first incumbent was likely Laura Speck.

> Mrs. Laura Speck, general assistant in the Library since 1894, died in St. Luke's Hospital on May 13, 1925. Besides general supervision of the information service at the main entrance to the Delivery Hall, Mrs. Speck had charge of numerous administrative details, and it was her duty as 'library hostess' (Mr. Crunden's first designation of this position) to welcome strangers to the Library and give them their first impression of its cordial hospitality. Her life residence in St. Louis and her very wide acquaintance among its citizens made her especially valuable in this post.[250]

Here the hostess was associated with "cordial hospitality," a hospitality based on her "life residence in St. Louis and her very wide acquaintance among its citizens." She probably had strong social skills and a large social network. This impression is given substance by Crunden in a series of five articles entitled "How Things are Done in One American Library," which meticulously described every aspect of library work at the SLPL, including the selection of books, the principle of collecting high-demand duplicates and "renting" them out for 10 cents (later 5 cents) for one week, registration and loan procedures, and the taking of inventory.[251] Crunden portrayed the hostess in the following terms.

> [W]e have a functionary that I do not recall having seen in any other public library, whose duties may be summed up in the title "official hostess." Her desk, bearing a large sign, "Information Desk," is in the middle of the delivery room. Most of the time, however, she is about the room, greeting diffident newcomers, anticipating inquiries, explaining the card catalogue or pointing out the finding lists, and, in general, trying to do for the public what a gracious hostess does for her guests. The present occupant of this position is a woman of exceptional tact and *savoir faire*, who speaks French and German fluently, accomplishments which she often has occasion to use.[252]

Later, he would expand his definition of the hostess's work. After receiving a library card at the registration counter, a patron "is referred for fuller instructions" to the Information Desk. Here, Speck had a multitude of responsibilities. Some were purely directional: "A child applying here is directed, or taken, to the 'Young Folks' Room' just opposite and about twenty-five feet away." Other responsibilities consisted of bibliographic instruction.

> The wishes of an adult, or adolescent, are ascertained, and he is instructed, and assisted, accordingly. He may want to know if the Library has Hudson's 'Law of Psychic Phenomena' ... [and] is told that we have the book named, and given a call-slip and shown how to fill it, receiving the suggestion to put down other titles, so that he may get a second choice in case the book most wanted is not in. Or ... she may ask if we have Mrs. Holmes' 'Works.' In response to this inquiry a drawer from the 'Index to Authors' is taken out, and the applicant is referred to the most soiled cards in the catalogue as furnishing a complete list of the desired 'works.' A woman wants to know what we have on French history. She is taken to the 'Classified Catalogue' and shown the drawer marked '94c, French history.' She is also reminded that some of the most interesting books relating to French history are to be found in personal memoirs, in the class Biography, 97b.

Still other responsibilities entailed answering readers' queries that Crunden, judging from his comments in "The Most Popular Books," had formerly handled himself. Unlike Crunden's approach, however, the hostess did not make recommendations or suggestions.

> [T]he reader may want merely a 'nice book' ... [and this patron] is directed, or accompanied, to the open-shelf room, where may be found new novels in one place, other new books (the latest accessions) arranged in classes, in another, and in other sections several hundred old novels of grades from fair to first-class, a compartment of 'Best novels,' shelves containing foreign fiction (German, French, Spanish, Italian and Polish), a selection of the best books in all classes, and lastly, filling four sections, the 'Collection of Duplicates.' Then there are the student, the club-woman preparing a paper, the seeker for information on some particular point. Many of these are directed to the reference room upstairs; but a majority want books they can take home. Reference to the catalogue is not sufficient: personal help must be given. When the information clerk cannot readily refer to the books wanted and is too busy to make research, she calls on the Assistant Librarian, who, during most of the day, is available for this work.[253]

To say the least, the hostess was a busy person—almost a tour guide providing directional assistance and practical help. She had her own centrally located desk, from which she went forth into all other areas of the library. Although it is not out of the question that, in those moments when numerous patrons were not soliciting her help, she discussed books in detail with patrons, the descriptions of her work given here suggest that she did not have extensive discussion about books with patrons. We can well imagine the sociable Speck greeting patrons, making them feel at ease, directing them to various other locations in the library, and offering them useful information. During Speck's time, the hostess was a multi-purpose assistant.

This characterization of her duties is given support by an unsigned editorial in *Public Libraries* in 1900 calling for the construction of a much-larger library building in St. Louis, an event which came to pass in 1912.[254] In 1900, the SLPL was housed on "the upper floors of a dark business block in the very heart of the city ... in cramped quarters and dingy rooms."[255] Notwithstanding its inhospitable external environment, the editorial writer was impressed with the functioning of the SLPL. Once inside the doors, he was immediately met by "[a] pleasant-faced woman" advancing toward him "from beside the placard which reads, Information Desk, at the first sign of bewilderment on the part of the visitor."[256] In the "most cordial [and] interested manner," she "shows him what he wants and how to get at it" despite a "steady stream" of patrons passing to the left and right and going about their business of returning books, borrowing books, or on their way to browse among the open-access book alcove.[257] In the new 1912 SLPL, where "the work of Readers' Advisory Service is combined with that of the Information Desk," Speck sat at one of "two desks near the main entrance in the Delivery Hall," with the other desk occupied by "Miss Helen Tutt, in charge of the public catalogue."[258] And even though Speck's post–1912 duties formally included readers' advisory, it is instructive to see how Arthur E. Bostwick, Crunden's successor, characterized her work in the SLPL's *Annual Report 1925–1926*, where he contrasted her with the person hired to replace her upon her death. "In filling [Speck's] place, the Library has been mindful of the growing interest ... in Adult Education, and the probability that many of the problems brought to the main information desk for solution would hereafter bear on this question. It has therefore been thought well to emphasize the advisory service to adult readers which has always been a feature of this Library."[259] Bostwick's implication was clear: Speck had not emphasized readers' advisory in the performance of her duties.

If Speck was more a multi-purpose assistant than readers' advisor, the PLDC's hostess was closer to the readers' advisor envisioned by Green in "Personal Relations between Librarians and Readers" and present in the early 1880s at BPL. George F. Bowerman, Librarian of PLDC, described his library's hostess in a 1906 article in *Charities and the Commons*.

> Still further to facilitate the use of books, to relieve the necessity of using the card catalogue on the part of the uninitiated or timid, an information desk has been established near the main entrance. This is placed in charge of a tactful and intelligent woman who acts as hostess and guide to all and especially to first visitors to the library. Does the visitor not know how to use the card catalogue? The reader's advisor will teach him or even look up the required book and make out the call slips. Is the reader hazy about the subject wanted? The advisor makes a shrewd guess. Does he want just "something to read" for himself or another? The advisor exercises her judgment concerning the mental, moral or social needs and capacities of the inquirer, with always an effort to improve the quality of the reading wherever possible, to supplant a good book by a better book.[260]

The extent to which a hostess metamorphosed into a readers' advisor varied from library to library. It all depended on the intellectual energy of the person so designated, as well as on the degree to which there was sufficient time and suitable space to engage in substantive discussion that was the hallmark of readers' advisory, instead of the often superficial social banter prevalent in busy environments. Bowerman's last sentence may stand as a shorthand formulation of the difference between hostess and readers' advisor. While the hostess showed a patron where books were located and quickly pointed out recent popular titles before rushing off to serve the next patron, readers' advisors had the time and will to "to supplant a good book by a better book."

By the middle 1910s, the work of the hostess at an information desk had become so multi-dimensional that readers' advisory barely existed. We can see this in Rachel Rhoades's 1914 article "The Work of a Library Information Desk," in which she identified herself as the "First Assistant" in the Reference Department.[261] She noted how her work at MCPL falls into seven parts: "Welcome to newcomers"; "Distribution of applications and guidance about the library"; "Assistance in the use of the catalog"; cooperation with the circulation department, school department, reference department, children's department, and clubs and university and extension classes; "Telephone calls"; "City information and miscellaneous service"; and "Routine work" such as "Newspaper indexing" and "List making."[262] And while "[m]any people stop at the Information desk for suggestions about fiction," most of the inquiries are from patrons who want to know whether they should read *David Copperfield* or Edward Noyes Westcott's 1899 bestselling phenomenon *David Harum* if they want "an American story about a horse race."[263] Occasionally, Rhoades suggested that a patron who is seeking a specific title should try another one instead. To a lonely man on Christmas Day who is looking for Eleanor Hallowell Abbott's *Molly Make-Believe*, she recommended Thomas Bailey Aldrich's *Marjorie Daw*, both examples of bestselling popular fiction.[264] But, for the most part, her time was spent explaining the card catalog, answering telephone reference questions such as "What day of the week was January 3d, 1891?" and informing people about "location of buildings, street numbers, cars to reach the suburbs, [and] free days at the Museum of Art."[265] Her position had few of the characteristics envisioned by Green in his 1876 "Personal Relations" essay, where reference work and readers' advisory were two distinct functions.

If Speck's and Rhoades's experiences were any indication, the position of library hostess had been subsumed by the position of information desk attendant by the 1910s. And, because the act of readers' advisory (when defined as a "process of self-culture," serious and purposeful reading, and meaningful educational progress) had at one time been linked with knowledgeable library hosts and hostesses who constantly tried to elevate patrons' reading tastes, readers' advisory itself had also been subsumed. In its place there appeared an adulterated version: a version based on popular and ephemeral fiction that generated impressive circulation statistics and that, as a result, permitted public libraries to become "ticket-offices" in which mechanical procedures dominated. It was readers' advisory that, because it believed that any kind of reading was good, sundered the connection between meaningful education (achieved by serious and purposeful reading) and progressive social reform. Instead of elevating the public through exposure to enduring fiction and nonfiction, it stressed the lowest-common denominator: popular and ephemeral fiction. One result was that the philosophy of educational, moral, and spiritual uplift at the core of late 19th-century librarianship—a philosophy that also informed the social-reform impulses of the WCTU—was in large measure dismissed from public librarianship in the late 1900s and early 1910s in its rush to become, following Dewey, mechanically efficient and "ignorant." Public librarians who saw a clear connection between elevated standards of reading and progressive social reform were marginalized as the mantra of "Buy only what your customers want, then you won't have any dead stock" turned into gospel.[266] It seemed that few librarians wanted to be reminded that adherence to "Cheap-John" management principles meant that they were "too much lacking in [a] just realization of the possibilities of their position" with regard to an "improvement in the character" of their patrons' reading and that they were consequently well on their way to becoming "mere book-delivery machine[s], or ... acquisition-registering and cataloging machine[s]."[267] Or, as Hill trenchantly put it, they were well on their way to practicing "librarianship by automatic figures."

Public Libraries as Social Centers

As Dewey's principles took hold, there was nevertheless resistance on the part of some public librarians who were influenced by the settlement-house movement, which laid the groundwork for the profession of social work.[268] These librarians were not strong proponents of Dewey, did not think that the WCTU had taken the correct approach with regard to "trashy" fiction, yet still believed in the possibility of elevating the general level of education and opportunity through reading. Focusing "on changing the environment" instead of "on saving individuals," the settlement-house movement consisted of social reformers who "established private, voluntary institutions to give advice, education, and care to the immigrant poor" in the densely populated inner cores of urban areas.[269] With the 1889 founding of Hull-House in Chicago, Jane Addams became its most visible figure. The spiritual heir of Brook Farm and the forerunner of 1960s' community-action programs,[270] the settlement-house movement "typically attracted educated, native born, middle-class and upper-middle class women and men, known as 'residents,' to live (settle) in poor urban neighborhoods."[271] In the beginning, Hull-House residents "provided kindergarten and day care facilities for the children of working mothers; an employment bureau; an art gallery; libraries; English and citizenship classes; and theater, music and art classes."[272] Later, as Hull-House expanded into 13 buildings, it "supported more clubs and activities such as a Labor Museum, the Jane Club for single working girls, meeting places for trade union groups, and a wide array of cultural events."[273] Yet Marvin Olasky in *The Tragedy of American Compassion* remarked that "its stress on societal transformation rather than personal change turned some of the settlement clients into means to an end," that "its emphasis on the material over the spiritual and the political over the personal" often led to "charity without challenge," and that the "cultivated young people" who took up settlement work were more interested in "sav[ing] the world, not the individual."[274]

Public librarians found much that was amenable in the settlement-house movement, especially its swirl of social activities. Extending library services into poverty-stricken areas of large cities, they focused on reaching underserved populations in what Cora Stewart described as a "necessarily scrappy" fashion, working out of storefronts in "thickly populated tenement house section[s]" of working-class and immigrant neighborhoods.[275] As they brought books to children and young adults through "home libraries," public librarians also reached their parents.[276] Occasionally librarians developed reading courses. Stewart tells how she designed a reading course for a 14-year old who wanted to "take up French history by myself and not have it dry."[277]

> She read the Champney books, *Old Touraine,* books on Anne of Brittany, Joan of Arc, Agnes Sorel, Bayard. Because the Italians of the same period are almost inseparable and yet form points of comparison and contrast, she read Armstrong's *Lorenzo de Medici,* Rea's *Tuscan and Venetian art,* Hewlett's *Little novels of Italy,* a sketch of Vittoria Colonna, and Cartwright's *Beatrice d' Este.* We aimed for books which would bring out enthusiasm—brief biographies, novels— sometimes those throwing sidelights, like *When knighthood was in flower.* In the spring she was ready for Dumas, and she read his novels of the Renaissance period. Though protesting that she was wading through massacres and intrigues, she was quite prepared to see that the same France of the massacres and intrigues produced Joan of Arc and Bayard.[278]

Here we see a good example of readers' advisory, with Stewart intelligently and sensitively guiding the patron through the thicket of European history, alerting her to connections among books, pointing out how one book informs another, urging her to undertake a broad program of challenging and often difficult reading. But it is an example that stands out because of its comparative rarity.

Imbued with the principles of the settlement-house movement, librarians also worked to extend public-library service to adults. As a lengthy report in the 1905 *Library Journal* showed, many public libraries in large American cities formed partnerships with organizations such as the Jewish Education Alliance, the Anti-Tuberculosis League, charities helping the blind, churches working in immigrant settlement areas, workhouses, and prisons, as well as continuing their more traditional involvement with women's clubs, art and historical societies, and public schools.[279] The Enoch Pratt Free Library (Baltimore, Maryland) stated that it worked with "nearly 200 institutions, of which number about two-thirds are drawing books."[280] Among these were fire engine companies, police stations, military installations, and church clubs. The Buffalo Public Library reported that it had formed an "alliance with the settlement houses of the city" such that "[i]n two of these we maintain small branches, with about 800 books each, ... [which] are open one afternoon and one evening each week with one or two assistants in charge."[281] The Free Public Library of Newark had "small circulating libraries in 4 department stores, 5 police stations, 13 fire houses, 1 factory, [and] 189 school rooms."[282]

Soon, however, public libraries began to transform themselves into "social center[s]."[283] Some idea of what this entailed is provided in the following passage about a small library in Wisconsin.

> It is from [the public library], that the Christmas baskets are annually filled and distributed to the poor; there do the officers of the Visiting Nurse association hold their meetings; lectures given by the local clubs for mental and moral uplift of the community, tuberculosis exhibits, and entertainments to raise money for "sweet charity" are all held in the auditorium of the library. The housemaid temporarily out of a position, the scrub woman in need of work or funds, and the mother with nine children and a drunken husband all come with their tale of woe to Miss Lucy Pleasants, the librarian, feeling sure that in due time help will come from some benevolent society or private philanthropist.[284]

In his ALA presidential address for 1915, Hiller C. Wellman commented that public libraries were holding "aeroplane contests, athletic meets, and other entertainments," such as "fly-swatting contests" for children, concerts "with victrolas," and "moving picture shows."[285] Another library had "established a social center for young women where "all the various useful arts and handicrafts [can] be taught, free of charge."[286] The Rahway (New Jersey) Public Library went so far as to hold a series of annual flower shows for roses, asters, dahlias, and chrysanthemums.[287] It seemed that many public libraries wanted to become settlement houses, to take on the diverse range of activities that went on at Hull-House, and to become entertainment-oriented social centers instead of places in which to gain meaningful education. Hull-House, after all, had its social clubs, dances, music recitals, and athletic activities such as bowling and billiards. Why not public libraries?

In their enthusiasm, librarians sometimes forgot that the settlement-house movement tried to instill an appreciation for "those 'best results of civilization' upon which depend the finer and freer aspects of living."[288] In addition to classes in "domestic training" and "trade instruction," Hull-House members were exposed to Shakespeare, Dante, Browning, and Plato. In *Twenty Years at Hull-House*, Addams wrote about the 16-year existence of the Shakespeare club.

> I recall that one of its earliest members said that her mind was peopled with Shakespeare characters during her long hours of sewing in a shop, that she couldn't remember what she thought about before she joined the club, and concluded that she hadn't thought about anything at all. To feed the mind of the worker, to lift it above the monotony of his task, and to connect it with the larger world, outside of his immediate surroundings, has always been the object of art, perhaps never more nobly fulfilled than by the great English bard.[289]

Addams also fondly recalled how classes about Dante, Browning, and Plato—not to mention a lecture series by John Dewey on "Social Psychology"—turned into "genuine intellectual groups ... who were willing to make 'that effort from which we all shrink, the effort of thought.'"[290]

In what can be taken as an echo of Addams's words about "the effort of thought," Wellman, at the conclusion of his 1915 address, felt compelled to "plead" with librarians that "however occupied with executive cares, and whether engaged in supplying with books the *practical* needs of the community, or turning to work of wider social application," they should never forget that the "primary duty" and most "fundamental" of services offered by public libraries is "to make accessible to all men the best thought of mankind, whether it be found in the classic works of the older civilizations that preceded our own, or in the master intellects of a later day, or in the innumerable derivative writings of lesser minds."[291] Wellman thought that the pendulum had swung too far toward furthering "the material or ephemeral interests of our communities," and he reminded public librarians of their long-term duty to ensure the transmission to present and future generations of the "best" cultural and historical writings of previous civilizations because only the "pure, white flame" of "the things of the mind and of the spirit" was capable of "light[ing] man's pathway through the ages."[292] For Wellman, librarians were in danger of crossing the line separating Green's "rational entertainment," which was delivered through serious and purposeful reading, into what could be called irrational entertainment, which was an amalgam of social- and entertainment-oriented activities that neglected "the effort of thought."

Make no mistake: we are not saying that flower shows, concerts, domestic arts classes, and charity "entertainments" are not worthwhile in their own right. Yet it is an open question whether any meaningful educational goals were achieved through these social activities at public libraries, or whether any readers' advisory work that could lead patrons to the "best" cultural and historical writings from past and present eras was being done. Certainly, there is the example of Stewart and the reading course on French history, but, given the overall emphasis on turning public libraries into social centers that offered concerts and flower shows, Stewart's efforts seem more of a rare beacon than a daily event. While Stewart took time to guide her 14-year old patron towards a better understanding of historical relationships and events and urged her to persevere when the going got tough, her fellow librarians were busy with victrolas and concerts.

But the mere act of providing books or inviting people into the library, just like the mere act of putting on a lecture series or concert, is not sufficient in and of itself for true learning to occur. With regard to lectures, there is a qualitative difference between hearing, for the sake of amusement and excitement, a lecture "first sweetened up to make it palatable, and then kneaded into the smallest possible pills" and "[a] living comment quietly given to a class on a book they are earnestly reading."[293] So it is with books. People may read as many books as they wish, but in order to add real "[s]ignificance to reading, one must follow the injunctions of Matthew Arnold: "Culture is reading; but reading with a purpose to guide it and with system. He does a good work who does anything to help this; indeed, it is the one essential service now to be rendered to education."[294]

For systematic guidance to become a reality in public libraries, knowledgeable staff members were required. But Winser had explained that knowledgeable staff members were in short supply as libraries became obsessed with circulation statistics driven by popular fiction and Dewey's mechanical approach to librarianship. In 1911, Samuel H. Ranck of the GRPL reiterated Winser's concern about the lack of knowledgeable staff, complaining that GRPL's efforts to attract the area's skilled furniture workers and designers were suffering because of a dearth of "staff persons who know both the books and the men, have a knowledge of the processes of manufacture, and what the men in the factories really need."[295] Educated staff members, he concluded, were the only way to avoid the "awful mistakes made by library workers who simply did not know the one hundredth part as much about a subject as the man they were endeavoring to 'instruct.'"[296] But, as Wellman hinted, public librarians were becoming over-involved in turning their libraries into social centers. The result was that they neglected readers' advisory that elevated reading tastes toward serious and enduring literature, which in turn led to meaningful educational outcomes.

Constructing Librarianship

In 1890, Frank P. Hill, then Librarian of the Free Public Library of Newark, rhetorically asked: "[I]t is all very well to talk of educating the people, but if they refuse to be educated, what is to be done about it?"[297] For many librarians in the 1900s and early 1910s who were nonplussed that their institutions had become repositories of popular fiction and social centers, the answer was: very little. In 1903, Bostwick, who was then head of the Circulation Department of the New York Public Library, compared the library to a museum or a zoo.[298] People "go there for pure amusement, yet they gain in this way much valuable information that they probably would not otherwise have obtained."[299] Asserting that recreational use of a library "is at the same time an educational use," he urged librarians that, "instead of lamenting that a large proportion of our people prefer to get their history and travel, their sociology and psychology in the form of fiction, we should be glad that we have this means of conveying it to them."[300]

The legacy of moral, social, and intellectual improvement through serious and purposeful reading that was central to the belief systems of Crunden, Foster, Green, Agnes Hill,

Kite, Peck, Porter, Winser, Winsor, and other 19th-century librarians was starting to be demonized as a relic of a bygone era. That era, many felt, had been superseded by new and pressing demands that needed to be met with mechanical procedures (which included handing out popular fiction in a "ticket-office" model of "librarianship by automatic figures") and social- and entertainment-oriented programming (where public libraries became venues for flower shows, concerts, and fly-swatting contests). And if public librarians compared themselves to missionaries, some wondered whether "this missionary spirit manifest[s] itself aright when it takes the direction of an ambition to hand across the desk as many volumes as possible on a given day, regardless of their nature? Will the librarian forever be content to think in quantity rather than quality?"[301]

For this just-quoted anonymous observer of the library scene in 1905, the answer was all too obvious: "The librarian is not fulfilling his whole duty unless he endeavors to educate the young people ... to the point where they realize that the desire to read the six best-selling novels is at best a low ideal."[302] Another observer, Edwin E. Slosson, Literary Editor of *The Independent*, expressed similar thoughts in 1915.[303] For him, public libraries resembled "municipal amusements, like the band playing in the park on summer evenings and the fireworks on the Fourth."[304] He dreamed of a time when they would become "public utilities ... for all the people in their daily work," built not on a foundation of "detective stories [and] memoirs of dead French ladies,"[305] but rather on a foundation of newspapers, government information, the classics, and "recent and authoritative works on pending questions,"[306] such that a farmer could "see what is the red bug that is eating his box elder trees and what to do ... against it" or a mechanic could "find out what horse-power he can get from a windmill above his shop."[307]

Despite the gradual drift toward circulation-obsessed and social- and entertainment-oriented public librarianship in the 1900s and early 1910s, public librarians had developed an underlying philosophy of readers' advisory and a rich array of ideas to carry out that philosophy starting around 1870. Many of these ideas are still being used in readers' advisory work in the early 21st century, forming the nucleus of contemporary readers' advisory and thus belying the assertions of Crowley, Kimball, and Ross that pre–1920 readers' advisory was a wasteland. Proposed by individuals who considered public libraries to be entities dedicated to meaningful education based on the "best" fiction and nonfiction available, these readers' advisory ideas had one central goal: elevating patrons' reading tastes so that they might gain a meaningful education thorough serious, purposeful, and enduring literature. As public librarianship built on popular fiction and social activities came to the fore in the 1900s and 1910s, these ideas were put aside and temporarily lay dormant, waiting to be rediscovered and reused when circumstances warranted. Those circumstances, an unanticipated byproduct of the lessons learned during World War I, were not long in coming.

Chapter 4

The Commitment to Systematic Adult Education

The entry of the United States into World War I in 1917 inaugurated the second phase of readers' advisory service. Although the war itself was an unfathomable tragedy, it had a bracing effect on librarianship in North America, especially in its reinvigoration of readers' advisory. At its 1917 summer conference in Louisville, Kentucky, the ALA strongly supported the creation of a wartime library service, as recommended by Librarian of Congress Herbert Putnam's Preliminary War Library Committee. Later in 1917, as the military began to prepare troops for their duties, the Commission on Training Camp Activities invited the ALA "to assume the responsibility for providing adequate library facilities in ... camps and cantonments" in the continental United States and overseas, including France and Siberia.[1] The result was the ALA's Library War Service Program (LWSP), under the direction of Putnam, which oversaw the design, staffing, organization, and overall functioning of 36 camp libraries.[2] The buildings were "plain wooden structures" with dimensions of either 120 × 40 or 93 × 40 feet, with an interior that was "one large room with two bedrooms located at one end[,] ... open shelves accommodating about 10,000 volumes[,] [and] tables and chairs for about 200 readers."[3] By the end of 1919, "more than 700 librarians" had participated in LWSP in some capacity, and about seven million books "had been placed in [camp] libraries or distributed directly to Army and Navy personnel."[4] As they provided support for training and general education courses for the troops conducted by government and military entities and the Young Men's Christian Association (YMCA), camp librarians marveled at the unflagging and ravenous demand by soldiers for knowledge and information contained in books and magazines.

Many of the soldiers were poor, recent immigrants, or from rural areas. For one or all of these reasons, they had only intermittently, if ever, been exposed to schools and libraries: some librarians recounted that soldiers often asked how much it cost to borrow a book. Atlases, French-language manuals, technical handbooks, and books about astronomy, aviation, engineering, history, military science, technology, and psychology—to name only a few subjects—were extremely popular, so much so that one librarian reported that "90 percent of ... circulation is non-fiction."[5] In another library, 1,050 books were borrowed: "[o]f these 548 were works of fiction, 46 dealt with war, 52 were in the foreign languages, while the balance, 404, were works on technical military problems, educational topics, poetry, art, history and general literature."[6] To judge from the pictures in Theodore Wesley Koch's *War Service of the American Library Association* and *Books in the War: The Romance of Library War Service*, camp libraries were constantly being used by the troops, some of whom "come in practically every day for a fresh book."[7] In a more humorous vein, "one officer reported that ALA library buildings were the only places where the men felt secure from both rag-time and prayer meetings!"[8]

Librarians were often called upon to guide readers: "Many of the Men Need Aid in Book Selection" stated a caption beneath a picture of a library worker handing books to troops in Koch's *War Service*.[9] But just as often they marveled at the selections the recruits made for themselves: Shakespeare's *Pericles*; Boswell's *Life of Johnson*; Henri Bergson's *Creative Evolution*; Conrad; Hardy; Meredith; Virgil; and Goethe's *Faust*.[10] Koch reports that "[t]he librarian at Camp Greene had requests for Horace in the original and in English. Spencer's *Sociology* circulated regularly there, as did also James's *Pragmatism*. Several men wanted to read Ibsen, either in the original or in translation."[11] The morale officer at Camp Devens wrote to an official from the Massachusetts Free Public Library Commission: "our foreign-born men ... seem to be desirous of obtaining the works of the best authors, and appreciate the opportunity of having them available in the camp library."[12] Thus the camp libraries supplied "classics in Arabic," as well as books in Finnish, Italian, Polish, Russian, and Swedish, among others.[13]

Camp libraries helped to educate those troops who were functionally illiterate. Military officials concluded that "*one soldier in every four* could not take English literacy tests of an equivalent to the second grade, either because of lack of education itself or through unfamiliarity with the English language."[14] The librarian at Camp Wheeler, in Georgia, remarked that, initially, the 3,000 illiterate soldiers there constituted "quite a problem, but we tackled that in fine style. We taught them how to read and write and then we gave them the books after they learned to use them."[15] Camp libraries also functioned as adult-education centers for post-war civilian life.

> It is an undisputed fact that the men in the American army are returning to civil life far better educated than they were when they entered the service. In the accomplishment of this result the camp libraries have played no small part. They have been valuable auxiliaries to the courses in history, civics, literature, social conditions, geography, and practical science conducted by the Y.M.C.A. in the various cantonments, with a view to the cultivation of habits of study and reading. The method employed in carrying on this work was a combination of the preceptorial system and the university extension idea. Lecturers lived in the camps for a week at a time, and by moving from building to building conveyed their inspirational message to the entire camp. Special study classes under local volunteer preceptors were also formed, and reading clubs were organized to guide the men in their choice of literature.[16]

As Raymond B. Fosdick noted in *Scribner's Magazine*, the ALA supplied the required books and provided "correlative reading."[17] Camp libraries became more than places of mere entertainment because

> [t]he requirements for books in the camp libraries are more specialized than in ordinary city libraries. The standard as a whole is even higher. Men are being called to unaccustomed tasks; so they are doing a vast amount of "reading up." The growth of the reading habit among the soldiers has brought to light an interesting contradiction to the generally accepted theory that among a group of individuals the leveling process is a leveling downward. The men in the camps who are readers stimulate by their example the interest of those who are not.... Thus does Private Y get an incentive to taste the joys of literature. There is a tendency toward a leveling upward.[18]

The work accomplished in camp libraries was extensively covered in the *ALA Bulletin* during 1917–1918.[19] The entire ALA membership became profoundly aware that camp libraries— despite their makeshift, rudimentary, and crowded nature—were indispensable educational institutions of great benefit to previously underserved populations. As Lee observed, "providing personal guidance to readers" in the context of camp libraries had "an energizing effect on the profession as a whole."[20]

When Colonel Edward L. Munson thanked the ALA at its 1919 conference for the services its members had rendered during the war years in military camps, he pointedly requested that public librarians, upon returning to civilian life, continue to publicize "the availability of books and reading to all levels of readers," not just the "educated and student class," because libraries were "under the patriotic obligation of using every possible measure to extend their facilities and good offices to that class of citizenry which, though illiteracy, inertia, and unfamiliarity with the American language, customs and ideals have heretofore made little use of them."[21] Good books, Munson believed, were "essential agent[s] in education and instruction" and "ready channel[s] for the conveyance of suggestion and thought for the betterment of character and behavior."[22] Munson's plea did not fall on deaf ears. The experiences of camp librarians became a compelling illustration of the merits of instituting systematic adult education as a formal component of the public-library mission.

The Aftermath of the Library War Service Program

As soldiers began to return home, the ALA "printed several million copies of carefully selected lists of books on various trades," which "were sent to camp libraries, branch reading-rooms, welfare centers, and public libraries, and were even made available through ... armories, banks, clubs, chambers of commerce, employment bureaus, factories, hotels, post-offices, restaurants, stores, and waiting rooms."[23] Banners proclaiming "BACK TO THE JOB—WHAT JOB? BOOKS ON ALL JOBS AT THE PUBLIC LIBRARY, USE THEM" were strung across busy streets in Birmingham, Alabama, and elsewhere.[24] Although libraries emphasized vocational materials, there was also renewed interest in providing literary classics, which many soldiers had requested during their visits to camp libraries. This demand for classics may have been one reason that Paul M. Paine, of the Syracuse (New York) Public Library, urged his colleagues not to forget that "it is vastly more important that a man or woman should know how to live."[25] Such knowledge is found in "the priceless treasures of the past" that collectively constitute "good reading": histories, novels, and poetry that are capable of providing "that immortal thrill that Keats' explorer felt when he stared at the Pacific," that show "how much greater the soul is than any material thing can be, and how faith can move mountains," and that "can teach ... what the duty of the neighbor is between nations, what it is between the one who makes the profit and the one who gets the wages, what it is between society and the child, society and the weak, society and the sinner, [and] society and the man who lies on the ground beside the road to Jericho."[26]

For all their newfound enthusiasm, librarians' first formal attempt to define and structure, on a national level, an expanded role for public libraries in the realm of adult education was a dismal failure. Developed by an ALA committee in the latter half of 1919 and discussed throughout 1920, this attempt was called the "Enlarged Program" (EP) and was dependent upon raising $2 million over three years from foundations and individuals.[27] A central feature of the EP was a "nationwide promulgation of the library idea, designed to stimulate the extension and development of libraries and to increase the use of print."[28] More specifically, "[g]eneral adult education, library extension to unserved areas, and Americanization" of immigrants were important goals of the EP.[29] Other ideas included "[a] national examining board, empowered to grant certificates and to set standards for library schools" and "closer relations with the National Education Association" so that teachers and public librarians might work together.[30] The ALA published newsletters and pamphlets about its plan; the EP was also mentioned in about 300 magazine articles and 10,000 newspaper items, including *Good Housekeeping* and the *Saturday Evening Post*.[31] But, because of infighting about the plan's scope and rumors that it would be administered in New York instead of Chicago, the EP fundraising drive collected only $50,702 by the end of 1920.[32] Although the EP was "a humiliating defeat" and a "debacle," librarians had nevertheless ventured to sketch out a vision of what public-library service could be.[33] As Arthur P. Young concluded, their "dream" of an expanded role as an institution providing adult education was not dead; rather, it "would be deferred."[34]

If a national top-down effort foundered because of regional sensibilities and irreconcilable philosophical differences, there was nothing preventing individual public libraries, typically large institutions with strong leadership, from undertaking local efforts to institute adult-education programs. These programs assumed various shapes—service to individuals, service to groups, book talks, and discussion forums—but at their core was the readers' advisor. In 1922 the Detroit (Michigan) Public Library (DPL) and the Cleveland (Ohio) Public Library (CPL) inaugurated the first readers' advisory bureaus dedicated to adult education in North America.[35] They were quickly followed by public libraries in Chicago (1923), Milwaukee (1923), Indianapolis (1924), Cincinnati (1925), and Omaha (1925).[36] By the end of 1925, seven public libraries offered readers' advisory through independent bureaus or units.[37] Ruth Rutzen, head of the Circulation Department at DPL, recounted the early days of readers' advisory in Detroit. "At that time it meant a desk in the open-shelf room of the circulation department and a specially designated assistant to handle requests and to bring to users of the room a consciousness of a special service. A few years later it became necessary to establish the readers' adviser in a small separate room, admirably placed between the large delivery hall and the open-shelf room. This provided more adaptable arrangements for consultation and space for a separate book collection."[38] Marie A. Hanson, an early DPL readers' advisor, offered additional details about the new service, noting that "office privacy" contributed to the creation of an "informal-at-home atmosphere which invites the confidence of the patron" because the readers' advisor can display "a sincere and convincing interest" in the patron's "personal problems, ... life-story—backgrounds—inhibitions and reactions, and seemingly beside-the-point experiences."[39] The entire interview process, she concluded, "means a shattering of any preconceived ideas of a strictly book-dealing informational job," so much so that "the training of a psychiatrist and social worker" would have been useful to her.[40] The phrase "consciousness of a special service" indicated the distance traveled from the multi-purpose library hostess or information-desk attendants in St. Louis and Portland, Oregon, respectively, in the 1900s and 1910s, and from Green's 1876 description of a part-time readers' advisor. In the wake of the LWSP experience, public librarians realized that systematic adult education was such an important need that it called for a full-time designated employee and a separate room.

One of the ways to best appreciate this change is to consider the functioning of the readers' advisory office in Cleveland, where two of the most prominent personalities in the 1920s and 1930s were Lucia H. Sanderson and Mabel Booton.[41] The CPL had two tiers of readers' advisory service, each functioning independently, but in such a way that the relatively informal tier of readers' advisory—an updated library-hostess service located in the Popular Library division—often funneled patrons to the more formal tier located in the Main Library. The existence of two tiers was a recognition that readers' advisory was a serious endeavor that could not be carried out in a completely satisfying way through a quick encounter in busy surroundings. CPL's informal readers' advisor had a desk near the registration area, was mandated to help new registrants after they had received their library card, and approached browsing patrons "with ... offer[s] of help."[42] Conversations were inevitably brief. Often, patrons were happy with the suggestions they received from the informal readers' advisor, but just as often this readers' advisor was confronted with "real reading problems" for which "special help" was called for. In these cases, the patron was directed to formal readers' advisory service, which was housed in its own office.[43]

Patrons could bypass informal readers' advisory and go directly to its formal counterpart. Perhaps they had picked up one of the "silent advisers" (i.e., bookmarks) scattered around the library and designed to encourage "readers who are shy."[44] On one side of the bookmark was the following invitation: "READERS' CONSULTANT SERVICE. We can become acquainted with the peoples, the places, and the important interests of this world of ours through the systematic reading of books in travel, philosophy, biography, history, literature, the arts and the sciences. Reading plans on these subjects may be had in the Readers' Adviser's Office of the Main Library."[45] And so, upon entering CPL's Main Library, patrons noticed "a large sign" placed on "a standard near the Information Desk": "There is education and enjoyment for you in a reading plan: ask at the Readers' Adviser's Book Room."[46] In this way the CPL differentiated readers' advisory from other functions: it was a special service that required patrons to walk a few extra steps to "a small room opening off the southeast corner of Brett Hall, the main periodical reading room."[47] Here, "[g]reat pains" were taken "to make this room appear like a home library."[48]

> The walls are lined with low cases filled with bright-colored books and above the cases the walls are painted a soft green. Opposite the entrance hangs an unusually decorative painting. The drapes at the windows add more color to the room. There are several armchairs, a desk for the adviser, a globe, a small display stand which holds a book open at some interesting illustration.[49]

The intent was "to create a friendly, inviting atmosphere, to avoid noise, hurry and disorder" so that patrons "can grow thoughtful and can feel that their particular problems will have our whole attention."[50]

Just as the atmosphere of the room was designed to calm patrons, so was the interview, which was not meant to tell the patron "what he should read—a most undesirable situation."[51] Instead, the ideal interview turned into a relationship-building conversation, where "one reader talk[s] over his problem with another reader, a librarian familiar with books."[52] It was a conversation that required "much wisdom, knowledge, sympathetic understanding and patience"; it was "no place for a patronizing attitude, aloofness, nor a too easy familiarity."[53] In her or his role as "an active listener," the advisor elicited as much information as possible: "probable age," "formal schooling," "interests and hobbies," "kind of work," and "books and magazines" frequently read.[54] The advisor then focused on why the patron wanted a reading plan. Most patrons talked about their problem "in generalities," but "[u]nderneath there is usually a quite definite need which reveals itself after some digging."[55] There was the secretary who "majored in commercial subjects in high school and missed out on the classics"; or the teacher who, after taking an "auto trip through New England last summer," realized "how much history and literature I don't know"; or the businessman who, after hearing radio broadcasts of Shakespearean plays, was "seized" with "a strong desire to read about Shakespeare."[56]

Once an underlying reason was adduced, a solution was presented that did not entail making "an arbitrary choice" for the patron or becoming "a dictatorial sort of teacher."[57] After "gaug[ing] the reader's capacity, and ... find[ing] the point of intellectual curiosity at which the reader seems best fitted to begin," the advisor "work[s] with him, get[s] him to do something for himself, [and] suggest[s] ways of using books so that eventually he can carry on his program of reading for self-education by himself."[58] Particular stress was laid on the educational value of fiction: "how psychology may be dramatized in a good novel; how clearly a philosophy can be demonstrated; how vividly sociological and economic conditions can be presented; how alive history can be made; and that so many of the great books of literature are fiction."[59] This implied that readers' advisors had in-depth knowledge about a vast number of books such that they were able to recommend just the right novel. Equal emphasis was put on "urg[ing] the reader to combine study with reading for pleasure": "[a] reader may be working on a plan for definite information and along with it he may be reading poetry, essays, drama or novels for no other purpose at all except enjoyment and inspiration, truly the noblest end of reading."[60] Finally, patrons were encouraged to return to the readers' advisory office and "share with us ... delight in a book, not because it has been a means to some other end, but just because it is what it is."[61]

When creating reading plans, CPL readers' advisors were inventive. For two patrons who wished "to spend an afternoon together ... every week to learn about the countries least familiar to them" and for whom Italy was the first country of choice, the plan included "the reading of books," but it also comprised "the studying of maps, using the picture file in the Fine Arts Division, playing phonograph records in the soundproof music room, visiting the Art Museum, Alta Settlement House, Alta Branch Library and 'Little Italy,'" as well as an Italian restaurant.[62] For patrons interested in "a list of the great books of literature," a popular approach was to suggest reading John Macy's *The Story of the World's Literature* and making notes about "books and authors which especially appeal." Patrons could then chart their own path or, if more help was needed, the readers' advisor prepared "a reading plan from [the] notes."[63]

Systematic reading plans were the backbone of the CPL's readers' advisory service. Constructed individually for patrons, these plans were based on an expanding master list of annotated books in all subject areas that had been personally examined by the readers' advisor and categorized as to "how each book may be used; that is, whether it is a simple introduction, a scholarly work, [or] a survey."[64] Folded and placed in convenient pocket-size folders, plans were made "as attractive as possible, considering carefully the wording of annotations, and the arrangement of material on the page, so that the whole will have a neat and orderly appearance."[65] Readers were counseled about the benefits to be gained from "having at hand a dictionary, a map, possibly an encyclopedia, [and] a notebook in which to record questions and new ideas." They were also informed that their self-education should also include "periods for thinking about the truth and value of new ideas."[66] Naturally, it was hoped that all this advice and attention would stimulate sporadic readers to become inveterate readers. When this occurred, "small groups for the study of special subjects" were formed.[67] At first, "[s]uch nuclei make only a small showing when they start, but as interest deepens and new people become interested they develop into significant outlets for adult education activity."[68] Individuals who coalesced into informal groups often wished to enroll in formal adult-education classes. Here, too, the CPL was ready to help, since it established an "Extension Division for Adult Education," which included a coordinating office featuring about 600 unique titles that were "extensively duplicated" for use by classes conducted under the auspices of the Board of Education, business schools, and various immigrant organizations.[69]

At the CPL, the readers' advisor was at the center of adult education as the initiator of systematic reading programs that were the springboard for further independent reading, informal group discussions, or formal classes. Similar trajectories can be seen in the work of the Readers' Bureaus of the Chicago Public Library (ChiPL), the Milwaukee Public Library (MPL), the Indianapolis Public Library (IPL), and the Cincinnati Public Library (CinPL). At the ChiPL, the Readers' Bureau's (RB) emphasized its distinctiveness from circulation-driven (and hence popular fiction-driven) librarianship. As Alice M. Farquhar, the guiding spirit behind the RB in Chicago, noted, the implementation of this service "woke us from our lethargy and started us on a new appraisal of our educational possibilities."[70] By creating "more intimate personal relations between the individual and the vast and overwhelming resources of the public library," the RB served patrons "who have found the present methods, necessarily adapted to quantity distribution, not entirely satisfactory."[71] Organized as "a separate department"; centrally housed in an office "adjacent to the general reference room, the teachers' room, the college reading room, and the Civics Department"; and staffed by a full-time librarian and stenographer, the Chicago RB prepared "courses of reading and outline study for individuals" on both cultural and vocational topics after a wide-ranging "personal conference" between patron and librarian.[72] It also developed "study programs for clubs and other groups and provides a consultation service for those who wish advice about books but are not necessarily interested in courses of reading."[73]

The "avowedly experimental" RB at the ChiPL enjoyed instant success.[74] In its first 15 months, "230 different outlines on 177 subjects were prepared, and 337 individuals were reading" under its direction.[75] Ninety-eight of these courses were in the field of literature, "twenty-two of which were in modern literature [and] eleven in drama."[76] By the end of 1929, a total of 3,712 adults "were given individual attention and subsequent reading guidance," an average of 49.5 per month.[77] In 1927, some 1,682 adults in various branches undertook "special reading courses."[78] As the work of the RB expanded, so did its staffing. By 1924, there was a "chief and six assistants" with multiple duties, including the compilation of lists of adult-education courses in the Chicago area and a thorough review of new books such that "substantial books are not summarily dismissed from consideration simply because they lack the elements of popularity."[79] By 1940, Carleton Bruns Joeckel and Leon Carnovsky wrote that "[t]he proponent of individual guidance is on sound ground when he argues that serious reading pursued in an earnest endeavor to improve one's intellectual and cultural status is far more important, from the social standpoint, than much of the reading which is reflected in circulation statistics, even though the latter type of reading also falls within the proper scope of the library."[80] Thus, in order to diffuse more broadly "the values inherent in individual guidance," readers' advisors worked with "groups with homogenous interests, so that the members may be encouraged in the reading of similar materials."[81] Joeckel and Carnovsky hoped that reading guidance would become the cornerstone of the library's mission in a new "Adult Education Department" and be "conceived as a function of every major service agency in the library system."[82] After suitable training, "*many* readers' advisers, available at all branches, and capable of preparing systematic reading courses for the adult student" would expertly guide patrons.[83]

CinPL, IPL, and MPL all took pains to stress the personalized nature of their readers' advisory service. At the RB in Cincinnati, started and directed by Pauline J. Fihe, "[t]he subjects on which courses have been prepared are most varied and sharply defined," so much so that "[f]requently they are so highly individualized that very thorough investigation is necessary in order to find any books which treat them in a manner suited to the reader's requirements."[84] Catherine Bailey, the readers' advisor in Indianapolis, was proud that, after an initial interview, "[r]eaders are encouraged to return to the adviser for conference and discussion" so that, if necessary, "alterations in courses" can be made.[85] Miriam D. Tompkins, the readers' advisor in Milwaukee, developed 1,207 unique reading courses in 1927, all of which took much "effort ... thought, and ... care."[86] After forming an estimate of a patron's educational background, interests, capabilities, and enthusiasm during personal interviews, she consulted "with other departments of the library, and with teachers, technicians, [and] experts in many fields" before creating a patron's course.[87] Her painstaking work paid off, since 1,113 individuals had either completed the courses or were following them in the early months of 1928, a success rate far above the 6 percent of students who completed work at "privately operated correspondence schools."[88] The beneficiaries of Tompkins's work—including 122 stenographers, 82 office clerks, 32 factory workers, 14 electricians, and 125 salesmen and saleswomen—profited from courses in Literature, Travel, Psychology, History, Architecture, Pharmacy, Mining Engineering, Petroleum, and Hinduism.[89] For those wishing to pursue their studies, MPL offered information about "schools, classes, and other opportunities for instruction" and worked with these outside agencies to coordinate "opportunity for collateral reading."[90]

Codifying Local Initiatives

Contemporaneous with the early experiences of these large public libraries in the realm of adult education and readers' advisory were the ideas set forth in William S. Learned's *The American Public Library and the Diffusion of Knowledge*.[91] Originally prepared for the Carnegie Corporation as a memorandum and published in book form in 1924, Learned's influential work presented a plan to make the public library a "community intelligence service" staffed by "an intelligence personnel."[92] Learned felt that, as currently constituted, public libraries "defeat[ed] their purpose by placing in charge a staff assigned to the entire universe"—a circumstance that resulted in "[o]nly the vaguest and most casual service" from "experts" who were anything but.[93] It was a procedure that could be compared "to rotating courses alphabetically among the instructors on a college faculty."[94] Good colleges did not operate in that way. Why should public libraries, especially because "the demands for differentiation both in the extent of ground covered and the peculiar treatment required by each successive applicant in the adult group [at the public library] are far more exacting than in any college"?[95]

He therefore recommended that public libraries of the future be staffed by individuals with wide-ranging subject expertise, who would "command all of the college teacher's familiarity with the literature of a strictly limited field plus the power which the college teacher may, and often does, lack completely, namely, the power speedily to read [a patron's] mental equipment and point of view, and to sense intuitively the character of [the patron's] personal need."[96] For a city the size of Akron, Ohio, which had a population of about 200,000 people, there should be about 20 librarians who, together "with their assistants," will actively disclose to area residents the knowledge pertaining to their field of expertise.[97] "When a valuable book on new processes in rubber manufacture appears, the technical librarian will immediately see to it that the Akron factories are furnished with a good description of the book and an estimate of its precise value to them ... [and] [i]f fresh designs and color combinations are unearthed in ancient Egyptian pottery, the art division at once calls the attention of the Akron potters to the possibilities of their utilization."[98] The personnel of Learned's intelligence center would be "actively aggressive ... in discovering advantageous ways of preparing and presenting important material to students for the purpose of arousing their progressive interest," so much so that they quickly "would be the real pilots" of the "social, intellectual, and economic life" of a town or city.[99] Learned contrasts this new breed of librarian with previous versions.

Mere grubbers in books according to professional tradition or a prevalent conception of a public librarian will not do. They must indeed understand their several fields of knowledge, but they must also understand the world of men as well or better; their excellence is measured by their power to connect the two. They must have sensitized minds that in addition to a good education possess quick insight into new relations and novel applications. They must watch their community and attend its professional gatherings, not primarily to advertise their services, but to discover how knowledge in books may be selected and arranged the better to meet the changing demands or a shifting point of view. They should work beneath the surface in terms of truth and a wiser world.... Such counselors, constituting a sort of new clergy of the mind, would open a fresh career that could not fail to appeal powerfully to capable men and women.[100]

The counselor-librarian's main task is "to produce a general diffusion of knowledge among small, ill-defined, and constantly shifting groups, where each need is peculiar to the individual himself, and must be dealt with separately."[101]

Learned used examples from public libraries in Cleveland, Indianapolis, Chicago, and other urban centers to indicate that his plan was possible. Particularly germane for him was the RB in Chicago, which he saw as a model of how readers' advisory could become a focal point for adult education, since it relied on "groups of selected experts [in its own public library] in charge of various divisions of the books."[102] The system worked to perfection in the case of a "saleswoman in a china shop who desired to make a study of the marks on crockery and glass ware in preparation for becoming a buyer," since her request was met in two days.[103] Little wonder that the demand for readers' advisory was so overwhelming in Chicago that the initial notice advertising it "had to be withdrawn until the bureau should catch up."[104]

Judson T. Jennings, Librarian of the Seattle (Washington) Public Library, agreed with Learned. In his presidential address to the 1924 ALA convention, Jennings urged his audience to take substantive steps toward establishing adult-education opportunities in all public libraries. He believed that each library should have at least one readers' advisor "whose special function shall be to assist readers desiring to pursue courses of reading or study."[105] To support these readers' advisors, the ALA should embark on a large-scale operation to ensure a ready supply of reading courses on "both vocational and cultural subjects."[106] To help in the creation of courses on more specialized topics, state library associations and state libraries should provide public libraries with "a list of educators and experts who would be willing to assist librarians" in their tasks.[107] Working together with school administrative personnel, readers' advisors should conduct interviews to persuade adults "leaving grade school, high school, or college" to continue their education, bringing to their attention the resources of the public library in their spheres of interest.[108] Finally, the ALA should contract with authors to write subsidized books "that are interesting and readable to the average man" and with printing plants to publish them in inexpensive editions.[109]

It was an ambitious program, Jennings admitted, but it had the virtue of concentrating the efforts of public librarians on books and other print resources. In the recent past, librarians sometimes had the deplorable tendency to "acquire[] the attitude of the welfare worker" as they became involved in "things that perhaps 'we ought not to have done'" in a rush to prove their utility.[110] Although these impulses were "laudable," they were also a sign of a scatter-shot approach that characterized public librarians as unsure of their role: "Why is it the function of libraries to supply needs in related fields whenever they discover these needs? Why should we think that we are commissioned to correct faults in other institutions?"[111] Jennings felt that such presumption diluted the public library's power, making it a social center instead of an entity with a meaningful educational purpose. "Since our libraries lend cook books, should we not provide cook stoves in order that the anxious young housewife may test Mrs. Farmer's recipes before borrowing her delectable book? Since we have laboratories for dramatics, should we not also install laboratories for chemists, machine shops for mechanics, drafting rooms for engineers and architects, and studios for artists?"[112] Although many public librarians looked upon these activities in a positive light, Jennings was less sanguine. For him, it was far better to focus on adult education through the prism of serious and purposeful reading. Otherwise, the public library was at risk of defining itself as an institution that did not consider itself as "an integral part of public education," an institution to which, in its current state, the words of the Apostle Paul applied: "For the good that I would I do not; but the evil which I would not, that I do."[113] Jennings's speech in 1924 followed the same trajectory as Wellman's speech in 1915, concluding with the same call for a renewed focus on meaningful education.

Learned's innovative ideas, Jennings's views, and the success of readers' advisory initiatives in the cities described above combined to form a critical mass of opinion in favor of public libraries becoming important participants in adult education.[114] In 1924, the ALA established the Commission on the Library and Adult Education (CLAE), with Jennings as Chairman and with the heads of the Milwaukee, Indianapolis, and Cleveland public libraries as three of its other six members. Between 1924 and 1926, the CLAE was extremely busy as it worked towards its final report, issued in 1926.[115] In November 1924, it began publication of a bulletin entitled *Adult Education and the Library*, which was a vehicle for issuing "reports of its progress and tentative proposals [seven or eight times a year] in order that librarians might not have to wait two years and depend solely upon the final report for information about the study now being made."[116] After the CLAE passed its mantle to the Board on the Library on Adult Education (BLAE), *Adult Education and the Library* evolved into a quarterly journal that described adult-education programs developed by public libraries in the United States and Canada.[117] The CLAE also initiated the *Reading with a Purpose* series, discussed later, but its main contribution was the report *Libraries and Adult Education*, which codified the scope of public-library involvement with and responsibility for adult education and defined an eight-point program for the BLAE.[118]

According to the CLAE, all public libraries should adopt four practices pioneered in Cleveland, Chicago, Milwaukee, and other large urban public libraries: the implementation of readers' advisory service; the "organization" or "coordination" of study or discussion groups to give readers "the opportunity to discuss the subject of one's reading with other students and with a discussion leader well versed in the subject"; the provision of information about "local opportunities for adult education available outside the library"; and "the supplying of books and other printed material for adult education activities maintained by other organizations."[119] With regard to discussion groups, libraries could be "coordinating agenc[ies] between readers and discussion leaders" by "putting readers in touch with discussion groups already organized; by arranging for informal conferences between a public-spirited specialist and a few persons following the same reading course; [or] by an arrangement with other adult education agencies whereby they will furnish leaders for discussion and organize small groups of readers."[120] Some public libraries quickly organized discussion programs. As Lee noted, the Library Association of Portland, Oregon, formed 26 "Read-a-Book-Together clubs," and in the early 1930s, "several state library agencies" launched discussion groups "on world economic conditions."[121]

But readers' advisory was the primary way for public libraries to dispense cogent advice to individuals wishing "to pursue their studies alone."[122] To do so effectively, libraries must realize that "[t]here is a sharp distinction between the work of a readers' adviser and the work ordinarily done in circulation and reference departments."[123] Whereas the work of the former involved "carefully organiz[ing] courses of reading which are suited to particular individuals," the work of the latter was "frequently hurried and impersonal and is intended to meet only the immediate need."[124] Readers' advisory should be conducted "undisturbed by the public and other influences which might make the reader ill at ease"; it should dispense reading recommendations that adhered to the "governing principle" of "careful selection and limitation rather than inclusiveness."[125] Moreover, readers' advisors must possess "the highest qualifications" with regard to "both breadth and depth of knowledge," as well as "personality, tact, sympathy, enthusiasm, and an understanding of educational psychology comparable to that of the successful teacher," because they must be "able wisely to recommend suitable books on the same subject to men and women who differ widely in ability, education, and purpose."[126] Given the CLAE's parameters for reading courses, readers' advisors needed every bit of the "breadth and depth of knowledge" called for, since each course must set "[d]efinite objectives"; contain "books of such interest as to compel the attention of the reader once he has undertaken the course"; include "essential titles only" such that "each book chosen" makes "a definite contribution to the development of the subject; and not overlook "books representing different points of view when the subject so permits or warrants."[127] Each course should also contain "notes and commentaries on all of the books included" so that readers clearly understand "the reason for including a certain title in preference to others."[128]

The CLAE's emphasis on tact, sympathy, and enthusiasm recalls Green's desiderata in 1876 for readers' advisors. But in its insistence on an unhurried private atmosphere for interviews and its description of the tremendous intellectual capacity that readers' advisors must bring to the task of developing reading courses, we are far removed from the informal atmosphere for readers' advisory envisioned by Green and carried out, for instance, by the library hostess in the early 1900s in a busy public area. In the report of the CLAE, readers' advisory achieved a breathtaking maturity of vision based on two principles: individual and time-intensive service; and commitment to serious and purposeful reading that would allow meaningful education to occur. The individualized service offered by readers' advisors in the 1920s and 1930s was often a necessary forerunner of meaningful educational achievement. As the readers' advisor and patron discussed at length the hopes and plans of the patron with regard to reading and education, both intuitively understood that the public library was playing a central role in the patron's aspirations and future prospects. Given this, the reading material that was included in a patron's reading course had to be of the highest quality: serious, purposeful literature reflective of the seriousness and purposefulness with which the patron had approached the readers' advisor.

The *Reading with a Purpose* Series

Just as the 1926 *Libraries and Adult Education* document was a crystallization of Learned's study, the series *Reading with a Purpose* (RWAP) gave shape and form to the CLAE's vision of readers' advisory through guided courses. "[M]ade possible by a special grant from the Carnegie Corporation,"[129] the RWAP series was published by the ALA in 66 volumes from 1925 to 1933.[130] Each volume was priced at 50 cents for cloth covers and 35 cents for paper covers. By the end of 1931, some 850,000 copies had been sold.[131] Meant to provide an overview of a specific social, cultural, historical, or political issue for individuals interested in a program of self-education, each volume was written by a well-known expert, typically contained an introductory essay of about 20–30 pages on a well-defined subject, and an annotated list of about 6–10 books for further reading "in the order in which they should be read for further knowledge of the subject."[132] Some lists were longer: George H. Locke's *English History* recommended 28 titles.[133] Some were shorter: Alexander Meiklejohn's *Philosophy* suggested four titles, as did Blanche Colton Williams's *Short Story Writing*.[134] Most of the volumes were between 30 and 50 pages in length.[135] W. N. C. Carlton's *English Literature* was 74 pages, the longest in the series, while William F. Russell's *American Education* was the shortest, at 22 pages.[136] In the preface to each volume, the ALA positioned both the RWAP series and the public library as integral parts of adult education: "A good general knowledge of the subject should result from following through the course of reading suggested in this booklet— a knowledge greatly superior to that of the average citizen. If you wish to pursue the subject further, the librarian of your Public Library will be glad to make suggestions. If you desire to increase your knowledge in other fields, you are referred to the other courses in this *Reading with a Purpose* series, and to your Public Library."[137] In short, the knowledge resulting from self-education based on serious and purposeful reading was an invaluable asset.

Topics included biology, economics, the physical sciences, philosophy, religion, geography, architecture, twentieth-century American novels, Scandinavian literature, Russian literature, Latin America, advertising, evolution, international relations, English history, prehistoric man, and astronomy. Other books were entitled *The French Revolution as Told in Fiction; Conflicts in American Public Opinion; Invention and Society; Capital and Labor; The Romance of Modern Exploration; Farm Life: Problems and Opportunities; Adventures in Flower Gardening;* and *The Pacific Area in International Relations.* Except for six volumes written by librarians, the authors were professors, scientists, journalists, and cultural figures of the era, many with numerous essays and books to their credit.[138] Vernon Kellogg, who wrote the first volume in the series, *Biology,* was "permanent secretary of the National Research Council" and had served "for twenty-one years [as] professor of entomology and lecturer in bionomics at Stanford University."[139] Meiklejohn, who wrote *Philosophy,* was a professor at Brown University and the University of Wisconsin, as well as a former president of Amherst College. After making insightful analogies between "the problem of the self and that of the meaning of a poem—"But if the meaning is not a part of the letters [of the poem] then the self is not a part of the body"—Meiklejohn recommended books for further reading that "express views contrary to his own," thus putting a heavy "responsibility on the student."[140] Alain Locke, the author of *The Negro in America,* was "the preeminent black intellectual of his generation," well-known for his theory of "cultural pluralism," which "valued the uniqueness of different styles and values available within a democratic society."[141] A Rhodes Scholar and professor of philosophy at Howard University, Locke's views were meant to "stimulate" readers "to go further in their reading, weigh and balance, and reach their own conclusions."[142] An equally inspired choice was Wilfred T. Grenfell, who wrote *Religion in Everyday Life.* Grenfell, a physician for whom the "practice of medicine and ... religion are inseparable," ministered for five years "to the needs of fishermen of the North Sea and of Iceland under the Royal National Mission to Deep-Sea Fishermen." He then lived in Labrador, Canada, founding "six hospitals," "dental and child welfare clinics," and 20 elementary schools in "remote fishing villages."[143] His view of religion was a forthright one—"Labels do not necessarily insure arrival at the desired haven"—that made intriguing use of Thomas Carlyle's maxim that "[i]n each of us ... dwells a coward and a hero [and] [t]he appeal of religion is directly to the hero in us."[144]

Many authors went well beyond writing an overview and recommending 6–10 books. In *Scandinavian Literature,* Hanna Astrup Larsen discussed an additional 30 titles.[145] In *The Negro in America,* Locke provided a 12-part guided study outline, each with suggested chapter and page-range readings keyed to his list of "further reading" recommendations. Interested readers could read further about "The Negro in Slavery and Reconstruction," "The Economics of the Race Question," "The Urban and Rural Negro," "The Negro in Art and Literature," and "The World Problem of Color."[146] Like Locke, Philip N. Youtz, in *American Life in Architecture*, keyed his 12-part study outline to specific chapters and pages in his recommended readings, offering insight into "European Backgrounds of American Architecture" and "Late British Colonies in America."[147] Like Larsen, he listed 34 additional books that readers were invited to consult after working their way through the study outline. Robert C. Brooks's *Russia: The Soviet Way* contained at least five discussion questions about each of the 12 topics in his study outline.[148] There were 10 volumes with study guides, all published in 1931, 1932, or 1933 as the series was nearing completion.[149]

Almost all the volumes were written with infectious enthusiasm. J. Russell Smith, in *Geography and Our Need of It*, described the way in which political and economic geographies explain international disputes, as well as the way in which "the power of geographic environment" can "mold society" and "influence a culture," even to the extent of influencing conceptions of the afterlife.[150] In *The Negro in America*, Locke wrote passionately about how the history of African-Americans can be viewed as a "great folk-epic" in which the "long inferno" stage has been replaced by "a yet unfinished social purgatory of testing struggle and development"—an epic in which "[w]henever we think of the situation as a minority problem, we must instantly think of it also in its other aspect as a majority problem."[151] Consider also Avrahm Yarmolinsky's shrewd characterization of two Russian authors in *Russian Literature*: "You must see Turgenev as a tall big-bodied man, gentle, alert, with the poise of one who was a wealthy land-owner and a cosmopolite, the penetrating glance of a born observer, and a curious tendency toward flabbiness, both moral and physical. Picture Goncharov as a heavy, apathetic-looking bureaucrat, with eyes that have been described as those of 'a cooked fish' and that yet took in every last detail of the limited scene before him."[152] Lewis Mumford's *Architecture* was just as keenly observed. After explaining how "a building is a vital experience" inasmuch as "one's nervous tonus is lowered or heightened by it," he characterized most American buildings as either "barracks architecture" or "picture-book architecture," with pertinent observations about the implications of each for the national psyche.[153] In *American Life in Architecture*, Youtz noted that "[t]he architecture of the United States is in some ways a more accurate index to American character than its literature."[154] Railway terminals and hotels soar with a "grandeur" emblematic of the deification of constant movement, while colleges and universities that are designed in the Gothic or classic style make one wonder whether "the education that goes on" there "is not better adapted to medieval or classic civilization than to the rhythms of the modern age."[155]

In some cases, the volumes turned into well-wrought meditations about the American soul. In *Farm Life: Problems and Opportunities*, Clarence Poe eloquently argued that the so-called farm problem was really a society-wide problem insofar as modernity had failed to develop the bases for a "satisfying rural civilization."[156] Agricultural questions cannot be solved and agricultural progress cannot be achieved by ensuring "efficient production by an efficient producer."[157] The issue was much deeper, requiring structural changes that would transform the farmer from "a producer of raw materials solely" into someone who participates in the manufacturing, distribution, and marketing of products.[158] Moreover, social attitudes must evolve to where it is accepted that "the farmer is entitled to a civilization, culture, educational system, literature, art, drama, etc., which will recognize, reflect, and utilize the cultural influences of country life and its environment in the same degree in which present-day culture recognizes and reflects the influences of urban life."[159] This holistic approach to agricultural issues was reiterated in his reading list. In addition to nonfiction works about farming issues, Poe included fiction by David Grayson about a thriving rural community and nonfiction by Mary Meek Atkeson about farm women to show that agriculture is "a method" for living one's life.[160] In *The Westward March of American Settlement*, Hamlin Garland, the esteemed author of *A Son of the Middle Border* and *A Daughter of the Middle Border*, traced the receding frontier through the Allegheny Mountains, the Ohio Valley, and the plains states and beyond, suggesting apt metaphors to understand the inexorable westward push. The never-ending stream of settlers was "like the slow march of an army" where women, "wearing out long days in small, rude cabins, rearing their children in constant fear of snakes and wolves," "grew old and died in the front ranks of the battle line."[161] Progress always had a steep cost, Garland asserted, especially because "the hunger for land is, at bottom, a hunger for gold."[162] While some found their "fairy world, the beauty of which would insure content," others became disappointed as the thrill of exploration gave way to a "deepening rut of commonplace routine."[163]

Even this brief description of the RWAP series gives a sense of the untold riches awaiting systematic readers. Someone who read even a handful of these small volumes and made his or her way through some of the recommended readings would indeed possess "a knowledge greatly superior to that of the average citizen." The RWAP books were therefore obvious boons to local readers' advisors, who referred to them in their own work and suggested them as jumping-off points for interested patrons. Still, the RWAP series was not without controversy, and some of the elements of this controversy reveal much about the way in which some public librarians viewed patrons and their responsibilities toward them. As Margaret E. Monroe explained in *Library Adult Education: The Biography of an Idea*, John Cotton Dana was disturbed about the influence of the Carnegie Corporation on the ALA's involvement in adult education in general and its role in the RWAP series in particular.[164] Dana was also worried that, because "[n]o library has a staff large enough to spare more than a few minutes each day to the special demands of each of a few inquirers," the idea of adult education "as we are now interpreting it" is unrealistic, since it "asks us ... to act as guides and teachers to all adults we can persuade to come and ask us what they should read, and how, and to quiz them on their progress and advise them from day to day—all that is quite impossible."[165] As Monroe put it, "skeptics ... question[ed] this mystical activity called library adult education—since librarians have always guided readers."[166]

Dana's persistence led to an ALA Activities Committee Report in late 1930.[167] Here were chronicled members' views about the RWAP series. On the whole, the series received "a preponderance of favorable opinion," with some members wanting "harder books" and others calling for simpler guides, such as Emma Felsenthal's 1929 *Readable Books in Many Subjects*.[168] A readers' advisor in a "Large Public Library" contributed perhaps the most representative comment: "We have found the RWAP courses most useful, though at all times it does not seem feasible to use the course without some additions, subtractions or substitutions. Many times they fill the want exactly, and always include some fundamentals."[169] Thus, despite Dana's worries, most librarians seemed satisfied with the RWAP series: while not perfect, it was a solid base that they could modify to fit individual circumstances.

But Dana's concerns were one of the reasons that the BLAE decided to revise its strategy about readers' advisory. Declaring that "the number of readers' bureaus is far too few, and the idea is not yet so firmly established but that such a consultant is one of the first services to be dropped when a financial cut goes into effect," it published a flow chart at the top of which was the slogan "Every Library Worker a Readers' Adviser To Encourage Self-Education Through Books."[170] Henceforward there would no longer be an emphasis on designated readers' advisors housed in separate departments or offices. As a clear symbol of the new philosophy of diffusing responsibility for readers' advisory throughout public libraries, the journal *Adult Education and the Library* ceased its life as a stand-alone publication and, starting in 1931, was incorporated into the flagship ALA publication *ALA Bulletin*.[171] Although this philosophical change was portrayed as a positive development, the new 11-word slogan had an unintended consequence in busy public libraries. It rendered precarious the continued existence of the time-intensive personal service delivered by a knowledgeable readers' advisor, entrenching a service ethic in which superficial advice was dispensed mechanically in a few seconds or scant minutes by untrained staff.

In 1934, Edward F. Stevens, who had been appointed Librarian at the Pratt Institute Free Library in Brooklyn, New York, and director of the Pratt Institute School of Library Science in 1911, resumed criticism of the RWAP series, in the process revealing many of the stakes at issue in the RWAP controversy.[172] The RWAP series was written by "experts" who were "without knowledge of the needs of those who are invited to approach the subject."[173] Because a large majority of the books were written by non-librarians, Stevens felt that that the ALA had dealt "a severe blow to our professional pride, and the implied lack of confidence on the part of our own organization in its membership to do the work which is theirs to do, will take years to live down."[174] More importantly, he explained that, based on his 25 years of "close touch with the public," it was fallacious to say that "many [of those] who have entered upon the life school of experience crave culture, erudition and continuous progressive study and improvement."[175] And because the number of individuals wanting "progressive study and improvement" was low, it was folly to undertake "a recasting of our work in terms of the few."[176] In addition, creating a readers' advisory department with a designated readers' advisor left the impression that other staff members were incapable of giving salient advice and bled money from other library departments. Better to make "every member of the staff ... in effect ... a readers' adviser" through professional training.[177] But, as will be discussed later, professional training in librarianship in the 1930s remained just as geared toward mechanical procedures as in the day of Dewey. Stevens's belief that this training could willy-nilly generate an entire staff of intelligent readers' advisors would prove to be an illusion.

The implications of Stevens's statements were far-reaching. He suggested that most adults did not want to learn, and because they did not want to do so, public libraries should stop catering to the elite few who do want to learn and concentrate instead on the vast majority who presumably desire other (easier) reading materials not recommended by the RWAP series, which invariably focused on classics and serious literature. Public libraries should not reorient their service toward formal adult education and should not concentrate on "fewer and better readers."[178] As a result, reading guides prepared by subject experts were unnecessary, since they only served an elite few who wanted "progressive study and improvement" and cast librarians in a bad light because librarians were not asked to write the guides.

In some ways, Stevens's position echoed the debates of the early 1900s and anticipated the views of the "Give 'Em What They Want" school of thought animating readers' advisory in the late 20th and early 21st century. Calling into question the educational aspirations of a large number of Americans, he suggested that patrons would be best served by the motto "The Best Reading for the Greatest Number at the Least Cost."[179] But, at the beginning of the 20th century, as public libraries became obsessed with circulation statistics, that motto became shorthand for supplying high-demand popular fiction that could serve as proof of the library's usefulness. Stevens implied that public libraries should concentrate on supplying high-demand items to the many, thus burnishing their democratic credentials. Conversely, they should make few attempts to embark upon the much harder work of adult education by guiding individuals toward serious and purposeful reading, because that benefited only a small minority. In this context, expert-written subject guides had ambiguous value because they positioned the public library as something that it was not (i.e., a venue for adult education) and depicted public librarians as lacking in subject expertise when, in fact, they were not meant to be subject experts in the first place but rather "professionally trained and professionally minded" facilitators between patrons and, presumably, high-demand items.[180] The divide between a conception of public-library service as something provided by "professionally minded" librarian-facilitators trained in mechanical procedures and offering "advice" about high-demand items, on the one hand, and a conception of public-library service delivered by librarians possessing in-depth subject knowledge that would allow them to offer thoughtful readers' advisory based on serious and enduring literature, on the other, was fast becoming a chasm.

Stevens's views, however, were belied by the fact that the RWAP series sold over 850,000 copies by the end of 1931. It would be strange if at least some of the tens of thousands of people who purchased RWAP volumes were not interested in "progressive study and improvement." His views were also belied by the results of a program in which CinPL offered "graded individual reading guidance without personal contact" based on information supplied on questionnaire forms.[181] CinPL worked with the depression-era Civilian Conservation Corps (CCC), where participants lived in camps and performed forestry, soil conservation, and park maintenance work.[182] Although these camps had educational advisers and libraries, reading material was scarce. CinPL asked volunteers in three CCC camps in Southern Ohio and Northern Kentucky to complete an 11-part questionnaire that would help readers' advisors provide them with reading material according to their interests and abilities.[183] Based on the answers received, CinPL readers' advisors selected three books to send to each respondent. Each recipient was asked to indicate whether he liked or disliked the book and to write a short report about it, answering questions such as "What ideas did you get from the book?" and "Did it make you want to continue reading?"[184] CinPL staff members calculated that 73.6 percent of the books had been "liked and intelligently reported."[185] The most popular books were those "on the higher level approaching philosophical thinking" or that "give concrete information about some objective interest, such as vocational possibilities."[186] It would be hard not to conclude that individuals from all walks of life had lofty educational aspirations.

When small public libraries began to offer readers' advisory in the middle 1930s, the response was overwhelmingly positive. Take the example of Dunkirk, New York, a small town of 17,802 near Buffalo, where readers' advisory was established in 1936.[187] After talking with Buffalo public librarians about the workings of their Readers' Bureau; receiving a "generous supply of reading courses" from them; and "assembling all reading lists, syllabi, bibliographies and club programs available in our own library," Viarda Clark Brubeck, Dunkirk's librarian, advertised the birth of readers' advisory in her upstate New York town. The success of the new venture was immediate: "We very quickly discovered that our collection of 500 reading courses did not encompass many of the latest interests of our townspeople."[188] Brubeck received requests for courses on bacteriology, nursing, anatomy, bank loans, "the legal phases of banking," the "philosophy and religion of Tibet," and others.[189] While some of these specialized requests could not be met, Brubeck had no difficulty filling requests for reading courses on "Literary history and criticism," "Forestry," "A general background course in psychology," and "Modern religious problems."[190] In sum, there was pent-up demand for reading courses on serious topics, revealing a side of Dunkirk residents that the public library had heretofore failed to appreciate. The experience of one patron, a businessman, was especially informative, and it led Brubeck to ponder the effect of readers' advisory on her community.

> Is a readers' advisory service needed and appreciated? I am inclined to believe that it is when a business man will take the time to stop at my office to say that he read in the paper about this "readers' service" where one can get individual help in a course of planned reading to suit the individual's needs, and that he considered it "a real service." He went on to explain that while he came in the library occasionally for a mystery story, what he really wanted, although he didn't know where to begin or what to ask for, were books that would "get me some place"—something to give him a background in various fields of knowledge—"things that I missed years ago in an interrupted education." ¶ With new books, interesting exhibits, book review meetings with which we are reaching new readers every day, we had still failed to reach this man who had a keen desire to read, until we established a service where we set aside time to talk over individual reading programs.[191]

It is easy to imagine that this businessman spoke for many of his fellow citizens in numerous smaller towns across the United States and Canada. Only after the Dunkirk library began to offer readers' advisory—a Herculean task that, according to Brubeck, was undertaken with "*no additional outlay of money*" despite the immense amount of extra work—did he finally find real value in the public library through books that would "get him some place."[192] Before, the library had been a place simply to pick up mystery novels, an act to which he attached little, if any, value. In effect, the mystery novels had been a stopgap measure, since he did not realize that the library could do so much more for him. He was no doubt convinced that the provision of popular novels was the full extent of library service, given their ubiquity. His experience, of course, is anecdotal, but it raises anew the thorny question of the purpose of public libraries and their expenditure of funds for popular fiction, here represented as mystery novels. Like the Dunkirk businessman, many individuals would likely feel better served if their public libraries dispensed with providing ephemeral fiction and focused instead on readers' advisory that could "get them some place." The many testimonials about the positive effects of readers' advisory service that was oriented to "getting someone some place" can thus be interpreted as latent criticisms of public libraries that practiced circulation-driven librarianship by concentrating on popular and ephemeral fiction. Those libraries were incapable of helping someone "get some place," and their emphasis on circulation statistics masked a disinclination to be all that they could be.

Adding Science to Librarianship

If readers' advisory as envisioned by Learned and the CLAE was to become a nationwide reality, there was near unanimity that the nature of educating librarians needed to change.[193] In 1912, Mary Wright Plummer—a former director of the Pratt Institute School of Library Science, director of the New York Public Library School starting in 1911, and a member of the ALA Committee on Library Training (CLT)—wrote that existing library schools had "peculiarities and limitations" that likely would not be understood by outsiders.[194] Her opinion was decisive in convincing the CLT Chairman, Azariah Smith Root, not to petition the Carnegie Foundation for the Advancement of Teaching to grant funds for a study along the lines of Dr. Abraham Flexner's searching analysis of the state of medical education. Flexner's 1910 study, *Medical Education in the United States and Canada*, a harsh critique of existing medical schools that caused many of them to close, "triggered much-needed reforms in the standards, organization, and curriculum" of the remaining schools as they gradually conformed to "the German tradition of strong biomedical sciences together with hands-on clinical training."[195] In 1915, Alvin S. Johnson, commissioned by the Carnegie Corporation to examine "the results of the wide provision of Public Library Buildings by Mr. Carnegie,"[196] painted a worrisome picture of the abilities of librarians in small and mid-sized public libraries to provide effective service. Poor service compromised Carnegie's "huge investment" in the physical plant facilities of libraries.[197] It also discouraged those individuals who wanted to undertake meaningful self-education through a program of serious and purposeful reading. To ensure a steady supply of "adequately trained personnel" to staff public libraries, Johnson recommended that state library commissions, working with the Carnegie Corporation, "secure the establishment in a number of state universities of combined academic and professional library courses" insofar as "[m]ost state universities view with a friendly eye the incorporation of technical training designed to advance any branch of public service."[198]

The most devastating indictment of library education was another Carnegie Corporation-sponsored report: Charles C. Williamson's *Training for Library Service*, completed in 1921 and published in 1923. As Shera summarized, Williamson found "just about everything wrong" with existing library schools, from faculty members lacking in "appropriate academic education and professional experience," to curricula "crowded with inappropriate subjects," to an overmuch reliance on the lecture method.[199] With regard to faculty, "[o]nly 52 percent had graduated from college, 93 percent had no teacher training, and 80 percent had no previous teaching experience."[200] Differentiating between professional and clerical library work, he proposed that professional librarians should henceforward have a "broad, general education" consisting of "a thorough college course of four years" followed by a post-baccalaureate graduate degree from an accredited and university-affiliated school or "autonomous professional" school in which the first-year curricula offered "a general program in basic library subjects followed by a second year devoted to specialization, with an intervening year of practical experience."[201] Echoing Williamson's conclusions, Learned called for "the most vigorous and drastic changes" possible in the "professional preparation" of librarians if "wholesome development" of public libraries was to occur.[202]

Both the Williamson and Learned reports "helped focus ... the library profession's attention on education," especially because the Carnegie Corporation expressed strong interest in "receiv[ing] specific suggestions from qualified organizations or individuals" about "the establishment of a graduate school of librarianship" that was "to be an integral part of an American university."[203] Competition to become the site of the new school was intense, all the more so because the Carnegie Corporation promised a $1 million grant to the successful candidate, preferably not an existing library school.[204] As recounted by John V. Richardson Jr., the University of Iowa, Yale, and Northwestern University were strong contenders,[205] but ultimately the University of Chicago (UC) prevailed.[206] A central characteristic of UC's new Graduate Library School (GLS), which opened in 1928, was a strong emphasis on scientific research.[207] Speaking about his initial choices of faculty members, the first dean of the GLS, George A. Works stated, "I do not believe this school ... should put a person on the staff primarily for the purpose of teaching what is now generally accepted in cataloging and classification. We expect our students to have this equipment before they come. This school ... should devote its energies to those phases in which there are opportunities for research."[208] Works's statement evolved into policy: the GLS "allows other library schools to assume the responsibility for passing on to their students a body of principles and practices that have been found useful in the conduct of libraries," expects "such training" to be "an essential prerequisite for admission," but does not itself undertake it.[209]

The clearest statement about the central place of research at the GLS was Williamson's article "The Place of Research in Library Service," which was, symbolically, the lead article in the inaugural issue of *Library Quarterly*, a journal produced and edited by the faculty of the GLS to disseminate library-oriented research.[210] A printed version of an address delivered at the Founder's Day Exercises at the School of Library Science at Western Reserve (Cleveland, Ohio) University in 1930, Williamson's article was a call-to-arms for librarianship to adopt "the spirit and methods of research that are being found so effective" in education, medicine, aviation, wireless communication, and engineering.[211] Especially salient for him was the example of the business world, where "research has come to be regarded as one of the most important factors in successful management," where "[p]ersonal qualities of intelligence, courage, and initiative are no longer a guaranty of business success," and where "[e]fficiency of administration and quantity and quality of output are under the constant scrutiny of the research laboratory."[212] Conversely, librarianship was a field "guided solely by experience,"[213] one that "follows the grooves and ruts that custom wears, and has no track to follow when the groove disappears," which results in "[m]ental inertia, laziness, [and] unjustifiable conservatism."[214]

Answering those who might say that "there are no problems in library service that call for scientific research,"[215] Williamson highlighted readers' advisory work. "The great weakness of the readers' adviser service is its total lack of scientific basis," Williamson stated, noting that librarians are only vaguely aware about "the attitude of readers toward library service, of why certain classes do not use the library, [and] of the motives which bring people to the public library."[216] However, with scientific research leading the way, readers' advisory could soon be placed on an entirely new footing.

> I can see no inherent reason why the future reader's consultant should not when requested administer scientific intelligence tests, aptitude tests, comprehension tests, etc., and on the basis of scientific findings prescribe a program of reading. The time may come when for many adult patrons the public library will have on file psychological and other personal data as complete and as scientifically prepared as any to be found in the records of hospitals or social service clinics.[217]

By singling out readers' advisory as his main example of how scientific research could help librarianship toward a future characterized in terms of "successful management," Williamson signaled his dissatisfaction with current readers' advisory practices. The two elements heretofore at the core of readers' advisory—the in-depth individual interview that led to a carefully prepared course of reading—were too nebulously impressionistic, not susceptible to the generalizability necessary for "efficiency of administration and quantity and quality of output."

In light of Williamson's comments, it was fitting that the research agenda of Douglas Waples, one of the original faculty members of the GLS, was oriented towards adult-reading studies. Works had identified "the habits of reading" as a potential research area for the GLS, and Waples, who was working at the College of Education at the University of Chicago, was viewed by Works as someone who was likely to make valuable contributions in this area.[218] In late 1928, Waples was transferred "from the College of Education and promoted to a professorship of Educational Method" at the GLS.[219] An indication of the general direction of Waples's work was his 1930 article "Propaganda and Leisure Reading," contained in the *Journal of Higher Education*.[220] The article was an outgrowth of a controversy roiling the University of Missouri (MU) after social psychology instructors distributed a questionnaire in the late 1920s asking MU students about sexual situations, including the "unconventional" situations of unfaithfulness, divorce, extra-marital relations, premarital relations, and promiscuity. Critics alleged that "the questionnaire tended to disrupt students' morals, since except for such suggestions the students would not know the [five unconventional and controversial] situations existed."[221] Skeptical that students first learned about the existence of these sexual situations through the MU questionnaire, Waples performed a content analysis of recent plays, novels, and films to gauge the frequency of appearance of 27 sexual situations, grouped into three categories: unconventional, conventional, and unclassified. Waples concluded that "all but one of the five [unconventional and controversial situations] are above the median for frequency of appearance in current novels, plays, and films" and that "the situations which the [original MU] investigators were accused of putting into the students' minds are more frequently discussed in plays, novels, and films than the other unconventional situations."[222]

Waples's article may have gone relatively unnoticed had it not been for its contextual framework. Wanting to ensure that college students were not bombarded with "propaganda" that "falls considerably short of the whole truth" on those topics that "are not treated by systematic courses" of instruction in colleges and universities,[223] Waples recommended that college librarians adopt the following solution to address the risk that the leisure reading of students was inadequate.

> First, prepar[e] through faculty co-operation a list of the personal and social issues that immediately concern students and which are not specifically treated by one department; second, analyz[e] the elements of each issue as presented in popular media—plays, novels, story magazines, films, and radio—to determine the relative emphasis given to each element with a view to selecting the elements omitted or insufficiently or improperly represented; and third, provid[e] on display shelves in students' reading rooms or the college library such fiction or interesting non-fiction as may be found to present such elements adequately.[224]

From a theoretical perspective, Waples suggested that books could be reduced to a long list of elements and attributes, each of which could then be quantified: Book Z contains x instances of element y and q instances of attribute r. Once quantified, these elements could be used to define the precise nature of a book, thus making it a simple task for readers' advisors to make mechanical matches between, on the one hand, patrons with a given set of abilities who find themselves in given situations and express given interests and, on the other, books containing certain elements and attributes in sufficient quantities. Recall, too, that Williamson in his 1931 article hoped that patrons would someday be categorized on the basis of "scientific findings" so that readers' advisors would better be able to help them. Waples's 1930 research on sexual situations provided the basis for one half of the equation: in the interests of "successful management," books could now be disassembled into discrete elements and attributes. In effect, it was no longer sufficient to see books as indivisible and unique entities that could (or should) be read for their overall worth or value. It was only a matter of time before Waples would set about exploring the other half of the equation: categorization of readers.

In 1932, together with Ralph W. Tyler of the Bureau of Educational Research at Ohio State University, Waples published *What People Want to Read About: A Study of Group Interests and a Survey of Problems in Adult Reading* (WPWTRA).[225] As the title suggests, Waples and Tyler were not concerned with actual reading, but with the historical, social, cultural, and economic subject matter that groups of people with various demographic characteristics would prefer to read about if given the chance.[226] If these reading preferences could be scientifically identified, categorized, and ranked for groups of people, the data could be "one basis for the selection of books to be purchased by libraries or booksellers."[227] Although they were careful to add that "such evidence alone would not be sufficient" for collection development, they were convinced that "other things being equal, it is hard to see how the book-selecting authorities of a given public library would fail to benefit by evidence concerning the relative appeal of each subject on the list to the particular groups composing their clientèle."[228] Readers' advisors would also find WPWTRA data helpful. When speaking with patrons from a specific demographic group, they could use the group scores to identify topics or subjects that "are most likely to interest the members of a given group."[229] This in turn "would presumably be helpful to readers' advisers in selecting interesting books of non-fiction for [those] individual patrons."[230]

It could never be said that the WPWTRA study was not carefully conceived and conducted. First, "a representative list of all questions discussed in magazines addressed to the general reader and published in the United States during the last decade" was created.[231] These "questions" were then classified into divisions, topics, and sub-topics: there were "20 main divisions, 117 topics, and 585 subtopics."[232] Examples of divisions were: Interesting Personalities; the United States Government; Social Changes and Social Problems; Crime; Sex; Education; Religion and Beliefs; and Literature and the Arts.[233] Under each division was a series of topics. Under "Social Changes and Social Problems," topics included: Modern Civilization; Comments on Modern America; and Problems of the City.[234] Under "Crime," topics included "Detection and Prevention of Crime" and "Criminals and the Treatment of Criminals."[235] For each topic, there were five sub-topics. In the case of "Problems of the City," two of the five sub-topics were: "Will the country movement relieve city congestion?" and "How to stop reckless driving." In the case of "Criminals and the Treatment of Criminals," sub-topics included "How professional criminals get their training" and "What sort of men go to Sing Sing?"

Four main groups were chosen: professional workers; high-school students; vocational-school students; and non-professional workers. Each of these groups was further subdivided. The "professional workers" group included 11 sub-groups of teachers (e.g., female English teachers, male Science teachers, male and female teachers over 39 years of age, etc.), as well as 46 sub-groups of college students (e.g., women graduate students from the University of Minnesota, male students from Cornell College, etc.). The "non-professional workers" group consisted of 27 sub-groups, including female Chicago telephone operators between the ages of 20–49; male Vermont farmers; female clerks from a small town in Connecticut; businessmen from a small town in Virginia; male post-office employees from Milwaukee; prisoners; male skilled laborers from Cleveland; and San Francisco waiters and waitresses.[236] In total, there were 102 sub-groups categorized by six factors: sex; schooling (college or non-college); occupation; age; environment (urban or rural); and time spent per week in reading.[237] Each person in each group was then presented with the list of 585 sub-topics mentioned above and asked whether he or she would be "at all interested" in each of them.[238]

The microscopic divisions of topics and groups allowed Waples and Tyler to produce numerous tables showing ranked lists of topics preferred by various groups and sub-groups. Many of the tables had some variation of the following title: "The Topics Preferred and The Topics Avoided by Subgroup X," where X served as a placeholder for a demographic subgroup. Thus, male Chicago high school teachers preferred in ranked order "People of legend and history," "Statesmen and politicians," and "scientists."[239] First-year female students studying home economics at the University of Minnesota preferred in ranked order "International attitudes and problems," "Chemical inventions," and "Science and warfare."[240] Another set of tables analyzed the level of interest that each group of people displayed toward each of the 585 sub-topics grouped into 117 topics. Under the topic "United States

Government and Politics," post-office clerks had a high level of interest in reading about "Criticism of Government Policies"; farmers had low interest in "United States' Foreign Affairs"; and female high-school teachers had high interest in "Law and Legislation" but low interest in "Problems of State and City Government."[241] Under the topic "Values and Developments in Science," prisoners had high interest in "Developments in Aviation," but low interest in "Developments in Farming."[242] Tables taking a more macroscopic view were also generated. It was thus possible to see at a glance the topics preferred and avoided by broad groupings such as "all college men," "all college women," or "all non-college groups."[243] And, despite the fact that in a later study examining male and female textile factory workers, Waples found "no significantly positive relationship ... between the subjects of most interest and the subjects on which the industrial groups do most reading," he was nevertheless convinced that scientific identification of group-reading preferences was a valid approach to librarianship and readers' advisory because the textile workers had read what was most accessible to them, not what they had actually wanted to read.[244]

As data was accumulated and cross-tabulated about additional groups of people, it was easy to envision the readers' advisory encounter between patron and staff member as a purely mechanical act: once the demographic characteristics of a patron had been determined, the readers' advisor would refer to an appropriate WPWTRA-like table and then recommend specific books containing the desired elements or attributes. Waples had now provided the tools to quantify both sides of the reading equation. He had shown that a book could be dissected so as to create a list of elements and attributes therein contained, and he had also shown that readers could be minutely categorized according to their levels of theoretical interest in a wide variety of reading materials. The readers' advisor of the future would merely match a book containing numerous elements of x with a reader whose demographic profile indicated that he or she preferred a book dealing with or containing that same element x. As Waples and Tyler wrote, "[t]he data concerning the reading interests and needs of particular groups should be especially useful to public libraries which undertake to advise readers who ask advice in planning their reading."[245]

Because many public libraries were concerned that the time-intensive model of readers' advisory centered on an in-depth interview between librarian and patron was too costly and were therefore moving toward a more cost-effective service-delivery model as embodied in the slogan "Every Library Worker a Readers' Adviser To Encourage Self-Education Through Books," Waples's two studies provided an attractive template for streamlining readers' advisory service. After asking a patron a few demographic questions and then using WRWTRA-like tables, every library worker could quickly match a book to a patron. Here then was the "scientific basis" for readers' advisory that Williamson had written about in *Library Quarterly* in 1931. Readers' advisory could now be based on "scientifically prepared" files containing "psychological and other personal data" about patrons, thus contributing to "efficiency of administration" in the public library. Agnes Hill's dystopian vision of "librarianship by automatic figures" was creeping ever closer to reality[246]; the glimmer of user profiling was on the horizon.

Waples's 1930 article and 1932 co-authored book were precursors of research-based reading studies meant to put librarianship on a professional and scientific footing. Other studies soon followed. While Waples's 1932 co-authored book focused on defined groups of individuals (e.g., male post-office employees), later GLS-connected studies were community surveys of reading tastes. Four "Community Studies in Reading" were published between 1933 and 1939: "Reading in the Lower East Side [of New York]"; "Hinsdale, A Suburb of Chicago"; "Reading Habits of Adult Non-Users of the Public Library [of Flushing, New

York]"; and "A Middle-Western Manufacturing Community [Alliance, Ohio]."[247] In the Lower East Side, statistics were generated about the number of times three or more books were borrowed by various male and female occupational groups, as well as about the "occupational distribution of loans of eighty-two titles concerning modern social problems."[248] In Hinsdale, after dividing fiction into three categories (i.e., standard, good modern, and light modern), it was found that women "borrowed more good modern, both actually and proportionally, than did men."[249] In Alliance, Ohio, "[m]en in trade, professional men and women, clerical men and women, students, and housewives read well above the average in good fiction."[250]

Jeannette Howard Foster, in "An Approach to Fiction through the Characteristics of Its Readers," can be taken as a representative example of these community-based studies.[251] Foster analyzed the demographic data and reading tastes of 15,285 individuals, most of whom came from the Chicago area, including "6,586 [r]esidents of South Chicago, an industrial community of fairly low economic status and social organization," as well as 4,333 patrons of the Chicago Public Library living in apartments or residence-hotels in a "neighborhood distinctly superior to South Chicago."[252] She then arbitrarily classified fiction into 15 categories, including detective, adventure, romance, satiric, cheerful, humorous, character, family, psychological, philosophical, social and political problems, special groups, and setting. Each of these 15 categories was further divided into six quality levels, with authors assigned to each level. After statistically correlating readers' characteristics (e.g., sex and occupational group) with both subject type and quality level of their reading, Foster concluded that "shop-owners and salesmen show the highest interest listed (index value 2.87) in social and political problems."[253] Yet she also admitted that "this preference seems the only clear case of correspondence between occupation and reading interest" because "outside this their interests are mixed: humor, psychological novels, family chronicles, satire, detective stories."[254] Clerks and stenographers also "present a mixed picture, exhibiting the greatest enthusiasm of any group for humor and for philosophical problems," but "[s]atire, psychology, and stories involving special groups also interest them, as do character and love stories to an almost equal extent."[255] Although Foster suggested that age and education were significant factors with regard to the type of fiction read, the relevant statistical data showed that there are very slight, if any, differences.[256] In other words, reading tastes could not be pigeon-holed.

But the genie was out of the bottle. Some public librarians became fixated on the idea that people could be classified and thus understood based on demographic characteristics, occupations, and personality types. Hazel I. Medway identified 70 character types, listed about three or four novels or plays under each that purported to "represent" and "interpret" that character type, and urged readers' advisors to familiarize themselves with as many of these books and plays as possible so as to gain "a much more sympathetic understanding" of the represented types. As readers' advisors read the books listed under "The Timid and Inferior-Feeling Person," "The Drudge," "The Vocationally Unadjusted," "Divorced People," "The Flirtatious Girl," "The Criminal in the Making," "The Musician," "The Lonely Person," "The Factory Worker," "Small-Town People," or "The Low-Brow," they would be better able to determine their "needs and problems than we had before."[257]

Perhaps the most discussed offshoot of Waples's work was James Howard Wellard's *Book Selection: Its Principles and Practice*, published in 1937. Although Wellard was British, his book was widely read in American library circles, benefiting from a laudatory foreword by Louis Round Wilson, dean of the GLS starting in 1932. Drawing on Waples's and Foster's statistical approach to reading studies, Wellard argued that collection development in public libraries should start with a classification of readers "by homogenous and identifiable groups, and for this purpose will utilize social traits [such as sex, education, occupation, and age] which have been found the most trustworthy bases for the description of reading as a social activity."[258] He was convinced that, from a philosophical standpoint,

> it has long been known that similarity of material conditions is paralleled by similarity of interests (reading interests among them) within different social groups: that, in general, any group of men of the same race, nationality, sex, age, educational and occupational level, will like, think, and read much the same things. This does not envisage a social group as a number of identically similar individuals like the economic divisions in Huxley's Brave New World. There will, of course, be as many individual variations as there are individuals; yet, none the less, common environmental influences will tend to produce a common type. From the point of view of group security, it is fortunate that it does.[259]

Librarians responsible for collection development should not pay a great deal of attention to "the intrinsic value of the book," and they should not attempt to make their collection "well-rounded."[260] Neither should they pay much heed to isolated and "selected data" that show that "six automobile mechanics have borrowed novels by Thomas Hardy over a certain period of time," since that fact "signifies nothing concerning automobile mechanics in general."[261] Instead, using "small samples to discover the character of large populations," they should perform a community analysis of their "actual and potential" reading public, thus ensuring "a well-regulated system of book selection" in which books should not be on the shelves "because they are erudite, but because they are potentially useful to a known group or groups of readers."[262] Referring to and praising Foster's work, he produced a table that schematically mapped the way in which book selectors might approach the task of selecting books for specific occupational groups in their surrounding communities: men who are "professional: academic" prefer "special setting" fiction, but men who are "professional: business" prefer detective stories; male clerks gravitate toward detective, humor, and adventure fiction; women professionals prefer family chronicles; and female clerks prefer cheerful stories and costume romances.[263]

Wellard believed that readers' advisors could also profit from scientific community analysis, since they can "base [their] handling of particular cases on the general findings of the group study."

> Thus, if [a readers' advisor] learns that such and such a borrower belongs to such and such a group as specified in terms of sex, age, occupation, education, and expected reading interest, he will adapt his approach and treatment of the inquiry accordingly. The individual variations he may find necessary will not on the whole invalidate the work already done by the less fine tools of research.[264]

Although Wellard explicitly denied that his procedures reflected principles found in Huxley's Brave New World, it is difficult not to see a substantial portion of determinism in his—as well as Waples's and Foster's—approach to reading. In caveat-filled language meant to obscure their main theme, Waples, Foster, and Wellard all suggested that reading interests were a function of an individual's existing social position as a member of a defined group. It was a stance that made the tasks of collection development and readers' advisory less complex, but it was also a stance that denied the possibility of personal agency, aspiration, intellectual development, and will by enclosing an individual in a carapace of ineluctable characteristics (e.g., age, sex) and contingent past choices (e.g., education, occupation). The scientific research carried out by Waples and his followers heralded the rise of public libraries featuring a limited range of homogenous products geared to defined demographic groupings—public libraries that had difficulty accepting that some automobile mechanics like to read the novels of Thomas Hardy and other classics. Concentrating on pre-defined groups and supplying reading materials that these groups presumably want, public libraries overlooked hidden individual differences and yearnings that could be revealed through in-depth attention to personal circumstances.

The Backlash: Librarianship as Art

If the scientific approach to librarianship of Waples and the GLS inspired followers, it also gave much ammunition to skeptics and detractors. In the Carnegie Corporation's 1929 *Annual Report*, Frederick P. Keppel, president of the Corporation, made ambiguous comments about the GLS, observing that university "entrance requirements, degrees and the like" were "really matters of relatively minor importance" for library education, especially given that the Pratt Institute, which "offers no degree at all," remains "one of the best schools for the professional study of librarianship."[265] In his mind, the GLS was being too rigid: "In every branch of higher education there lies the danger of confusing high requirements for admission and advancement with an inelastic standardization which often loses sight of the needs and capacities of the individual student and his promise of usefulness to the profession in question."[266] Keppel's juxtaposition of "inelastic standardization" and "the individual" is an intriguing one, especially since he added that individuals "with scholarly tastes and training in letters" currently working or preparing to work in "the overcrowded field of English teaching" should be welcomed into librarianship.[267] His words suggest that the Carnegie Corporation had some misgivings about the direction that the GLS was taking away from a flexible humanities-centered program toward an "inelastic standardization" symbolized by Waples's scientific and statistical approach.

Abraham Flexner, in his 1930 *Universities: American, English, German*, was even more caustic about the efforts of librarianship to be recognized as a university-level program.[268] Placing librarianship in the same category as hotel management; labeling both as vocations that were attempting to upgrade themselves into professions by offering a series of dubious university-level courses; and specifically mentioning Keppel's 1929 comments implicating the GLS, Flexner contended that "universities need not and should not concern themselves with miscellaneous training at or near the vocational level."[269] Even Pierce Butler, one of Waples's colleagues at the GLS, had by 1937 realized the danger of the scientific approach.[270] In *The Literary History of Scholarship*, Butler claimed that social-science fields had become obsessed with "the statistical phase" of scientific endeavor, "zoom[ing] off" on "a mad tangent, into infinity" and thus neglecting the role of "extensive case studies" and "systematic speculation from general knowledge" in intellectual progress.[271] Butler's 1937 comments were all the more noteworthy, since he had, in his 1933 *An Introduction to Library Science*, made generally favorable, yet highly nuanced, comments about the role of scientific research in librarianship—comments that were interpreted "as a symbol" of his support of "rigorous, empirical research supported by quantitative methods."[272] As perhaps the most visible of the GLS professors involved in scientific research, Waples must have felt that at least some of these criticisms were directed at him.

The ALA was also not happy with the GLS. In resigning the deanship of the GLS in 1929 after only a few short years at the helm, Works made it clear that interference by the ALA with regard to the philosophy and research agenda of the GLS had been—and would continue to be—detrimental to the future success of the GLS and progress in librarianship.[273] Some of the most scathing comments about the GLS in general, and about

Waples in particular, came from working librarians. For them, Waples's research was a synecdoche of the scientific and statistical approach to librarianship as embodied by the GLS. When they criticized Waples, they were criticizing the scientific and statistical orientation of the GLS; when they criticized the scientific and statistical orientation of the GLS, they were criticizing Waples and the growth of "inelastic standardization." In 1929, Margery Doud went right to the point, hoping that any new "research" in librarianship would take into account "an extended and understanding experience with people as well." "Otherwise," she continued, "innocent book-loving men and women who support and enjoy public libraries, are in danger of being translated into 'case records'—of being separated into their component parts and juggled about on statistical sheets."[274] Avoiding statistical juggling and separation of the individual into component parts was especially important in readers' advisory work, she believed, because "[i]n interviewing a reader before planning a [reading] course, we 'gather' so much more about him than we can tabulate on any standard form."[275]

Doud may have had in mind something like William S. Gray and Ruth Munroe's *The Reading Interests and Habits of Adults: A Preliminary Report* (1930), which concluded that, while the reading activities of business and professional men, college students, college alumni, young industrial workers, loggers, and rural people were different, "[e]ven more striking ... are the variations in the reading activities of members of given groups."[276] Individual factors were the key to understanding patrons because a wide variety of "influences" in a particular group "determine[s] to a large extent the amount and character of the reading that is done."[277] To support their point, Gray and Munroe presented "intensive case studies" of readers, many of whom described reading tastes that Wellard would likely dismiss as so many examples of auto mechanics reading the novels of Thomas Hardy.[278] The first case study described "Mrs. S." as someone who had completed only the eighth grade, whose "family and friends show little inclination toward books," and who had worked outside her own home as a stenographer, domestic caretaker, and housekeeper.[279] During her last job she decided that she should read books that would "do her good," and so she chose, for reasons unknown, to follow a reading course on the French Revolution prepared by a readers' advisor.[280] After working her way through novels and biographies on this topic, she expanded her range to include works by H. G. Wells, Anatole France, Balzac, Galsworthy, Tolstoy, and Fielding. The reading tastes of "Mr. B." were also on a high level. To put it mildly, "Mr. B." had a difficult life. He was "born in a primitive village of western Russia."[281] At the age of nine, he was "sent out daily to watch the village herd of goats," where "[t]he long lonely hours out of doors awakened in him a love for the beautiful in nature" and where he began to read "Hebrew poets and novelists."[282] Immigrating to the United States as a teenager, "he was placed in first grade because he knew no English."[283] Because of illness in his family, "he has been obliged to give up school" and work "as a pressman" in order "to contribute to the support of his family."[284] But, after joining a poetry group at the local library, he voraciously began to read poetry. And, after coming into contact with a readers' advisor, he broadened his reading to include biographies of famous men, political and social histories of their respective eras, novels, Chinese poetry, and travel books.[285]

Although antedating Waples's early 1930s' research, Gray and Munroe's work, especially their compendium of case studies, validated public librarians' views about the broad range of individual reading interests that simply could not be predicted by group allegiance or statistical formulas. They understood, as James I. Wyer put it in his 1930 *Reference Work: A Textbook for Students of Library Work*, that, even though it was both time- and thought-intensive, readers' advisory tailored to a patron's personal circumstances was "highly significant and advantageous for the individual when compared with at least some of the 'mass production' attempted by correspondence schools and other commercial educating agencies."[286] Further validation was provided in 1934 by Charles H. Compton's *Who Reads What? Essays on the Readers of Mark Twain, Hardy, Sandburg, Shaw, William James, the Greek Classics*, which brought together case studies that he had conducted in the late 1920s and early 1930s.[287] To a certain extent, we have already met Compton's work, since Wellard alluded to it when he disparagingly referred to auto mechanics who read Thomas Hardy. Compton, who was Assistant Librarian of the St. Louis Public Library starting in 1921 and chief Librarian from 1938,[288] looked at the circulation records of many hundreds of readers of Twain, Hardy, James, Shaw, Homer, Aeschylus, Sophocles, and Euripides. He discovered that "the bulk" of the readers "came from what we consider the uncultured and certainly the humble occupations."[289] Readers of the philosophical works of William James included "a trunk maker, a machinist, stenographers, a saleswoman, a laundry worker, a common laborer, a maintenance man in a soap factory, [and] a colored salesman."[290] Readers of the Greek Classics included "printers, clerks, salesmen, a cabinet maker, a draftsman, stenographers, a musician at a vaudeville theater, a colored insurance agent, a hairdresser, a chauffeur, a drug store clerk, a beauty specialist, a butcher, a telephone operator, a reporter and a railroad brakeman's wife."[291] And Hardy attracted bookkeepers, carpenters, cooks, maids, plasterers, house painters, coopers, blacksmiths, soda dispensers, electricians, Pullman conductors, street car conductors, bus drivers, telephone operators, waiters and waitresses, and factory workers.[292] His conclusion was simplicity itself: "[l]owbrows read good books."[293] Despite repeated assertions from GLS-related researchers that his work was "[t]oo limited in scope to be of great significance in the direction of prediction or defining the reading of sex, occupational, or other groups,"[294] Compton showed that conclusions about individual reading tastes could not be made from aggregated statistical data. Anyone who used aggregated data to develop book collections or advise readers was committing a grave error, not to mention underestimating the level of reading tastes of a broad cross-section of the public.

Against this disputatious background C. Seymour Thompson, Assistant Librarian at the University of Pennsylvania, delivered a landmark speech entitled "Do We Want a Library Science?" in the summer of 1931.[295] Although the audience greeted the speech with "thunderous applause," later commentators typically interpreted it as the querulous byproduct of a dyspeptic temperament.[296] We respectfully differ. Thompson's forthright answer to the question he posed in the title of his speech was no: "if we can have a science only by adopting the psycho-sociological laboratory methods that are being urged upon us, my answer is, No, we do not want librarianship to be a science. Let it be an art; a Fine Art,—untouched by science."[297] Singling out Waples's "Propaganda and Leisure Reading" study for virulent criticism, Thompson identified what was for him the core issue. Judging from the direction in which the scientific research of the GLS was headed, he feared that library shelves would no longer hold "best-book collections" for "the purpose of cultivating appreciation of books and broad acquaintance with literature in all its branches."[298] If Waples had his way, that time-honored principle would be discarded, to be replaced by library collections based on "the idea of promoting the reading of books which present certain elements" that are not represented elsewhere in other media.[299]

Although Thompson's words came prior to Waples's 1932 co-authored book, he nevertheless limned the ideological underpinnings of Waples's work: the reduction of holistic entities—whether books or people—into divisible components or elements such that one component (or a limited number of components) could be made to define the once-whole entity. While this would make library work easier and more efficient from a managerial perspective, it would also "divert the attention of the profession still further from the need of better educational equipment and greater knowledge of books," two qualities sorely lacking in current library staff members.[300] His observations were all the more salient because he drew attention to Williamson's observation that readers' advisory lacked a scientific basis. Intuiting that Waples's work could be used to give readers' advisory its missing scientific foundation, Thompson also understood that this scientific base would make readers' advisory work superficial and trivial because it would cause all library staff members to think that they could perform it simply by categorizing an individual into a defined group. Directed toward books that matched their artificial profile, patrons would not necessarily be exposed to "best-book collections," nor would they gain a "broad acquaintance with literature in all its branches." The slogan "Every Library Worker a Readers' Adviser" would become "Every Library Worker a Scientist"—a development that, Thompson felt, would distance librarianship even further from a much-needed *bibliothecal* spirit" carried out by educated library personnel with a broad knowledge of books.[301]

In *Living with Books*, first published in 1935, and, more crucially, in her 1938 commencement address "Technics or Humanization in Librarianship?" at the School of Library Science at Western Reserve University, Helen E. Haines expanded on many of Thompson's concerns regarding statistical research and its detrimental effect on reading.[302] While primarily a book about developing library collections, *Living with Books* also touched upon questions important for readers' advisory because it situated reading as an activity through which character was formed and knowledge of the world was accumulated. A revered figure in the library world, Haines served as the managing editor of *Library Journal* from 1892–1908; professor of Book Selection at the Library School of the Los Angeles Public Library from 1914–1931; and, starting in 1924, a visiting or adjunct professor at the Columbia University School of Library Service, the Library School of the University of California, and the University of Southern California School of Library Science.[303]

Through books, Haines said, individuals gained "the historic sense of progress through the ages."[304] Admitting that "[a]ll reading, any reading, is better than none" and that "[e]ven books born only to die, like the coral insect have left their trace of vital substance in the substructure of the world of literature," she insisted that "good reading" was only possible when individuals had a ready grasp of and appreciation for acknowledged fiction and nonfiction masterpieces and classics in all fields.[305] Only when individuals become armed with this background knowledge could they make sound judgments and evaluations about the contemporary world. Only then could they best appreciate "every new subject contemplated, studied, or enjoyed" because they had at their disposal contextual threads by which "the whole panorama of the world's life, past and present, becomes constantly more varied and interesting, while at the same time the mind's own powers of reflection and judgment are exercised and strengthened."[306] And if "[t]he whole fabric of public library reading is a texture woven of different strands—weak and strong, gay and somber, shoddy and genuine; and the reading of the individual is of the texture of the whole," it was nonetheless true that most individuals possessed "an instinctive craving for beauty and wisdom in books, of purpose to enlarge opportunities and improve environment."[307] It would be counterintuitive if the librarian's task did not comprise supplying books that encouraged intellectual growth, since intellectual growth alone could lead "to broader, deeper understanding, to deeper insight and freer range" and to "the enduring materials of knowledge, prepared for us through centuries of thought and labor."[308] And so it behooved public librarians to apply five tests when selecting books, especially novels: tests of time, compensation, significance, effect on reader, and comparison.[309] They should consider the question of "the permanence of appeal"; they should inquire into "whether sufficient profit of any kind ensues from reading the book to compensate for the time spent on it instead of on a different book."[310] Most importantly, they should determine how a book "measure[s] up, quality by quality, alongside works of the same kind that have passed the test of time"—a task that "demands a broad background of book knowledge."[311]

Given all this, the statistical approaches of Waples and Wellard were disconcerting, since they foreshadowed the "scientific-mathematical mechanization of library functions," where "the warm personal understanding and use of book-values in human relationships" were being replaced by "an impersonal acceptance of model formulas that is impervious to universals of human experience and unaware of the richness and stimulus of creative art."[312] For Haines, "statistical mass-analysis of readers' interests as indicated by elaborate questionnaires" did not lead to the selection of books, but rather to the "selection of subjects."[313] This effectively devalued the type of readers' advisory offered by Katherine Yerxa at the Minneapolis Public Library, where "groping minds have been brought into vital relationship with the world of books, by librarians who draw from rich personal stores of book knowledge, who maintain friendly skilful guidance, who establish a mutual interest, and who select books according to their individual substance for individual readers."[314] With their emphasis on "technics," Waples and Wellard sounded the death knell for the "[h]umanization of book service" and "fuller acceptance[] of the values of creative literature," transforming books into "tools of professional routine or ... ready-cut building material for the library's structure of public service."[315]

The art of librarianship, as conceptualized by Thompson and Haines, was fully on display in the work of Jennie M. Flexner of the New York Public Library (NYPL). Jennie Flexner, whose uncle Abraham Flexner wrote *Medical Education in the United States and Canada*, was a key figure at the Louisville (Kentucky) Free Public Library in the 1910s and 1920s, where she developed the ideas contained in her 1927 textbook *Circulation of Books in Public Libraries*.[316] In 1928, she was hired by the NYPL to establish a readers' advisory service at its central location, a service inaugurated on March 4, 1929.[317] Her experiences organizing, publicizing, implementing, and evaluating the NYPL's "scheme of education outside of schools" were recounted in *A Readers' Advisory Service*, co-authored by Flexner and Sigrid A. Edge, and *Readers' Advisers at Work: A Survey of Development in the New York Public Library*, co-authored by Flexner and Byron C. Hopkins.[318] Although both books provide useful information about the demographic characteristics of patrons using the service, the subject areas most in demand, and the number of recommended items that patrons actually read (32.7 percent), their central value lay in their formulation of an ethics of readers' advisory—an ethics permeated by "a sensitiveness to the dignity attaching to the individual and his needs."[319]

Set up "in a corridor converted by means of screens and comfortable chairs into an attractive room," the NYPL readers' advisory office, like its predecessors in other urban libraries, prided itself on individual service that would "supply guidance and assistance to the adult reader interested in self-education" through systematic reading.[320] Between 1933 and 1939, Flexner and her staff received 5,561 individual requests and 665 group requests for reading advice and conducted 5,336 personal interviews.[321] Building on the success of its central office, the NYPL expanded readers' advisory to 30 branch libraries by 1941.[322] The diffusion of readers' advisory to branches after successful implementation at a central location followed the pattern established in the 1880s at the BPL. A regular interchange of staff members between NYPL's central readers' advisory office and the branches occurred, a process that helped to create system-wide support for the importance of the service. Flexner also implemented a training program for branch readers' advisors who, after conducting interviews at their dispersed locations, came to the central office to prepare reading courses.[323] As readers' advisory in the NYPL branches expanded in the late 1930s, there was an increased emphasis on "floor work."[324] This development built on the insight of Lillian C. Gates, the readers' advisor at the Omaha Public Library in the middle 1920s, who felt that "[a] casual remark made while we are browsing among the books gives the assistant a glimpse of the reader's wants. Suddenly we know of a variety of personalities with whom he would love to become acquainted."[325] The Cleveland Public Library also had a readers' advisor who browsed among patrons.

Personal interviews, which took the form of "general conversation" designed to elicit as much useful information as possible about a patron's unique circumstances, and anno-tated book lists, which required constant attention to "the needs and capacities of the reader" and served as "an entering wedge" to in-depth knowledge, were at the center of read-ers' advisory at the NYPL.[326] As Flexner and Edge noted, "[t]he more information gained from the reader about his tastes and interests the more complex he becomes."[327] While lists were also prepared for groups, including the League of Women Voters and the Women's Trade Union League,[328] the majority of work was conducted with individuals.

> All come with at least the desire to read already formed, and more often with reading habits which need only direction or stimulation. No statistics will ever disclose the human needs behind these requests—the unhappiness, lonesomeness, bewilderment, ambition and curiosity—all hidden behind the oft repeated request for 'systematic reading.' A healthy dissatisfaction is usually manifest not only with conditions in life but also with conditions in libraries.[329]

The statement about the unfathomable complexity of individuals is particularly relevant, since the statistical approach of Waples and his followers was incapable of taking the meas-ure of this complexity. Flexner and Edge specifically called attention to their refusal to cat-egorize and pigeon-hole, explaining that they had "[a] firm determination not to develop a service resembling the case investigation of social agencies."[330] They likely would have agreed with Helen L. Butler who, in her 1940 "An Inquiry into the Statement of Motives by Read-ers," concluded that, because individuals read specific items for an overwhelming number of reasons, it was necessary to move beyond easily identified "dominating motives," such as "information-getting" and "recreation, with its implication primarily of emotional satisfac-tion," to the deeper issues undergirding any expressed reading need.[331] "[T]he occasion which has prompted interest in the subject and the satisfaction which is likely to be derived" must be explored, but "[s]ince these may have started far back in some trait of the reader's per-sonality or in some real or vicarious experience, the answer is not easily obtained."[332]

To discover all the complex facets of individuals and their reading needs, Flexner and Edge believed that the central requirement was a readers' advisor "released from the pres-sure of routine, freed from many of the necessarily hampering restrictions of the general schedule—a librarian at the disposal of the reader, trying to make easier and more satisfy-ing the connection between the reader and books."[333] This librarian could "spend little or much time [with the patron], depending on the need and purpose of the reader and the wider implications of the request."[334] This librarian should also have "maturity, experience, and as broad an educational background as can be achieved," possess "the ability to discuss definite books with readers," and be an "avid" and enthusiastic reader who nevertheless has "an honestly critical attitude which shall make for a weighing of processes rather than a quick acceptance of what appears in print."[335] These characteristics were essential because Flexner and Edge, like Haines, believed that books should be "an integral part of a scheme of life involving continual education and expanding interests."[336] And if some of the books that had proved to be most valuable to patrons of the NYPL's readers' advisory office were any indication (e.g., *Story of the World's Literature*, *Stream of History*, *Story of Philosophy*, and *Rise of American Civilization*), patrons also believed that serious and purposeful reading was a meaningful educational activity that could fill what Haines called their "instinctive craving for beauty and wisdom in books, of purpose to enlarge opportunities and improve environment."[337]

Flexner and Edge's four main criteria for successful readers' advisory—time, wisdom, sensitivity, and maturity—were crucial prerequisites if patrons were to gain meaningful education through reading. Absent these factors, readers' advisory ran the risk of being superficial, of hurting the reputation of the public library more than helping it. In Robert S. Lynd and Helen Merrell Lynd's 1929 *Middletown: A Study in American Culture*, one of the 14 "business class women" interviewed about their reading habits described her interaction with a person who was likely a readers' advisor at the local public library: "I would take up some definite study. I am really interested in intellectual work, but I have so little time for it. I have tried to get one of the librarians ... to make me out a list of books on history but it doesn't work very well. My reading is so scattered, due to my children being small, and I want to organize it."[338] We can imagine an overworked and overwhelmed readers' advisor quickly making out a list that "doesn't work very well." Possibly the reader's advisor did not possess much subject expertise in history and therefore relied on generic suggestions not specifically tailored to the personal circumstances of the "business class woman" in question after a hurried interview that failed to uncover relevant personal information. Had this Middletown business-woman spoken with Flexner or Edge at the NYPL, we can imagine a much different outcome: an annotated reading course prepared by a discerning, well-read, and knowledgeable public librarian who took the time to weigh the choice of books in light of the patron's unique circumstances and motivations, which were discussed at length during an expansive interview. As Flexner and Hopkins documented, the reasons that individuals seek out readers' advisors were serious ones. In the period 1933–1939, on average 36.5 percent of patrons came for occupational reasons, 45.5 percent came to gain a liberal education, and 7 percent came for political education.[339] Because the reasons that patrons seek readers' advisory service were serious ones, the readers' advisory service that patrons received should by definition be just as serious.

Appraising the Role of Public Libraries in Adult Education

When Alvin S. Johnson, an economist and one of the founders in 1918 of the New School for Social Research in New York (of which he served as director beginning in 1922), wrote *The Public Library—A People's University* in 1938, he was trying to ensure that the educational needs and intellectual aspirations of Middletown business-women everywhere would always be met in a satisfactory manner.[340] Founded by a "rebellious group of scholars" who were inspired by Thorstein Veblen's *The Higher Learning in America: A Memorandum on the Conduct of Universities by Business Men* (1918), a critique of "the intrusion of business principles" and vocational training into institutions of higher education and the resulting "substitution of impersonal, mechanical relations, standards and tests, in the place of personal conference, guidance and association between teachers and students,"[341] the New School "emphasized a 'progressive' adult education as well as an independent social science research institute."[342] Johnson's book appeared at a time when the slogan "Every Library Worker a Readers' Adviser" was broadly accepted as the reigning paradigm for readers' advisory work.

Some libraries, like the NYPL, retained specialized readers' advisory offices, but as Monroe shows, the responsibility for adult education and readers' advisory was being diffused throughout the public library between 1936 and 1940 and placed "upon all professional staff serving adult readers."[343]

Especially important for enshrining the principle of diffusion was the Princeton Conference in 1936, although the Board on the Library on Adult Education (BLAE) had paved the way in 1931. At the Princeton Conference, the "synonymous relationship" between adult education and readers' advisory was set aside, with the result that "adult education became identified among library leaders as a quality of service or a philosophy, as the use of library materials to fulfill educational purposes and to meet social needs."[344] John Chancellor, who was readers' advisor at the New Haven (Connecticut) Free Public Library from 1927–1930 before becoming the "supervising librarian of libraries in ... Federal prisons, 1930–34" and the ALA's specialist in adult education starting in 1934, agreed with this new direction, suggesting that "a motive of informal education" needed to be put "into all library planning and practice, into book selection, cataloging, reference, desk work and publicity."[345] But there was both opportunity and danger in the new philosophy. It was all very well, as Chancellor recommended, to set "a main objective" and let each public library "work toward it in [its] own way and as the details of [its] immediate situation permit,"[346] but there was risk of a "dilution of the quality of service if staff were not trained and skilled or were without commitment to the adult education objectives."[347]

Johnson was not impressed with the philosophy of diffused adult education in public libraries, viewing it as a return to the principles of "pure librarianship," which he saw as "suicidal mania" because it meant "the mere supplying of books without regard to any influence they may exert" and basking in "the humble glory of standing neutrally to serve the wise man in his pursuit of wisdom, the fool in his folly, indifferently."[348] On a symbolic level, "pure librarianship" had the same qualities as Veblen's "impersonal, mechanical relations." It was ludicrous to think that the patron who "comes to a library every Friday evening to carry away an armful of westerns or detective stories" was receiving "an educational service, in any meaningful sense of the term."[349] Thus, when public librarians advanced the "commonplace" arguments that "[t]he best book in a field may not be the best for the general reader" or that high demand for a book signified that the book was "best" in the eyes of many readers and that therefore multiple copies of it had to be purchased, they were merely indulging their "neurosis of mechanism, common to overworked and underesteemed professions" and erecting "quantitative criteria" into a "stultifying ... system."[350] It was passive service, the antithesis of service based on "personal conference, guidance and association," which was the essence of meaningful education.

Johnson identified the Free Public Library of Newark (NPL) as a facility offering "pure librarianship." After examining "the reading records of a thousand persons [using the NPL] through a period of six months," he concluded that many of these patrons "offer few indications of getting anywhere" because they are "[r]eading at random."[351] For Johnson, this was troubling, since it raised the question of "whether, after all, adult education is as well served in Newark as it would be if the able and helpful staff who carry on Mr. Dana's work were in a position to deal more directly with the individual reader and with the groups it would be possible to form."[352] If we recall that Dana had been the head of the NPL from 1902–1929 and that Dana was instrumental in the adoption of the "Every Library Worker a Readers' Adviser" slogan, Johnson implied that Dana's belief that adult education could be delivered through "pure librarianship" was false. Diffusing adult-education responsibilities so that all staff members became readers' advisors did not enhance adult education, but diluted its promise to the point of non-existence. The result was service that had "no time for anything but the most cursory consideration of the reader's needs" and offered advice "based mainly on hunches."[353] Hesitating "to come to grips with the individual reader" because individual contact required time and thought, readers' advisory instituted under the aegis of "pure librarianship" models was "dominated by conceptions of coverage" and "extending the volume of general reading."[354]

One of the most widespread manifestations of this philosophy was "stereotyped [reading] lists," where "the educational intent [is] incidental" and which involved "the minimum of discretionary judgment and the widest possible application of the service."[355] Johnson called them "agglutinative" reading lists.[356] Their overriding function, he said, was to "produce impressive statistical results," and so they had little, if any, "developmental" value or "definite educational purpose."[357]

> This is likely to be the case with lists for summer reading, lists on travel, lists of books bearing upon some event of local interest, a play, a pageant, an anniversary. Hosts of lists group books together simply on the basis of particular readers' interests. If a number of readers appear interested in a popular historical novel, these same readers might be interested in other novels by the same writer, or dealing with the same historical period.[358]

But public libraries could take significant steps toward creating developmental lists or reading courses should they so desire. Take the example of a recent Supreme Court case. Many public libraries, Johnson explained, "prepared lists of books and magazine articles bearing upon this particular problem," but "[t]o a large extent the principle of list making was the juxtaposition of pros and cons, useful for debates and forum discussions."[359] There was an element of adult education in these lists, but "the interests of adult education would have been better served by exploiting the opportunity for placing the issue in the context of American history" so that documents, luminaries, and events such as "*The Federalist*, John Marshall, Taney, Chase, the Supreme Court discussions of the 1890s, ... [and] broad historical movements" were included.[360] In this way, "an inquiring layman" could become "a liberal scholar."[361] Johnson recognized that the creation of "developmental" lists was no easy task, yet he noted that public libraries often had access to expert faculty members from nearby colleges and universities who could prepare lists and infuse them with their deep learning and "expositional skill."[362] Ultimately, it was a matter of priorities. If public libraries were truly interested in adult education, they would ensure that thoughtful and wide-ranging developmental lists were created. But if they were content to provide "coverage" so as to generate high circulation statistics, then they would continue with the production of agglutinative lists.[363]

To reach their full potential, public libraries should abandon their role of filling shelves with books "that meet a transient demand but are worth little or nothing" and, instead, become people's universities wholly consecrated to adult education.[364] No longer should they feel compelled to follow "the misplaced commercial principle of giving the public what it wants" such that "an excessive proportion of the library funds is devoted to the purchase of books of no real educational significance" and that attract the public through "the seductive getup of a blurb or the whim of a famous reviewer who never reads books."[365] After all, "if Judy O'Grady and the Colonel's lady had not had a chance to read last year a book they would not touch this year, where was the loss?"[366] Why should public funds subsidize private entertainment? If individuals want entertaining books, they should "join a circulating library or book club and pay for [their] entertainment, as [they] pay[] for movies and other harmless pastimes."[367]

Another consequence of focusing on high-demand and entertainment-based books that swelled circulation statistics was that overworked staff members lacked the time or energy to provide knowledgeable and thoughtful service in the manner of NYPL's Jennie Flexner. Praising Flexner's work as "part of a great system that is working confidently toward an expanding future" in which public libraries would become people's universities,[368] Johnson envisioned libraries staffed by educated librarians with comprehensive knowledge of the humanities and social sciences presiding over discussion forums, lecture courses, and classes.[369] Here, readers' advisors would have both the time and expertise to create developmental reading courses that would meet the requirements of a business-woman from Middletown. He most decidedly did not want public libraries to resemble department stores, which used the too-easy criterion of public demand to justify "offering for sale good merchandise, vulgar merchandise, [and] merchandise that can float only on the folly of the purchaser."[370] By narrowly defining public wants as the "expressed wish for particular books," public libraries overlooked the unarticulated needs of patrons, which were often nebulous and inchoate but no less real. The result was that public libraries spent their time slaking public demand for popular and ephemeral novels, all the while stumbling to provide meaningful educational opportunities.

As the storm clouds of World War II gathered, Johnson viewed the adult-education efforts of public libraries as vital democratic bulwarks against the scourge of ignorance that could be exploited by ruthless leaders. "The crux of the adult educational problem is concerned with the civic and cultural development of the individual," he wrote, since "a democratic civilization can maintain itself and make progress only through a wide diffusion of sound ideas, political, social, and cultural."[371] As witnessed by the establishment of the New School, Johnson agreed with Veblen that many existing American colleges and universities, modeled on an "underlying business-like presumption" in which "learning is a merchantable commodity, to be produced on a piece-rate plan, rated, bought and sold by standard units, measured, counted and reduced to staple equivalence by impersonal, mechanical tests," were not offering their students a sound liberal education, the prerequisite for rigorous independent thinking.[372] In *The Public Library—A People's University*, Johnson made a similar assessment about the current state of public libraries. Like American colleges and universities, public libraries had the potential to be so much more, if only they wanted to be. That they were not moving to reach their potential in any systematic manner—that they were mostly content to adopt a philosophy of "businesslike standardization" that generated impressive statistics but also imposed a "regime of graduated sterility,"[373] as in their obsession with agglutinative lists—was a mystery to him, a searing commentary on their unwillingness to assume greater responsibility for meaningful adult education. Public libraries should not be content to play an ancillary role with regard to their educational responsibilities, since there is "nothing adequate to which [they] may be ancillary."[374]

Recognizing that Johnson's assessment was at least partially accurate, the ALA in its 1939 "A National Plan for Libraries" argued that public libraries should have four goals, the first three of which were "education, culture, scholarship," with "recreation" in fourth position.[375] Public libraries should stimulate "intellectual curiosity" so as to "advance the educational and cultural objectives of the nation and the community."[376] Patrons should expect to find "skilled personal advice and counseling necessary to effective self-study" at their libraries, as well as librarians who "encourage reading on subjects of vital importance to the community."[377] Most importantly, readers' advisory must be "perfect[ed] and extend[ed]" so that patrons receive "some kind of after-use" of what they read in order to better "make it [their] own."[378] Public libraries therefore "should foster formal and informal discussion among readers, and aid in any other practical way to complete the educational process which begins with reading."[379]

World War II (1939–1945) and Its Legacy

Arguably, the World War II period in readers' advisory begins with four documents that in many ways grew organically out of the thematic concerns discussed so far. One was "People and Libraries" by Waples, a speech delivered in the late summer of 1938 and published in 1939.[380] The other three were "The Psychology of the Reader," "Personality Adjustment through Reading," and "The Reader as a Person," all by Alice I. Bryan and all published in 1939 or 1940.[381] At first glance, the pairing of Bryan and Waples is odd, yet their combined views describe a readers' advisory service equally respectful of the underlying needs and motivations of people and the possibility of meeting those needs through serious and purposeful reading of classics—the basis of liberal education and independent thinking.

Waples was a complex individual who changed his intellectual interests during the early 1940s to "the fledgling field of communication science" and later "joined the United States army studying psychological warfare and propaganda."[382] Two events set the stage for his 1938 speech. First, in a 1936 speech to The Library Institute at the University of Chicago, he spoke "about the dangers caused by low-quality reading, mainly totalitarian propaganda and commercial trash, and how such print threatened to exacerbate the contemporary crisis in the United States and to lead to the destruction of its democratic society."[383] Second, in his 1937 book *People and Print: Social Aspects of Reading in the Depression*, he suggested that "near monopolistic" control of publishing outlets by profit-oriented media companies contributes to the production of "mass literature" that "regiment[s]" readers, "dulls their sensitivities," and "makes them easy to manipulate."[384] In 1938–1939 in "People and Libraries," he argued that public libraries that persisted in stocking their shelves with "mass literature" were doing a disservice to the community at large because they were offering books that could just as easily be found in "Mike Flanagan's drug store" and other commercial establishments.[385] These public libraries were not performing their fundamental educational function.

The most enduring and valuable libraries were those that "continually sought the excellent book in the given field—whether law, medicine, art, or literature," those that "held fast to books and paid small attention to people."[386] Thus, instead of succumbing to "the pull of large circulations" and blithely letting the public believe that "quantity of service" represents "a proper evaluation of library service," public librarians should realize that the best way to render "the greatest service to the cause of popular education" was by satisfying "the demands of scholarship," defined as the "best books" in any given field.[387] Giving patrons ephemeral, sensationalistic, and "trashy" books may satisfy librarians' sense of self-importance as ready providers of an in-demand service, but it ultimately does nothing to raise the level of educational attainment of patrons, who continue to read unchallenging materials simply because these materials are readily provided by public libraries.

Granted, reading good books is difficult, but "the way to learn to read good books is to try to read them, not to read something else."[388] But, by making few attempts to meaningfully educate patrons, public libraries effectively abandon them to lowest-common denominator reading, with possibly dire social and political consequences. If they are to be more than glorified drug or department stores that offer "sound recreation," public libraries must focus on books that will provide "sound education" to "serious readers."[389] In "People and Libraries," Waples did not repudiate his earlier work, but, like Johnson in *The*

Public Library–A People's University, he recognized that, as the horror of World War II loomed, the stakes were just too high to allow the "drug store" model of librarianship to continue. For both writers, the central mission of the public library should not be agglutinative, but developmental. If Waples was more dogmatic in formulating his views than Johnson, they shared a common interest in making public libraries meaningful institutions of adult education where serious and purposeful reading and learning occurred, not replicas of "Mike Flanagan's drug store."

The idea that books contained important developmental possibilities played a seminal role in Bryan's three articles from 1939 and 1940. While Johnson and Waples focused on educational development through books, Bryan concentrated on the power of books to assist readers in their psychological development, which she viewed from a holistic perspective that included educational development as an important component. Her vehicle to accomplish psychological development was bibliotherapy, which she felt should become an important part of mainstream librarianship.[390] Bryan's formal training was in psychology, and she was recruited to the School of Library Service (SLS) at Columbia University by its then dean, Charles C. Williamson, to teach courses in research methods and "psychology for practicing librarians." Appointed as an assistant professor in 1939, she became "the first woman in the history of SLS to attain a full professorship" in 1956 after a serpentine and often tumultuous journey through academia.[391]

Although the term "bibliotherapy" was likely first used by Samuel McChord Crothers in 1916—he defined it as "[t]he employment of books and the reading of them in the treatment of nervous disease"—the concept of bibliotherapy had a long history.[392] As Rhea Joyce Rubin pointed out in *Using Bibliotherapy: A Guide to Theory and Practice*, the ancient Greeks considered their libraries as "repositories" for "medicine for the soul."[393] The Roman encyclopedist Aulus Cornelius Celsus "suggested that works of great orators be read by patients in order to improve their judgment."[394] An early use of bibliotherapy in hospital settings was in 1272 at the Al-Mansur Hospital in Cairo, Egypt, which "provided readings of the Koran as a part of treatment."[395] Bibliotherapy was introduced to the United States by Benjamin Rush in the early 1800s.[396] Rush recommended religious and nonreligious materials in his 1812 *Medical Inquiries and Observations upon the Diseases of the Mind*: "when there is no relish for the simple and interesting stories contained in the Bible, the reading of novels should be recommended to our patients."[397] John Minson Galt II's article "On Reading, Recreation and Amusements for the Insane" in 1853 explained that the act of selecting books "to fit the special needs of patients" should be conducted in the same careful manner as the selection of "additional medicine to treat some rare physical symptom."[398] As Eleanor Frances Brown remarked in *Bibliotherapy and Its Widening Applications*, Galt "thought of a library as a kind of intellectual pharmacy stocked with remedies for every kind of emotional disorder and he stressed the importance of proper guidance and supervision."[399] In 1904, "E. Kathleen Jones, administrator of libraries at the McLean Hospital in Waverly, Mass., was the first trained librarian to use books in the treatment of the mentally ill."[400] In the 1920s at the 135th Street Branch of the NYPL, Sadie Peterson Delaney developed some of the bibliotherapy principles that she would later implement at the Veterans Administration (VA) Hospital in Tuskegee, Alabama, where she increased the size of the collection from 200 volumes to about 4,000 volumes and the monthly circulation from about 275 loans to 10,000 loans during her tenure.[401] Her work became "a model" for other VA hospital libraries, and "library schools in Illinois, North Carolina, and Georgia sent students to study her programs and methods."[402] Collectively, VA hospitals "played a large role" in the dissemination of bibliotherapy practices in the United States during the 1930s and 1940s.[403]

Because literature had therapeutic properties, bibliotherapy was the act of "harnessing ... the power of literature into a specific activity."[404] Most bibliotherapy was either "institutional bibliotherapy" (which was "primarily didactic" and was used with "individual institutionalized clients") or "clinical bibliotherapy" (which used imaginative literature "with groups of clients with emotional or behavioral problems").[405] The third type of bibliotherapy was "developmental bibliotherapy," which was "the use of both imaginative and didactic literature with groups of 'normal' individuals."[406] Developmental bibliotherapy helped individuals with the accomplishment of what Robert Havighurst called "developmental tasks," which arise "at or about a certain period in the life of the individual, successful achievement of which lead[] to his happiness and to success with later tasks, while failure leads to unhappiness in the individual, disapproval by society, and difficulty with future tasks."[407] It also helped them "cope with individual problems such as divorce, pregnancy, death, and prejudice, all of which are refinements of developmental tasks."[408]

Bryan was convinced that the concept of developmental bibliotherapy could profitably be transferred into the realm of public libraries. For her, psychological development included educational development, since it meant exposing adults, through the auspices of public libraries, to "the essence of a liberal education," defined as "the distilled wisdom and inspiration of the sages, saints and scientists, the poets and statesmen, the historians and critics of all times whose writings have been preserved to us" and the thought and writings of "the great minds of the past and present."[409] It also meant understanding that "[e]very time a librarian hands a book across the counter to a waiting reader, he participates in a social situation" involving the librarian, the patron, and the author of the book.[410] The librarian functions as a "host or hostess" introducing two guests to each other, and like a good host or hostess, the librarian must ensure that "no time will be lost in unprofitable or discouraging exploration of inappropriate or inferior material."[411] Librarians should therefore possess "some knowledge of the general characteristics of human behavior" as well as "an appreciation of the great range of individual differences through which these common traits may express themselves in the life pattern of each particular person."[412] In addition to taking stock of a patron's "intellectual status," librarians must understand which of the four human spiritual drives, values, or wishes (or some combination thereof) motivates the patron.[413] These four drives are: security, subdivided as the need for economic, philosophical, or social security; new experience; recognition; and response, defined as "the universal craving for love and affection, friendship, companionship."[414] Taken together, these drives "are basic to the personality development of everyone," and "[t]hey should be recognized as inborn, legitimate needs, the fulfillment of which, for each individual, society must find some way to make possible."[415] Often these drives conflict, and "[i]f the librarian can understand the nature of these conflicts and can help guide the individual at these moments of crucial decision to reading materials which will influence his choice toward the wisest possible solution, he will be fulfilling the highest function possible as an adviser."[416]

Bibliotherapy should thus become part of the continuum of reading guidance performed by readers' advisors at public libraries. The psychological approach inherent in bibliotherapy, Bryan explained, should prove especially valuable during "the present period of conflict, chaos, and crisis" and in the "dangerous and difficult times [that] lie ahead" because individuals are searching "to comprehend and adjust to the changing conditions of life."[417] In these circumstances, thoughtful reading guidance can "give insight into the nature of the problems the world is facing ... [and] help the individual to retain his emotional and intellectual balance while values and standards shift, change, and disappear."[418] And so "novels, poetry, plays, works on philosophy and ethics, religion, art, history, and science [should] be placed in readers' hands for the specific purpose of helping them to face their life problems more effectively and to gain greater freedom and happiness in their personal adjustments."[419]

But it should also be remembered that readers cannot be "classified according to some developmental or sociological typology" because, in that case, the individual "as a dynamic personality" would "remain completely undiscovered."[420] If readers' advisors want to avoid giving "a very superficial service," they must understand the reader as "a whole personality" with specific "needs, goals, frustrations, and conflicts" that may not always be revealed in their first (surface) request for a book or reading course on a specific topic. As Bryan demonstrated, three people who want "a course of reading on contemporary affairs" may indicate three different reasons for wanting to read on that subject to a readers' advisor, but their interest in contemporary affairs may conceal a deeper personal drive or motivation that can only be addressed by books not related to current events.[421]

Her most extended example involved a female patron who asked a public librarian for thrilling detective stories "to help keep her husband home for an evening or two."[422] But, as the librarian soon discovered after probing further, the patron's situation turned out to be much more complex than the initial request for detective fiction indicated. Unemployed for three or four years, the patrons' husband had recently found a low-level factory job. Determined to succeed at this job so as to be able to move out of his wife's parents' home, rebuild their savings, and provide a better future for their two young children, he spent all his leisure hours at home either doing work that he had brought from the factory or studying in order to be promoted. As his wife began to complain that he had little time for her and their children, he began to spend all his time at the factory. The patron therefore decided that detective stories, which her husband had liked in the past, might be a way to convince him to spend more time at home and enjoy family life. But as Bryan pointed out, while detective fiction might have a "slight constructive value" if the husband looked upon it as "an act of genuine consideration for his needs, free from censorious and ulterior motivation," it "would have practically no value" as a solution to the underlying problem.[423] The patron had failed to see that her husband "was attempting to make a really constructive adjustment to his underlying need, which was the restoration of his confidence and self-esteem" through the act of trying "to re-establish himself vocationally," which despite "[t]emporary deprivation and irritations" might lead to the prospect of "their own home even on a very limited income and at the sacrifice of [the relative] material comforts and conveniences" present in their current situation.[424] Instead of acceding to the patron's request for detective fiction, an astute and sensitive readers' advisor "could begin by offering some novel which dealt constructively with the problem of unemployment and which might be expected to give the wife a more sympathetic understanding of her husband's emotional reactions."[425] Subsequently, "[o]ther fictional materials might be found helpful in building up a more mature appreciation of the values to be found in marriage, apart from material considerations, ... and [t]hese might be followed by some practical books on child guidance which stressed the importance to the child of a harmonious relationship between the parents."[426]

Bibliotherapy as practiced by public librarians could therefore serve as "reader education in its most fruitful and valid form"[427] as long as librarians realized that they should attempt to grapple with "broad objectives" on "a deeper level" in dealing with the issues and questions presented to them by patrons. As in the example above, it was not enough to acquiesce when a patron asked for detective fiction, since that was an easy answer that merely addressed "surface idiosyncrasies."[428] Instead, through "carefully selected reading materials," patrons can be shown that they are "not the first person to encounter" a particular problem, that "more than one solution is possible and that some choice can be made in the way it is handled."[429] These materials could "[h]elp" patrons to understand "the basic motivation of the people involved in the situation," as well "[h]elp ... to see the values involved, in human rather than material terms."[430] And although Bryan remarked that current bestsellers could occasionally be used to initiate the "deeper level" process of psychological development, her comments in "The Reader as a Person" that the essence of liberal education was "the distilled wisdom and inspiration of the sages, saints and scientists, the poets and statesmen, the historians and critics of all times whose writings have been preserved to us" suggest that she believed that human motivations and values could most vividly be seen in books written by "the great minds of the past and present." This implied that the more knowledge about serious and enduring fiction and nonfiction that a readers' advisor had, the more help that the readers' advisor could be to a patron in need of psychological and educational development.

Bryan's core idea that books were capable of helping individuals find abiding values in troubled times through bibliotherapy techniques was given support in the years immediately after World War II in Cyril O. Houle's "Chicago Public Library Staff Studies Adult Education."[431] Houle, an associate professor of education and dean of University College at the University of Chicago, explored in a discussion group with librarians from the Chicago Public Library the nature of public libraries' responsibilities in the realm of adult education. Convinced that it was not enough simply to keep busy by "increasing the number of books which one catalogs and circulates, multiplying the visits one makes to social groups of various sorts, or extending the detailed knowledge one has about the community the library serves," the group read four books (Sir Richard Livingstone's *The Future in Education*; John Dewey's *Experience and Education*; Sidney L. Pressey, Joseph Elliott Janney, and Raymond G. Kuhlen's *Life: A Psychological Survey*; and Carl R. Rogers's *Counseling and Psychotherapy*) so as "to study the principles of adult education in order to determine how best the library might apply them."[432] They concluded that public librarians should further the ideals of education, defined as "the process of changing people's skills, knowledge, attitudes, and understandings so that they might be helped to formulate and achieve worthwhile social and personal goals,"[433] through a philosophy of service that Rogers described as a counselor approach whose aim was "the greater independence and integration of the individual."[434] One of the best ways to operationalize this service philosophy was to set goals "both for individuals and for the community served," thus discarding the "widespread notion" that the public library is "merely a service agency, ready with whatever anyone might want, with the librarian a handmaiden to, rather than a leading force in, personal or social improvement."[435] Once librarians determined the "immediate and ultimate social needs" of the community and set goals to meet those needs, they could then embark on a program of adult education to meet the desired goals by working with individual patrons and groups in a way that took into account "adult psychological factors."[436]

Houle's work with Chicago public librarians was part of the postwar debate about the place of public libraries in adult education. In many ways, Flexner and other readers' advisors in the 1930s were following on a daily basis Houle's philosophical orientation by gauging the drives, motivations, and abilities of the patrons who came to them for reading courses. But Houle's emphasis on the need to establish community-wide goals was relatively new, and this emphasis implied trying to reach more people than was possible through individual readers' advisory interviews. One answer was the formation of guided group-reading programs or great-books programs,[437] which were the direct descendants of the study groups that Adolph

Peck conducted in the 1890s at the Gloversville Public Library about social and political issues and the discussion groups recommended by the CLAE in 1926. Guided group-reading programs functioned as group developmental bibliotherapy sessions and as the "after-use" groups suggested by the ALA's 1939 "A National Plan for Libraries." They generated intense and lively discussions that, because they did not supply "ready-made conclusions" and were not led by experts, encouraged participants to "reflect[] further between meetings on the unsettled issues."[438] Embodying Johnson's view that "[t]he crux of the adult educational problem is concerned with the civic and cultural development of the individual," these groups provided the same kind of "stimulation and guidance of purposeful reading" that was a central accomplishment of readers' advisory during the 1920s and 1930s. John Powell, one of the initiators of postwar guided group-reading, invoked the heritage of the reading courses prepared by pre-war readers' advisors and the *Reading with a Purpose* series to situate group-reading as a natural extension of "the individual guidance services already established."[439]

Powell's guided group-reading program at the Public Library of the District of Columbia (PLDC), launched in 1945, is usually credited with being the first of its kind. It was soon followed and subsumed by the Great Books guided group-reading project in Chicago, where 27 of the 34 reading groups were organized by and held in public libraries.[440] By late 1946 and early 1947, the Great Books program, sponsored by the Great Books Foundation, "a nonprofit, independent body with headquarters at the University of Chicago," had expanded nationally and was taking the first steps toward the publication of a 54-volume set of ancient and modern classics in cooperation with the Encyclopedia Britannica.[441] Public libraries, colleges, and universities in 25 cities in the United States and Canada—including Buffalo, New York, Cleveland, Detroit, Louisville, St. Louis, Topeka (Kansas), Manhattan (Kansas), Seattle, Salem (Oregon), and Vancouver—conducted Great Books programs in 1947.[442]

Inspired by the vision of Robert M. Hutchins, chancellor of the University of Chicago, and Mortimer J. Adler, author of *How to Read a Book: The Art of Getting a Liberal Education*, the Great Books program had two key features. First, the materials read were "harder" than members would "ordinarily read by themselves."[443] While the PDLC program was not technically under the Great Books umbrella, the books read were of the great-books variety, including Flaubert, Gide, Hobbes, Kant, Marx, Plato, Rousseau, Shakespeare, and Tolstoy.[444] In the Chicago Great Books project, typical fare included Aristotle, Chaucer, Descartes, Freud, Homer, William James, Locke, Machiavelli, Milton, Nietzsche, Rabelais, Thoreau, and Thucydides.[445] Second, the groups were led by ordinary individuals who were not experts, since "[e]xperts tend to suffer from the fallacy of 'having the answers,' and from the urge to impart knowledge in the form of instruction."[446] Group leaders posed a series of questions, and their main preparation consisted in "having read and thought about the problem more than" other group members.[447] In a group discussing Goethe's *Faust*, "no time would be wasted in talking about things that only professors know, such as the life of Goethe, the condition of Europe during that time, and the influences that he felt or exerted."[448] Although the selected books were classics and thus seemingly more difficult, discussion did not falter. As Powell noted, discussion was stimulated.

> The themes of group discussion are pretty much the same, whatever angle of them the reading may be used to illuminate. They are the perennial problems that confront working adults as citizens, as parents, as Americans, as members of the human family. They are themes of personal ethics and belief, of social action and reaction, of individual purpose and accomplishment, of human freedom and responsibility. They arise in, and lead to, discussions of history, politics, economics; of life and character; of science, art, and morals; of the sources of knowledge, the motives of action and the methods and standards of making judgments.[449]

Classic literature, whether in the form of Greek, French, or English philosophers or dramatists, was capable of addressing contemporary social and cultural concerns and generating intense personal reflection that caused individuals to think critically about their place and role in their communities. As Hutchins remarked, "[t]he difficulty in leading a Great Books class is to keep the group off the modern problems long enough to get the author's ideas clear."[450]

Guided reading groups became developmentally therapeutic because they made "the wisdom distilled from the world's experience ... an active ingredient in the community's current thinking," thus leading to a "richer, more satisfying, more humane" life.[451] Hutchins observed that "[t]he object is to talk about issues important to every one of us in the light of what some great writer has said."[452] In this way "education for the future" would occur through "the Civilization of the Dialogue, which conceives of history as one long conversation leading to clarification and understanding"[453] after a period of "a good kind of confusion," which leads "everybody to continue thinking about the unresolved issues."[454] Adult education conceptualized in terms of "shared inquiry"[455] would not only help participants develop the habit of lifelong learning through exposure to the "process of liberal education,"[456] but also enhance their "individuality" because they would no longer be afraid "to assert any difference between them[selves] and the majority."[457] No longer at the mercy of conformity-inducing and profit-driven bestsellers, digests, book reviews, or movies, participants would see themselves as part of a historical continuum in which "[t]hey as individuals find themselves concerned with mankind's perennial problems: the questions of evil posed by Antigone and Job; the problems raised by the existence of democracy and tyranny together in the Athenian state; the demands made by a dead past on a living present in *Hamlet*."[458] Finally, "individuals who have difficulty with the human drama of Plato or the sweeping narrative of Thucydides when they enter a class are observed a year later dealing with the close reasoning of Aristotle and the scientific insight of Bacon."[459] Waples's statement in "People and Libraries" that "the way to learn to read good books is to try to read them, not to read something else" was startlingly prescient.

Continuity and Evolution

Guided group-reading programs were meaningful adult-education initiatives for serious times. They responded to the ALA's 1941 statement that "[l]ibraries have an opportunity to promote the reading of thought-provoking books on socially significant questions; they have an obligation to make it difficult for people to escape the influence of such books."[460] They also responded to the 1943 *Post-War Standards for Public Libraries*, which named "education" as the primary and "perhaps the most important" function of public libraries, with "recreation" last.[461] Public libraries should do everything possible to strengthen their roles as "people's universit[ies]," the *Post-War Standards* stated, noting that many commentators believed that "the future of democracy depends in a genuine sense upon adult education" and that public libraries were uniquely positioned to become "focal point[s] for service to the citizen in the examination of the problems of public affairs."[462] In 1947, Margery Doud, Chief of the Readers' Advisory Service at the St. Louis Public Library, explained that returning veterans typically sought out "books and periodicals having to do with the world of ideas."[463] Quoting Charles Bolte's *The New Veteran*, she attributed this "passionate earnestness" to the veteran's realization that "the world of political and economic security he fought for as a soldier" could only be achieved if a similar fight is continued on the domestic front.[464] "Such determination," Doud concluded, "is a spur to the finest kind of adult education, the kind that might be called 'Pursuit of Understanding.'"[465]

To meet the challenge of delivering "the finest kind of adult education," public librarians were urged to become as serious as the times in which they lived. Mary U. Rothrock, in her 1947 ALA presidential address, declared that, because "[e]vents have placed on today's libraries, as on other institutions concerned with education and enlightenment, a more positive responsibility for getting the insides of books into the minds of men," librarians should spend more time becoming knowledgeable about various issues and subjects, such as atomic energy, than with selecting, classifying, or circulating the books that deal with those subjects.[466] She therefore recommended that "at least half" of the meeting time at library conferences be devoted "to such nonlibrary subjects" as atomic energy or international relations insofar as most conference attendees "would go home better and more intelligent librarians for having given some of their time to ideas and the subject content of books instead of to the technical processes of libraries."[467] In A National Plan for Public Library Service (1948), the ideal public library was envisioned as an "intellectual force" staffed by model librarians who spoke knowledgeably about topics such as labor history, economic theory, and child psychology to relevant groups, led fruitful discussions on important socio-cultural issues, and offered "personal guidance" to readers.[468]

The emphasis on knowledgeable and informed public librarians was in part designed to reverse the situation, reported in 1949 by Bernard Berelson in The Library's Public, that "[o]nly 6 percent of a national cross-section named librarians as a source of 'ideas about books to read' as against 35 percent who credited friends, 27 percent advertisements, 23 percent reviews, and 17 percent other people."[469] Public librarians were not well-respected, Berelson implied, and this lack of respect stemmed from the fact that librarians measured their performance quantitatively (e.g., circulation per capita, percent of population registered).[470] If public librarians really wanted to deliver "responsible public service" and were "really concerned about the educational services" that they offered, they would choose to measure the effectiveness of their services in terms of "social, political, and psychological processes" such as "the promotion of group understanding, the clarification of the goals and values of the society, the encouragement of interest in politics, [and] the development of greater rationality in political decisions."[471] In other words, they should turn their attention to serious matters.

As a sign of its commitment to seriousness and purposefulness, the ALA initiated two programs: the Great Issues program (1948) and the American Heritage Project (1951).[472] Great Issues was a multi-dimensional effort based on displays, exhibits, and reading lists about significant contemporary topics such as "The Marshall Plan" and "Inflation-Deflation." Emphasis was placed on lectures and community discussion groups; all library staff members received training so that they could "understand the arguments for and against" the topic in question.[473] Public libraries were to become actively involved in "spreading information and stimulating citizen action upon the solution of [various] problems if our nation is to avoid disaster."[474] American Heritage, sponsored by the Fund for Adult Education of the Ford Foundation and conceptually similar to Great Books in that it focused on outstanding examples of American fiction and nonfiction, could serve as a model for "adult community discussion under library leadership all over the country."[475] Far from being "a flag-waving program ... to prove American superiority to the world," it gave "the average citizen a chance to examine his heritage and decide what it stands for; to realize where we have achieved the dream of our forefathers; where we have failed; and what we might do about the failures."[476] Although Great Issues had limited success,[477] it paved the way for American Heritage, which "was the most extensive adult education program ever undertaken" by American public libraries.[478] Between 1951 and 1955, a total of 28,476 adults participated in 1,474 discussion groups, where they talked about "current political, social, and economic problems in the light of the basic documents, ideas, and experiences which constituted the American Heritage."[479] As John Dale Henderson of the Los Angeles County Public Library remarked, the program had immense value: "The tolerance and the understanding and the interest in other points of view, the new horizons that were opened to them through the reading and through the communion and exchange of ideas, was a great revelation to our people in the group."[480]

When Robert D. Leigh, a non-librarian with a rich career in the academic world—he was "the first and organizing president of Bennington College" (1928–1941) and later a visiting professor of political science at the University of Chicago, where he also served as "director of the Commission on Freedom of the Press (1944 to 1946) under the chairmanship of Robert M. Hutchins"[481]—published the final version of *The Public Library in the United States* in 1950, a consensus had formed among library leaders that public libraries were educational institutions that should focus their limited resources on serious readers who came to the library for meaningful "personal enrichment and enlightenment."[482] Leigh's report was the culmination of the three-year Public Library Inquiry (1947–1950), commissioned by the ALA to study public-library objectives, with participation from the Social Science Research Council and the Carnegie Corporation. Leigh felt that, because "commercial media are motivated and well equipped to perform" the functions of "entertainment, relaxation, and escape," public libraries should focus on "other social needs to which the commercial media do not minister as adequately as the library can."[483] He noted that, although "[s]alability is not an acknowledged basis for the selection of books by an institution performing an educational function," "present library selection of current books is determined for them to a considerable extent by promotion at the hands of commercial media," with their emphasis on "celebrity-building," "sensationalism," "personalization," and "the unusual or the forbidden, such as murder, scandal, and sex, or ... the dream worlds of mystery and romance."[484] The publication of sensationalistic and celebrity-oriented popular fiction and nonfiction was one way that commercial media entities met their profit-oriented goals. For Leigh, public libraries and commercial media should not have overlapping roles. Were they to overlap, "the standards of mass production, distribution, and consumption" would be erected as public-library goals, thus de-emphasizing scholarship and contributing to homogeneous library collections and potentially homogeneous thought among library patrons.[485] Instead, social objectives would be best served if public libraries concentrated on being "general center[s] of reliable information" and places that "provide opportunity and encouragement for people of all ages to educate themselves continuously" through serious and purposeful reading.[486] They could best do so by "awaken[ing] interest, stimulat[ing] reading and discussion on crucial problems" and "help[ing] people develop a constructively critical attitude toward all public issues and ... remov[ing] ignorance regarding them."[487] Public librarians could contribute to this process by being active guides in assisting patrons toward meaningful educational opportunities, "selecting subjects for emphasis with the view to replacing indifference by interest, and of exercising an influence on what people think about, without attempting to tell them what conclusions they should reach."[488] Public libraries must define their services in terms of "positive personal and social value" and then "seek[] maximum quality and maximum audiences for these services" by ensuring that the "natural public library audience" undergoes continual "enlargement."[489]

In 1954, Leigh's vision about the inherent responsibility of public libraries to provide meaningful education was reiterated at the Allerton Park Conference in Monticello, Illinois.[490] In a summary of the conference, Lester Asheim wrote that the purpose of public libraries was the provision of "equal opportunities for access to ideas," variously defined as keeping up with current events, learning "what the great minds of the past have had to say on the great questions of continuing importance," filling in "gaps in formal schooling," increasing knowledge about specific techniques or skills, enlarging "appreciation of the arts and skills of others," and "renewing the mind through constructive relaxation or sharpening it through intellectual discipline."[491] Libraries could accomplish these goals by taking a dynamic leadership role "in the patron's search for self-education" through a process of "active" adult education, which was formally defined as part of the "total educational process" and as something that was "marked by a defined goal."[492] Moreover, it resulted in "a continuing cumulative educational experience for those who participate" and required "special planning and organization."[493] Adult education could be delivered in three ways: active cooperation with other educational institutions; "discussion series, film forums, and other sequential programs planned around a topic or theme and organized to give continuity and direction to the educational process"; and, most importantly, readers' advisory service, which was defined as "a planned program of readings specifically designed for a particular individual or group, involving analysis of specific needs, guided progression, and specific educational objectives over and beyond the promotion of reading in general or the provision of pleasant entertainment."[494]

In other words, readers' advisory as practiced by Jennie Flexner and her peers in the 1920s and 1930s was recognized as an inherently valuable component of adult education at the Allerton Park Conference. And since the underlying principle of readers' advisory in the 1920s and 1930s had always been to encourage patrons toward serious and purposeful reading through the auspices of planned programs, the conception of readers' advisory in the 1950s was little different from what it had been in the era of readers' advisors such as Farquhar, Fihe, Flexner, Sanderson, Tompkins, and others. The work of readers' advisory was very much alive. As Leona Durkes explained in 1959, at the NYPL there was little change from Flexner's original initiatives: "[e]xpert help is still being given both through oral suggestion of titles and through the preparation of book lists tailored to fit the needs of individuals or groups whenever such a list is requested or seems indicated."[495] The Readers' Bureau of the Cincinnati Public Library (CinPL) also continued its work. CinPL consultants "planned 207 courses in 1955," ensuring that the reading lists "were tailored to special needs" and holding "frequent conferences, sometimes weekly, ... with those students who need it."[496] In 1959, CinPL started "a supervised home study program" in which "more than 200 individuals" participated on a regular basis.[497] The Enoch Pratt Free Library had a central readers' advisory office headed "by an experienced adult co-ordinator" who worked closely with subject departments and branches "to maintain the quality of reader guidance" through "a program of in-service training" and the publication of "informal reading guides."[498] The Detroit Public Library under the direction of Ralph A. Ulveling instituted a department called Home Reading Services (HRS), to be differentiated from its subject-based Reference-Research departments.[499] The Detroit HRS, which saw as its mandate "the best personal development of people through existing knowledge, rather than with the refinement and extension of knowledge itself," concentrated on selecting books that are "the best and the most usable ... at varying levels" and then embarked on a concerted strategy of "stimulation and guidance" so as to "promote" the reading of those books.[500] These efforts, it was hoped, would contribute to patrons' "fullest development as individuals, as members of a family, as citizens."[501] Still other libraries combined "responsibility for individual and group advisory service, including audio-visual, in a single office."[502] Nevertheless, "fewer than ten large libraries" retained "the position of readers' adviser" by 1959,[503] down from 44 public libraries in 1935.

To compensate for the decrease in formal designated positions, readers' advisory, while retaining its foundational emphasis on serious and purposeful reading, broadened its scope to include group activities "planned around a topic or theme and organized to give continuity and direction to the educational process."[504] Examples of these programs were Great Books, Great Issues, American Heritage, and, starting in 1957, Great Decisions.[505] Readers' advisory also relied to a greater extent on subject specialists in separate departments because the number of patrons seeking help with "more specific needs than general self-development" increased, thus "overtaxing the time and energy of the one or two people" that were assigned to a special readers' advisory office.[506] Yet these were not entirely new directions. As discussed in chapter 3, Alice Farquhar in Chicago and Miriam Tompkins in Milwaukee, among others, consulted subject specialists and outside experts in the 1920s and 1930s to help them in preparing annotated lists for patrons such as the "saleswoman in a china shop who desired to make a study of the marks on crockery and glass ware in preparation for becoming a buyer." The Cleveland Public Library foresaw in the 1920s and 1930s that patrons who received individual readers' advisory attention would eventually coalesce into small discussion groups and then into more formal adult-education classes, and the CLAE's 1926 report identified discussion groups as one of the four main pillars of adult education.

Public libraries' commitment to discussion groups in the 1950s also benefited from librarians' involvement in the founding of the Adult Education Association (AEA), which emphasized "small group discussion, education for democracy, and concern for reasonable discussion as a preface to action."[507] As Helen Hugenor Lyman explained, the discussion group format lent itself to "direct experience in democratic beliefs and methods" because it was "a frame in which the individual, differing and different, comes together with others to say what he thinks, to listen to others, to be stimulated to know more—to read, learn, agree and disagree."[508] As participants acquired knowledge and insights about crucial issues and expressed their views on the same issues, they also gained insight about "forming decisions and learning how to work together," which were invaluable tools in an "incomplete and frustrating" modern world rife with seemingly intractable problems.[509] Inspired by the lessons of American Heritage and the AEA, 36.9 percent of all public libraries by the end of 1953 planned, organized, and administered activities such as "world affairs forums, reading and discussion group programs, [and] study groups," with the largest public libraries doing so at a rate of 59.4 percent.[510] Judging from Henderson's comments, the groups were bibliotherapeutic, and so met the criteria envisioned by Bryan for active developmental guidance that gave individuals "insight into the nature of the problems the world is facing" and helped them "to retain [their] emotional and intellectual balance while values and standards shift, change, and disappear."

It was thus natural that readers' advisory work became an integral part of the mandate of the ALA's newly formed Adult Education Division, later renamed the Adult Services Division (ASD), established in 1957. As described by Grace Thomas Stevenson, the Deputy Executive Director of the ALA and the Director of the ALA's Office for Adult Education, the ASD offered both "[i]ndirect guidance services" and "[a]dvisory services to the individual," which consisted of "on the floor" or "over the desk" advisory assistance and "[p]lanned reading guidance" in the form of "preparation of the reading list."[511] In addition, public libraries contributed to adult self-education through library-sponsored group programs, community advisory services, and program-planning assistance for groups and organizations.[512] On a symbolic level, the expansive philosophy of the ASD with regard to adult self-education was echoed by the equally expansive Library Services Act (LSA), which was passed in 1957 to bring "library service to rural areas of less than 10,000 population which had no library service or inadequate or substandard service" and to stimulate "the use of state and local funds for the improvement of library service through the use of federal funds."[513]

In the same way that the LSA recognized that funds from one source would be insufficient to bring adequate library service to the approximately "27 million people in the United States" that were without it in 1956,[514] so the ASD program recognized that adult education could best be accomplished through a multi-pronged approach. Individualized readers' advisory was an important component of that approach, but guided group discussions and the creation of planned programs for external organizations were also significant elements. And irrespective of the number of people directly served, annotated reading lists and courses were at the heart of readers' advisory in the 1950s, just as in the 1920s and 1930s. As discussed in this chapter and in chapter 3, readers' advisory throughout its history was an amalgam of individual guidance and group guidance as readers' advisors employed the technique(s) best suited to the circumstances at hand to lead patrons toward serious and purposeful reading. The ASD statement thus enshrined some 90 years of developments and innovations in readers' advisory in a formal, coherent, and multi-dimensional program that retained the same sense of seriousness and purposefulness that readers' advisory had exhibited from its origins.

As an eloquent statement about the continuity of readers' advisory work in the ASD era, one of its first initiatives was the planning and publication of a new series of annotated reading courses. Very much in the tradition of the RWAP series in the 1920s and the 1930s, the new series, called *Reading for an Age of Change* (RFAC), was first proposed in 1958 by Florence Anderson, secretary of the Carnegie Corporation, and enthusiastically supported by the ASD.[515] Funded by a Carnegie grant in 1960, the RFAC series consisted of 10 books of the same general size and style as the RWAP books.[516] Their purpose was also similar: to help readers "comprehend more fully important areas of knowledge" by means of "an essay by a recognized authority surveying the broad outlines of the subject, and an annotated list of books selected by a group of librarians and the author of the essay for background and for understanding current trends and developments."[517] Five RFAC volumes were published in 1962 and 1963, and five more between 1965 and 1968 in contentious circumstances that marked the end of the series.[518] Among the authors were William O. Douglas, an associate justice of the United States Supreme Court, who wrote *Freedom of the Mind*; Robert L. Heilbroner, a lecturer at the New School for Social Research, who wrote *The World of Economics*; Marston Bates, a professor of zoology at the University of Michigan, who wrote *Expanding Population in a Shrinking World*; and Bartlett H. Hays Jr., Director of the Addison Gallery of American Art, who wrote *The Contemporary Arts*. And just like many of the books in the RWAP series, the early volumes in the RFAC series were characterized by an accessible and lively writing style that provided numerous discerning insights for general readers.

Three examples will suffice. In *Freedom of the Mind*, a searching examination of the factors leading to conformity, Douglas identified mass communications, the scientific revolution and technology, and the financial interests funding the scientific revolution, among others, as contributors to the loss of freedom of thought and autonomy in American life.[519] As one of his 12 annotated suggestions for future reading, he included Rachel Carson's *Silent Spring* alongside more traditional choices such as Walter Gelhorn's *American Rights: The Constitution in Action*, thus putting readers on alert that the erosion of freedom was a systemic phenomenon operating on multiple levels.[520] Heilbroner, in *The World of*

Economics, portrayed economics as the science of human tragedy, showing how "[m]an's immediate enemy in seeking to secure his own regular and sufficient provisioning," no matter the system used, has always been the inability to "share out the common harvest among his fellow men."[521] Among his 17 primary and 34 supplementary reading recommendations, he mentioned three titles by Thorstein Veblen, including *The Theory of the Leisure Class* and *The Theory of Business Enterprise*, both sure to give readers trenchant analyses about the roots of American affluence.[522] In *The Contemporary Arts*, Hays suggested that abstract art is profitably understood as music, which "inspires moods and prompts associations which are part of the non-musical matrix of human experience, yet it conveys no precise message to all alike."[523] With 10 plates and 14 lengthy annotations of books for future reading, Hay's book showed how abstract art perfectly signifies the "molecular, atomic, and cosmic realities" of the age.[524] In the 1920s and 1930s, it was said that patrons reading the RWAP volumes would gain "a knowledge greatly superior to that of the average citizen." Those words apply equally to the RFAC series.

In 1962, when the ALA published Helen Huguenor Lyman's *Reader's Guidance Service in a Small Public Library*, readers' advisors still had a ready arsenal of tools with which to reaffirm the public library's "specific role and responsibility to make individuals aware of information and ideas" so that they could embark upon intelligent reading for the purposes of "continuing self-education and enrichment."[525] Lyman recapitulated the purposes of reading guidance and advisory service, which included "help[ing] the random reader or the non-reader become a purposeful reader; "extend[ing] the individual's frontier of knowledge by making possible ever wider reading choices"; and "develop[ing] a lasting interest in ideas" in the reader.[526] To accomplish these goals, public librarians should offer "positive guidance service," defined as "a written plan to be followed in the guidance of all individuals in the use of books for education, information, and enjoyment."[527] And to produce compelling written plans, they should "be familiar with a range of materials representing the knowledge and ideas in the modern world" and be prepared to "advise and counsel" patrons "in personal conversation, consultations, and group activities."[528] In the 1950s and early 1960s, readers' advisory was therefore still operating within the same philosophical framework as in the 1920s and 1930s: the importance of providing meaningful educational opportunities to patrons on significant past and current social, political, and cultural issues through serious and purposeful reading courses and guided group-discussion programs.

Chapter 5

The Devolution
into Entertainment

In addition to the factors discussed in chapter 1 and chapter 2 for the rise of entertainment-oriented readers' advisory in the middle and late 1960s and 1970s, there were two other factors that deserve mention. As a group, these factors coalesced to produce a series of events in the 1980s that mutually reinforced each other, entrenching the "Give 'Em What They Want" philosophy as the basis for public librarianship and allowing genre titles, bestsellers, celebrity-authored books, and prize-winning titles to define the parameters of readers' advisory work.

First, Leigh's *The Public Library in the United States* was not welcomed by everyone. Many observers were taken aback by its emphasis on serving "opinion leaders," who were to be supplied with "the widest possible range of reliable information on which to base their judgments and action" even if that meant "some curtailment of acquisition of popular and general materials."[1] They castigated him for excluding from "the public library's natural audience" three groups: the illiterate or those who were "incapable of learning through reading"; those who "innately lack the capacity to deal with abstract concepts, who cannot generalize beyond a very limited point"; and those who "have little or no serious concern with the world outside their immediate daily surroundings."[2] But, Leigh observed, these groups were already well-served by "commercial agencies of public communication," which provided them with "obvious amusements, sports, and other entertainments, rather than material designed for serious personal enrichment or enlightenment."[3] Public libraries should therefore concentrate on individuals who aspired to "serious personal enrichment and enlightenment" for two reasons: they were invariably "leaders of opinion and culture in their communities" and commercial media do not adequately furnish them with the serious materials they need.[4] These were individuals who exhibited interest in public affairs, science, literature, and art, and they therefore develop "unofficial, informal, and flexible ... circles of influence."[5] Although many of these individuals possessed high levels of formal education, this was not always the case: "In one New England village where the subtle process of influence and discipleship was plotted out in detail, the village barber and a banker's widow were found to be the most-widely accepted leaders of opinion."[6] "[E]xcellent service" to this "existing and potential group of natural library users [has] a social value much greater than the gross numbers involved."[7]

Although Leigh was adamant that "nothing in this general analysis" implied "that furnishing entertainment, relaxation, and escape to people is unimportant," critics accused him of elitism.[8] At best, this was debatable. As he stated, "[t]he public library's concept of audience starts with a definition of services of positive personal and social value and seeks maximum quality and maximum audiences for these services."[9] Public libraries should not offer the services that commercial media do a much better job of offering (i.e., popular fiction for "entertainment, relaxation, and escape"). Public libraries should fill the "social needs" area to which commercial media "do not minister with any adequacy."[10] Then, by using various strategies of active stimulation and guidance, libraries could slowly work toward an "enlargement" of their audience, including the three groups mentioned above.[11] Working in conjunction with other agencies of adult education, public libraries could help to increase "the competence of people to form sound judgments and to realize that they should not only understand about important public problems, but also express their opinions and act in accordance with their judgment."[12] In Leigh's view, by offering popular fiction for "entertainment, relaxation, and escape," public libraries set up "the standards of mass production, distribution, and consumption" as their goals, with inevitable consequences such as the "central purchase of uniformly popular books and periodicals"; staff members "selected for qualities of salesmanship rather than scholarship"; and "results judged entirely in terms of volume of circulation and numbers of users."[13] Public libraries thus abdicated their responsibility to encourage "serious personal enrichment and enlightenment" in the wider community. For Leigh, this abdication was the real elitism, since it naively entrusted the provision of "serious ... enlightenment" to market forces.

Still, many public librarians felt comfortable providing entertainment, with one survey reporting that 83 percent were in favor of circulating popular fiction.[14] In addition to their philosophical objections to Leigh's report, these librarians were responding to the widespread expansion of higher education in the United States after World War II.[15] This expansion was spurred by skyrocketing enrolments that can be traced to the Servicemen's Readjustment Act of 1944 (commonly known as the G. I. Bill), which granted returning veterans up to $500 per year "for tuition, books, fees, and other training costs" at colleges and universities.[16] In the "peak year" of 1947, "veterans accounted for 49 percent of college enrollment,"[17] the same year that a presidential commission proposed that "one-third of all youth should attend college."[18] Formal educational opportunities for veterans and non-veterans abounded, especially in light of Vannevar Bush's 1945 report *Science, the Endless Frontier*, which led to unprecedented federal grants for infrastructure and military and scientific research in the 1950s and 1960s.[19] Money and students poured into colleges and universities, so much so that "between 1960 and 1970, college enrollments jumped from 3.6 to 8 million students, with aggregate expenditures rising from $5.8 to $21.5 billion."[20] One of the most spectacular developments was the redefinition and rebirth of the community college network. Although they "had been a fixture since the early 1900s," their role changed in the early 1960s.[21]

[A] new vision for such an institution—explicit community-relatedness, open-door admissions, and high status for vocational-technical studies—emerged. Soon, every community wanted its own "democracy's college," as community colleges came to be known. In the course of the decade, new community colleges opened for business at the rate of one per week—a total of 500 in ten years. Enrollments soared from 453,000 students to 2.2 million.... [A]lthough two-thirds of the earlier enrollments were in programs designed for transfer to a four-year program, by the 1970s, 80 percent of all community college students were in shorter-term programs—preparing to be engineering technicians, health care workers, law enforcement officers, among dozens of occupations. If a community needed trained workers for a new plant, adult basic education, certificate programs for day-care workers, or English-language training for recent immigrants, its community college was there to respond.[22]

Against the background of these developments, many public librarians believed that Leigh's emphasis on "serious ... enlightenment"—not to mention Learned's vision of a readers' advisor as a college faculty member and fulcrum of an "intelligence center"—were anachronistic because college and university educators had assumed responsibility for meaningful education. As a result, they felt that public libraries were free to focus on entertainment, pleasure, and recreation in the form of popular and ephemeral fiction and nonfiction, which they shrewdly positioned as a service that was more democratic than the service envisioned by Leigh.

Yet, despite the rapid growth of community colleges, colleges, and universities in the 1960s and 1970s, millions of North American residents still lacked the financial resources to attend institutions of higher learning. In times past, these individuals could have turned to public libraries, secure in the knowledge that they would find there a broad array of adult-education opportunities for "serious personal enrichment and enlightenment." In the 1920s and 1930s, adult education at public libraries was mainly delivered through reading courses prepared by knowledgeable readers' advisors, while in the 1940s and 1950s it took the form of group discussions, as well as personal guidance by readers' advisors. But in the post–1963 era, when librarians devoted an increasing amount of their time to valorizing popular culture, these individuals were effectively shut out from opportunities for adult education at public libraries. In their emphasis on "light, quick, escapist" books that were certainly popular but also ephemeral, public librarians contributed to the entrenchment of an entertainment-oriented "society of the spectacle" more concerned with what Lasch termed "[t]he banality of pseudo-self-awareness"[23] than with serious and purposeful reading capable of leading to meaningful education.

Of course, education-based readers' advisory in public libraries did not vanish in a puff of smoke in 1963. It lingered on—an evanescent, almost ghostly, presence whose fate was inexorable. By the middle 1980s, readers' advisory as an activity leading to meaningful education was effectively dead, metaphorically buried by the headlong rush of public librarians toward the rhetorical panacea of user-centered responsiveness. But this rhetoric of responsiveness, most visibly on display in the "Give 'Em What They Want" slogan but also insinuating itself into every aspect of post–1980s' library work, masked an embrace of the structural power of market forces and the narcissistic society of the spectacle. What made this embrace particularly troubling was that public librarians claimed that it was for the benefit of patrons, that post–1980s' entertainment-oriented readers' advisory was superior to pre–1963 readers' advisory based on meaningful education. It was an imposture that bore witness to the evolution of public librarianship in the final two decades of the 20th century.

Vestiges of Readers' Advisory Based on Meaningful Education

From June 29 to July 2, 1965, the University of Wisconsin Library School and the University Extension Division, Department of Library Science, held a Reading Guidance Institute in Madison, Wisconsin, which was attended by 110 librarians.[24] Sponsored by the ASD, the gathered librarians heard from many notable speakers, including Helen Huguenor Lyman, Margaret E. Monroe, and Richard D. Altick, professor of English at Ohio State University (with a specialty in Victorian studies) and author of *The English Common Reader*. Invoking her 1962 publication *Readers' Guidance in a Small Public Library*, Lyman reiterated her beliefs about the ongoing importance of readers' guidance, calling it "an educational process and technique ... [that] must effect learning, that is, bring about changes in the individual involved."[25] Paraphrasing Cyril O. Houle and Charles A. Nelson about the learning process, she stated that reading guidance must be "planned and carried out in ways that will help the individual and the librarian discover [the learner's] 'nature and needs,' utilize a method in which he participates, and finally achieves goals previously determined and which the material and the learning process aimed to fulfill."[26] Readers' advisors must therefore develop "the art of the book" and "the art of annotation," which meant attaining "intellectual maturity" to critically understand and analyze books so that this same maturity can be subsequently passed on to readers.[27]

Like readers' advisors in the 1920s and 1930s, Lyman believed that the individual consultation, which required "privacy, [a] quiet and relaxed atmosphere, and sufficient time to establish confidence," was the preferred method for ensuring that patrons reach their learning goals and achieve intellectual maturity.[28] Only then could annotated reading courses be created "to effect a cumulative learning experience"; these courses had "purpose and direction" because "[t]he selections are arranged in a sequence designed to help the reader progress through the development of content and ideas."[29] Other techniques—such as the creation of reader-interest files, notification services, guidance in building a home library, topical lists, book talks, and group discussion—were also helpful insofar as they increased patrons' knowledge in a systematic and cumulative way about diverse topics. Monroe agreed, situating readers' advisory as "a service relationship to the reader with an educational objective; a commitment to encouraging and enabling the reader increasingly to exercise critical judgment in the use of books and to exercise intellectual freedom by the widest possible examination of relevant materials."[30] The goal of this "fundamental" service was "intensive, purposeful, increasingly independent book use" by patrons who willingly take on the work of "self-education."[31]

Altick was even more adamant than Lyman and Monroe that readers' advisory should be directed toward meaningful education, especially in the 1960s, which he characterized as a decade populated by "millions whom we might call the disadvantaged educated" because of "the mass education to which our society is committed."[32] For him, it was precisely because of "the frantic expansion" of the college and university system that public libraries should (re)commit themselves to providing patrons with the opportunity to gain a liberal education, since "the intellectual level of American higher education, low though it has already been, is bound to fall much lower in the next few years" because of "the radically altered requirements of this age of specialized technologies."[33] Public librarians must therefore become "surrogate teacher[s]" who guide readers to the best reading in all fields, including imaginative literature: "[i]f anyone is to spend some time reading ... he might as well read novels or plays or essays or poems of recognized literary worth."[34] They must be "well-informed critic[s]," not "routine dispenser[s] of information," possessing "the ability to discriminate between shoddy books and sound ones; and [they] must always have in mind [their] responsibility for directing the reader, not merely to convenient books about a subject, but to the books that ... can be trusted."[35]

For this to occur, there must be a reconceptualization of librarianship in general and readers' advisory in particular because, currently, readers' advisors mechanically suggest books based on criteria of "convenience [and] recency,"[36] not quality or truth. They recommend biographical "technicolor confections" or "sensational sociology,"[37] not to mention books that are reviewed in popular reviewing and reference tools, such as *Guide to Reference Books, Book Week, Saturday Review*, the *New York Times Book Review*, or the *New York Review of Books*.[38] In these reviewing publications, "approval and even high praise are continually being meted out to books which dismay, and sometimes veritably outrage, the people who really know the subjects under discussion."[39] Readers' advisors should therefore "make themselves as knowledgeable as they can be about the differences between books which are superficially authoritative and those which are genuinely so."[40] One way to do so is to undertake "considerable advanced academic work in one or more of the various disciplines, so that they have been exposed to and, hopefully, have acquired as part of their permanent professional equipment an acute sense of critical discrimination ... [and] an abiding awareness that certain standards of scholarly dependability apply to books in all fields of knowledge."[41] Only by differentiating "between books that are meretricious in substance and manner and books that are readable and dependable" could readers' advisors hope to fill their "growing responsibility as an educator who teaches outside the classroom."[42]

As Lynn E. Birge observed, the Institute "encouraged many librarians to return to their libraries with renewed commitment to individualized library service."[43] One indication of this commitment was that, by mid–1972, despite widespread departmentalization of public libraries into subject areas staffed by specialists, 23 American public libraries of various sizes had a "fully designated position, reader's adviser or its equivalent, whose responsibility it was to suggest, guide and develop patron's book reading habits."[44] Three libraries stated that this service was provided "upon request." Another two libraries offered a "Reader Interest Service," where patrons were notified when the library received new books that matched their indicated reading interests.[45] Readers' advisors spent "from three-quarters to almost all their time working on an individual basis" with patrons; remaining time was spent "in reading and other background work."[46]

Another indication that readers' advisory was still deemed important was a growing interest in the application of bibliotherapy to public librarianship. This interest reached a peak in the middle and late 1970s with the publication of three books devoted to various aspects of bibliotherapy: Eleanor Frances Brown's *Bibliotherapy and Its Widening Applications*; Rhea Joyce Rubin's *Using Bibliotherapy: A Guide to Theory and Practice*; and Rubin's *Bibliotherapy Sourcebook*.[47] This interest was catalyzed by a special issue devoted to bibliotherapy in 1962 in *Library Trends*,[48] a bibliotherapy workshop held in 1964,[49] and Margaret C. Hannigan's "Counseling and Bibliotherapy for the General Reader," delivered at the Reading Guidance Institute in 1965.[50] Although most of the discussion about bibliotherapy revolved around its application to institutional settings, its role vis-à-vis general readers at public libraries was also invoked. In this context, Evalene P. Jackson's "Bibliotherapy and Reading Guidance: A Tentative Approach to Theory" was important.[51] Jackson argued that, since "education is not clearly separable from therapy" and "[t]he librarian is apparently attempting to educate by means of books," reading can have therapeutic properties for library patrons insofar as books may reduce alienation, thus "counteracting the meagerness of the environment and the limits of those who are parts of interpersonal situations."[52]

Jackson referred extensively to Caroline Shrodes's 1949 dissertation *Bibliotherapy: A Theoretical and Clinical-Experimental Study*,[53] which explained that literature was "an instance of the process of symbolization" such that characters, themes, events, moods, and conversations in books become "symbolic equivalents" of actual experiences in the lives of readers.[54] By undergoing a process of identification, transference, and catharsis with regard to the situations presented to them in imaginative literature, readers gained important insights about themselves and their environments.[55] Most importantly, "[s]ince it is in the nature of man to move toward something larger than the individual self," literature "permits the reader to consider and weigh the relative satisfaction inherent in a diverse number of occupations and professions, and to evaluate a variety of ways and means of achieving 'the good life.'"[56] It also allows readers to "examine the joys that come from mature human relationships, from the enjoyment of nature and of the arts, from the explorations of science and philosophy, from the dedication to causes greater than the self."[57] For Shrodes, it was important to know in great detail the life stories and circumstances of individuals to whom a book was recommended: only then could a suggested book serve a meaningful therapeutic purpose.[58] And if the examples of effective therapeutic literature that she presented were any indication, she believed that classic literature was an inexhaustible source of significant insights about matters "larger than the individual self": Eugene O'Neill's *The Great God Brown*; John Steinbeck's *The Grapes of Wrath*; numerous Shakespearean plays; James Joyce; Marcel Proust; Virginia Woolf's *To the Lighthouse*; Samuel Butler's *The Way of All Flesh*; D. H. Lawrence's *Sons and Lovers*; and Sherwood Anderson's *Winesburg, Ohio*.[59]

The rich potential that Jackson saw in Shrodes's approach for general readers led her to suggest that "[t]he education of some librarians should also include advanced courses in psychology and literature."[60] Here she echoed Bryan's 1939 recommendations that "library schools should include in their curriculum a course in psychological adjustments, designed to give the librarian the background he needs for understanding the psychology of the reader" or that public libraries "should employ a consulting psychologist, either full- or part-time, to cooperate with the readers' adviser in diagnosing the needs and problems of readers who appear to require this service."[61] Jackson, like Bryan, believed that readers' advisory was crucial work. Librarians therefore required extensive specialized knowledge to perform it well, especially because she foresaw that "[w]hile imaginative literature is promising" as a start for meaningful readers' advisory, "there are times when carefully planned courses designed to provide a more formal learning experience will be required."[62] Despite Jackson's article, bibliotherapy in public libraries in the 1960s and 1970s came to be associated almost exclusively with working with special and/or troubled groups, including recently released patients from psychiatric institutions, patients at local hospitals and retirement homes, and troubled teenagers as identified by school counselors, social workers, or psychologists.[63] As bibliotherapy gradually returned to its clinical roots, its developmental possibilities for general readers were de-emphasized.

A final indication of interest in education-based readers' advisory was the participation of some public libraries in the "non-traditional education" movement, which was analyzed in 1971 by the Commission on Non-Traditional Study (CNTS), sponsored by the College Entrance Examination Board (CEEB) and the Educational Testing Service (ETS) and funded by the Carnegie Corporation.[64] CNTS was chaired by Samuel B. Gold, chancellor emeritus of the State University of New York, with significant contributions from Cyril O. Houle, among others. It produced the report *Diversity by Design*.[65] As defined by the CNTS, non-traditional education "has concern for the learner of any age and circumstance, for the degree aspirant as well as the person who finds sufficient reward in enriching life through constant, periodic or occasional study."[66] It started from the premise that, despite the rapid expansion of educational institutions in the past three decades, "there is a quickened and even urgent sense that the long-sought dream of universal and broadly based educational opportunities is still much too far from accomplishment."[67] The CNTS thus recommended that "[t]he public library should be strengthened to become a far more powerful instrument for non-traditional education than is now the case" because there is "a very large group of people outside the formal structure of education with obvious educational needs."[68] Castigating public libraries for being "passive conveyors of information or recreation, available when needed, but not playing, or expected to play, active roles in the educational process," the CNTS suggested that public libraries should return to their historic roots, becoming "the primary community resource for individual intellectual growth."[69] The public library should once again see itself as "literally a college around the corner."[70] But the CNTS recognized that this transformation would not be an easy one, since there would be inevitable "[c]onflicts" between a vision of the public library as an educational center and "those who favor the library as a cultural center or as a place for undirected reading, recreation, and information-giving."[71] Still, if public libraries truly wanted to provide "unlimited knowledge" and "unlimited opportunity" for individuals from all walks of life, they should become "active planners and collaborators" in educational programs.[72]

Some libraries did not wait for the completed CNTS report to develop innovative programs. In 1971, the Dallas Public Library (DaPL) implemented its "Independent Study Project" (ISP); the Denver Public Library's "On Your Own" and Chicago Public Library's "Study Unlimited" projects were also significant. ISP was undertaken in partnership with the CEEB through its College Level Examination Program (CLEP). The CEEB had "become increasingly involved in nontraditional education" and, through CLEP, "provided opportunities for obtaining college credit in a variety of subjects by passing nationally standardized exams."[73] Officials at the CEEB, led by Jose Orlando Toro, who was then assistant director of its CLEP program, presented DaPL leaders with a plan in which the public library would become "a Counseling and Independent Study Center for Achieving a Two-Year College Education."[74] Toro hoped that public libraries would build on the readers' advisory service that they had offered in the past, expanding it "into a more complete educational guidance and counseling activity" so that they would become "more involved in assisting independent students."[75] The result was the DaPL-ISP, which cooperated with Southern Methodist University "in assisting adults pursuing self-education directed to academic recognition in area colleges and universities and [in providing] information about those and other colleges and universities."[76]

Encouraged by the success of the DaPL-ISP, the CEEB developed the Adult Independent Learning (AIL) project in 1973, with Toro as its director. Together with the CNTS, Toro believed that public libraries were not living up to their vast potential, confining themselves to an "informal" role that, because it lacked "purpose and direction," was tantamount to a "happening."[77] Again, Toro placed readers' advisory at the core of the AIL, observing that properly trained readers' advisors could "[h]elp the learner plan a program of study" and "[g]uid[e] the learner in the selection and use of study materials."[78] Within the parameters of the AIL, the term readers' advisors eventually became learners' advisors, whose task it was to conduct interviews with interested individuals "concerning personal goals and interests, educational attainments and experience, and then, based on the accrued information, the librarian helped the individual assess the nature of the intended learning project and locate appropriate resources."[79] In this way, the library became a "library-college," where the independent learner "formulates his or her own curriculum, choosing with the librarian's help basic treatments of the subject ... while discovering autonomously other relevant materials within the range of personal intellectual capacity."[80] As the learner continued to work with the learners' advisor, "a sense of inner order and unity" arose as "concepts are successively mastered," to the extent that the learner could begin to compare concepts, which led "to the formulation of judgments and even to new conceptual systems and insights."[81] Eleven large public libraries participated in the AIL, including Salt Lake City (Utah) and Atlanta (Georgia),[82] with 86.9 percent of learners' advisors helping students "select materials" for study and 60 percent of them helping students "develop [a] study plan."[83]

To judge by the words of Gerald R. Shields, many librarians looked askance at AIL-like projects. Labeling the AIL movement as "circus time" and "a big, ornate, and gaudy bandwagon" that public librarians should let "pass by, horns blowing as if it were midnight," Shields stated that participation in AIL programs would compromise libraries' independence, not to mention their limited financial resources.[84] "We must remember that libraries are independent places for independent people. They must remain that way. We can not afford to go the route of U.S. mass education, or we, too, will be an institution that the learner will shun."[85] However, as Birge observed, this reticence often served as "a screen, utilized by many librarians who still were unable to embrace a change in professional emphasis, from educational support through materials collection, organization, and supply to direct educational services through mediation between library and community resources and adult learners, involving individual guidance and the increased responsibility of the librarian in such service."[86] By 1978, the AIL had disappeared from public libraries as "the influence of [its] goals, objectives, and ideals ... rapidly waned and professional interest and concern were largely redirected."[87] Its disappearance also represented the symbolic disappearance of any vestigial trace of readers' advisory for the purpose of meaningful education. The "happening" mindset referred to by Toro, already present in post–1963 public libraries, was slowly but surely colonizing the entire public-library landscape.

The Legitimization of Popular Culture

While the increased presence of popular culture in post–1963 public libraries was closely tied to the Baltimore County Public Library (BCPL) and its "Give 'Em What They Want" slogan, there were broad socio-cultural currents and philosophical principles that enabled "Give 'Em What They Want" to gain legitimacy. We discussed these in chapter 2. Wanting to see their institutions as forward-looking participants in the wave of dissent washing over American society, librarians began to cast a critical eye at the long-esteemed educational mandate of public libraries, associating that mandate with oppressive social structures and phenomena. As they demonized meaningful education and the serious fiction and nonfiction books that inevitably led to it, they valorized their opposites: the genre titles, bestsellers, celebrity-authored books, and prize-winning titles that led to narcissistic edutainment for their middle- and upper-middle-class users. The idea that public libraries should be responsive to users' demands became a timely and attractive justification to turn libraries away from their traditional role as institutions dedicated to meaningful education. At the same time, the idea of responsiveness steered public librarianship toward a business model emphasizing maximum consumption of a product at the least cost to the organization delivering the product—a model that initiated the process of deskilling in libraries.

We can see the structural framework behind the "Give 'Em What They Want" approach in an interview with Charlie Robinson and Jean-Barry Molz, director and deputy director of the BCPL, respectively, from the early 1960s until their dual retirements in 1996.[88] When they first arrived at the BCPL, they were intent on making it a "good library" that contained "the definitive works of literature."[89] But they soon realized that this aspiration was "ridiculous" and "insane," and so they adopted a policy whereby a book that failed to circulate, no matter how important, was not retained. The "Give 'Em What They Want" approach was born. How-to books on lawn care and heat pumps became mainstays of the collection rather than culturally and historically important literature, a stance made all the more convenient by Robinson's assertion that "[g]reat literature puts me instantly to sleep. I read military histories, Tom Clancy, and how-to books."[90] Here, then, was a succinct encapsulation of the "Give 'Em What They Want" approach: entertainment-oriented genre fiction and how-to books. It was the late 20th-century version of Agnes Hill's "librarianship by automatic figures,"[91] where librarians mechanically handed out books as if they worked in a "ticket-office," and Johnson's "pure librarianship," where librarians encouraged patrons "to carry away an armful of westerns or detective stories."[92]

Little wonder that the BCPL became know as "the best seller library" and "the bookstore library."[93] Furthermore, Robinson and Molz believed that "jobs, housing, and education" were problems that "[l]ibraries can't do anything about."[94] The task of public libraries was to supply multiple copies of high-demand books for entertainment, pleasure, and recreation to the middle class. To this end, Robinson and Molz preferred to run their library with paraprofessionals, seeing no value in graduate library education. "The library degree is very important for keeping the mayor's cousin out of the library and as a union card. Other than that, we can teach people more library skills over a year than a library school can."[95] Graduate library schools taught students too much about the philosophical aspects of librarianship and not enough about needed practical skills; besides, they argued, paraprofessionals were more cost-effective.[96] In this regard, Robinson proudly compared public libraries with banks, which trained employees to perform their jobs without thinking about larger philosophical questions. It was a telling comment about how business models defined the BCPL's conception of library work.

It was no accident that the BCPL's emphasis on the "Give 'Em What They Want" approach was linked with its beliefs about the benefits of cost-effective paraprofessionals. Just as the BCPL minimized the importance of "the definitive works of literature," it also minimized the importance of librarians dedicated to achieving meaningful educational opportunities for patrons through the kind of thoughtful book-selection processes described by Haines in *Living with Books*. Purchasing genre titles, bestsellers, celebrity-authored books, and prize-winning titles was a mechanical procedure that could be done from a centralized location by paraprofessionals specifically trained for this task. Robinson was more than caustic about the way in which librarians had heretofore practiced collection development, judging it to be an unproductive waste of time that resulted in the selection of unread books. Collection development could therefore be deskilled. Knowledgeable and critical evaluation about books on the part of librarians was no longer necessary, since high-demand was the only valid criteria. And because it was not within the purview of public libraries to think about providing meaningful educational opportunities for patrons through serious fiction and nonfiction, professional librarians were superfluous. In effect, the BCPL contended that library work could be deskilled because the print materials in public libraries were being de-intellectualized in order to show that libraries were not plodding, irrelevant, and undemocratic institutions focused on "the definitive works of literature" that Robinson said put people "instantly to sleep." Instead, they were lively and "happening" venues focused on empowering patrons by mechanically giving them what they wanted, when they wanted it: multiple copies of ephemeral fiction and nonfiction.[97] It was a policy shift that was perfectly in tune with the ephemerality and narcissism of the times, captured in Robinson's self-assessment that he quickly lost interest in things and Molz's characterization of him as someone with "a short attention span."[98]

If collections were now to be developed mechanically by paraprofessionals working in the BCPL ethos, it was only a short time until someone suggested that readers' advisory should also be mechanized and automated. In a 1965 article entitled "Advisers Anonymous, Arise!" May Shortt, Assistant Librarian at the Bathurst Heights Branch of the North York (Ontario) Public Library, did just that. Convinced that public libraries should be officially recognized as "the true temples of pop art" and be proud of "the aesthetic qualities" of the literary equivalents of "comic strips, advertisements and plaster sundaes," Shortt regretted that library schools did not teach future librarians about popular fiction titles written by authors such as Georgette Heyer, Elizabeth Seifert, Victor Canning, and Dennis Wheatley.[99] Her scorn of librarians who dared speak to patrons about Tolstoy or Charlotte Brontë instead of Leon Uris or Isabella Holt was palpable: "If the library schools are to cease unloading broken reeds on the public each year, they must gear their advisory courses to the fiction the students will have to work with.... Think not because we are virtuous there shall be no more *Peyton Place*."[100] But, she continued, the hope that library schools will suddenly start discussing "popular writers who happen to be second- or third-rate" is unrealistic, and so "[a]ll things considered, the time may be ripe for automating advisory work."[101]

> Probably some library down in New Jersey or California already has a simple punch-card system on the job. The patron pushes one of a series of buttons indicating the type of story desired: Family—Love—Humour—Doctors, and then chooses between Historical/Modern[,] English/American[,] Long/Short. The machine, which is stocked with cards representing the whole collection, selects all the titles meeting the indicated tastes, and delivers a list of sure-fire suggestions.[102]

She thus foresaw a time when all public libraries had "Advisermatiks, which give you a title and not an argument when you ask for a good book."[103]

Building on the Waples-led scientific movement to define books by their component parts and presciently anticipating the development of electronic databases such as NoveList, Shortt was an inadvertent visionary whose proposal for "Advisermatiks" was made half in jest, half in earnest. Nevertheless, she worked from the same premises as the BCPL. She believed that the purpose of public libraries was to be as responsive as possible. If patrons wanted popular fiction and other entertainment-oriented literature, then readers' advisors, in as mechanical and efficient a manner as possible, should direct them to, for example, humorous family novels featuring romance and doctors, or to the novels of Georgette Heyer or Leon Uris. In all cases, readers' advisors must forego the "broken reed" temptation to elevate reading tastes and provide meaningful education through serious literature. Here we catch an echo of Lindsay Swift's 1899 characterization of "the feeble and incomplete" individuals who wanted to turn libraries into "quasi-educational institutions" instead of venues for independent readers who wanted robust and vigorous books. For Shortt, popular culture, whether in the form of comic strips, plaster sundaes, or third-rate novels, had "aesthetic qualities" that made it inherently worthy. Public libraries first had to ensure that they mechanically and cost-effectively purchased sufficient stock of these high-demand items. Then they had to ensure that they mechanically and efficiently suggested these same titles to patrons by disassembling a book into as many component parts as possible, thus facilitating the matching of components to patrons. As collection development and readers' advisory were framed in these terms, little room remained for knowledgeable librarians thoughtfully creating meaningful educational opportunities for patrons through recommendations of serious fiction and nonfiction. Taken together, the beliefs of Robinson, Molz, and Shortt legitimized the participation of public libraries and readers' advisory not only in the age of edutainment, but also in a deprofessionalized and deskilled work environment relying on mechanical procedures and "librarianship by automatic figures." "Pure librarianship" was on its way to becoming deskilled librarianship.

The Return of Agglutinative Lists

Once it was accepted that public libraries should have responsive collections consisting largely of popular fiction and nonfiction, it was a small step to suggest that the current alphabetical-by-author shelving system was difficult for patrons to navigate as they searched for books. As Annelise Mark Pejtersen remarked, existing organization systems were of little help to patrons looking for "an exciting book, but not with too many problems or politics."[104] They did not "make it easier for the user to find the type of novel desired"[105] because those systems did not take into account the "subjective and subconscious reading criteria of users."[106] To help solve these problems, attempts at developing fiction classification systems were undertaken during the late 1970s and early 1980s. Many of these explored the utility of classifying fiction by genre. But unlike the fiction classification systems developed by Rathbone and Borden in the 1900s, whose central aim was to elevate the reading tastes of patrons, the systems proposed in the late 1970s and 1980s revolved around making it easy for patrons to find books within their preferred genres, which had the corollary benefit for libraries of increasing circulation statistics, which in their eyes testified to their public value. This in turn meant that, since their value was already established by demand-driven circulation statistics based on entertainment-oriented reading, public libraries need not concern themselves with demonstrating their value in other ways, such as the provision of meaningful educational opportunities through the reading of serious literature.

In 1978, Pejtersen began working toward a thematic approach to classifying fiction that, as her examples suggested, was oriented toward genre.[107] Thus, under the broad user-defined rubrics of "subject matter," "frame," "author's intention/attitude," and "accessibility," she located genres such as mysteries, love stories, family chronicles, humor, historical novels, psychological suspense, and action/adventure books. In 1988, Sharon L. Baker conducted an experiment in which she physically separated romances and mysteries from the regular fiction collection at three small branches of the Davidson County (North Carolina) Public Library system and appended genre-identifying spine labels to interfiled romances at one of these branches.[108] She compared circulation statistics for these two experimental groups with control groups of romance and mysteries that were not labeled nor physically separated. Physically separating romances and mysteries from the general collection increased their circulation. Moreover, "the size of the circulation increase of the *classed* titles was directly related to the library's size"[109]; the larger the library's overall collection, the larger the increase of classed-title circulation. Increased circulation was also found for labeled and interfiled romance novels, as well as for other less-popular genre titles within a specific genre. Baker concluded that "fiction classification appears to narrow the patron's selection to the desired genre category, while at the same time decreasing his reliance on known authors and broadening his use of books by other authors within that genre."[110] Baker's results were replicated by Jeffrey Cannell and Eileen McCluskey in the Cumberland County (North Carolina) Public Library system, where they undertook physical separation of genre categories such as science fiction and mysteries.[111] Calling their plan "genrefication," they pointed to a total circulation rate increase of 36 percent in their target branch library, commenting that patrons who were unable to find a new book by their favorite author likely found themselves standing in front of and borrowing books by authors "who have similar stories to tell."[112]

Public libraries intuitively knew that genrefication worked, but these studies gave added impetus to an implementation of genre-identification systems. In a survey of 49 public libraries serving a population of 100,000 or more, Gail Harrell found in 1984 that 46 of them used genre-identification techniques such as distinct shelving and spine labels. Of the 26 genre categories identified, the five most popular were: science fiction/fantasy (98 percent); westerns (96 percent); mysteries/suspense (93 percent); short stories (28 percent); and love/romance (20 percent). Other categories included biographies, adventure, humor, movie and TV, psychological, and prizewinners. In an expanded version of the survey in 1993 that included 86 libraries serving populations of 50,000 or more, Harrell again found 26 genre categories being used. Not counting the addition of the "large print" category in 1993, the five most popular genre-identification categories in 1984 were also the most popular in 1993.[113]

Even more impetus to genrefication was given by the appearance of the *Genreflecting* series, which made its debut in 1982 and whose spectacular growth we discussed in chapter 1. There was a flagship *Genreflecting*, which covered all genres, and there were also separate volumes that dealt exclusively with one genre. *Genreflecting* owed its birth to Betty Rosenberg, a former senior lecturer at the Graduate School of Library Science, University of California, Los Angeles. Rosenberg's "First Law of Reading," which was "Never apologize for your reading tastes," served as a justification for her "blissfully squandered reading life" spent among genre fiction and "read[ing] only what I enjoyed."[114] Positioning genre fiction as an important aspect of popular culture that had incurred the wrath of intellectuals throughout the ages but that, starting in the 1960s, had begun to be respectfully studied and analyzed in universities, Rosenberg saw it as a welcome entertainment-oriented antidote to "the exigencies of a formal education."[115] "[I]ts intent is to divert and amuse, to hold the mind in enjoyment. Reading for pleasure is carefree; purposeful reading to improve the mind is not within its province. Not for genre fiction is the evasion used by early writers for children; to edify *and* amuse, the amusement a tool to ensure edification."[116] Rosenberg's statement caught the spirit of 1960s' New Left cultural dissent, rhetorically equating edification with "early writers for children" and situating meaningful education as the preserve of antiquated individuals such as Edmund Wilson, whom she quoted as saying that detective novels were intellectually degrading.[117] For Rosenberg, Wilson—"widely regarded as the preeminent American man of letters of the twentieth century"; the author of influential essays on English, American, Russian, and French classic authors; and a guiding force in the conception of *The Library of America* series[118]—was someone upon whom to heap scorn, an emblem of the period 1920–1950 whose time had passed and who would mercifully be submerged by waves of popular culture, which would provide people with much-needed carefree entertainment and pleasure masquerading as edutainment.

One of the characteristic features of the *Genreflecting* volumes, whether flagship or genre-specific, was their reliance on what Johnson in 1938 in *The Public Library—A People's University* had called agglutinative lists, whose central purpose was to "produce impressive statistical results."[119] Johnson suggested that these were the easiest kinds of lists for librarians to make, contrasting them with lists that had clear developmental and educational value and that took time, thought, and knowledge to create. The second major feature of the *Genreflecting* volumes was the division of fiction into ever-smaller sub-genres and sub-sub-genres such as comic horror, science fiction detective stories, or historical romantic suspense. Each of the six editions of the flagship *Genreflecting* provides good examples of the agglutinative technique and microscopic sub-divisions, but the fifth edition by Diana Tixier Herald is particularly illuminating.[120] After brief overviews of the major genres, Herald compiled lengthy list after lengthy list of sub-genres and sub-sub-genres. Under the Horror genre, the sub-genres included: Cosmic Paranoia; Demonic Possession and Exorcism; Haunted Houses; Witches and Warlocks; Monsters; Vampires; Satanism, Demonology, and Black Magic; Animals Run Rampant, Werewolves; Mind Control; Medical Horror and Evil Science; Psychological Horror; and Splatterpunk.[121] Under the Fantasy and Science Fiction Romance sub-genre of the Romance genre, sub-sub-genres included Time Travel; Paranormal Beings; and Futuristic/Science Fiction.[122] Under the Womanly Romance sub-genre of the Romance genre, sub-sub-genres included Soap Opera and Fantasies of Passion.[123] The Science Fiction genre had 29 sub-genres, including Psionic Powers and Detectives in Science Fiction, while the western genre had 32 sub-genres, including Hired Man on Horseback and Celebrity Characters.[124] Most of the lists under each of the sub-genres or sub-sub-genres were comprised of unannotated titles that often stretched on for pages at a time. The Alien Beings sub-genre of the Science Fiction genre contained 77 unannotated titles by 47 authors.[125] The sub-genre Political Intrigue and Terrorism of the Adventure genre contained 77 unannotated titles by 59 authors.[126] In the Parallel Worlds sub-genre of the Fantasy genre, there were 114 titles, five of which had annotations ranging from 2 to 44 words, by 35 authors.[127]

The genre-specific *Genreflecting* volumes followed the same general pattern as the flagship title, but with more frequent and longer annotations. *Hooked on Horror* sub-divided the horror genre into 13 sub-genres, including Telekinesis and Hypnosis; Small Town Horror; Technohorror; Ecological Horror; and Comic Horror.[128] *Christian Fiction* contained sub-genres such as Romancing the West and Fantasy and Science Fiction, with sub-sub-genres such as Romantic Westerns; Historical Romance; Problem Romance; Unequally Yoked; Alternate Universe; and Spiritual Warfare.[129] *Fluent in Fantasy* contained 16 sub-genres, including Shared Worlds; A Bestiary; and Dark Fantasy, with sub-sub-genres such as Wizards, Sorcerers, and Enchantresses; The Human Condition; and Shapeshifters.[130] *Historical Fiction*, one of the largest *Genreflecting* volumes at 813 pages, contained 13 sub-genres, including Historical Fantasy; Time-Slip Novels; Historical Thrillers; Christian Historical Fiction; Literary Historical Novels; Historical Mysteries; Adventures in History; and Sagas. Each of these had multiple sub-sub-genres. The sub-genre of Sagas included the sub-sub-genres of Sagas with a Sense of Place and Glitz, Glamour, and Riches. Under the sub-genre of Adventures in History, sub-sub-genres such as Swashbuckling Adventure and Exotic Adventure were included. Under the Time-Slip Novels sub-genre, there were three sub-sub-genres: Time Travel; Reincarnation; and Past in the Present. One of these, Time Travel, contained four additional sub-sub-sub-genres, including Romantic and Science Fiction.[131] Given the characteristics of the *Genreflecting* series described here, Johnson's indictment of agglutinative lists in the late 1930s as an abdication of librarians' responsibility for meaningful education also applied in the early 2000s.

The idea of genrefication became so popular that prize-winning titles evolved into a separate genre. Consider that, in the NoveList database, under the "Browse Lists" tab, the first option presented was "Best Fiction," defined as "Awards, honors, and recommended lists." Under the subsequent "Literary" sub-division, this option contained 36 awards, prizes, and "notable" lists.[132] By making prize-winning books a genre of its own, readers' advisors enshrined the notion that fiction was no longer primarily to be read because of intrinsic worth, cultural value, or historical and social importance. Rather, it was to be read because it had been deemed a winner in what English referred to as "the economy of prestige,"[133] the supreme accolade in a culture obsessed with making social comparisons in every area. As well, "classics" evolved into its own genre category, symbolically turning these books into just another market segment instead of the cornerstone of meaningful education.

While genre identification of fiction ostensibly started out as a way to make it easier for patrons to find exactly the type of novel they were looking for, it also effectively fragmented the reading public into a bewildering array of specialized micro-niches consisting of avid readers breathlessly waiting for the next novel. Urged on by publishers, authors catered to locked-in audiences for specific sub-genres and sub-sub-genres by repeatedly including what had been determined to be the most popular elements of those sub-genres and sub-sub-genres in new novels. Often there were rules established by publishers "governing plot and characters," as well as "taboos."[134] Just as often genre authors wrote under multiple pseudonyms for the purpose of turning out as many titles as possible—about one a month—to feed the seemingly insatiable market for them.[135] Genre fiction was nothing less than Bourdieu's industrial literature, an important constituent of Debord's society of the spectacle. It certainly raised the circulation statistics of public libraries, but it also made them venues where the economic logic and power of commercial cultural producers was consecrated.

Toward Profiling

Because much of the popularity of genre fiction stemmed from the fact that each sub-genre and sub-sub-genre had its own set of conventions and rules, each book was highly structured and formulaic, with many recognizable components that specifically appealed to the audience of that sub-genre or sub-sub-genre. This characteristic of genre fiction was an important factor in the development of Saricks and Brown's appeal-elements theory, which became a progressively more important part of each of the three editions (published in 1989, 1997, 2005) of their *Readers' Advisory Service in the Public Library*, the last of which Saricks wrote without Brown. Saricks retired in 2004 after nearly 27 years as the Literature and Audio Services coordinator at the Downers Grove (Illinois) Public Library, located in a wealthy Chicago suburb.[136] In 1989, Saricks and Brown wrote that "[w]hen readers' advisors begin grouping books together into genres," the question of appeal was uppermost in their mind: "[i]n studying each genre, we first tried to identify the genre's appeal elements and its standardized patterns."[137] By 1997, appeal-elements theory was fully formed. It argued that reading choices were dependent on pacing, characterization, story line, and frame,[138] a fourfold division that may have been inspired by Pejtersen's 1978 discussion about "subject matter," "frame," "author's intention/attitude," and "accessibility." Taken together, appeal elements described "more accurately the 'feel' of a book ... and reveal more of [a] novel's essence."[139]

It was therefore important for readers' advisors to take a "systematic approach" to understanding which elements "singly and in combination, seem to address the ways in which books affect readers."[140] To this end, each of the four main elements was sub-divided: pacing had eight sub-elements; characterization had seven; and story line and frame each had three. Under pacing, readers were asked to define their preferences in the following terms: "Are characters and plot quickly revealed or slowly unveiled?"; "Is there more dialogue or description?"; "Is the book densely written?"; "Are there short sentences, short paragraphs, and short chapters?"; "Are there multiple plot lines, flashbacks, alternating chapters related from different points of view; or is there a straight-line plot?"; "Do characters act or react to events?"; "Is the book end oriented or open ended?"; and "What is the pattern of the pacing?"[141] Under characterization, readers were asked to define their preferences as follows: "Are the characters developed over time, or are they stereotypes we recognize immediately?"; "Is the focus on a single character or on several whose lives are intertwined?"; "What is the point of view from which the story is told?"; "Is characterization the most important aspect of the book?"; "Is the reader expected to identify with the characters or observe them?"; "Are there series characters, followed through and developed over several related novels?"; and "Are there memorable and important secondary characters?"[142] Finally, under story line and frame, readers were asked to consider the following questions: "Does the story emphasize people or situations and events?"; "What is the author's intention in regard to story line?"; "Is the focus of the story more interior and psychological or exterior or action oriented?"; "Is the background detailed or minimal?"; "Does the frame affect the tone or atmosphere?"; and "Is there a special background frame?"[143] In 2005, Saricks developed a detailed checklist of terms describing each appeal element, and readers' advisors were urged to use the list as a guide to further pinpoint patrons' reading preferences.[144]

Once readers' advisors elicited this detailed information about preferred components, they were theoretically able to make a mechanical match between the patrons' preferences and a book meeting those preferences. Genre identification thus subtly merged with the idea of appeal elements, forming a toxic mix that disassembled books into their component parts. This merger was perhaps best on display in Saricks's *The Readers' Advisory Guide to Genre Fiction* (2001), where each of 15 genres was dissected from the perspective of its appeal elements, then listed in tabular form.[145] Books became commodities whose value was judged on the altar of user satisfaction and on the presence or absence of features or elements. The idea of appeal elements became so popular that in Nancy Pearl's *Now Read This: A Guide to Mainstream Fiction, 1978–1998* and *Now Read This II: A Guide to Mainstream Fiction, 1990–2001*, books were subdivided according to the four appeal elements of setting, story, characters, and language, further entrenching fiction as something that should be selected on the basis of component parts instead of overall factors related to artistic value and cultural importance.[146] Popular fiction reigned supreme, whether in the form of genre titles, bestsellers, celebrity-authored books, or prize-winning titles, since they were part of a safe and predictable entertainment universe in which patrons indicated their preferred appeal elements in order to customize their experience to their exact specifications. It was also a universe where standards of literary and cultural excellence were eschewed. As Saricks and Brown stated, "readers' advisors do not measure books by literary and critical standards, but by readers' perceptions,"[147] which meant that they should not "recommend" titles to patrons, but rather "suggest" titles.[148] And, in an attempt to be as non-judgmental as possible, readers' advisors were told not to refer to a book as "slow paced," but instead use the phrase "*slowly unfolding*."[149]

The readers' advisory interview in the post–1980 era was therefore different from the interviews described in chapter 4. Similarly, the recommended background knowledge for readers' advisors in the post–1980 era was different from the backgrounds of readers' advisors in the 1920s and 1930s, since post–1980 readers' advisory was almost exclusively concerned with popular fiction and nonfiction. Interviews no longer took place in a separate room with a designated readers' advisor, precluding the kind of serious discussion that was the first step to the creation of a reading course leading to meaningful education. Instead, they were "conversations" between staff members and patrons about books that occurred as staff members worked at "busy service desks" answering all types of questions.[150] Because this conversation "usually occurs in an open area, it is rarely a two-person encounter," with numerous "eavesdroppers" who "chime in with their impressions."[151] In other words, we re-entered the world of Rachel Rhoades and Laura Speck, both of whom had omnibus duties and therefore could only make the most superficial of reading suggestions.

The informality of Saricks's approach was striking, all the more so because she stated that "[t]he measure of success for the readers' advisory interview is not whether the reader takes and reads the books the readers' advisor offers[,] [but] ... when readers perceive, based on the service they receive, that the library is a place where they can talk about books and obtain suggestions and resources to meet their reading needs."[152] Still, these conversations were necessarily brief, since they had to be quantified as reference "interactions" to show legislators that public libraries deserved continued financial support.[153] In Saricks's emphasis on conversation and place, it is not hard to recognize the rhetoric of the "civic library" movement, where the public library is a "community front porch" that functions as an "attraction" and "instrument for civic and social life."[154] But it was the kind of "community front porch" whose foundations rested on genre titles and ephemeral bestsellers produced by entertainment conglomerates that created demand for them. Little room remained for meaningful education.

When Saricks discussed the interview (or conversation) proper and its preliminaries, the difference between 1920s-1930s' readers' advisory and its post–1980 incarnation was even more apparent. Whereas readers' advisors such as Farquhar and Flexner devoted considerable time and energy to gaining in-depth knowledge of and recommending only high-quality books so that patrons could take the first steps toward meaningful education, Saricks's suggestions about how best to prepare for readers' advisory work emphasized acquiring trivial knowledge of recent entertainment- and pleasure-oriented fiction and nonfiction. First, readers' advisors should have a suitable background in genre fiction, a primary component of which was "speed-reading," in particular the "How to Read a Novel in Ten Minutes" a method developed by Georgine N. Olson.[155] Here, readers' advisors were told, among other things, to: "Hold the book and look at its basic features. Is it heavy? When you open it, do the pages lie flat?"; "Look at the typeface.... Is there much white space?"; "Look at the cover. What does it tell you about the book ... ?"; "Read the blurb. Does it give you an idea of the story line?"; "Skim and read bits and pieces here and there throughout the book. Does it seem to flow? What's your general impression of the book?"; "Read the end ... Is there a conclusion or is it open-ended?"[156] Second, staff members should devote themselves to "organized genre study," where they were urged to discuss questions such as "What is the difference between Grafton's books and Private Investigator Mysteries and Police Procedural Mysteries that feature women characters, such as those by Stephanie Booth, Elizabeth George, and Jill McGown?"[157] Third, readers' advisors should construct "sure bets" lists, which function as "failsafe[s]" and "lifeline[s]" and should contain titles such as Dorothy Gilman's *Caravan*, Robert Littell's *The Amateur*, Margaret Truman's *First Ladies*, Joseph Garber's *Vertical Run*, and Harlan Coben's *Tell No One*.[158] Fourth, they should know how to make "popular fiction" and "popular nonfiction" lists according to provided models.[159] For example, Danielle Steel was one of the authors featured in the "Women's Lives and Relationships" list, while the biographies of Kitty Kelley were included in a "Memoirs and Biography" list. Fifth, they should regularly do "readers' advisory assignments," where skills were honed by answering questions such as "Years ago there was a series of Mysteries in which the detective is a dwarf. Who wrote them, and what is the detective's name?"[160]

Finally, Saricks urged librarians to perform "warm-up exercises" immediately before working a shift at the service desk.[161] These exercises uncannily resembled the exercises that retail establishments required their floor staff to perform before meeting customers: familiarizing themselves with available stock, especially the most popular and bestselling items, all in the interests of moving merchandise. In the library context, Saricks recommended that readers' advisors "preview[] ... what is available that day," paying particular attention to "Romantic Suspense, Cozy Mysteries, Thrillers, Romances, Travelogues, or whatever else is being asked for,"[162] as well as bestseller lists contained in the *New York Times Book Review* and other publications.[163] Familiarity with the bestseller list was especially important. Just as retail sales managers told their staffs to steer customers toward another item if their first choice was unavailable, so Saricks suggested that readers' advisors substitute, for example, "other Romance and Romantic Suspense Fiction" for the unavailable bestselling Nora Roberts book.[164]

Once these preparations had been accomplished, readers' advisors were ready for the "rigors" of conversation, the fundamental premise of which was "paraphrasing" the patron's requests and responses, then breaking them down into appeal elements so as to be better able to compartmentalize and match a patron's request with in-stock items having those same elements.[165] For patrons, readers' advisory conversations turned into retail encounters, where sales clerks, using their knowledge of genre titles and bestsellers acquired during ten-minute speed-reading sessions, displayed vapid cheeriness and employed marketing techniques to suggest fashionable or seasonal reading options. When Saricks praised the following opening gambit—"'Looking for something light for the summer?' makes a good beginning on hot July days"—one could be forgiven for not knowing whether one had entered a public library or a clothing store.[166] Both now offered seasonally fashionable and ephemeral items to economically advantaged consumers convinced by the promotional reach of the entertainment industry that the ethos contained in the "Give 'Em What They Want" slogan was the essence of democratic freedom, not a manifestation of market censorship.

In one sense, it was an appropriate development, given that books had become industrialized commodities. In another sense, it was an acute commentary on the way in which public librarians conceived of themselves and the library. As they convinced themselves that adherence to the "Give 'Em What They Want" slogan constituted valuable public service, they also laid the groundwork for a deprofessionalized work environment relying on mechanical and automated procedures and validated the premises of an entertainment-oriented promotional culture. Robinson and Molz felt that schools of library science overemphasized the philosophical aspects of librarianship and did not spend enough time giving their graduates practical skills. They preferred to hire paraprofessionals at the BCPL and provided them with task-specific on-the-job training that effectively deskilled librarianship. Based on speed-reading and marketing techniques, Saricks's mechanical system of readers' advisory was another step toward deprofessionalizing librarianship. In the early 1900s, Hill criticized the "ticket-office" ideal of librarianship in which the lending of popular fiction assumed pride of place, where public libraries "tried every possible mechanical device except librarianship by automatic figures," and where educational values were given short shrift.[167] Together with Beatrice Winser, Hill was worried about the specter of deskilling in librarianship, even though what she perceived as a slow slide toward deskilling was looked upon by Dewey and others as the bedrock of professionalism: a business-like approach where principles of order, efficiency, and technical prowess dominated. In the late 1930s, Johnson castigated the principles of "pure librarianship," expressing the same concerns as Hill some 30 years earlier. Firmly lodged within the "Give 'Em What They Want" ethos and the natural heir of "librarianship by automatic figures" and "pure librarianship," Saricks's approach to readers' advisory was also permeated by Robinson and Molz's embrace of mechanized procedures, which they presented as an efficient and cost-effective development, but which ultimately led to deskilling.

For readers' advisors, the institutionalization of genre fiction and nonfiction and the mechanical implementation of appeal-elements theory allowed them to think that they understood the totality of individuals' reading needs based on their expressed past preferences for specific sub-genres, sub-sub-genres, or one or more discrete features. This pigeon-holing of individuals according to their preferred genre categories or appeal elements was the first step toward user profiling. Reading choice was narrowed to one or two sub-genres or sub-sub-genres. Once the choice was narrowed, readers could explore widely in that sub-genre, but it was the type of freedom that was artificial, confining the patron to familiar and safe possibilities. For readers searching for specific appeal elements, books no longer were culturally or historically resonant entities to be experienced in their rich and complex totality, but delivery mechanisms for a user's perfect combination of mixed-and-matched elements. Following Saricks and Brown's appeal-elements outline, a reader could, for example, ask for a book that had mostly dialogue; alternating viewpoints; detailed backgrounds; "characters developed over time"; "memorable ... secondary characters"; satiric authorial intent; interior and psychological focus; no flashbacks; and foreboding atmosphere.[168] It was a process that, taken to its extreme, reduced the reading experience to an empty, mechanical, and alienating consumerist endeavor under the guise of making fiction and nonfiction easily accessible. In its minute specification of desired elements perfectly tailored to personal tastes, it was also a process that recalled David Brooks's description in *Bobos in Paradise* of the intricate and ultimately narcissistic coffee orders placed at Starbucks in the late 20th century by bourgeois bohemians, who ordered "a double espresso, half decaf—half-caffeinated, with mocha and room for milk" or "a vente almond Frappuccino made from the Angolan blend with raw sugar and a hint of cinnamon."[169] Just as Brooks's "cultivated" consumers returned again and again to Starbucks to place the same specialized order,[170] so readers gravitated toward homogenous reading material that fit their exact entertainment-oriented requirements. The possibility of meaningful education at public libraries had disappeared, swept away by genrefication, agglutinative lists, and books defined exclusively in terms of appeal elements. As public libraries strove to gentrify, they also strove to genreficate, with troubling consequences for individuals in search of meaningful education.

Solidifying Support for Popular Fiction and Nonfiction

Readers' advisors welcomed these developments with open arms and more than a hint of defiance. Saricks's e-mail signature proudly included a quote from Marshall McLuhan: "Anyone who tries to make a distinction between education and entertainment doesn't know the first thing about either."[171] And so, in the wake of Rosenberg's first edition of *Genreflecting* in 1982, Saricks, along with Ted Balcom, director of the Villa Park (Illinois) Public Library until his retirement in 1999, was instrumental in the founding of the Adult Reading Round Table (ARRT) in 1984: "[A] group of adult services librarians working in the suburbs of Chicago decided they'd had enough, and they weren't going to take it anymore. What upset them was the lack of continuing education available on both the national and local level relevant to their specific area of librarianship: readers' advisory for adults. If the professional associations don't provide what we need, we'll create it for ourselves, they concurred."[172] Here began the ideas that culminated in Saricks's authorship and co-authorship of three editions of *Readers' Advisory Service in the Public Library*. As they participated in evening meetings; all-day workshops featuring Rosenberg, Baker, and others; newsletters; and book discussions, ARRT members became a significant force in setting the direction for readers' advisory in North America in the post–1980 era. Claiming that they wanted to put "'high touch' back into library service," Saricks, Balcom, and other ARRT members nonchalantly placed themselves within the framework of "media hype."[173] Balcom bluntly asked: "But isn't 'media hype' just another form of readers' advisory except this time it's coming from the publishers?"[174] And so he praised those "active" readers' advisors who not only "keep abreast of what's coming up on the television channels and in the movie theaters," but who also "refer constantly to a publication called 'The Get-Ready Sheet,' which gives them advance information about titles which will be featured in the media."[175] As an indication of the role readers' advisors played in entrenching an ethos of entertainment-oriented reading based on the artificial creation of consumer demand,

Balcom's observations were hard to surpass. For him, as well as for ARRT in general, there was little difference in the work that readers' advisory in public libraries should perform and the work performed by what he considered another kind of readers' advisory: publishers' "media hype."

As readers' advisors in the Chicago suburbs congratulated themselves in 1984 about their decision not "to take it anymore," they saw themselves as courageous rebels standing up for the right to read and discuss popular fiction and nonfiction without having to apologize for their reading tastes. But in championing the right of individuals to read popular fiction and nonfiction, they effectively abandoned the historic commitment of public libraries to provide meaningful education. Seeing nothing wrong in being adjuncts of "media hype" and convinced that their patrons must be given what they want, they were blissfully unaware—or chose to overlook—that they were actually giving patrons what media conglomerates wanted patrons to want. Instead of being unapologetic rebels standing up against prevailing powers on behalf of the right of people to read what they wanted, they became co-opted apologists for and eager participants in corporate promotional prowess. It was a sad irony, especially given the shining heritage of pre–1963 readers' advisory.

For ARRT members, the work of scholars such as Radway and Ross, as well as reception analysis and reader-response theory in general, was a balm: here was evidence that popular fiction and nonfiction were valuable. But, as pointed out in chapter 2 in our discussion of Radway, audience ethnographies lauding "interpretive communities" of active readers who appropriated commodified cultural items for their own purposes tended, falsely, "to cheerfully equate 'active' with 'powerful,' in the sense of 'taking control' at an enduring, structural or institutional level."[176] Ross's work was part of the same scholarly tradition as Radway's, and so a similar assessment can be made of it. This is not to deny the validity of some of Ross's observations. In her 1991 study "Readers' Advisory Service: New Directions," she wrote that readers constantly informed her that

> Books provide confirmation that others have gone through similar experiences and survived. Books help me clarify my feelings, change my way of thinking about things, help me think through problems in my own life, help me make a decision, and give me the strength and courage to make major changes in my own life. They give me a sense of mastery and control, give me courage to fight on, make me think that if the hero(ine) can overcome obstacles then so can I, give me the hope to rebuild my life, and help me accept things I cannot change. They put me in touch with a larger, more spacious world.[177]

In "Finding without Seeking: The Information Encounter in the Context of Reading for Pleasure," she reiterated these points, stating that books provided: "awakening/new perspective/enlargement of possibilities"; "models for identity"; "reassurance, comfort, confirmation of self-worth, strength"; "connection with others/awareness of not being alone"; "courage to make a change"; "acceptance"; and "disinterested understanding of the world."[178] Nonetheless, many of these reasons fell within the general parameters of what Brooks identified as the "Less Rembrandt, more Me. Fewer theologians, more dietitians" ethos, where a prevailing culture of narcissism sanctioned entertainment-oriented reading whose primary purpose was personal meaning-making.

Her findings in these two studies, as well as the conclusions of much of her other research,[179] were based on a study of 194 "heavy readers," a category that makes up "10 percent of the North American population."[180] Moreover, among these "heavy readers," "[t]he level of education was generally high."[181] And while some of these readers gravitated to serious literature, including the works of Austen, Anthony Trollope, and Mihail Bulgakov, most of them returned repeatedly to genre fiction. Ross commented that "more than 60 percent of the interviewed readers spontaneously mentioned having read series books as children," and "[n]ot unexpectedly, for many adult readers, genre books provided the same advantage of familiarity that series books had provided for them as children."[182] Her "heavy readers" were therefore "heavy" (and proud) readers of genre fiction who spoke in glowing terms of being able to "call[] the shots now" and having the "freedom"[183] to choose authors such as Rosemund Pilcher, Robert Ludlum, Tom Clancy, John Grisham, Stephen King, and Danielle Steel.[184] Since "genre reading makes up such a large component of pleasure reading,"[185] Ross urged librarians to encourage pleasure reading of series and genre books, concluding that "research-based insights" on reading "legitimate[] what you are doing to support reading for pleasure as a central function of a public library."[186] Specifically praising Saricks and Brown's appeal-elements theory, she divided readers' reasons for choosing a book into 26 sub-categories under six broad categories: "pacing"; "kind of action represented"; "characters"; "the nature of the world represented"; "emotional impact on the reader"; and "demands placed on the reader."[187] Assigning each of these sub-categories a letter, Ross concluded that "[a] reader who agrees with statements ALOS is clearly looking for a very different book from the reader who agrees with statements EJNT and so on."[188] The task of readers' advisors was therefore to induce readers "to describe reading preferences by matching three or four of these statements."[189] While Ross believed that this was a process that would enhance, professionalize, and "revolutionize" readers' advisory in the way envisioned by Saricks,[190] it was also another important step toward its mechanization and deskilling: the slotting of readers and books into categories reminiscent of Waples's scientific and statistical approach.

Underlying Ross's confidence in the value of genre titles and bestsellers as pleasure reading was her belief that bestseller lists were beneficial tools "to reduce [information and choice] overload"; as such, they were "marker[s] of quality," with the additional function of "track[ing] consumer behavior."[191] Moreover, referring to the work of Alan T. Sorensen, she observed that the bestseller phenomenon does not "steal[]" sales that "would otherwise go to non-best-selling books," but "au contraire, it expands the total numbers of books sold and increases demand for *all* books."[192] For her, bestseller lists were a boon, since they expanded reading of all kinds. But Sorensen's research was nuanced.[193] First, he stated that "the data available are clearly insufficient to provide a direct answer" to the question of whether bestseller lists increase demand for all books.[194] "The ideal experiment might be one in which a large set of consumers makes purchases in the presence of a bestseller list, and another set of consumers makes purchases without having any exposure to the best-seller list (either through the media or at the retail outlet itself). The ubiquity of the *New York Times* list makes it virtually impossible to find any group of book purchasers that resem-bles such a control group."[195] As a substitute for this impossible experiment, he created an "average subject similarity" equation in which "the estimated coefficients seem to suggest a complementarity between bestsellers and non-bestsellers" such that "weeks in which books of a particular genre first appear on the bestseller list tend to be strong-selling weeks for non-bestsellers of the same genre."[196] He concluded that "[t]his pattern could plausibly reflect multiple-book purchases: for example, weeks in which a new romance novel hit the best-seller list draw more than the usual fraction of romance enthusiasts into bookstores, and they may buy several romance novels when visiting the store."[197] Sorensen's research showed that, instead of expanding the reading horizons of individuals, bestseller lists narrowed those horizons still further, confining individuals to a preferred genre in which they read greater and greater quantities. Bourdieu's statements about the ever-increasing presence of industrial literature seemed more appropriate than ever.

Personal meaning-making through entertainment-oriented reading may be preferred by the educated individuals studied by Ross, but by focusing on them Ross overlooked that, as Thomas Mortenson explained, "higher education is now causing most of the growing inequality and strengthening class structure of the United States."[198] In the early 2000s, "the gap between rich and poor is widening," as "[s]tudents in the poorest quarter of the population have an 8.6 percent chance of getting a college degree [but] [s]tudents in the top quarter have a 74.9 per cent chance."[199] As Brooks noticed, educational stratification turns into economic stratification, which then "translat[es] into social stratification."[200] When Ross told public librarians to continue encouraging patrons to read series books, genre titles, and bestsellers for pleasure based on research that these books had proved valuable to educated and economically advantaged patrons, she contributed to enshrining not only the economic and social stratification discussed by Mortenson and Brooks, but also "our culture's enshrinement of subjectivity—'moi' as a modus operandi for processing the world."[201] As well, her defense of bestseller lists reinforced what Alain Roy called "the tacit and tactical alliance between cultural industries, the discourse of publicity, sponsoring agencies, and the mass media"[202] and what Andrew Wernick labeled "promotional culture,"[203] turning public libraries into monoscapes of commodified literature read by voracious consumers caught up in Debord's society of the spectacle.

Providing meaningful educational opportunities through serious and purposeful reading for less-advantaged individuals thus became a lower priority for public libraries as they concentrated on satisfying the "enshrinement of subjectivity" of economically advantaged patrons through popular fiction and nonfiction. Wanting to "call the shots" with regard to their reading choices, these patrons rejected the idea that their tastes had been manufactured by "media hype" or bestseller lists and asserted that they had a right to read as much genre fiction and bestsellers as they wanted. Having received meaningful educational opportunities at colleges and universities, they felt that public libraries should be venues for entertainment-oriented reading that served their pleasure and recreational needs, not small-scale replicas of the educational institutions from which they had graduated. It was an attitude that said "give me what I want," and so librarians "Gave 'Em What They Wanted." By valorizing and validating popular fiction and nonfiction, librarians situated the public library as a favored location for economically advantaged patrons. As public libraries genreficated, they also gentrified, excluding individuals for whom entertainment-oriented reading was a luxury as they struggled to gain meaningful educational opportunities outside colleges and universities, to which they had little chance of being admitted. Just as the poorest quarter of the population was disproportionately excluded from gaining an education at colleges and universities, librarians' emphasis on popular culture excluded the poor from an opportunity to gain meaningful education through serious and purposeful reading at public libraries. Razieh's words in *Reading Lolita in Tehran* resonate clearly: "I don't know why people who are better off always think that those less fortunate than themselves don't want to have the good things—that they don't want to listen to good music, eat good food or read Henry James." Public libraries that emphasized entertainment-oriented reading of genre titles and bestsellers perpetuated economic and social stratification, creating "a hereditary meritocratic class that reinforces itself generation after generation."[204]

Ross's research thus legitimized what ARRT members felt intuitively about the value of popular fiction and nonfiction. And by praising Saricks and Brown's theory of appeal elements as something that should form the basis of readers' advisory, Ross also legitimized the view that books could be disassembled into component parts; defined in detail on the basis of those elements; and then matched with a patron who expressed a desire for a book containing, for example, elements ALOS or EJNT. Books became products that delivered pre-determined and customized sensations, feelings, and experiences; they were no longer complex and indivisible entities valued for their significant cultural and historical contributions or for their ability to provide meaningful education and stimulate independent thought. As Janet Evanovich stated about books: "You have to look at it in the way you would look at any business.... You have to meet consumer expectations. You give them value for their money and give them a product that they need."[205] Readers' advisory was now ready for its next step. Because genre titles (both fiction and nonfiction) and bestsellers had formulaic elements, matching those titles to a patron's checklist of preferences (e.g., ALOS, EJNT, etc.) was something that readily lent itself to automation.

Automating Readers' Advisory

As described in chapter 4, the path that eventually led to the automation of readers' advisory service began with Waples's scientific and statistical analyses in the early 1930s in the *Journal of Higher Education* and *What People Want to Read About*. In the 1960s, Shortt's proposal for "Advisermatiks" summarized the evolving "Give 'Em What They Want" consensus and anticipated the viewpoints of Rosenberg, Saricks, and Ross: if patrons wanted popular fiction and other entertainment-oriented literature, then readers' advisors, in as mechanical and efficient a manner as possible, should direct them to novels that had the exact combination of desired elements. It was only a matter of time before Shortt's wish for "Advisermatiks" was fulfilled.

The relationship between popular fiction and automation was clearly on display in Duncan Smith's account of the germination of the idea for NoveList, an electronic database produced by EBSCO Publishing that inaugurated automated readers' advisory.

> In the 80s, I became a branch manager at the Forsyth County (North Carolina) Public Library's Kernersville Branch.... The first 'information' question I got was from a reader who wanted another author who wrote just like Danielle Steel.... I really hoped that this question would go away but it kept coming back—only the author's name kept changing. If it wasn't Steel, it was King, or Robert Ludlum, or John D. MacDonald.... And what was worse for me at the time was discovering that 50 percent of my branches' circulation was adult fiction, and the authors who were driving those numbers were not Dickens or Dostoevsky or ... Jane Austen.[206]

Smith subsequently videotaped readers "talking about books they read and enjoyed" and embarked upon a series of nationwide workshops about popular fiction in public libraries.[207] Because workshop participants "kept asking for a resource that could help them do this work," Smith, together with Roger Rohweder and John Strickler, "began mapping out what an electronic readers' advisory resource would look like" in 1991.[208] In March of 1994, "Joyce Saricks at Downers Grove Public Library bought the first copy of NoveList. The copy of NoveList that we shipped to her came with its own computer, a DOS-based application with a text interface that contained about 20,000 adult fiction titles and 1,200 full-text reviews."[209] By 2004, NoveList had become "a Web-based application that provides information on over 120,000 fiction titles for readers of all ages, contains over 90,000 full-text reviews and also has author read-alike lists for popular authors, book discussion guides, book talks, and a complete 4-hour course in basic readers' advisory service."[210] Smith was especially proud that NoveList, which used over 36,000 subject headings, could retrieve and "group titles along the multiple combinations that readers like—a woman detective in a small town who has a relationship with her father."[211]

> NoveList lets the staff member focus on the reader and guiding the reader through the titles that NoveList provides instead of standing there trying to remember if she (the staff member) knows

of any authors who write about women detectives and set their stories in small town and, oh, by the way, have a father-daughter relationship as part of the story. ¶ When NoveList is used as part of this work, ... the reader becomes an active part of the process of finding his own books. For many readers, this results in an interaction with staff that makes finding a book to read as engaging and as satisfying as reading one.[212]

But, as the first case study in chapter 6 shows, while NoveList may have been able to adroitly "group titles along the multiple combinations that readers like—a woman detective in a small town who has a relationship with her father," many readers did not find NoveList particularly helpful in its descriptions of books nor useful in suggesting titles that they actually liked as complete entities.

It is little wonder that Saricks was the first customer for NoveList, since it fit perfectly with her conception of a mechanical approach to readers' advisory. With the advent of NoveList, mechanical and automated readers' advisory gradually became the norm, all the more so because Smith, by praising the authors of the *Genreflecting* series; Saricks and Brown's appeal-elements theory; and Ross's studies about popular fiction, saw NoveList as a natural extension of their beliefs. As a co-creator of NoveList and its Product Manager for EBSCO, Smith naturally thought that NoveList was a positive development. From a philosophical perspective, however, NoveList reproduced in the electronic realm the mechanical and deskilled approach to readers' advisory based on popular culture suggested by Shortt, codified by Saricks and Brown, and justified by Ross. As such, it was also the first step toward outsourced readers' advisory service, which is discussed in greater detail in a subsequent section of this chapter.

The ideological process by which readers' advisory became deskilled can be seen in "Reinventing Readers' Advisory," where Smith set up an opposition between what he viewed as competency-based readers' advisory that relied, on the one hand, on mechanical procedures and electronic resources and, on the other, on what he implied to be old-fashioned, amateurish, and serendipitous readers' advisory that stressed reading and counseling.[213] He made use of two studies (one by Kenneth Shearer[214]; the other by Anne K. May, Elizabeth Olesh, Anne Weinlich Miltenberg, and Catherine Patricia Lackner[215]) to state that readers' advisory service as currently constituted had "failed to fully meet readers' needs."[216] One reason for this, Smith suggested, was reading: "Library staff members have worked in an environment where the central message is ... '[i]n order to provide excellent readers' advisory service you must read, read, read. In cases where you are not able to meet a patron's request for assistance in this area, you should read in that area so you can respond to patrons' requests in the future.'"[217] For Smith, reading was an insufficient answer, since there never was any certainty that consistently good readers' advisory would result from it. An equally important reason was that many librarians unsuccessfully tried to apply Carol Collier Kuhlthau's counselor model of librarianship to readers' advisory. But the counselor role "is one that only the most dedicated, adept, and passionate readers' advisors employ. It is a role that few have been educated to assume and that many may not choose to accept. It is a role that may also be very difficult to consistently employ in today's library context."[218]

For readers' advisory to improve, Smith recommended that electronic resources such as NoveList be used because they help staff "to cope with gaps in book knowledge by serving as added memory."[219] Electronic resources "can reduce the complexity of performing readers' advisory work" and "could help move readers' advisory service out of the realm of Kuhlthau's counselor model, a realm that is uncomfortable for many of us, into the more familiar standard reference intervention of the identifier role."[220] The result was "a more standardized approach to providing readers' advisory service," which Smith hoped would not sacrifice "the depth of this service."[221] As an example of the standardized approach, he envisaged that electronic resources would contain built-in prompts and scripts.

> Prompts could help guide inexperienced or overwhelmed staff through the readers' advisory transaction, who then use it as part of their conversation with the reader. One prompt in such a resource might say 'Ask the reader to describe a book read and enjoyed.' The next prompt might include sample elements to listen for: 'Did the reader identify a genre, a location, a topic, or theme?' 'Did the patron use words such as 'fast-paced' or give detailed descriptions of characters?' In this case, the resource would be guiding the staff member through the process of the readers' advisory transaction.[222]

After sequencing through these prompts and scripts, staff members would offer patrons a machine-generated list of titles. Here, the staff member's contribution was to mechanically follow directions appearing on a screen and key in relevant information.

This was in keeping with Smith and Suzanne Mahmoodi's *Talking with Readers: A Workbook for Readers' Advisory*, published by EBSCO in 2000.[223] This manual formalized readers' advisory into a series of 130 competencies divided among four broad areas: "background in fiction and nonfiction"; "understanding people as readers and readers as people"; "the appeal of books"; and "the readers' advisory transaction."[224] While outlining the importance of enthusiasm and paraphrasing patrons' statements, *Talking with Readers* was centered on "knowledge of eighty popular authors and their titles," including John Grisham, Tom Clancy, Jean Auel, and J. K. Rowling.[225] The mechanical approach was also in keeping with the introduction in 2004 of Book Index with Reviews (BIR), a database developed by "EBSCO Publishing's NoveList team in cooperation with Baker and Taylor" in response to "requests from our users for a NoveList-'like' resource for nonfiction titles—a resource that could help staff and readers find books in popular areas like biography, true crime, and crafts."[226] Containing information "on around 3.8 million titles and 800,000 full-text, fully searchable reviews," BIR allowed readers' advisors to search for appeal-element words and phrases, such as fast-paced or flashbacks, that were contained in its reviews.[227] But its primary characteristic was its four-star popularity rating system, which was "based on ordering information from thousands of libraries and retail outlets across the country, over the past seven years, making sure that your readers can quickly find the titles that everyone is talking about, or reading."[228] For Smith, popularity was equivalent to quality: "[f]or example, someone interested in biographies of Ronald Reagan can not only get a list of those titles but also sort the list so the most popular ones appear at the top. Just think of all of those times you have done a search for a reader only to be asked—but which ones of these are good? Our popularity ranking lets library staff show a reader which titles are popular."[229] BIR therefore enshrined a readers' advisory ethos in which library staff relied on sales data to determine suggestions or recommendations. When popularity rankings and popularity-sort capabilities were included in NoveList in 2006, its developers boasted about these new features by telling readers' advisors that "[e]ven when you haven't read the book, you now have a way to guide your readers to the most widely read books in any genre or on any topic."[230] The reverence of market forces had reached an apotheosis: that which was popular was also good and worthwhile.

Smith's definition of improved readers' advisory service, which encompassed such concepts as "reduce the complexity," "standardized," "prompts," and "popularity," called into question Kuhlthau's counselor model of librarianship. As described in *Seeking Meaning: A Process Approach to Library and Information Services*, the counselor's role was centered on an in-depth interview between user and librarian where, among other things, "[t]he recommended sequence of sources of information emerges as the topic or problem evolves in a highly individual way," where "[t]he [c]ounselor establishes a dialogue that leads to an exploration of strategy and to a sequence of learning," and where "the user and the [c]ounselor redefine the problem, determine a strategy, identify additional sources, and a sequence for use." [231] At the counselor level of librarianship, Kuhlthau concluded, "two forms of intervention, mediation and education, merge into one interactive service of guidance."[232] In its emphasis on in-depth interviews, sequences of learning, and education, Kuhlthau's description of the counselor's role captured many aspects of the type of readers' advisory conducted by Flexner and her peers in the 1920s and 1930s, where well-read and knowledgeable librarians recommended serious literature for the purpose of meaningful education. Smith's rejection of the counselor approach was therefore a rejection of readers' advisory leading to meaningful education. Instead, valorizing an elaborate "Give 'Em What They Want" approach based on a mechanical determination of reading tastes and relying on sales data as an indicator of quality, he updated Hill's "ticket-office" ideal of librarianship and legitimized "librarianship by automatic figures."

While Smith claimed that "standardized" and prompt-based service would allow staff members "to focus on the reader,"[233] the opposite was more likely to happen. As staff mechanically cycled through prompts and scripts and suggested the most popular titles to patrons, little opportunity for meaningful education remained. Readers' advisory was deskilled, reduced to a series of competencies enabling staff members to identify and be enthusiastic about authors such as Jean Auel and John Grisham, key in appeal elements such as "fast-paced" on BIR or check off "father-daughter relationship" on NoveList, and steer readers to the most popular titles as determined by sales rankings. The emphasis on popularity symbolically marked the distance that readers' advisory had traveled from its origins to the early 2000s. Rather than trying to elevate patrons' reading tastes by recommending serious and purposeful reading for meaningful education, readers' advisors mechanically enforced homogeneous reading choices as determined by sales data, which in turn was a function of the type of books entertainment-oriented media conglomerates chose to publish and promote.

The McProfiling Phenomenon

While Smith automated the mechanical process of disassembling popular fiction and nonfiction into component parts so as to profile a patron's reading preferences, Sharon L. Baker, in "What Patrons Read and Why: The Link between Personality and Reading," recommended that readers' advisors take an additional step in creating a patron's profile. She suggested that patrons should be categorized according to the Myers-Briggs Type Indicator (MBTI), which "provides a useful framework for understanding personality type, since it categorizes people into four different preference groups that seem to have some implications for reading preference: extroverts versus introverts; sensing versus intuition; thinking versus feeling; and judgment versus perception."[234] Each of the eight personality types in the four groups could then be linked to a type of book or even to a specific author. For example, "extroverts prefer action-oriented works to works that are more literary"; sensors may enjoy fiction "in which the writing is highly concrete," such as "works by Ed McBain," who "tends to write in highly concrete terms"; intuitors who like mysteries would likely prefer G. K. Chesterton, whose fiction is "figurative" and makes people "read in between the lines"; and thinking types, who prefer that "information be presented logically and objectively," might "relate well" to "Tom Clancy's complicated thrillers."[235] In addition, combinations of type preferences might also "influence reading choice."[236]

[S]ensing judgers, people who tend to be precise and detail oriented and who like fairly traditional ways of doing things, might enjoy historical fiction. Sensing perceivers, who gather information through doing concrete things, might like concrete, action-oriented adventures like those
written by Ernest Hemingway or Mickey Spillane. Intuitive feelers, who like reading about possibilities and who emphasize human values, might enjoy science fiction that addresses human values (like Ray Bradbury's *Fahrenheit 451*), fiction where the main character is highly idealistic (like
Dorothy Gilman's Mrs. Polifax novels), or fantasy that expresses moral values (like that written
by Ursula LeGuin).[237]

Baker was optimistic about the value of her idea: "my own experience and that of other
librarians with whom this work has been shared suggest that the approach presented here
may enrich our understanding of why patrons like or dislike certain works and improve our
abilities to match patrons with books they will enjoy reading."[238]

Yet her proposals for readers' advisory amounted to what Stephen Mihm called
"McProfiling," defined as the ability of McDonald's and other fast-food outlets to accurately
predict a customer's order after analyzing, through a video camera mounted on the restaurant's roof, the size and shape of that customer's vehicle as it pulled into the parking lot.[239]
"By the time you've opened the door [of your vehicle], a computer has analyzed the image
and, based on previous encounters with vehicles the size and shape of the one you're driving, classified you as a likely consumer of, say, chicken nuggets and fries."[240] By slotting
patrons into narrowly defined categories based on personality type, Baker's ideas were part
of a general trend to recommendation systems based on customer profiling and market segmentation. These ideas presented the perfect complement to Smith's automation of Saricks's mechanical disaggregation of books into appeal elements. If books could be
disassembled into components, individuals also could be reduced to and defined by a cluster of personality or demographic traits, propensities, and behaviors. An algorithm would
then determine a match between a book with certain elements and an individual's cluster
of characteristics.

But personalization-through-profiling was ultimately a business strategy designed to
increase consumption, and the fact that such personalization was equated with "old-
fashioned" individual attention was a clear indication of the success of that strategy. In general, there were two types of profiling: content-based and collaborative filtering. Both started
from a simple premise: the more information that could be gathered about an individual,
the more that could be sold to that individual.[241] In content-based profiling, "a profile is
composed out of the user's history of past interests," with the result that an individual is
told that he or she will like Item A because he or she also liked Item B and C.[242] In collaborative filtering, "one gathers knowledge on general user traits, and models this into a
profile."[243] Here, "other peoples' choices, aggregated on a massive scale, are likely to hold
valuable information that can be applied to [an] individual case."[244] An example of collaborative filtering was Amazon.com, which "compares your purchase history with those of other
shoppers on the site and tries to use this information to recommend books that you are
likely to enjoy."[245] "[G]athering large amounts of data about the buyers of a product to make
recommendations based on demographics and interests,"[246] collaborative filtering expanded
to match "customer tastes across Web businesses, using knowledge of a customer's tastes in
music to try to sell them books, for example."[247]

At the heart of these processes was identification and categorization of microscopic
appeal elements and the grouping of people into behavioral, attitudinal, or demographic
clusters and market segments. ChoiceStream, a company that devised recommendation systems for "AOL, Yahoo Music, and eMusic, among others," categorized new movies and

music "based on about 25 attributes, such as 'macho,' 'romantic,' 'mainstream,' and 'obscure'" and then relied on an algorithm based on users' previous choices to make new recommendations.[248] The Music Genome Project, which classified "about 8,000 songs per month," identified "a song's fundamental traits from among 400 possibilities" such as "melodic songwriting" and "a clear focus on recording studio production" before making recommendations to users.[249] Total Research, a company based in Princeton, New Jersey, segmented individuals into seven categories: "Intellects, Conformists, Popularity Seekers, Relief Seekers, Sentimentalists, Pragmatists and Actives."[250] Claritas, which described itself as the "the pre-eminent source of accurate, up-to-date demographic data and target marketing information about the population, consumer behavior segmentation, consumer spending, households and businesses within any specific geographic market area in the United States" segmented the United States into 66 "demographically and behaviorally distinct" lifestyle clusters (e.g., "Second City Elite," "Blue Blood Estates," and "Pools & Patios"). Based on "nearly 10,000 behaviors and hundreds of demographic predictor variables at different geographic levels," these 66 clusters defined the "likes, dislikes, lifestyles and purchase behavior" of individuals comprising those clusters, thus allowing companies and organizations to "target them more efficiently with tailored messages and products designed just for them."[251] In employee hiring, researchers developed a process called "synthetic validity, where a particular job was broken down into a series of behaviors—common building blocks that could be assembled in different combinations to describe any kind of work" and then matched with an applicant's abilities and characteristics, which had been determined by a series of questionnaires and/or psychological tests.[252]

No matter their various permutations and levels of technological sophistication, these profiling systems were instances of what Jon Katz identified as "behavioral monitoring,"[253] fitting individuals into socio-cultural and socio-economic niches so that "personalized" commodities—whether products, jobs, or something else—could be "pushed" to them. But, by "filter[ing] the world on your behalf," profiling systems also contributed to "the death of serendipity."[254] As Richard Waters asked, "[i]f a media or commercial organisation uses its knowledge of your behaviour to feed back more of what it knows you already like, then where is the potential for surprise?"[255] Another risk was that "social groups will become increasingly fragmented and insular as the preferences of the majority are used to shape the experiences of the group as a whole."[256] In this regard, John Hagel observed that profiling systems created a "self-reinforcing cycle" such that "[w]hen all the information presented to you has been filtered to match your world view, how will you encounter ideas that make you think again?"[257]

When Smith identified collaborative filtering in "Reinventing Readers' Advisory" as a promising resource that would allow readers' advisors "to engage all readers in productive conversations regardless of our personal knowledge of books or our knowledge of the reader we are serving and the books that reader enjoys,"[258] he was pointing toward a time when deskilled readers' advisors treated patrons as disaggregated, segmented, and profiled constructs whose future reading preferences could be mechanically predicted. It was a future where individuals did not read for the sake of gaining meaningful education through serious literature; rather, it was a future where individuals focused on entertainment-oriented reading that contained elements and characteristics tailored to their profiles. Although readers thought they were receiving personalized attention, they were really being slotted into fragmented micro-categories where they consumed homogenous commodities that were only superficially different. Smith foretold an age where the phrase "more me" would resound all the time, drowning out all else.

Although Altick wrote only some 30 years before Baker's article about the MBTI psychological test and about 40 years before Smith's BIR, his words seem to come from a different century. While Altick wanted readers' advisors to stop being "routine dispenser[s] of information" and, instead, become discerning and well-informed "surrogate teacher[s]" with an "acute sense of critical discrimination" who guided readers to books of "recognized literary worth,"[259] Smith urged readers' advisors not only to equate popularity with quality, thus effectively sanctioning market censorship, but also to explore the possibilities inherent in collaborative filtering. While Altick urged librarians to engage in "advanced academic work" in subject fields because they had a "growing responsibility as ... educator[s] who teach[] outside the classroom,"[260] Baker recommended categorizing people into four psychologically oriented preference groups and suggesting books based on those categories. These differences encapsulated the deskilling phenomenon in readers' advisory. Where once readers' advisory had been conceptualized as the realm of surrogate teachers able to help patrons gain meaningful education through exposure to books of "recognized literary worth," it now devolved into a set of mechanical procedures where BCPL-like paraprofessionals "Gave 'Em What They Wanted" by following prompts and scripts; inputting gathered information; segmenting and profiling patrons according to personality type, behavioral and sociodemographic information, or past preferences; and generating an agglutinative list of books ranked by nationwide sales data.

The Lust for Book Lists

In the late 1980s and early 1990s, some librarians realized that the "Give 'Em What They Want" movement may have gone too far. Nancy Pearl, then Coordinating Librarian for Adult Resources and Head of Acquisitions at the Tulsa City-County (Oklahoma) Library (TCCL), was among them. In 1992, along with co-author Craig Buthod, she described her frustration in "Upgrading the 'McLibrary,'" observing that public libraries were often besieged by "droves" of patrons "expecting to find every best seller and new video release on the shelf."[261] Under pressure "to deliver the titles the book and video industries were promoting," public libraries were losing sight of their "higher purpose" of "cultural enrichment" and neglecting their "historical role" as "a center of education" as they struggled to cater to "the 'me' decade's expectation of immediate satisfaction" of their "cravings."[262] Taking as their motto John Ruskin's statement that "All books are divisible into two classes—the books of the hour, and books of all time,"[263] Tulsa librarians adopted a policy whereby they focused less on "reactive buying"—defined as "keeping up with new releases from mainstream publishers" as reviewed in *Library Journal, Booklist, Publishers Weekly, Kirkus Reviews,* and *Choice*—and concentrated more on "building collections of enduring value."[264] TCCL thus undertook a thorough analysis of existing collections; made use of non-librarian subject experts in the community to identify collecting gaps and recommend ways to fill those gaps; and instituted a long-term collection philosophy with a "commonly understood direction."[265] The result was a series of collection projects that enhanced holdings in areas including "plays, screenplays, and scripts; the classics; the homeless; basic life skills; aging; and secondary works of major authors."[266] Although Pearl and Buthod admitted that "[w]e have probably disenfranchised some readers of romances, who grumble that we don't have enough for them to read," TCCL's emphasis on collection quality sent a strong message that at least one library was listening to Ruskin.

By 1999, Pearl's views about the value of "new releases from mainstream publishers" had evolved, judging by her two *Now Read This* volumes for the *Genreflecting* series, both of which were compendia of recent mainstream fiction organized around Saricks and Brown's appeal elements. Of course, mainstream fiction titles were not genre fiction titles, but they were still the type of books that were regularly reviewed in publications such as *Library Journal*, *Booklist*, *Publishers Weekly*, and *Kirkus Reviews*, which Pearl in 1992 had identified as organs promoting "reactive buying" and, presumably, reactive reading. In *Book Lust: Recommended Reading for Every Mood, Moment, and Reason* in 2003 and its sequel *More Book Lust* in 2005, she compiled book lists about topics such as "Academic Mysteries"; "Bicycling"; "California, Here We Come"; "Czech It Out"; "Dick Lit"; "Do Clothes Make the Man (or Woman)?"; "Gallivanting in the Graveyard"; "A Holiday Shopping List"; "Idaho: And Nary a Potato to Be Seen"; "It Was a Dark and Stormy Novel"; "Jersey Guys and Gals"; "Legal Eagles in Nonfiction"; and "True Adventures."[267] There were more serious topics as well: "The Alpha, Beta, Gammas of Greece"; "Balkan Specters"; "Civil Rights and Wrongs"; "Founding Fathers"; "Lewis and Clarke: Adventurers Extraordinaire"; "The Middle East"; and "Sri Lanka: Exotic and Troubled."[268] In the final analysis, however, *Book Lust* and *More Book Lust* were examples of self-celebration, diary-like records filled with often breathless opinions about personal preferences whose purpose seemed to be more ostentatious self-aggrandizement about the breadth of her reading than the provision of meaningful cultural enrichment or education.

As blogs multiplied in the early 21st century, allowing anyone to electronically post comments, no matter how trivial, about any aspect of their own lives or the lives of others on the web, it was not surprising that Pearl's books were wildly successful. The blurbs about *Book Lust* on the opening page of *More Book Lust* testified to her fame.[269] The *New York Times* said that "She's the talk of librarian circles." The *Los Angeles Times* observed that *Book Lust* was "[a] tour de force that would thrill any listmaker.... This is one lusty librarian." Invoking the sensation caused by the creation of a Nancy Pearl-"action figure" plastic doll,[270] *Bust* magazine stated that she had "become pretty much the librarian version of a rock star." And Will Manley in *American Libraries* noted that "Just when I was ready to put the last nail into the coffin of readers' advisory services, up pops the best book ever written on the subject. In fact, this may be the best book ever written by a librarian."[271]

Some of Pearl's views on readers' advisory were refreshing, especially given the emphasis on mechanical "Give 'Em What They Want" readers' advisory based on genre titles and bestsellers.

> How do you define 'good stuff'? I think the librarian's role is to help people find the books they will enjoy reading, whether or not you as the readers' advisor or librarian consider that book good literature. The first rule of readers' advisory is that it's not about you, not about what you like or read or don't like or don't read, but rather what that person in front of you loves to read. ¶ On the other hand, I believe that one of the things that we can do best is broaden a person's experience with works of literature, so that we shouldn't necessarily be constrained when someone says they only read westerns and thus not offer them the option of books like *Pioneer Women* or a biography of Wyatt Earp, or a history of the War of Texas Independence, or novels that aren't necessarily considered westerns, like Pete Dexter's *Deadwood*, or Clair Huffaker's *The Cowboy and the Cossack*, both wonderful books that won't be shelved with the westerns or probably even given the western labeling that a Louis L'Amour would have.[272]

But while her approach in *Book Lust* and *More Book Lust* was "celebratory" of the written word,[273] it was also celebratory of herself. Pearl was a self-absorbed chronicler of her own reading life, jauntily commenting on a wide array of subjects from the perspective that "reading should be pure pleasure" and individuals should read only about 50 pages of a book before deciding "to commit yourself to reading it."[274] It was a good example of what

Kakutani called "our culture's enshrinement of subjectivity—'moi' as a modus operandi for processing the world,"[275] especially since Pearl announced that "[b]elieve me, nobody is going to get any points in heaven by miserably slogging their way through a book they aren't enjoying but think they ought to read" and that authors were responsible for the fact that a reader did not like a book.[276] Although not commenting directly on Pearl's books, Brian Fawcett perceptively identified the tradition in which they partook: "the transformation of Western cultural discourse from that of structured enquiry into a marketplace of opinion and belief."[277]

Calling herself both "an addicted reader" and "a promiscuous reader," Pearl summarized her approach to reading as follows.

> I basically read anything, as long as it's well written and has interesting characters. And there's no subject in which you won't find books that meet those criteria. As I write this, stacked next to my bed are these books, waiting patiently for me to read or reread them: *Collected Poems* by Donald Justice; Robert Byron's classic travel book, *The Road To Oxiana*; James Muirden's *Shakespeare Well-Versed: A Rhyming Guide to All His Plays*; *Why Didn't They Ask Evans?* by Agatha Christie; Francine Prose's *A Changed Man*; *Boys and Girls Together* by William Goldman; *Sheila Levine is Dead and Living in New York* by Gail Parent; *The Children's Blizzard* by David Laskin; *Vanity Fair* by William Makepeace Thackeray; *Mantrapped* by Fay Weldon; *Mrs. Daffodil* by Gladys Taber; and *The Saturdays* by Elizabeth Enright. A frighteningly eclectic list, to be sure.[278]

And she constantly sprinkled her annotations with the words "I" and "my favorite": "I have an inordinate fondness for first novels"[279]; "I was introduced to Iris Murdoch's novels in the early 1980s, and I read them ... in a flurry of delight and awe, thoroughly convinced that she was among the most brilliant writers I had ever encountered, an opinion I still hold. Even when I read a novel of hers that didn't quite click with me, I knew I was in the presence of a major twentieth-century writer"[280]; "Although in the years since Stout's death I find myself going back and rereading his entire oeuvre every year or two, I return with particular pleasure to these five novels"[281]; "But for some reason, these three books ... are favorites of mine"[282]; "Of my two favorite contemporary essayists...."[283]; "One of my top ten favorite novels in any category is Stephanie Plowman's *The Road To Sardis*"[284]; and "Here are some of my very favorite novels that I'm glad I didn't judge by their covers."[285]

But, as discussed in the second case study of chapter 6, her exuberant style often concealed recommendations that were superficial, as befitted "a professional reader" who approached books as stand-alone entities with little or no awareness of how a specific book fit into a larger context.[286] Of course, Pearl did not claim that she was a subject expert on such topics as "The Middle East" or "Founding Fathers," but her lack of subject expertise drew attention to the gulf between, on the one hand, *Book Lust* and *More Book Lust* and, on the other, the *Reading with a Purpose* series in the 1920s and 1930s and the *Reading for an Age of Change* series in the early 1960s. As described in chapter 4, both of these series were written by subject experts who produced context-rich overviews about their topics and provided systematic reading plans for meaningful education. After comparing the volumes in these two series with Pearl's books, the inescapable conclusion is that Altick's vision of readers' advisors—surrogate teachers who, through concerted and systematic study, would "make themselves as knowledgeable as they can be about the differences between books which are superficially authoritative and those which are genuinely so"—was indeed a thing of the past.[287] If NoveList-based readers' advisory was the literal embodiment of Agnes Hill's "librarianship by automatic figures," then Pearl's type of readers' advisory was its symbolic equivalent, since it invariably relied on "reactive" reading and recommendation of recent books made popular by the tentacular reach of what Wernick called "promotional culture."

In 2005, Pearl assumed a leading role as a consultant for the H. W. Wilson Company, publisher of five Standard Catalogs—*Fiction Catalog* (FC) and *Public Library Catalog* (PLC), as well as three other catalogs for children and high school students. These catalogs were standardized listings of fiction and nonfiction titles that many public, academic, and school libraries used to evaluate their own collections. The more FC- and PLC-listed titles that a given library owned, the more complete and worthwhile its collection was deemed to be. When R. R. Bowker formed a partnership with H. W. Wilson such that Bowker's Book Analysis System (BAS) was integrated into Wilson's Standard Catalogs, Pearl became an important marketing presence for the new product, described as "a long-awaited collection development tool which automates a laborious manual comparison process" by performing "quick core and gap analyses of ... book collections by subject."[288] As the press release announcing the partnership explained, "subscribers to H. W. Wilson's electronic Standard Catalogs will be able to view a comparison of those appropriate core titles with their own library's collection, identifying specific titles they would like to purchase" by "assess[ing] their collection[s] based on the core selections of Wilson's highly esteemed advisors and subject specialists, such as Nancy Pearl, author of *Book Lust*."[289]

Under the guise of performing readers' advisory, Pearl wrote two volumes of recommendations that focused on the books she herself had liked. Because *Book Lust* and *More Book Lust* reached a wide audience, her favorites became the choices of thousands of other people. Then her recommendations were incorporated into FC and PLC, which were in turn merged with Bowker's BAS. Pearl's *Book Lust* and *More Book Lust* recommendations became standardized; they were now understood to be integral components of all good library collections. As numerous North American public libraries evaluated their collections against H. W. Wilson catalogs using Bowker's BAS, Pearl's recommendations were a baseline by which to judge the extent and quality of a library's collection. But, as Juris Dilevko and Lisa Gottlieb showed in "The Politics of Standard Selection Guides," a study of PLC-recommended titles in 23 subject areas, major lacunae existed in the way in which PLC covered subjects, including "missing theoretical perspectives," "overemphasis of a particular facet or theory within a field," "missing voices," and the lack of "a comprehensive framework."[290] As public libraries strove to buy PLC- and FC-recommended books, they homogenized not only their collections on the basis of recommendations by individuals (such as Pearl) who were not subject experts, but also their readers' advisory service, which was necessarily based on their collections. If 19th-century librarians and readers' advisors were criticized for perpetuating a canon based on a set of works labeled as the classics, then Pearl could just as easily be criticized for participating in another type of canon formation—one premised on Debord's society of the spectacle, cultural commodification, and personal taste transmuted into public fiat.

Online and Outsourced Readers' Advisory

In the final analysis, Pearl's book lists were not much different from the book lists found in the *Genreflecting* series or on the web sites of North American public libraries. All were entertainment-oriented lists of mostly popular fiction and nonfiction that, at best, might provide instances of edutainment, but not the kind of meaningful educational opportunities available through the *Reading with a Purpose* or the *Reading for an Age of Change* series. When Saricks identified five readers' advisory web pages as models for other public libraries to emulate, she established them not only as benchmarks, but also as the primary means of delivering readers' advisory service in the early 21st century. Hosted by the

Johnson County (Kansas) Library (JCL); the Public Library of Charlotte and Mecklenburg (North Carolina) County; the Morton Grove (Illinois) Public Library; the Williamsburg (Virginia) Regional Library; and the Waterboro (Maine) Public Library (WPL),[291] these model web pages (as well as other similar pages hosted by thousands of other North American public libraries) were characterized by their vast array of lists, which invariably contained one- or two-sentence annotations that often seemed to be drawn directly from publishers' promotional materials and book jackets.

To be sure, many readers' advisory web sites offered more than just lists. The "Great Reads" site of the Columbus (Ohio) Metropolitan Library (CML), rated as the top large public library in the United States in 2005 by Hennen's American Public Library ratings service,[292] featured links to and information about online book-discussion groups, as well as book reviews by staff members.[293] Its "Book of the Month" club presented a new book each month "with links to discussion questions, similar titles, and related information." In addition to book reviews by patrons, the "Readers' Café" area of the Halifax (Nova Scotia) Public Libraries (HPL) web site offered a librarian-moderated online book-discussion group, where registered members contributed to a discussion about a monthly topic and relevant books pertaining to that topic. Interested readers could "choose to participate in the discussion as little or as much" as they liked, certain that they would "receive a copy of every email message posted to the group in [their] email box for as long as [they] wish[ed] to subscribe."[294]

But even at the CML and HPL web sites, lists were by far the main component, with genre-specific lists, award lists, and bestseller lists from the *New York Times*, *Essence*, *USA Today*, *Book Sense*, and *Publishers Weekly* prominently displayed. At the JCL web site, there were 12 thematic categories containing 83 fiction booklists, including "Mysteries are Academic"; "Fiction about Flight"; "Family Skeletons"; "Street Fiction"; "Rented Rooms"; "Views from the Minaret"; "Nautical Yarns"; "Quarky Fiction"; "From the Korean War to Elvis"; and "Heaven & Hell on Earth."[295] When users clicked on any of these 83 lists, they were presented with lengthy lists of individual titles that were either unannotated (e.g., "Business Fiction," "Fiction about Flight") or described in one sentence (e.g., "Mysteries are Academic," "Rented Rooms"). For nonfiction, there were 19 thematic categories, including "Beyond the World We Know"; "Traces of Evidence"; and "True Survival." A similar dynamic was present at the WPL web site.[296] Here, the adult-fiction booklist contained 78 broad categories, each of which was further divided into additional categories linked "to more than fourteen hundred reading lists"[297] created by libraries across North America and the world. For example, the category "Adventure/Military Fiction" was sub-divided into 30 subcategories, including "Espionage Thrillers"; "Action Adventure"; and "Masters and Commanders." The category "Fiction Featuring Modes of Transportation" had nine sub-categories, including "Driving Stories" and "Fiction with Trains." The category "Domestic Fiction" featured five sub-categories, each of which had additional sub-sub-categories. Under the sub-category of "Friends and Families," there were 20 sub-sub-categories, including "O My Papa" and "Divorce Novels, Poems, and Short Stories." Under the sub-category of "Food and Drink," there were five sub-sub-categories, each of which contained sub-sub-sub-categories, such as "Food in Fiction"; "Coffee-Related Books"; and "Chocolate Fiction." It was a veritable explosion of lists, where every topic, no matter how specialized, had its own list.

These online lists were the basis of virtual readers' advisory service. As defined by Saricks, virtual readers' advisory used "the same technology available for virtual reference" and "promotes 24/7 access to trained staff who offer book suggestions and assist with other readers' advisory queries."[298] One example was the ReadThisNow (RTN) program of the Cleveland Public Library and the CLEVNET consortium of Ohio libraries, which was "rolled into the broader statewide virtual-reference consortium, KnowItNow" in late 2004.[299] Available to all Ohio public libraries, RTN offered round-the-clock access to "genre geniuses,"[300] including "overnight service ... handled by sixty-two librarians independently contracted for the project ... who were selected after successfully completing tests of their reference and technology skills."[301] One aspect of the online world reinforced the other. In the same way that virtual-reference staff "pushed" web pages to users, virtual readers' advisors pushed one or more ready-made online lists to potential readers according to their expressed preferences.

Increasingly, these preferences were determined by elaborate online questionnaires (forms) that effectively segmented patrons into categories based on appeal elements. Once a patron's form was submitted and analyzed, the patron's profile was established and list(s) that best matched that profile could then be pushed to the patron. Since profile analysis took time, e-mail-based readers' advisory was preferred. As Barry Trott explained, just as there were two types of virtual-reference service, there were two types of virtual readers' advisory service: "synchronous (chat-based) or asynchronous (e-mail based)."[302] While chat-based service had the advantage of providing immediate reading suggestions and encouraged follow-up questions that could clarify users' needs, e-mail-based readers' advisory had more potential because it could be automated through the use of standardized forms and was therefore "scaleable."[303] It also offered staff "the opportunity to practice readers' advisory work in a less threatening atmosphere, without the direct pressure of a waiting patron."[304] Providing examples of forms from, among others, the Lincoln City (Nebraska) Libraries (LCL); the Massillon (Ohio) Public Library; and the Williamsburg (Virginia) Regional Library (WRL), Trott noted that form-based service was "within the reach of most libraries"[305] because it could be based on appeal-elements theory.

Despite Trott's assertion that "the more in-depth forms actually provide a closer approximation of a readers' advisory interaction in that the choices the reader makes from the menu of offerings draw out the reader's interests in a way that simply listing titles does not do,"[306] these forms were another step in the deskilling of readers' advisory. Based on a series of multiple-choice clickable menu options, they defined users as the sum of their clicks, paving the way for mechanical and automated analyses of reading preferences. The LCL form asked readers to "[p]ick the top five types of fiction you most enjoy reading" and then offered 25 choices, not counting "other." They then indicated their favorite authors; preference for male or female protagonists; preferred appeal elements such as "snappy dialogue"; and the existence of "any hobbies or interests that you'd like to read about in the plot of a fiction novel." If an individual wanted nonfiction, a similar set of questions was provided. At the end of the form, there was a question asking about "any subject areas, world issues, political or social views, etc. that you would rather *not* read about, in either fiction or non-fiction," as well as an opportunity "to tell us anything else about yourself and your personal reading interests that has not been covered by the questions above."[307]

One of the most in-depth forms was developed by WRL. Here, users indicated whether they had "high interest," "OK [interest]," or "No [interest]" in 20 genres and formats. After listing five favorite books/authors and five least-favorite books/authors, they rated on a seven-point Likert scale their preferences for 10 tone, style, mood, and language elements. Did they want their book to be "Happy, Light, Uplifting" or "Dark, Ironic"? Did they want it to have a "Resolved Ending" or one that left them "thinking"? Did they want it to be "Sentimental, Emotional Style" or stark and realistic? Did they want a book that was "Safe, Relaxing" or "Suspenseful, Tense"? They were also asked to indicate high, medium, or low interest in appeal elements such as: characters; action and events; issues and ideas; clever dialogue; and absurd humor. They specified their preference for "characters who are sure of themselves" or "conflicted characters"; the age, gender, ethnicity, and relationship status of their preferred characters; and their preferred geographical and demographic settings. They were asked whether they wanted their book to avoid or include 15 elements such as: sexual themes; violence; death; sympathetic portrayals of crime; dark or cynical humor; technology; anti-religious themes or statements; pro-religious themes or statements; right wing politics; left wing politics; or addiction. Finally, they were asked whether they wanted a book that dealt with or avoided 31 subjects, including animals; gardens; disasters; other cultures; romantic relationships; outdoor activities; food; holidays; and medicine and health.[308] To say the least, the WRL form was a microscopic fragmentation of reading tastes into component parts that segmented and profiled users, then provided them with a book or book list best suited to their precise specifications. But it was also an exercise that left little room for the broadening of horizons or the exploration of alternative viewpoints. It did not provide the opportunity for meaningful education that had been the hallmark of readers' advisory in the pre–1963 period.

Although these forms were still in their infancy at the beginning of 2006 and were physically processed by local readers' advisors, they were susceptible to analysis by algorithm-based profiling software that would segment users into micro-categories and generate lists of books that had been deemed to meet users' criteria. It was only a matter of time before readers were divided into 66 Claritas-like lifestyle or preference clusters, each of which could then be further subdivided into as many "mini-clusters" as desired. Once a patron's profile was determined, a ranked list (e.g., "Science Fiction: Ironic; Resolved Ending; Emotional Style; Conflicted Characters; Includes Cynical Humor; Excludes Outdoor Activities" or "Romances: Uplifting; Requires Thinking; Tense; Includes Animals") of books adhering as closely as possible to the profile would be "pushed" to the patron. This in turn depended on two things: first, the development of "a controlled vocabulary of appeal,"[309] the basis of which had already been established by Saricks; and, second, the segmentation of books according to that controlled vocabulary. When Ross explained that readers' preferences could be indicated by letter combinations such as ALOS or EJNT, it was a short step to defining those preferences by even lengthier (and weighted) numeric and letter combinations of the kind made possible by elaborate WRL-like forms and then matching these results algorithmically against a list of books that had been assigned weighted values on a wide range of appeal elements defined in terms of controlled vocabulary. Just as Robinson and Molz at the BCPL had relied on task-trained paraprofessionals for collection development and other services, so readers' advisory based on a controlled vocabulary of appeal presaged task-trained paraprofessionals or deskilled librarians feeding WRL-like forms through profiling software that would generate lists of recent popular fiction and nonfiction to match readers' preferences. Every library worker could indeed be a readers' advisor, but it was superficial and deskilled readers' advisory with no meaningful educational purpose.

Of course, all this presupposed that readers' advisory would remain an in-house endeavor. For some public libraries, this was undoubtedly the case. Even though libraries such as the JCL, WPL, and WRL offered ready-made lists and profiling forms, these lists and forms at least had the virtue of being either in-house creations or links to the in-house creations of other public libraries. But, in the same way that cataloging and collection development were first deskilled and then outsourced when technological advances segmented, routinized, and automated formerly high-level library specializations that had been predominantly performed by relatively well-paid female professional librarians,[310] many public libraries in the middle 2000s began to view readers' advisory work as something that could be outsourced. Perhaps this was inevitable, given the gradual deskilling of readers' advisory described in previous sections of this chapter. As Roma M. Harris and Victoria Marshall pointed out, when tasks that had once been intellectually intensive were simplified, fragmented, and mechanized, they were pushed "down the organizational hierarchy," where they were carried out by "less expensive nonprofessional staff."[311] But when these same tasks became even more simplified and automated, they "may be pushed entirely out of the waged work structure in libraries."[312] This was an elegant way of saying that libraries outsourced once-valorized functions that had demanded a high degree of knowledge and care, turning to external companies and organizations that promised them significant financial savings to perform now-deskilled and devalorized tasks as quickly and inexpensively as possible.

If NoveList had pushed readers' advisory "down the organizational hierarchy" such that it could be performed by "less expensive nonprofessional staff," companies and products such as DearReader, BookLetters, EBSCO's NextReads, and whichbook.net signaled that readers' advisory was ready to be "pushed entirely out of the waged work structure in libraries." Emphasizing how much time and effort their turnkey services would save library staff, they assumed an increasingly larger share of readers' advisory work in public libraries.[313] DearReader's signature product was e-mail book clubs, but it also provided outbound e-newsletter-lists and moderated virtual discussion groups.[314] Patrons who registered for one or more of DearReader's 11 book clubs—for example, Business, Fiction, Nonfiction, Good News, Horror, Mystery, Romance, and Science Fiction—through their library's web page were sent by e-mail a daily "5-minute sample from a book," typically a genre title or a best-seller, such that "[b]y the end of the week, you'll have read 2–3 chapters."[315] Targeted at multi-tasking and time-strapped individuals, DearReader's e-mail book clubs were an important part of the readers' advisory web pages of 760 library systems and 3,000 individual libraries,[316] including the Gwinnett County (Georgia) Public Library and the Los Angeles Public Library. Indeed, "over 300,000 people start[ed] their morning with a [DearReader] 5-minute read from their local library." DearReader also prepared "21 genre related newsletters" that libraries could post on their web pages and/or send to patrons. These newsletters were enhanced lists of recent titles, providing "book jackets, descriptions, book reviews, author commentaries, links to [a library's] card catalog and discussion questions." In addition, library staff could create "customized" newsletter-lists by using "easily generated" "content" from "book databases that [DearReader] provide[d] from Ingram and *Publishers Weekly*." Newsletter-lists and web pages were "automatically branded so they integrate seamlessly into your current web site," thus "requiring no staff intervention." Finally, libraries could avail themselves of a DearReader-moderated online book-discussion forum, as well as readers' advisory marketing assistance, including web design, programming, art work, flyers, and promotional ideas.

Proud that all its services could "be up and running at your library in a few days, with virtually no [library] staff time required," DearReader may have been the very embodiment of a responsive supplier, but it also ensured the complete deskilling of readers' advisory work. Library staff members were relieved of the burden of recommending or suggesting meaningful books for patrons on an individual basis; they no longer had to expend thought and energy creating intellectually meaningful reading courses; and they no longer had to spend time participating in reading groups. Everything was done for them by DearReader. With its cloying "Thanks for reading with me. It's so good to read with friends" slogan, DearReader substituted unctuousness for substance, aligning itself with the kind of superficial, entertainment-oriented, and "Less Rembrandt, more Me" reading that could be done in five-minute increments. As commodified pleasure reading became the norm, the idea that readers' advisory could be a force for meaningful education was nothing but a distant memory. By contracting with DearReader and similar companies, public-library administrators relegated their staff members to the role of "automatic figures" who ensured a ready supply of recent genre titles and bestsellers at their institutions or cut-and-pasted DearReader-supplied content into newsletter-lists. Downplaying the value of educated, knowledgeable, and analytical librarians capable of in-depth critical discussion about culturally and historically significant books, public libraries also downplayed the central role of culturally and historically significant books in the acquisition of meaningful education.

Much like DearReader, BookLetters offered public libraries genre-based e-newsletter-lists, custom e-newsletter-lists, regularly updated bestseller and award lists, and online book clubs to enhance their readers' advisory service.[317] As with DearReader, emphasis was placed on easing the burden on library staff. To judge by some of BookLetters's promotional copy, library staff members were next to superfluous: "Some of the [subscribing] libraries don't touch BookLetters for months, but most spend about an hour per week." Or again: "Since listings [provided by BookLetters] carry the library identity and link to [the] library OPAC, they appear as if created by library staff." Equally important was the low price of its products, with base "[a]nnual costs" of $600 and an additional $30 per 1,000 patrons, "up to a maximum of $5,000 per year." Eager customers included the Wellesley (Massachusetts) Free Library, Highland Park (Illinois) Public Library, and the Lawrence (Kansas) Public Library.

Once patrons of these and other libraries clicked on the BookLetters icon on their libraries' web pages, they could choose to receive e-newsletter-lists such as "Book Sizzle" ("Stay up-to-date on books in the news. From authors on the air to the latest movie adaptations, you'll always know what's on"); "New Fiction" ("Stay informed on what's hot in fiction, from young sensations to established literary masters.... [Y]ou'll get reviews of tomorrow's bestsellers, with selections in women's fiction, historical novels, suspense and more"); "Mystery" ("Get the lowdown on the hottest whodunits"); and hardcover fiction and nonfiction bestseller lists from the *New York Times*. These lists could also be posted on libraries' web pages. In addition, libraries could subscribe to the BookLetters Daily program. After patrons signed up for one or more of the Fiction, Nonfiction, Mystery, and Teen book clubs, they "receive[d] a daily e-mail carrying [the subscribing] library's name, address and contact information that includes BookPage content (reviews and interviews), a brief book excerpt and insightful comments from our knowledgeable club hosts." For staff members who were too "[t]ired of updating bestseller lists each week, or scouring the web to find the latest award winners," BookLetters supplied an easy-to-install link such that "your library will never have to worry about updating those listings again." In light of the comprehensive nature of these services, it was almost as if public libraries had become BookLetter franchises, with library employees in ancillary roles.

Certainly, library staff could cut and paste generic descriptions of recent books from BookLetters-supplied bibliographic databases into "custom" newsletter-lists, thus controlling their "look and feel" by inserting vendor-supplied "stock messages," "Book Covers and Annotations," and "Spotlight Pages" into "[c]ustom e-Newsletter message blocks" and introductions. But this supposed customization of newsletter-lists by deskilled library staff members was an apt metaphor for the state of reading experience at North American public libraries in the early 21st century. Just as customized newsletter-lists were a pastiche of ready-made elements waiting to be sorted into various combinations that gave only the illusion of difference to the finished product, so the reading experiences of many library patrons consisted of entertainment-oriented and "more Me" genre titles and bestsellers whose essential unidimensionality was cloaked by what at first glance seemed to be a plethora of different appeal elements, but on closer examination was nothing more than a set of formulas that delivered pre-determined sensations, feelings, and experiences.

Although NextReads, "a subscription email service developed by the creators of NoveList" to compete with BookLetters, claimed that it went beyond bestsellers to include read-alikes on its lists for those times "[w]hen all of your copies of the best sellers [or new releases] are out" and "there are long hold lists" for them, there was scant difference between NextReads and its competitors on a structural level.[318] NextReads provided 20 genre-based e-mail lists, including fantasy, inspirational fiction, historical fiction, romance, horror, mystery, science fiction, armchair travel, business and marketing, mind and body fitness, history and current events, and popular culture. Each of the lists contained three sections: new releases; alternative read-alikes; and "forthcoming titles in the genre or some hot theme tied to the list topic or genre." Brief two- or three-sentence descriptions accompanied each listed title. Just like DearReader and BookLetters, NextReads emphasized that "[l]ittle or no additional work is required by library staff after initial set-up—NextReads supports and manages the email application, content archives, reading lists, the works!" Library staff members were also offered a special "Book Display Ideas" list that served as "[a] starting point of ideas and titles for creating book displays that will highlight your midlist and capture the attention of your patrons." Although NextReads stated that its lists were customizable, it also noted that "[a]n Advance List of all the titles ... in forthcoming Newsletters is sent at least two months prior to the Newsletters' distribution to subscribers so that lists can be checked against your collection," thus allowing libraries "to order and/or process titles to meet anticipated demand." When all was said and done, this was a recipe for homogenous entertainment-oriented and NextReads-driven collections based on genre-specific popular fiction and nonfiction, especially in light of NextReads' admission that "sales rating[s]" were one of the factors used in determining book choices. It was as if library staff no longer even had to think or generate their own ideas.

With whichbook.net, a database developed by United Kingdom-based (UK) Applied Psychology Research Ltd. and Opening the Mind Ltd. that was offered for free to UK public libraries, the microscopic fragmentation of reading tastes according to appeal elements reached dizzying heights.[319] Allowing "each individual to build the elements of that elusive 'good read' we are all looking for but don't quite know how to define," whichbook provided readers a choice of "building" their next reading experience according to either "mood and style" elements or "plot, character and setting." If they chose to use "mood and style," they were presented with 12 scales, including "safe-disturbing," "gentle-violent," "optimistic-bleak," "beautiful-disgusting," and "larger than life-down to earth." Picking up to four of these scales, they could indicate, by way of a sliding cursor, the precise degree of "mood and style" they wanted: "you can look for a book that is unpredictable, very romantic and a little bit sad. Or a challenging book that's also funny with plenty of sex." Readers could also select according to plot, character, and setting, specifying that they wanted, for example, a book containing a "mixed race" straight female character (age 50+) with a "success against the odds" plot set in East Africa or a book featuring a "lots of twists and turns" plot set in Argentina whose main character was a black gay man between the ages of 26 and 50. Once they had made their parameter selections, the database returned a list of "best," "good," and "fair" book matches. After scrolling through the list and choosing a matched title, users were presented with the comments of other readers who had read the book in question and "[t]he titles of and authors of three books or films considered to be parallels" to it. Although it certainly was a "cool tool[],"[320] whichbook made library staff members little more than low-paid, deskilled, and devalorized check-out clerks mechanically processing books suggested by impersonal Advisermatik-like devices. This became even more the case when UK public libraries were offered access to another online tool (also developed by Opening the Book Ltd.) called reader2reader.net, which permitted readers to review, discuss, recommend, or disparage books.[321] As readers chatted among themselves on reader2reader.net about books they had selected using whichbook, public libraries became the equivalents of warehouses dispensing products.

Boasting that "20 million different individual permutations [were] possible," whichbook appeared to offer limitless choice, but it was a choice based on the fragmentation of books into minute segments, which were enshrined in what amounted to a weighted "controlled vocabulary of appeal" assigned by a "specially trained" person. Books were no longer integral and artistically indivisible wholes, but a series of commodified mix-and-match menu options catering to lifestyle choices and preferences. Even more so than the WRL-type forms described above, whichbook reduced reading to a consumerist act: books were disassembled into their component parts and then re-built to suit customized specifications. As readers busied themselves with sliding their cursors this way and that on whichbook scales, books were seen in terms of desired appeal elements rather than their social, cultural, or historical importance. Reading was all about entertainment, personalization, customization, and "more Me," not about meaningful education through serious and purposeful literature that did not necessarily suit an individual's precise menu order.

DearReader, BookLetters, NextReads, and whichbook certainly made readers' advisory work easier for participating libraries, but they also consecrated them as "ticket-offices" where deskilled librarians and paraprofessionals practiced "librarianship by automatic figures," circulating entertainment-oriented bestselling books that had been chosen by and filtered through distant organizations. Although these services appeared to be personalized or customized, it was personalization and customization masquerading as a managerial strategy to cut labor costs and maximize delivery of bestselling fiction and nonfiction to library users. As such, it was a far cry from the individual and in-depth attention that knowledgeable readers' advisors had given patrons in the 1920s and 1930s in order to set them on the road toward meaningful education. Instead, readers' advisors in the early 21st century resigned themselves to being delivery mechanisms for popular and ephemeral fiction and nonfiction that benefited not only from the structural power of corporate publishers, but also from the intercession of secondary agents such as DearReader, BookLetters, NextReads, and whichbook. And, in allowing these secondary agents to take over the mechanical slotting of patrons into categories based on genre or appeal-element preferences, public librarians forsook any pretense that readers' advisory was concerned with intensive individual attention, let alone the type of reading that led to meaningful education.

In Bourdieu's terms, readers' advisory was now a field that had been conquered by "the logic of commercial production" that emphasized entertainment-oriented commodities.[322] It was a field that accepted at face value the assertions of "promotional culture"[323] and "the empire of the economy"[324] that industrial literature and compromised middle-brow literature were worthy. It was a field that, by validating the argument that pleasure reading of any kind contributed to personal meaning-making, had sold its soul to entertainment and edutainment. It was a field that had abandoned those searching for meaningful educational opportunities through serious and purposeful reading of books that had enduring cultural, historical, philosophical, or social value: the type of books that, in the words of the Dunkirk, New York, businessman referred to in chapter 4, could "get me some place."

Chapter 6

Case Studies of Readers' Advisory Resources in the Early 21st Century

Case Study 1: The NoveList Database

BACKGROUND INFORMATION

This case study has two parts. In two iterations of a Readers' Advisory course taught by the first-named author at a major Canadian university in the summer 2004 term and the winter 2005 term, students were asked to complete two assignments that form the basis of this case study. In the first assignment, they examined the NoveList informational record (IR) for their favorite novel. Did the NoveList IR (i.e., subject headings, descriptions, and accompanying reviews) give a good sense of that novel? This assignment attempted to take stock of the quality of IRs available in NoveList. Specific instructions for this assignment are contained in appendix A. Of the 77 students enrolled in the two iterations of the above-mentioned course, 69 (89.6 percent) allowed us to analyze their responses for the first assignment. The second assignment asked students to simulate finding a novel that was similar to their favorite novel. Using the "Find Similar Books" feature in NoveList, they were asked to define their favorite novel in whatever terms they wanted from the available subject headings; then pick one of the novels that NoveList suggested as being similar to their favorite novel; read that novel; and, finally, comment about NoveList's suggested choice. Specific instructions for this assignment are contained in appendix A. This assignment attempted to gauge overall satisfaction levels with NoveList reading suggestions. Of the 77 students enrolled in the two iterations of the above-mentioned course, 69 (89.6 percent) allowed us to analyze their responses for the second assignment.

ASSESSING THE QUALITY OF NOVELIST INFORMATIONAL RECORDS (IRs)

Sixty-seven unique novels were selected by the 69 participating students.[1] Some of the novels identified as favorites were: Yasunari Kawabata's *Thousand Cranes*; Douglas Coupland's *Microserfs*; Jamie O'Neill's *At Swim Two Boys*; Andrew Pyper's *Lost Girls*; Kazuo Ishiguro's *The Unconsoled*; Emily Brontë's *Wuthering Heights*; John Grisham's *The Firm*; Virginia Woolf's *To the Lighthouse*; Judith Guest's *Ordinary People*; Jack Kerouac's *On the Road*; Guy Gavriel Kay's *Tigana*; Donna Tartt's *The Little Friend*; Gustave Flaubert's *Bouvard and Pécuchet*;

Anita Diamant's *The Red Tent*; Jane Austen's *Pride and Prejudice*; William Faulkner's *Absalom, Absalom!*; Toni Morrison's *Beloved*; and Chuck Palahniuk's *Survivor*.

The mean rating for all 69 IRs was 32.3 on a scale of 0–50, where 45–50 was "excellent," 40–44 was "very good to good," 30–39 was "acceptable," 20–29 was "inadequate," and 0–19 was "laughable." Four of the 69 participating students rated their IRs as "excellent" (5.8 percent); 16 as "very good to good" (23.2 percent); 27 as "acceptable" (39.1 percent); 14 as "inadequate" (20.3 percent); and 8 as "laughable" (11.6 percent). The three highest scores were 48, 47, and 46 (Kate Atkinson's *Behind the Scenes at the Museum*; Gabriel García Márquez's *One Hundred Years of Solitude*; Grisham's *The Firm*, respectively). The three lowest scores were 10, 9, and 1 (Larry Niven and Jerry Pournelle's *The Mote in God's Eye*; Alistair MacLeod's *No Great Mischief*; and Kawabata's *Thousand Cranes*, respectively). Three rating groups emerged: the "excellent" and "very good to good" group (29 percent); the "acceptable" group (39.1 percent); and the "inadequate" and "laughable" group (31.9 percent). Depending on whether one chose to see the middle "acceptable" group as part of the first or third group, NoveList IRs were either very good or inadequate. In addition to quantitative ratings, students were asked to provide written comments to explain their numeric ratings. A content analysis of the 69 assignments was performed to identify predominant themes and issues, which are summarized in table 1 of appendix B. Because each student's assignment could contain multiple themes or issues, the figures in table 1 of appendix B do not add to 69. Definitions for terminology used were taken from *The Concise Oxford Dictionary of Literary Terms* and M. H. Abram's *A Glossary of Literary Terms* (7th ed.).[2] Overall, these comments showed that, while some NoveList IRs performed their work commendably, many others had serious shortcomings. Table 2 in appendix B displays the relationship among student ratings, the number of subject headings in the IR, and the number of accompanying reviews in the IR. In broad terms, the greater the number of subject headings and reviews in an IR, the greater the chances that the IR would be rated as "excellent," "very good to good," or "acceptable."

Positive Comments about NoveList Informational Records

Reviews were especially praised for giving insight into "how the writing style ... impacted the reader" and in helping "capture the intangible aspects of the books, such as the mood, atmosphere, and themes." A student commenting about the IR for Mark Dunn's *Ella Minnow Pea* wrote that "The reviews paint the most accurate picture of the book. References to the works of Vonnegut, Orwell, and Bradbury serve to embed this novel within a certain thematic realm, and give the reader an idea of what type of tone and attitude might be forthcoming. Within the reviews, most of the components that are missing from the subject headings are ... enumerated." The student writing about Paulo Coelho's *The Alchemist* concurred, explaining that the reviews "aptly capture[] the tone of the novel." Other students commented how the book reviews for *At Swim Two Boys* were able to communicate "my own feeling of urgency"; how the reviews for *Beloved* perfectly described its structure as "a fluid but fragmented continuum of past and present" delivered through "intense visual images"; or how the reviews for Anne Michaels's *Fugitive Pieces* conveyed the author's use of language "to create joy and great pathos." In sum, reviews provided "a bigger picture of the novel."

Negative Comments about NoveList Informational Records

Students whose favorite novels were classics were particularly disappointed in NoveList IRs, characterizing them as misleading or simply inaccurate. The student who chose

Absalom, Absalom! rued that "[t]here is no indication of the chronologically- and character-specific surround levels of the story. Nor is there any indication of the kind of narrative, linguistic, and stylistic complexities that permeate this book, and are such an important aspect of its tone and themes. Moreover, the relation of this central plot is at best arguable and at worst misleading, because it reduces what happens to only one possible explanation, something that the book itself takes pains to suggest may not be possible (perhaps one of the novel's guiding structural principles)." The student who chose Charlotte Brontë's *Villette* observed that it "is a gleefully subversive gothic ghost story, wedding Victorian psychology, drug induced hallucinations and wickedly funny feminist social critique in an experimental style that not only simulates madness but also pointedly subverts novelistic conventions. But NoveList provides a misleading bibliographic description and summary, inadequate subject headings, and gives little sense of the novel's genre, literary connections or influence. The lack of reviews and more thorough synopses provided outside the novel's own page suggests organizational problems endemic to the database itself." The IR for Philip Roth's *Portnoy's Complaint* was taken to task because it "evinces none of the novel's intrinsic comic value." The subject headings in the IR for *Bouvard and Pécuchet* "render an inadequate representation of the work in terms of its themes, narrative, characters, and subject matter. A single subject heading with two free-floating subdivisions has been assigned to describe the content of the work (i.e., French fiction—19th century—Translations into English).... It is no exaggeration to state that [this] could equally apply to thousands of titles of nineteenth-century French fiction."

Perhaps the most outraged comments came from the student who selected *Dune*. "If Frank Herbert had ever heard NoveList's description of his beloved *Dune*, I believe he would have turned in his grave. The 'savages,' so inadequately described by NoveList, are a race of people Herbert modeled after the Bedouin tribes of North Africa. The 'Fremen' are a nomadic race of people that were the first to colonize Arrakis, a planet that has absolutely no open water and very little moisture. The Fremen are hardly savages, they practise Zen-Buddhism, they are expert fighters, they have managed to adapt to their environment by designing suits that retain their water, they harvest 90 percent of all the spice used in the empire, and it was through their efforts that Paul was able to usurp the emperor. Not only were the Fremen not savages, they also did not struggle over water; instead, they fought for control of the spice."

The IRs for somewhat less well-known novels were also harshly criticized. The IR for *Ordinary People* was judged to be "laughable" because "[t]he description gives no indication of the many nuances of the story and the writing, and gives little sense of the intelligent way that the material is handled. In addition, the description is misleading about what is fundamentally a hopeful, life-affirming book." The IR for *The Mote in God's Eye* was found to be "not particularly accurate." The IR for Maeve Binchey's *Quentins* was deemed to be misleading: "If I did not know this book, I would come away thinking that this book was mostly about a restaurant called Quentins, and through Ella's filming of a documentary, we heard stories about the restaurant and its patrons. When in actuality, this novel was about a girl entering adulthood and the experiences she had along the way. The author covered her family, love life, career, and friends." Equally misleading was the IR for Rosamunde Pilcher's *The Shell Seekers*, which characterized the book as romantic fiction despite the fact that about 80 percent of the book is "about an elderly woman facing death, and her desire to understand her past and leave a legacy to her children."

The IR for Mary Janice Davidson's *Undead and Unwed* seemed to miss the point completely: "Betsy may be the stereotypical dumb blond, who does all the stereotypical girly things, but she does not subscribe to the male-dominant/female subservient idea and consequently the book has a strong female empowerment aspect. Betsy beats up rapists, muggers, pedophiles, and murderers. By juxtaposing the stereotype and the female empowerment the author is devaluing the stereotype. I like a feminist perspective in my books, but NoveList doesn't provide that option in the subject headings, and, in fact, seems to be emphasizing the stereotype in the description." And the IR for *Lost Girls* omitted "the fact that this novel is a coming of age story and that the other elements (murder, trial, etc.) are less prevalent in the text—the book is misrepresented. The database has neglected its responsibilities to the reader, the author and to the book to properly represent it; instead they have created a standard book profile that is very generic."

As a result, many students said that they never would have read their favorite novel in the first place if they had only read the NoveList IR for it. "I probably would not pick *On the Road* if I had to rely on [the] NoveList description alone. It presents readers with a form, a mere shell of a wonderful and vivid novel." The student whose favorite book was *Microserfs* offered the same assessment, as did the student whose favorite book was *Ordinary People*. For these students, the skeletal nature of NoveList IRs defeated the purpose of the entire database, which they assumed was to expand, not restrict, readers' horizons. The student who wrote about *Villette* had perhaps the most comprehensive evaluation of the gaps in its IR: "The subject headings, while technically accurate, are overly general and incomplete: *Love stories, English; Autobiographical novels; Teachers–Brussels; England–Social life and customs–19th century.* More problematically, the disregard for more accurate available headings frustrates finding connections to similar works" such as *Wuthering Heights*, "Henry James' story of a sexually/socially repressed governess who may or may not be seeing ghosts, *The Turn of the Screw*," or Charlotte Perkins Gilman's *The Yellow Wallpaper*, a narrative about "socially induced delusions instilled by the rest cure."

The student who wrote about the IR for Mervyn Peake's *Titus Groan* shared the previous assessment: "[t]he description is perfectly accurate, but short, simple and factual, and gives few clues to suggest what the book is really like.... The subject headings provided by NoveList do little to specify this work, which makes it doubtful that NoveList has done enough to capture its nature to identify other works that are actually similar out of the mass of existing literature." A similar complaint was raised by the student who wrote about the IR for Cormac McCarthy's *All the Pretty Horses*. Here, the IR made no mention that the "novel is part of a new breed of Westerns but has its roots deep in the traditions of southern writers like Faulkner; strangely, NoveList makes no mention of genre whatsoever." As the student writing about the IR for Laurie R. King's *Folly* observed, "NoveList descriptions cater to the lowest common denominator-type reader. NoveList, in fact, does such a poor job of linking similar books, I do not believe sophisticated readers will find it useful at all."

Students also criticized NoveList's inability to capture "intangible aspects such as feelings, tone, stylistic elements, mood, atmosphere, etc." The student whose favorite novel was Gary Jennings's *Aztec* was especially distressed about this. "The characters and places in *Aztec* are living, breathing, full of sights and sounds; not dry, dusty places time forgot. Having read a lot of historical fiction, there are few authors who can match Jennings for his ability to recreate lost worlds. The NoveList entry for this book contains a brief description, publishing information, subject headings, notes regarding sequels and a reference to the author's website.... I found this entry to be terribly lacking in capturing anything about the novel, let alone 'important aspects.'" The IR for *Microserfs* was equally uninformative: "The entry fails to acknowledge the book's pastiche writing style, which, containing sophisticated literary techniques as well as amusing pop culture references, offers both 'high brow' and 'low brow' elements—and yet deliberately explodes rather than unifies or straddles them." The student who selected William Maxwell's *So Long, See You Tomorrow* was disconcerted to find that its IR lacked any mention of the book's prose, which was "sparse, yet remarkably evocative, recalling events with lyricism and poignancy." It also failed to convey "the book's sense of wisdom and accompanying tone of moderation and sympathy." The IR for *The Unconsoled* overlooked the novel's relationship to magical realism and its experimental writing techniques. The IR for T. H. White's *The Once and Future King* lacked just about everything the student loved about the book: its "serious philosophical speculation"; its "deliberate anachronisms"; and its unique combination of profundity and humor. The IR for *On the Road* did not even hint at "the fascinating simplicity and beauty of the language used in the novel. Sentences flow naturally, and long after I read the novel I found out that it was literally written in one breath—in three weeks on a single roll of paper. It seems that the book so full of life could be created only in such a laborious outburst of energy." Finally, the IR for Michel Faber's *The Crimson Petal and the White*, "lacks any reference to the novel's intangible aspects such as its complex themes—religion, gender, love, etc.—and stylistic elements—elaborate and carefully detailed descriptions, intense dialogue, and gripping narrative." By neglecting to consider the complex totality of a book, NoveList missed numerous opportunities to create intriguing linkages between and among different kinds of books—a fact that one student said was especially important with genre-bending "lateral works."

CONCLUDING OBSERVATIONS ABOUT NOVELIST INFORMATIONAL RECORDS

Three comments summarized many of the concerns expressed so far. A student whose favorite book was *Tigana* observed that NoveList's fundamental flaw was "its inability to deal with novels that exceed the boundaries for their genre. It was created for novels that have conventional plots and easily identified themes, character types and setting. This shortcoming reflects the reality that most readers want to be directed quickly and easily to novels that fall within the conventional boundaries of their preferred genre. NoveList, to encourage readers to reach beyond these limits, should create a section called 'Best in the Genre' for those readers who want to read the finest novelist in their class, not just the latest paperback churned out for the best seller's list." A student whose favorite book was Rohinton Mistry's *A Fine Balance* concluded that "[a]lthough one can break down a book into its individual components and try to identify appeal factors, no amount of analysis can truly capture the essence of an individual's personal experience of a book. The best method for understanding the meaning of a book to a reader is to read, too. And though any two people might react differently to the same book, any avid reader will understand the sensation one experiences when reading a book that truly touches them. The best reader's advisory, therefore, will always be a human being—not a computer." Another student agreed, noting that "[w]hen a librarian describes a book they use their own emotions and body language to show how much a book meant to them. A review has no way of conferring the same excitement, boredom or disgust as a real person." All three students sensed that books could not be reduced to a convenient list of appeal elements, since each book revealed itself most fully as a complex and indivisible whole that addressed each reader on numerous psychological and intellectual levels.

THE QUALITY OF NOVELIST SUGGESTIONS OR RECOMMENDATIONS

For assignment 2, students were asked whether they would suggest or recommend to a library patron the novel that NoveList suggested or recommended as being similar to their favorite novel. As shown in table 1 of appendix C, 13 percent would unequivocally do so, while another 5.8 percent would do so for the most part. If these two categories are combined, then only 18.8 percent would suggest or recommend to a library patron the NoveList-recommended novel. On the other hand, 39.1 percent would unequivocally not suggest the NoveList-recommended novel, while another 18.8 percent would for the most part not suggest it. Adding these two categories, 57.97 percent would not suggest the NoveList-recommended novel. Another 23.2 percent of students were ambivalent.

Students were given the option of selecting the first-, second-, third-, or fourth-listed NoveList recommendation as their single choice for the novel that appeared to them to be most similar to their favorite novel. As shown in table 2 of appendix C, 25 students chose the novel ranked first by NoveList; 11 chose the second-ranked novel; 10 chose the third-ranked novel; and 15 chose the fourth-ranked novel. Eight students were not satisfied with any of the first four NoveList suggestions, and so opted to select a title that appeared later in the NoveList-recommended list. But no matter whether the novel was ranked first, second, third, fourth, or beyond in NoveList, 50 percent or more of students said that they were either unequivocally or for the most part dissatisfied with that choice. Overall, 40 students (59.97 percent) would not suggest to patrons the NoveList-recommended novel. Their reasons are summarized in table 3 of appendix C. Often a student mentioned multiple reasons, and so the figures appearing in table 3 of appendix C do not add to 69. Finally, based on their in-depth knowledge of their favorite book, 45 students included the name of a novel that they would suggest instead of the NoveList-recommended title.

POSITIVE COMMENTS ABOUT NOVELIST RECOMMENDATIONS

One of the most positive assessments came from the student whose favorite novel was *Fugitive Pieces* and whose choice of "required" and "desired" elements led to Carol Shields's *Unless*. After commenting that both authors "tend to be lyrical and poetical" and that both "use internal monologue of their narrators to wax philosophic on matters both great and small," this student observed that "[o]n numerous occasions, they were able to swing from poetical prose to horrific description, successfully engendering that emotion that can only be described as lump-in-your-throat.... Michaels almost drowns you in poetry and emotions, making you feel like you're in a whirlpool, leaving you breathless and exhausted. Shields is more subtle, drawing you into what you think is a domestic drama about a family suffering loss, then blindsiding you with philosophy and theory.... Although these styles seem at odds with each other, they are only two different ways of approaching the same goal: to expand the mind of the reader without making the subjects at hand dull or trivial." For the student whose favorite novel was Mark Haddon's *The Curious Incident of the Dog in the Night-time*, NoveList's first-ranked suggestion of Robert Barnard's *Out of the Blackout* was ideal because "[t]he character development of each of the main characters includes some form of psychological and physiological trauma that influences their experience of life and the challenges they seek to overcome in their lives." One reason for their satisfaction may have been that they both indicated many search parameters when searching for a novel like their favorite: seven (1 required; 6 desired) and eleven (2 required; 9 desired), respectively.

But it was not always necessary to have detailed search parameters. Even with only three search parameters checked (1 required; 2 desired), the student who selected *How To Be Good* by Nick Hornby as her/his favorite novel was suitably impressed with NoveList's recommendation of John Mortimer's *Felix in the Underworld*. This student wrote: "[B]oth novels address more serious topics beneath the comedy—themes of the decline of British society, homelessness, the definition of goodness, and others. Both novels share a general feeling of mild despair for the state of British society—in *How to Be Good*, David's initial anger and cynicism reflects this mood, while in *Felix in the Underworld*, the feeling is of a society gone off the rails, with lawyers who don't seem too concerned about justice and publishers and readers who don't care about literary values."

Even when the NoveList-recommended novel was not really similar to the student's favorite novel, some students found the NoveList recommendations compelling. A student whose favorite novel was John Irving's *The Cider House Rules* selected *Cold Times* by Elizabeth Jordan Moore from among the first four NoveList recommendations: "While there were a lot of elements missing from the subject list of my original choice in the second book, I must say that *Cold Times* did satisfy my reading tastes. Unlike NoveList would have us believe, it is not necessary to always read books similar or identical to those that we currently like to read. Many gems can be found if we are willing to take some risks with unknown authors and book titles." What this student particularly appreciated in *Cold Times* was that its author "uses empathy and care in revealing her characters and their motivations. She does a very good job showing the reader why some baffling choices might have been selected in certain situations."

AMBIGUOUS COMMENTS ABOUT NOVELIST RECOMMENDATIONS

One central theme dominated the comments of students who found NoveList recommendations ambiguous. Although they found that their favorite novels and the NoveList-recommended novels superficially resembled one another at the level of plot and theme, they often discovered that, as in the case of the student who compared her favorite novel *Mirror Image* (by Sandra Brown) with the NoveList-recommended *Half Moon Bay* (by Meryl Sawyer), "[i]n terms of tone and stylistic content, Sandra Brown's novel is far superior to Meryl Sawyer's novel in that Brown's writing style is more eloquent, introspective, detailed, and poetic. The characters in Brown's novel are believable, three-dimensional, and painstakingly created to evoke sympathy, pity, and anger from the readers. In Sawyer's novel, the characters appear two-dimensional, quirky, simple-minded, and predictable."

The student whose favorite novel was *Absalom, Absalom!* and who ended up reading Tom Franklin's *Hell at the Breech* based on the NoveList recommendation agreed, remarking that "[t]here are undoubtedly similarities between the two, but they are mainly superficial ones having to do with setting and subject." Specifically, *Hell at the Breech* "[a]ll in all ... was not a bad book," but it "lacks the stylistic and tonal qualities that are such a big part of what I like about [Faulkner], and which seems to pull you into the details of the story in part through the idiosyncrasies of the main characters' individual voices." This student thus had major reservations about "the feasibility of NoveList as a readers' advisory tool."

> By its own parameters, NoveList can only tell me about the more-or-less concrete elements like characters, setting, subject, genre, number of pages, etc. In fact, I doubt that the service does very well by its clients even if they purport to be interested in only these things. When it comes to fiction (and arguably any other kind of writing) I have no doubt that the way that such elements are handled by the author is crucial to the reader's enjoyment and understanding. And this is a factor that is really above and beyond the tangible elements of the story. While I understand the economic and otherwise practical reasons behind developing such a system ('it's better than nothing?'), the NoveList model of readers' advisory seems premised on the idea that subject headings are what one needs to make a choice about what to read; and furthermore, that they can and will mean the same thing to everyone.

A similar concern was expressed by the student whose favorite novel was *The Crimson Petal and the White*. In this case, the student selected the NoveList recommendation

Slammerkin by Emma Donoghue, mainly because "[b]oth novels were well-written historical fiction (pre-modern Britain) that focused on young prostitutes trying to better their lives by infiltrating themselves into particular families. And both novels do a good job of exploring some of the same themes, poverty, gender, home/family." Nevertheless, the student continued: "I would have to warn the reader that if he or she liked *The Crimson Petal and the White* because of its complex and rich narrative, characters, and mood/atmosphere, the reader may not enjoy *Slammerkin* because he or she would not find the same degree of those aspects in the novel. NoveList's 'find similar books' allows the reader to choose the right 'bones' of a book but does not let the reader choose the intangible aspects already discussed. The NoveList user has to rely on the summary and reviews to determine if the similar book has similar intangible aspects, but ... some descriptions do not provide reviews and some summaries are not very good."

Given these views, the student noted that it was imperative that readers' advisors conduct in-depth interviews with patrons because "some books have a certain *je ne sais quoi* quality about them that would be hard to express on screen or even verbally. But at least in person a librarian would be able to conduct the right kind of interview to determine the reader's likes and dislikes and have a proper discussion about certain qualities of books in question, even qualities that are often intangible." The need for in-depth interviews was also brought up by the student whose favorite novel was Kurt Vonnegut's *Slaughterhouse-Five* and who chose Timothy Findley's *The Wars* even though it was NoveList's fifth-ranked recommendation. "'Anti-war stories' was the only subject heading that survived in the list produced by NoveList and so I was provided with an excellent antiwar novel. Whether or not I would recommend *The Wars* to a patron who wanted to find a book similar to *Slaughterhouse-Five* depends on a few variables. It would first of all be necessary to find out why this person liked *Slaughterhouse-Five* and what aspects of the book they were looking for in other books. If the patron decided that the antiwar aspect of the novel was the reason for its appeal and that this was the most important characteristic, then *The Wars* would be an excellent book to recommend. However if a patron was ultimately enamoured with the style of Kurt Vonnegut and more specifically the style of *Slaughterhouse-Five*, *The Wars* would not come to mind immediately."

In many ways, the student whose favorite novel was Ann-Marie Macdonald's *Fall on Your Knees* eloquently summarized NoveList's advantages and disadvantages, again stressing the necessity of a readers' advisor who reads widely and broadly. "If a patron were to come into the library requesting a book similar to *Fall on Your Knees* and I had not read [Marilyn Bowering's] *Visible Worlds* I may have suggested it. The two books are indeed similar in all the ways I specified on the NoveList database. The criteria deemed as required was that the novel be Canadian fiction but I listed as desired 20th century, family, family chronicle (Canadian), family secrets, interpersonal relations and sisters. It makes perfect sense that the criteria I provided NoveList with would suggest this novel, for Bowering's novel contained all of these criteria. Therefore if I was using NoveList to aid a library patron, I would certainly suggest Bowering's novel. However, having read Bowering's novel I would now ask the patron to give me more explicit reasons they enjoyed *Fall on Your Knees* before suggesting they read *Visible Worlds*. People like books for different reasons and the fact that I did not enjoy *Visible Worlds* does not mean that the patron will not, for it does indeed contain all the criteria I suggested for NoveList."

NEGATIVE COMMENTS ABOUT NOVELIST RECOMMENDATIONS

NoveList successes were far outweighed by its failures, no matter how many or few search parameters a student designated. The student whose favorite novel was Isabel Allende's

The House of the Spirits indicated seven search parameters, including "Magic Realism" and "Psychics," and was presented with a recommendation for Lucius Shepard's *Life during Wartime*, which was unsuitable. "*The House of the Spirits* voice or attitude is calmer, even at times of cruelty and crisis, such as the abduction of the daughter; the story unravels slowly and gently. On the other hand, throughout *Life During Wartime* the attitudes of the narrator is negative, condescending, angry, irrational, vengeful, confusing, lustful, cold, uncaring and unfeeling. The atmosphere of *The House of the Spirits* is steady, careful, and gentle, almost as if the times are happy and harmonious among the people." For this student, a much better choice would have been Tompson Highway's *The Kiss of the Fur Queen* "because of the First Nations cultural aspects, his flowing writing style, humour, vivid imagery and pretty magic elements, such as dropping a child gently from a star into a woman's womb, makes this a more appealing fiction to read."

A student whose favorite novel was *A Fine Balance* indicated six "desired" subject headings when searching for a book similar to Mistry's novel, which generated Siddhartha Deb's *The Point of Return* as NoveList's top-ranked recommendation. The student was initially happy with this recommendation, because "[t]here were similar subject headings between *Balance* and *Return*, including: Political Corruption-India, India-History-1947–1971, India-Politics and Government-1947–1971, and Indic Fiction. There were also subject headings that made me think *Return* would be similar to *Balance*, such as, Alienation in Men, Generation Gap, Violence, Memories, Coming-of-age stories." Yet for all these similarities, the two books were "nothing like" each other because, in part, "[t]he settings are completely different. In *Balance* you feel the grit of the city; you experience the poverty and degradation. You feel claustrophobic and smell the retched stink. In *Return* the surroundings seem quite nice by comparison. The countryside and the forests make you feel at ease. Unlike *Balance* where you experience physical discomfort. The depth is very different in each novel. The Mistry book provides a meaty story. A story that can be consumed by the reader. Deb's novel is more of an overview. The reader is not drawn in and enveloped. Mistry's book is longer but that is not the reason for the depth of the story. The biggest difference between the two novels is the writing style. NoveList could not warn you about Deb's writing style in relation to Mistry's style." Instead, this student would "absolutely suggest" *Mirage* by Bandula Chandraratna. "Although the physical setting for this novel is a different country, it is set in the Middle East, it is very similar to Mistry's writing style and level of tragedy. This is a very small novel, about the size of *Return*, but the story is so engrossing and intense. You fall in love with the main character and his humble ways. The writing flows so effortlessly that it draws you in and you become part of the story. As in Mistry's novel, this novel allows you to smell the city, feel the grit, and experience the poverty."

For the student whose favorite novel was Francine Rivers's *As Sure as the Dawn*, it was inexplicable that the best of the top-four NoveList recommendations turned out to be Thomas Kinkade's *Cape Light*. After specifying "Christian fiction," "Christian love stories," and "Early church 30–600" as required and desired subject headings, this student found that "[a]s for mood, tone and style, *Cape Light* does not have the fire and passion of [Rivers's novel]. It is a simple, more modern love story, beautiful but forgettable.... The authors' characters are completely different in personality, the era and setting are different, and the story, plot and tone of each novel are in stark contrast. The only common theme is love, which is not enough to class these together." Lew Wallace's *Ben-Hur* would have been infinitely preferable. The student whose favorite novel was *Villette* complained that NoveList was unable to find true analogues to Brontë's novel because "[t]he paucity of adequate subject headings in the database entry for *Villette* initially led to a variety of poor matches in unrelated genres that needed to be weeded out. The ability of critics/reviewers/librarians to make connections unanticipated or unnoticed by the deployment of a standardized set of subject headings is still paramount." Databases are unable, for example, to suggest intriguing choices such as *The Turn of the Screw*, *The Yellow Wallpaper*, or "Mary Hay's *Memoirs of Emma Courtney* in which the heroine's radically independent epistolary pursuit of the man she loves borders on mad entrapment and Sinclair Ross' prairie Gothic *As For Me and My House* in which the narrators' frantic desire for a child may (or may not) have led her to arrange another woman's pregnancy and murder provide two further examples."

Often, the information contained in the IR of NoveList's top-ranked recommendation made it appear that it was very similar to a student's favorite book, but when the student read the recommended book, all question of similarity disappeared, even with regard to intangible aspects. The student whose favorite novel was *Beloved* chose Lalita Tademy's *Cane River* because "[t]he reviews of the novel ... focused on its portrayal of the inter-relations between slaves, free people of colour, and the Creole French plantation owners [and so] I hoped to learn more about the psychological aspects of relationships based on race during this period." To this student's dismay, however, the books differed significantly in character development and language. "In *Cane River* there are many characters; so many it is easy to lose track. This means that few are developed in a comprehensive way and generally contributes to a sense that the characters are uni-dimensional. Exacerbating this problem is Tademy's plain, literal language. Morrison's lyrical prose, on the other hand, more subtly points to the complexities of black-white relations. By focusing on the four main characters of Sethe, Paul D, Denver and Beloved, Morrison is able to create complex characters and weave them into an emotionally-rich story. The experience of the reader of *Beloved* is an intense and personal one; whereas with *Cane River*, emotional involvement between characters and reader is limited, remote." According to this student, a much better recommendation would have been Zora Neale Hurston's classic *Their Eyes Were Watching God*, which not only "picks up" where *Beloved* left off, but also "provide[s] a complex and emotional reading experience for anyone interested in learning more about the African-American experience."

The student whose favorite novel was *On the Road* and who selected NoveList's top-ranked recommendation of Jim Dodge's *Not Fade Away* did so because the reviews in its IR stated that "this novel was an energetic and inventive writing which reflected 'America's fascination with rock 'n' roll, automobiles, and the open road.' The description looked as if this one would be very close to the energy displayed in Kerouac's book. In addition, the review promised imaginative description, a writer's command of language and a plot the 'flows with grace and rhythm.'" But the student's excitement at finding a book that promised Kerouac-like energy soon turned to disappointment. "*On the Road* represents very positive and uplifting writing. If there is one thing that the book stands for, it is pulsating energy that grabs a reader. One cannot but be embraced by Kerouac's excitement for everything, from food to women to his friends to sun and constant moving. A reader has this desire to feel the heat of the Mexican night, taste Californian grapes or get soaked in the rain somewhere on the East Coast. *Not Fade Away* not only does not match Kerouac's energy, but it often tends to be a negative and depressing book. It is a different writing and in many ways it looks like a spent Charles Bukowski; stretches of dark feelings, suppressed anger, aimless drinking and Benzedrine addiction. There simply is no enthusiasm coming out of Dodge's writing." For this aficionado of Kerouac, a more worthy recommendation would have been "the works of Jack London," especially *The Game*, because of its "enthusiastic writing, simple but powerful syntax and above all raw energy" mixed with "a dose of naivete."

For the student who loved *Lost Girls* and who chose NoveList's second-ranked recommendation of Gil Courtemanche's *A Sunday at the Pool in Kigali* because of the presence in both books of a psychological journey and "the theme of death, of love, of a quest, of being in a foreign element, the main setting of a hotel, and the fact that NoveList insinuated that the book had dark elements that could make it frightening," there was only deception. Not only were the psychological journeys of the protagonists vastly different, but "[t]he NoveList-recommended book also lacks the spooky quality and is instead horrific and grim reminder of the negative qualities that can lurk in our society. *Lost Girls* is meant to allow the individual reader to decide the fate and outcome of the protagonist's journey to self-discovery and that allows ... reader[s] to see themselves reflected in the work as it can become applicable to them by not estranging them from the work. *A Sunday at the Pool in Kigali* alienates its audience by both reminding the reader that it is based on historical events ... and by removing all hope of there really being any major change in African culture." Because of its "subversive" and "spooky" qualities, Jim Grimsley's coming-of-age story, *Dream Boy*, would have been a much wiser recommendation.

The student whose favorite book was *Microserfs* was keenly anticipating reading Ellen Ullman's *The Bug* after learning from NoveList's IR record that it "connoted aspects of *Microserfs* that I took pleasure in": it was wryly and darkly humorous; poetic and philosophical; peopled with uncertain and anxious characters; and, in the final analysis, humanistic. Yet, after reading *The Bug*, the student could only conclude that "*Microserfs* shows dark storm clouds but never lets it do anything more than drizzle; *The Bug* is a dreary, dismal day that rains non-stop. In tone, the two books are nothing alike." One of the books that this student would have recommended instead was Kurt Vonnegut's *Cat's Cradle*, an "irreverent" look at the events that lead to the destruction of life on Earth." Trusting NoveList's description of Anna Maxted's *Running in Heels* as hilarious and touching, the student whose favorite novel was Helen Fielding's *Bridget Jones's Diary* was appalled at Maxted's book. "*Running in Heels* [RIH] is utterly lacking the charm and humour of [Fielding's novel]. I did not find [it] funny at all. The characters in RIH are either unsympathetic or downright vile," whereas Bridget is a "charming" "optimist" in what is essentially "a joyful novel." Instead of Maxted's book, this student would recommend *Pride and Prejudice*, partly because "Austen's style is so engaging that a reluctant reader might be enticed. I think a reader might find comparing *Bridget Jones's Diary* [BJD] to *Pride and Prejudice* much more interesting and pleasurable than reading an inadequate BJD clone."

The student whose favorite book was *Survivor* was excitedly looking forward to the NoveList-recommended *Kangaroo Notebook* (by Kobo Abe) because it "seemed to discuss similar subjects, be of the same genre, and have the same tone as Survivor" (black humor; commercialization; cults; and religion). Unfortunately, after reading Abe's book, nothing could have been further from the truth, since it was "boring, esoteric, and confusing," with a plot that was insufficiently suspenseful and that "moved along too slowly." As a result, this student was "unsure whether I would use [NoveList's] services again" because it "failed to account for writing style." Instead, this student would have relied on his/her own knowledge to recommend Bret Easton Ellis's *American Psycho* "because it deals with similar subjects, and possesses similar stylist[ic] elements and tone. This novel satirizes American culture, and like *Survivor*, it begs the reader to question excesses of consumer culture. *American Psycho* also has a similar morbid and bleak tone, and is quite graphic."

A similar initial excitement and subsequent disappointment characterized the comments of the student whose favorite book was John Irving's *A Widow for One Year*. "Based on the reviews for LaVyrle Spencer's *Family Blessing* I thought that this title would be very similar to *A Widow for One Year* not just in respect to the selection criteria (subject headings) I chose, but also in terms of mood and writing style," this student wrote. Enthusiasm, however, was short-lived. Unlike Irving, Spencer did not provide "a detailed description of people, places, things, and situations and letting the reader come to their own interpretation, [but] writes the meanings behind character's intentions and situations out for us, so that no thinking is necessary." Furthermore, "Irving's novel is a haunting tale of family tragedy that traces the aftermath of a horrific accident in several characters' lives. There is nothing haunting about Spencer's story, and the loss of the son seems little more than an excuse for the May-December romance that is really the 'aboutness' of this book." Instead of *Family Blessing*, this student suggested that a more-inspired choice would have been Reynolds Price's *Love and Work*.

Concluding Observations About NoveList Recommendations

As table 1 of appendix C and the above comments demonstrate, NoveList recommendations left much to be desired. As one student stated, "active critical intervention" on the part of readers' advisors is required. But, as another student observed, "I think part of the problem is the database itself, because the subject headings are not always accurate in their reflection of the book to which they are attributed. Also, the meaning I derive from a book is coloured by my own life experiences and therefore for a database to provide a good recommendation it would need to know who I am and the context of my life. I do not believe a database can do that." Readers' advisors should therefore have in-depth understanding of the individual patrons with whom they discuss books.

The example of Mary Gay Shipley, owner of a small independent bookstore in Blytheville, Arkansas, is therefore instructive.[3] Shipley, who has lived in the same place for 23 years, is proficient at identifying books that her customers would like to read because she realizes that "to predict correctly whether you'll like something, the person making the recommendation really has to know something about you."[4] But she knows her customers not just as customers, but as people.

> For example, [Shipley] really likes David Guterson's new novel, *East of the Mountains*, but she's not about to recommend it to anyone. It's about a doctor who has cancer and plans his own death and, she says, 'there are some people dealing with a death in their family for whom this is not the book to read right now.' She had similar reservations about Charles Frazier's *Cold Mountain*. 'There were people I know who I didn't think would like it,' Shipley said. 'And I'd tell them that. It's a journey story. It's not what happens at the end that matters, and there are some people for whom that's just not satisfying. I don't want them to take it home, try to read it, not like it, then not go back to that writer.'[5]

Shipley must not only know every aspect of the books she suggests and recommends; she must also be thoroughly aware of all events in her community, and how these events are likely to affect individuals. As she explained, "not every book that's liked by the 'right' people is going to be liked by you. It could be that you're not ready to read a certain author, as I myself found. Then look what happens: You won't give that author the same chance again. There are just lots of people out there who'll never buy anything else that author writes because they read him when they shouldn't have."[6] In other words, she must have read widely and intelligently in books, as well as in the social and cultural mores of Blythesville, Arkansas.

Shipley's last comment was directed at Malcolm Gladwell, who wrote about her for *The New Yorker* magazine. Gladwell portrayed her in terms of collaborative filtering, which he defined as "a simple way to build your very own Mary Gay Shipley" insofar as it was "an attempt to approximate [her] kind of insider knowledge" through the creation of a system that "sifts through the opinions and preferences of thousands of people and systematically finds your doppelgänger," using "its knowledge about you to steer you toward choices you wouldn't normally know about."[7] Structurally, Shipley's sharp response to Gladwell parallels the many negative student responses to NoveList described above. Just as collaborative filtering is a poor substitute for Shipley, so databases such as NoveList, despite their claims, are poor substitutes for "active critical intervention" on the part of readers' advisors. Additionally, by suggesting that automated intervention that generates mechanical recommendations can replace, complement, or serve as "added memory" for readers' advisors, NoveList's promoters deskilled and deprofessionalized readers' advisory by positioning it as a narrowly conceived skill-set that relied on standardized protocols and prompts. In so doing, they discouraged readers' advisory from being perceived as an intellectually rigorous pursuit, one that required extensive critical knowledge about books, a strong commitment to analytical reading, and a deep acquaintance with community developments.

Case Study 2: *Book Lust* and *More Book Lust*

The readers' advisory practiced by Nancy Pearl in *Book Lust* and *More Book Lust* meets many of the criteria described by Shipley. Pearl is obviously a voluminous reader, but as this second case study shows, there was a lack of intellectual rigor in many of her lists. This lack tilted or skewed her lists toward one viewpoint or another, obscuring fundamental issues and neglecting alternative perspectives. Readers who followed in her reading-choice footsteps were effectively led astray, convinced by the authority of a celebrity recommendation to think that they had a comprehensive understanding about a specific topic when in fact they only possessed incomplete information. These concerns applied particularly to her lists about "Winston Churchill"[8]; "Founding Fathers"[9]; "American Indian Literature" and "Asian American Experiences"[10]; "Vietnam" and "The 1960s in Fact and Fiction"[11]; and "The Middle East" and "The Islamic World."[12]

WINSTON CHURCHILL

Although Pearl briefly mentions Ted Morgan's *Churchill: Young Man in a Hurry, 1874–1915*, which recounts flaws of the younger Churchill as so many examples of his "desire to prove to his father as well as to himself that he was worthy of the great career for which he hungered,"[13] her essay on Winston Churchill focused on the biographies that institutionalized and cemented the Churchillian myth. The works of Martin Gilbert, William Manchester, and Roy Jenkins are therefore prominently featured. Pearl also referred to Churchill's "wonderful memoirs," noting that they spurred her "down some fascinating highways and byways." In short, she chose to highlight works that portrayed Churchill admiringly as the "greatest human being ever to occupy 10 Downing Street"[14] and that depicted a heroic Churchill at the center of world events, "a lone figure, single-mindedly and unrelentingly warning the world of an avoidable war and the need for strong defence measures."[15] In Gilbert's biography, Churchill's heroic view of himself "is thus unmediated—and to a great extent uncriticised—by a man who, perhaps inevitably, came over thirty years of exposure to that remarkable personality to be one of his very greatest admirers."[16] Indeed, Gilbert's biographical volumes were so influential in establishing the heroic myth of Churchill that other historians, including Manchester and Jenkins, "succumbed to Gilbert's tendencies—

over-concentration on the heroic periods of Churchill's life and writing at excessive length because Churchill seems so giant a figure."[17] Writing about Manchester's biography, one reviewer observed that it was "[a] pedestrian effort to popularize the stateman's life ... [that] provides neither a new perspective nor illuminating new material. Its effect on the reader is simply that of a very long, and not particularly well-narrated, newsreel of Churchill's life.... There is lots of pageantry and color, too little analysis and insight."[18] As an indicator of the tone of Jenkins's biography, Rudolph Giuliani, Mayor of New York City during the crisis of September, 2001, recalled that he "had consciously sought out Jenkins' book in order to drink deep at the Churchillian spring."[19]

While Pearl called Churchill's memoirs "wonderful," numerous scholars characterized them as blatant examples of "self-promotion"[20] that revealed a "paucity of historical knowledge, lack of analytical power, and an ignorance of economic, social and intellectual history of staggering proportions."[21] Because "[t]hey were based on special access to the records and had extensive quotations from his letters, memoranda and dispatches which were impressively integrated into a coherent and dramatic narrative," the memoirs "gave an aura of authenticity and impressed even the best informed." But they were highly selective because "[o]nly Churchill's successes were recorded, not his failures and his rejected proposals. His own words might have been quoted in extenso but there was much less coverage of replies and reaction. This had the distorting effect of making Churchill appear at the heart of virtually everything of significance."[22]

Pearl's praise of key bibliographic components of the Churchillian myth was thus part of a wider phenomenon where "[m]ost readers don't want serious historical analysis, they want an uplifting story" that satisfied their "craving for glorious myth and ... need for heroes."[23] Opting not to explore revisionist historical perspectives about Churchill, Pearl skimmed the surface of understanding, content to direct readers to books that repeated truisms and did not do much to broaden their horizons. At least three books could have provided necessary correctives about the Churchillian myth: John Ramsden's *Man of the Century: Winston Churchill and his Legend since 1945*; Clive Ponting's *Churchill*; and John Charmley's *Churchill: The End of Glory*.[24]

Critics admitted that many would find Ramsden's book "loathsome" because Churchill had "become a symbol of all things sublime [and] [t]o question his achievements is rather like spitting on the Cenotaph," but nevertheless praised it as the work of "a highly talented historian at the peak of his prowess."[25] In fact, Ramsden was "particularly suited to this topic because of his unashamed admiration for the Conservative Party. Had this book been written by a leftist historian it would be easily dismissed as socialist small-mindedness. But when Ramsden claims that Churchill was 'more petty and selfish than almost any other British prime minister,' one is inclined to believe him."[26] In tracing the ways in which the Churchill legend was manufactured after 1945, Ramsden showed the contingent nature of fame, demonstrating how the Churchillian myth "owed a great deal to his own words," which "helped him to win ... the historical conflict over his own reputation."[27]

Ponting's book was even more controversial, since it revealed Churchill "the reactionary, the bigot, the racist, the imperialist, the class warrior, the aristocrat whose only real concern in politics was to ensure himself a place in history."[28] Churchill, Ponting explained, "wanted forcibly to sterilize 100,000 'mentally degenerate' Britons and send tens of thousands of others to labor camps. He failed to oppose appeasement of the Nazis in the 1930s and, after World War II, proposed a pre-emptive nuclear strike on the Soviet Union. He disliked democracy, preferring rule by a small aristocratic elite, and had huge problems in his marriage and his family."[29] Finally, Charmley's biography depicted a man who was "an almost unmitigated disaster to his country"[30] and "a romantic imperialist whose views had hardly changed since the 1890s [and who] was out of touch with the realities of British power and politics in the twentieth century."[31] By emphasizing books that showed Churchill in a hagiographic light, Pearl certainly took a popular path, but it was not a path that provided a well-rounded appraisal of Churchill.

FOUNDING FATHERS

Pearl's exclusive focus on books about George Washington, Benjamin Franklin, and Alexander Hamilton in "Founding Fathers" presented a surprisingly incomplete picture of the American Revolution, especially given the wealth of books that challenge the celebratory views of "the new school of founding fathers historians."[32] "Founding fathers historians" included Joseph J. Ellis, Walter Isaacson, Gordon S. Wood, Ron Chernow, and David McCullough, all lauded by Pearl.[33] As Barry Gewen observed, "the new school of founding fathers historians" established itself in the 1990s as a reaction to the outpouring of histories that looked at the American Revolution from a bottom-up perspective.[34] It was partly "[a] reaction against distortions and exaggerations" of the kind contained in Howard Zinn's *A People's History of the United States,* which found "little or nothing to praise" in American history[35] and which Pearl referred to in "American History: Nonfiction" in *Book Lust.* Founding Fathers historians, "basking in Reaganesque optimism and victory in the cold war," resurrected the "great man" model of history and immediately jumped to the bestseller lists. As Gewen noted, "Ellis's *Founding Brothers* was a best seller in hardback for almost a year, and a best seller in paperback for more than a year. Isaacson's *Benjamin Franklin* spent 26 weeks on the best-seller list; McCullough's *John Adams* entered the list at No.1, staying there for 13 weeks, rivaling for a while the popularity of novels by the likes of John Grisham and Danielle Steel. Chernow's *Alexander Hamilton* and Ellis's *His Excellency: George Washington* both made the best-seller list [in 2004]."[36]

By concentrating on bestseller "great man" interpretations of the founding of the United States, Pearl not only overlooked a large body of nuanced (i.e., non-Zinn-like) scholarship about "the formative years of the republic" in which ordinary Americans were just as much Founding Fathers as elites,[37] but also failed to acknowledge its very existence. Anyone glancing at Pearl's recommendations in "Founding Fathers" would come away with the idea that Washington, Franklin, and Hamilton were primarily responsible for the founding of America, which was not the case. By not discussing the various intellectual traditions and counter-traditions that animated American Revolutionary history, Pearl left readers adrift without context, reinforcing the view that the only books that matter on a given topic are comparatively recent bestsellers or books that became celebrated because of their mention in the *New York Times Book Review* or other mainstream publications.

Forced Founders: Indians, Debtors, Slaves, and the Making of the American Revolution in Virginia by Woody Holton was a sterling example of a bottom-up historical perspective neglected by Pearl.[38] Holton's book, wrote one critic, was "a fascinating reinterpretation of the coming of the Revolution in Virginia" because he explained how "the agency of smallholders, slaves, and Indians ... pushed Virginia's leaders [Thomas Jefferson, George Washington, and others] toward 'the most important decision white Americans ever made.'"[39] For Holton, the American Revolution "was not a freedom struggle led by a confident gentry, but, rather the result of several freedom struggles launched by nonelites to protect their own interests."[40] Another critic remarked that "*Forced Founders* strips away the patriotic veneer that has long surrounded the leadership of Virginia and exposes a grasping elite, committed most of all to preserving its class interest. The 'real' American Revolution in which we now take pride—the movement for greater liberty, equality, and democracy—was carried as much by allies of the Crown, notably, slaves and Indians, as by the white farmers who pushed the gentry into declaring independence."[41] In Holton's book, the gentry was not only "selfish but also shallow, driven mainly by short-term considerations of advantage. Its members possess interests, not ideas. Not a single ideal animates their actions." In sum, it was a "powerful expose of gentry self-seeking" that "will dismay remaining believers in the Great White Men of the Old Dominion."[42]

Brendan McConville's *These Daring Disturbers of the Public Peace: The Struggle for Property and Power in Early New Jersey* extends Holton's thesis.[43] Showing "how many of the ideas and conflicts thought to have been unleashed by the Revolution had their origins in a near century-long contest over title to New Jersey lands," McConville argued that "for New Jersey yeomen, the crucible of Revolutionary ideology was a longstanding internal struggle between ordinary settlers (who claimed the land by purchase from land speculators, Indians, or by right of settlement) and the colony's genteel proprietors (who asserted ownership by right of royal grant)."[44] This land conflict "eventually developed into a power struggle over fundamental issues of sovereignty and governance" that foreshadowed Revolutionary conflict as "farmers began equating a good society with a government that placed the interests of ordinary farmers ahead of a propertied aristocracy."[45] Bruce E. Johansen's *Forgotten Founders: How the American Indian Helped Shape Democracy*[46] approached the question from a different angle, suggesting "that tenets of the Iroquois Confederation directly influenced Benjamin Franklin and Thomas Jefferson in their drafting of the Declaration of Independence and Articles of Confederation."[47] Many structural features of American federalism were present in Iroquois federalism as enshrined in The Great Law of Peace (e.g., two houses of Congress; presidential veto and Congressional override; and the relationship of states to the union), and Franklin's friendship with individuals who participated in Iroquois governing bodies ensured that he knew about their traditions.

This re-examination of the origins of the United States owed much to Gary B. Nash and his landmark works *The Urban Crucible: Social Change, Political Consciousness, and the Origins of the American Revolution* and *Race, Class, and Politics: Essays on American Colonial and Revolutionary Society*.[48] *Urban Crucible* explored "the relationship of economic inequality to the revolution," thus rejecting the consensus interpretation that the American Revolution could primarily be explained in terms of ideas in which the primary actors were elites such as Washington and Franklin who rebelled against arbitrary English rule.[49] Documenting how "the rise of a market economy" led to social and economic stratification in Boston, Philadelphia, and New York that evolved into "lower-class discontent" and "an increasingly radical political consciousness,"[50] Nash argued that "plebeian urban dwellers forced their way into the political arena ... through street demonstrations, mass meetings, extralegal committees that assumed governmental powers, the intimidation of their enemies, and, in some cases, spirited defenses of traditional norms."[51] These factors coalesced to form "a world in which revolution was possible,"[52] where "social strains," "social discontent," and "economic disturbances" gave rise to a "revolutionary predisposition" in which "ordinary people, in bold opposition to their superiors ... were creating power and suggesting solutions to problems affecting their daily lives,"[53] often spurring reluctant elites to action.

AMERICAN INDIAN LITERATURE AND ASIAN AMERICAN EXPERIENCES

"American Indian Literature" and "Asian American Experiences" were particularly noteworthy for their lack of intellectual context, offering bare-bones lists of Pearl's favorite novels and anthologies without recognition of the underlying debates and issues permeating those literary traditions. When she did mention one book that provides such context (Craig S. Womack's *Red on Red: Native American Literary Separatism*), it was a single-sentence reference that was immediately undercut by a long list of mainstream "favorite" novels that "present Indian populations as simply gatherings of exiles, emigrants, refugees, strangers to themselves and their lands, pawns in the control of white manipulators, mixed-bloods searching for identity."[54] Readers are left with the impression that these literatures are non-ideological entities, that the novels Pearl identifies as her "favorites" offer handy shortcuts to the totality of Native American or Asian American life. This is far from the truth.

Most of the American Indian books listed by Pearl fall under the rubric of what Elizabeth Cook-Lynn identified as "the mixed-blood literary movement."[55] She defined this movement as follows: "While there is in the writings of these intellectuals much lip service given to the condemnation of America's treatment of the First Nations there are few useful expressions of resistance and opposition to the colonial history at the core of Indian/White relations. Instead, there is explicit and implicit accommodation to the colonialism of the 'West' that has resulted in ... three intellectual characteristics in fiction, nonfiction, and poetry: an aesthetic that is pathetic or cynical, a tacit notion of the failure of tribal governments as Native institutions and of sovereignty as a concept, and an Indian identity which focuses on individualism rather than First Nation ideology."[56] Cook-Lynn was particularly scathing about Louise Erdrich, Michael Dorris, James Welch, and Sherman Alexie, and she also wondered whether N. Scott Momaday and Leslie Marmon Silko in her early works "may also have moved away from nationalistic concerns in order to gain the interest of mainstream readers."[57] Focused on their mixed-blood "liberation and individualism," these writers and other like them "argue their shared victimhood through America's favorite subjects about Indians, i.e., despair, rootlessness, and assimilation."[58] Creating "Chief Doom School" books that were inhabited by characters "who appeal to mainstream audiences because 'they are dressed in America's favorite subjects when it comes to Indians: tragedy and despair,'"[59] mixed-blood writers gravitated toward "violence, self-hate, romanticism, blame, mournfulness, loss, or anger."[60] This left "little room ... and little use for nationalistic/tribal resistance"[61] and signaled that "a return to tribal sovereignty on tribal homelands seems to be a lost cause, and American individualism will [win] out."[62] For Cook-Lynn, the mixed-blood literary movement was a movement of "disengagement," "assimilation," and "Americanization"[63] that overlooked "the presence of the Indian nation as cultural force" and did not see much value "in establishing the myths and metaphors of sovereign nationalism; the places, the mythological beings, the genre structures and plots of the oral traditions; the wars and war leaders, [and] the treaties and accords with other nations."[64] There were, however, hundreds of "traditional native thinkers" and writers such as Vine Deloria Jr. who were interested in "decolonization and the revival of nationalistic paradigms."[65]

Pearl's emphasis on acclaimed mainstream novels such as Silko's *Ceremony* and Momaday's *House Made of Dawn* thus "limit the perceptual paradigms of Indian literature and Indian experience by diverting attention away from narratives of tribal sovereignty and other crucial paradigms of Indian experience."[66] In addition, when writers such as Silko tried to break away from their early writings to forge something new such as *Almanac of the Dead*, their critical standing and popularity suffered.[67] It is therefore telling that Pearl chose to overlook *Almanac of the Dead*, which not only explored "what it would mean for a racially or culturally marginalized group to rise up and resist state and corporate actions that put their families and environments at risk,"[68] but also discussed "the links between race, class, and environmental exploitation by tracing the historical formation of 'class' in terms of colonialism and imperialism" in a way that respects tribal/nation status.[69] Most importantly, Silko's use of elements of "the most ancient 'American' literature—the Mayan almanacs" was a deliberate rejection of "the notion of a renaissance in American Indian writing" and an affirmation that "indigenous peoples have been writing and articulating their cultures and beliefs for hundreds and even thousands of years."[70] Among other things, it directly belied Pearl's assertion that "American Indian literature began coming into its own in the 1960s"[71] and gave support to Cook-Lynn's view that literary depictions of "native nationalism" (where, for example, "tidal waves of South and North American Indians wipe out borders and reclaim lands"[72]) cannot be fruitfully processed through Euro-American aesthetic standards that have acclaimed the mixed-blood literary movement and dispossessed "autonomous models" of literature grounded in "tribal nationhood."[73]

In the case of "Asian American Experiences," Pearl defined this tradition in terms of popular coming-of-age stories such as Amy Tan's *The Joy Luck Club*, Jade Snow Wong's *Fifth Chinese Daughter*, and Maxine Hong Kingston's *The Woman Warrior*. But, as the editors of *The Big Aiiieeeee!* pointed out, these books do nothing more than "ventriloquiz[e] the same old white Christian fantasy of little Chinese victims of 'the original sin of being born to a brutish, sadomasochistic culture of cruelty and victimization' fleeing to America in search of freedom from everything Chinese and seeking white acceptance, and of being victimized by stupid white racists and then being reborn in acculturation and honorary whiteness."[74] Moreover, just as these books "boldly fake" traditional Chinese stories and fairy tales, they also "fake all of Asian American history and literature" by arguing that "the immigrants who settled and established Chinese America lost touch with Chinese culture."[75] In fact, "Chinese and Japanese immigrants were a literate people from literate civilizations whose presses, theaters, opera houses, and artistic enterprises rose as quickly as their social and political institutions."[76] The portraits of China and Chinese Americans presented by Tan, Wong, and Kingston were therefore "products of white racist imagination" that had nothing to do with real Chinese history and culture as found in, for example, "the texts of Chinese childhood literature, the ethics that the fairy tales and heroic traditions teach, and the sensibility that they express."[77] Again succumbing to the convenient temptation to valorize mainstream bestsellers that perpetuate stereotypes, Pearl neglected thorny questions about the existence of alternate traditions and viewpoints.

VIETNAM AND THE 1960S IN FACT AND FICTION

Taken as a whole, Pearl's recommendations in "Vietnam" and "The 1960s in Fact and Fiction" emphasized the positive, romantic, and dynamic aspects of the 1960s' New Left cultural revolution and portrayed the Vietnam War as an unwarranted military adventure. When she did recommend fiction books that presented an equivocal portrait of the 1960s— Neil Gordon's *The Company You Keep*, Susan Choi's *American Woman*, and Marge Piercy's *Vida*—they all focused on underground political radicals, especially members and sympathizers of the Weather Underground and the Symbionese Liberation Army. In so doing, Pearl drew a sharp demarcation between these violent groups and what she saw as the many beneficial outcomes of New Left cultural dissent. Even so, both Gordon's and Choi's books presented the 1960s' radical political movement as a "kind of substitute for or imitation of family."[78] Laura Miller wrote that, while Choi's heroine saw the kidnappers "as achingly young, naive, reckless, vainglorious and cruel," she nevertheless helped them not only because of the "rightness" of their cause, but also because "[t]he 'secretive family dimension' of their shared radicalism wins out over her reservations about their tactics."[79] Gordon, moreover, "clearly sympathizes with the militants" because of their loyalty to each other and the loyalty they engendered in "various counterculture hangouts" where no one turned them over to the police.[80] As Miller noted, "[t]his is the much-vaunted sense of community that post–60's leftists yearn for. The radicals in *The Company You Keep* make enormous sacrifices on one another's behalf. Though the book begins as a former radical's apologia to his daughter, it ends up portraying the underground as a kind of extended family, better in some ways than any group united by mere blood."[81] Pearl's fiction choices did not include T. C. Boyle's *Drop City*, which, in exposing the pretentiousness and "self-righteous proselytizing" of the era,[82] was a stunning "rebuke of hippie culture that would make Abbie Hoffman put on a tie and write a humble apology on Crane's stationary."[83]

But it was Pearl's nonfiction choices that best revealed her acceptance of mainstream thinking about Vietnam and the 1960s. By praising David Halberstam's *The Making of a Quagmire*, Frances Fitzgerald's *Fire in the Lake*, and Neil Sheehan's *A Bright Shining Lie*, Pearl led readers toward "the conventional wisdom" that "America succumbed to mindless anticommunism and intervened in a war—a civil war, really—that it couldn't win, even while using excessive force, and wound up humiliating itself and killing fifty-eight thousand GIs and hundreds of thousands of Vietnamese in vain."[84] But, as recounted by William Prochnau in *Once upon a Distant War: Young War Correspondents and the Early Vietnam Battles*, Halberstam and Sheehan were far from unbiased observers, but rather more like "two overgrown college boys, determined to use the school newspaper to do in the football coach and have fun in the process."[85] Understanding that their "personal success" depended on adopting an anti-American viewpoint, they forgot that their personal views had a "significant impact on the outcome in Vietnam and the long shadow it casts over a generation of American life."[86] In emphasizing the conventional, Pearl overlooked revisionist books such as Michael Lind's *Vietnam: The Necessary War* and Lewis Sorley's *A Better War: The Unexamined Victories and Final Tragedy of America's Last Years in Vietnam*, which explained that "America was right to intervene militarily, for the worldwide consequences would have been far worse for the non-Communist world if it hadn't" and that "[n]ot only was the war winnable, but it had actually been won by sometime in 1970."[87] Also neglected were titles such as Norman Podhoertz's *Why We Were in Vietnam*, which argued that the United States was "morally right to have been involved in the war, and the effort to end that involvement will bear history's moral censure."[88]

With regard to nonfiction books about the 1960s, Pearl's recommendations concentrated on New Left cultural dissent, reflected in such books as David Hajdu's *Positively 4th Street*; Mark Kurlansky's *1968: The Year that Rocked the World*; Kirkpatrick Sale's *SDS: Ten Years Toward a Revolution*; and Ken Kesey's *The Further Inquiry*. Books that documented other aspects of the 1960s were missing. Three such examples were: Paul Lyons's *Class of '66: Living in Suburban America*, which examined the lives of people in the 1960s who did not participate in anti-war protests or social rebellion; Lisa McGirr's *Suburban Warriors: The Origins of the New American Right*, which traced the rise of the conservative movement from its beginnings in Orange County, California; and John A. Andrew III's *The Other Side of the Sixties: Young Americans for Freedom and the Rise of Conservative Politics*, which described the beliefs and philosophies of numerous 1960s' conservative social groups. Finally, Pearl excluded books that discussed the often negative social consequences of New Left cultural dissent, including Roger Kimball's *The Long March: How the Cultural Revolution of the 1960s Changed America*; Gertrude Himmelfarb's *One Nation, Two Cultures: A Searching Examination of American Society in the Aftermath of Our Cultural Revolution*; David Horowitz's *Radical Son: A Generational Odyssey*; *The Betrayal of Liberalism: How the Disciples of Freedom and Equality Helped Foster the Illiberal Politics of Coercion and Control*, edited by Hilton Kramer and Roger Kimball; Jeffrey Hart's *Smiling Through the Cultural Catastrophe: Toward the Revival of Higher Education*; and Peter Collier and David Horowitz's *Destructive Generation: Second Thoughts About the 60's*. The titles alone of these books indicate that the 1960s was anything but a one-dimensional decade.

THE MIDDLE EAST AND THE ISLAMIC WORLD

In a now familiar pattern, Pearl's recommendations in "The Middle East" and "The Islamic World" consisted of books that were praised by mainstream reviewing outlets, especially the *New York Times*. Yet many of these books were problematic, providing a distorted picture of crucial issues and calling into question Pearl's enthusiastic assertions about their value. By praising Thomas Friedman's *From Beirut to Jerusalem* and *The Lexus and the Olive Tree*; Michael B. Oren's *Six Days of War*; Bernard Lewis's *The Middle East: A Brief History of the Last 2,000 Years*; Karen Armstrong's *Islam: A Short History*; and Mary Anne Weaver's *A Portrait of Egypt*, Pearl again skimmed the surface of things, content to accept the judgments of mainstream reviewers and bestseller lists and to claim that these books "provide a much-needed context for our thoughts about this region of the world."[89] In addition, her misplaced emphasis in "The Islamic World" on "militant Islam" not only framed Islam as a monolithic construct, but also excluded books that would "open up Islam's worlds as pertaining to the living, the experienced, the connected-to-us, rather than to shut it down, rigidly codifying it and stuffing it into a box labeled 'Dangerous—do not disturb.'"[90] As a result, titles such as Muhammad Asad's *The Road to Mecca*, Malcolm X's memoirs, or Taha Hussein's *The Stream of Days* were neglected.[91]

Particularly dismaying was her inclusion of Lewis, who is a polarizing figure denounced by, among others, Edward Said as a pseudo-authority who depicts Islam as "an irrational herd or mass phenomenon ... ruling Muslims by passions, instincts, and unreflecting hatreds" and as something that "never changes."[92] Lewis "seems unaffected by new ideas or insights, even though among most Middle East experts his work has been both bypassed and discredited by the many recent advances in knowledge about particular forms of Islamic experience."[93] For anyone who reads Lewis, "there was no surprise, no discovery to be made from anything [he] wrote, since it all added up in his view to confirmations of the Islamic tendency to violence, anger, antimodernism, as well as Islam's (and especially the Arabs') closed-mindedness, its fondness for slavery, Muslims' inability to be concerned with anything but themselves, and the like."[94] Often, Lewis was duplicitous, highlighting the democratic failings of Arab nations and omitting or downplaying the Israeli "invasion and colonization of Palestine despite and in conflict with the native Arab inhabitants," "the dozens of illegal settlements on the militarily occupied West Bank of Gaza," and "the absence of human rights for Arabs ... in former Palestine."[95] In many ways, Lewis was the "spokesman for the guild of Orientalists"[96] that Said criticized in *Orientalism*, a book that, in analyzing the negative stereotypes of Arabs and Muslims prevalent in the Western world, suggested that such misrepresentations were the product of a long-standing "cultural enterprise."[97] Pearl, of course, did not mention Said's *Orientalism*. Instead, Said's only appearance in *Book Lust* and *More*

Book Lust was in "Essaying Essays," where his *Reflections and on Exile and Other Essays* was unceremoniously grouped with a long list of anthologies (e.g., *The Best American Essays of the Century*) and literary essays by authors such as Joseph Brodsky and John Updike.[98]

Pearl's other choices were little better. Armstrong's bestselling book contained "potted history that chronicles events since Muhammad's birth without much insight or particularly fresh knowledge. The reader would get as much out of a good encyclopedia article on 'Islam' as from Armstrong, who seems to be a very industrious if not especially knowledgeable author.... [L]ike Lewis's book, [it] too frequently suggests great distance and dehumanization rather than closeness to the experience of Islam in all its tremendous variety."[99] Weaver's account was more about Weaver than anything else, and thus failed to explain much of anything. One critic observes that "[h]er continuous laments over the diminishment of the elitist expatriate life she had in the 1970's Cairo is insufferable. This tendency ... makes Weaver seem slightly out of touch and parasitic.... [S]he seems unaware of the ironic strands of her own situation—that the bygone Cairo she nostalgically dreams of and the involvement of people like her in sustaining it was itself a factor in the rise of militant Islam."[100]

Numerous commentators expressed dissatisfaction with Oren's book, which, they said, contained "misleading accounts of factual issues and unacceptable omissions in analysis" insofar as it neglects or "lightly slides over crucial aspects of Israel's policies and behavior, especially its treatment of the Palestinians"; "tends to play down the significance of Israel's military provocations ... as well as its refusal to engage with serious Egyptian and Syrian proposals for a political settlement"; "denies that a significant portion of the hundreds of thousands of Syrian and Palestinian civilians who left the Golan Heights and the West Bank in the aftermath of the 1967 war were either expelled outright or 'encouraged' to leave in a variety of ways by the conquering Israeli armies"; and sidesteps "the escalating conflict between Israel and the Palestinians in the wake of the establishment of the Israeli settlements in the West Bank and Gaza Strip."[101] As Norman G. Finkelstein remarked, Oren "skews the historical record" in fundamental ways despite the fact that the *New York Times* "lavished unstinting praise on the book," using such adjectives as "gripping," "fascinating," "masterly," and "fabulous."[102]

According to many critics, Friedman was a younger Lewis, recapitulating Orientalist thinking in *From Beirut to Jerusalem*, where he explained that "politics in all Middle East countries is based on a combination of 'tribe-like' traditions, 'primordial identities' and the imperatives of authoritarianism and modernization."[103] Not only was the book marked by "superficial observations on the nature of Arab polities," but it also "pays little attention to the impact of uneven economic development and class conflict on the internal dynamic of repressed groups," choosing instead to fall back on "the know-nothing explanation of primitivism" and an overmuch concentration on "personalities."[104] Despite this and other serious criticisms, Pearl labeled *From Beirut to Jerusalem* "eminently readable, vital, and engaging," blithely recommending that readers also turn to Friedman's *The Lexus and the Olive Tree* (LOT). As Pearl informed readers that this book "too" was "[w]orth reading,"[105] it was clear that she was merely follow bestselling trends. Indeed, the inclusion of LOT—an unapologetic paean to "excellent globalizing economic forces" in which the Lexus automobile represented "the modernizing free market global economy" and where the olive tree, a characteristic feature of many Middle Eastern countries, represented "foolish backward regionalism"[106]—in a list of books meant to give insight about the Middle East was, to put it mildly, awkward.

Critics were virulent about LOT. In addition to pointing out its "blatant errors" and commenting that it belonged to the genre of "madly triumphalist TV commercial," Thomas Frank observed that "[s]o grandiose is the tone of arrogance Friedman adopts that one suspects he has taken leave of his senses."[107] Castigating Friedman for "embod[ying] the stereotype of the Ugly American so aptly that he almost becomes a caricature," Amitabh Pal stated that LOT was "such a collection of cliches, generalizations, and superficial observations that you felt like you would choke."[108] William A. McWhirter derided Friedman's "gloating triumphalism that becomes increasingly troubling and unattractive."[109] Jackson Lears dismissed Friedman's "stupefyingly bland and simple vision of globalization."[110] And David C. Korten, noting that LOT was nothing more than an "elitist corporate puff piece" that "accepts unjust and destructive institutional structures as immutable givens and focuses on how to gain the greatest personal or national advantage," concluded that "people like Friedman serve as cheerleaders for injustice."[111]

Instead of giving readers insightful analyses, Pearl's recommendations in "The Middle East" and "The Islamic World" were glib bestsellers riding the crest of events. Yet there were many books that offered in-depth understanding about these topics from valuable perspectives, including Albert Hourani's A History of the Arab Peoples; Benny Morris's Righteous Victims: A History of the Zionist-Arab Conflict and The Birth of the Palestinian Refugee Problem, 1947–1949; Avi Shlaim's Iron Wall: Israel and the Arab World; David Grossman's The Yellow Wind; John Esposito's The Islamic Threat?: Myth or Reality and Islam: The Straight Path; and Rashid Khalidi's Palestinian Identity: The Construction of Modern National Consciousness. Perhaps one of the more eloquent contributions was Ammiel Alcalay's After Jews and Arabs: Remaking Levantine Culture, which did not see the Middle East as "a battleground between Arab and Jews," but as "a Mediterranean culture common to both peoples."[112]

Conclusion

Pearl thought of herself as "a professional reader."[113] But, as our analysis of selected essays in Book Lust and More Book Lust demonstrates, being "a professional reader" is not the same as being a knowledgeable and analytic reader able to intelligently contextualize and situate books within their specific domains and traditions, thereby providing a comprehensive picture of any given issue or topic. For Pearl, "professional" reading amounted to frenetic consumption of bestselling books that often won prizes, but were just as often lacking in meaningful insights. Taken as a group, the books Pearl recommended in each of the essays examined above displayed many of the faults identified by Dilevko and Gottlieb in "The Politics of Standard Selection Guides": "missing theoretical perspectives"; "overemphasis of a particular facet or theory within a field"; and "missing voices."[114] Her involvement with H. W. Wilson's Standard Catalogs and Bowker's BAS system was therefore all the more troubling, since many of her recommendations were likely integrated into these vendors' products and thus ultimately became the building-blocks of numerous North American public-library collections, as well as the basis of readers' advisory suggestions. Based on "reactive" reading, Pearl's recommendations contributed to the formation of a homogenized reading landscape consisting of bestsellers consecrated by mainstream media. Although she was revered by many as the very model of an informed readers' advisor, Pearl's type of readers' advisory had many of the same characteristics as NoveList-based readers' advisory. Both were part of what Agnes Hill called "librarianship by automatic figures": a deskilled and superficial approach to readers' advisory work that relied, in the case of NoveList, on mechanical profiling and, in the case of Pearl, on books consecrated by bestseller lists and "promotional culture."

Chapter 7

The Future of Readers'
Advisory Service

In many respects, the history of readers' advisory service can be seen through the prism of George Kyle's life. Kyle, a library clerk at the Carpenter Branch of the St. Louis Public Library died in 2005 at the age of 88.[1] Constructed in 1927, the Carpenter Branch was "one of the last libraries in the nation built with money provided by the Andrew Carnegie Endowment." Invariably wearing a "pressed, white dress shirt and ... maroon tie," Kyle was a modest and frugal man who brought "a bologna sandwich on white bread, with two graham crackers, ... and a thermos of milk" to work every day for 46 years. He knew "most of the regular patrons by name." He was familiar with "children's titles as well as adult ones, and never tired of talking about books with the youngsters." He "loved to talk about what he read, everything from the big bang theory to calculus." Judging from the comments of a local minister's wife, he had detailed knowledge about the Bible and numerous other religious and philosophical issues. Shortly after his death, his extensive book collection was donated "to the library of Concordia Seminary in Clayton [Missouri]."

Other than the fact that he bequeathed some $350,000 for collection development at the Carpenter Branch, the obituaries do not tell us much more than that about Kyle. He retired in 1985, which meant that he began working at Carpenter around 1939–1940.[2] We can imagine him infused with Carnegie's self-education ethos—an ethos based on serious and purposeful reading symbolized by his interest in astrophysics, calculus, philosophy, and religion. When Kyle began work, this ethos constituted the backbone of readers' advisory, defined then in terms of meaningful education. And although he most likely did read novels, we can easily imagine those novels as classics, part of the great-books tradition.

We can also imagine him agreeing with Murray C. Bob, who in 1982 wrote that "consumers' tastes are largely shaped by what is available, which, in turn, is governed by economies of scale."[3] The notion of "consumer sovereignty" was illusory, Bob stated, since "tastes are easily manipulated" by industries spending millions of dollars each year on advertising, which "promote[s] consensus, otherwise known as conformity, to the greatest extent possible and thus achieve[s] economies of scale."[4] "[O]ver-emphasizing the lowest common denominator," which in the world of books "is very often the best seller," showed "contempt for people's capacities" and made public libraries into "fast-food chains of the mind."[5] Unless librarians wanted to be victims of "mass production and mass marketing" and transform libraries into yet "another imitative and redundant instrument of massification," they must realize that "[j]ust as the increased sale of junk foods weakens us physically, the increased circulation of schlock diminishes us intellectually."[6]

In an almost too-perfect coincidence, Kyle's retirement in 1985 occurred at approximately the same moment that Rosenberg published the first *Genreflecting* volume (1982) and that ARRT was founded (1984). These two events were watershed moments in the history of readers' advisory in the late 20th century. After becoming strong advocates of popular culture in the wake of 1960s-1970s' social turmoil, many public librarians in the early and middle 1980s began to codify their embrace of genre fiction, bestsellers, celebrity-authored books, and prize-winning titles in professional organizations and publications. As public libraries welcomed commodified and ephemeral entertainment-oriented fiction and nonfiction, they reaffirmed their participation in what Toro in the early 1970s had decried as "happenings" that lacked "purpose and direction."[7] Turning their backs on the type of serious and purposeful reading represented by Kyle, public libraries frowned upon being considered "library-colleges"[8] or people's universities. Those aspirations now seemed too old-fashioned and too quaint to carry much weight with Rosenberg or ARRT members, who were intent on asserting the benefits of genre titles and bestsellers.

Popular culture, of course, had many defenders. Rosenberg, ARRT members, Radway, and the 4MA book group were not the only ones to sing its praises. But the defense of popular culture often took unexpected turns, revealing unanticipated connections. A good example of this was Steven Johnson's book *Everything Bad is Good for You*, which argued that video games and television were "growing more sophisticated, demanding more cognitive engagement with each passing year," thus "making our minds sharper, as we soak in entertainment usually dismissed as so much lowbrow stuff."[9] Video games compelled players "to decide, to choose, to prioritize,"[10] encouraging them toward "probing," "telescoping," and "participatory analysis and thinking."[11] Television shows became "increasingly rigorous," demanding more "cognitive work" from viewers as they followed "multiple threads" and made sense "of information that has been either deliberately withheld or deliberately left obscure."[12] For Johnson, these qualities represented the essence of learning because "learning how to think is ultimately about learning to make the right decisions: weighing evidence, analyzing situations, consulting your long-term goals, and then deciding."[13] As the subtitle of his book proclaimed, "Today's Popular Culture is Actually Making Us Smarter." Yet Johnson's long list of the benefits of popular culture sounded curiously like the skills that early 21st-century corporations wanted their workers to possess in order that they might become compliant and conformist team- and career-oriented employees, as opposed to independent thinkers with actual subject knowledge about economic, cultural, historical, and political events and issues.

As John C. Beck and Mitchell Wade noticed in *Got Game*, gaming was "an amazingly effective training camp for critical business skills" because "[a]ll those hours immersed in game culture have created masses of employees with unique attributes: bold but measured risk taking, an amazing ability to multitask, and unexpected leadership skills."[14] Indeed, some of the essential values of gaming culture—players are "the center of attention of every game"; real life can be manipulated as one chooses; "[e]verything is possible" and "(unrealistically) simple"; "[l]ike shopping, the whole experience is designed for your satisfaction and entertainment"; each player is "a tough guy" constantly "competing" "even if you collaborate"; players "always get the star's role" and the opportunity to be "[b]e a hero"; an escapist "[t]une out and have fun" ethos dominates—"have surprising potential to drive great professional performance."[15] Thomas Friedman, in *The World Is Flat*, was even more enthusiastic than Beck and Wade about the business-productivity potential of "zippie culture" (effectively a synonym for gaming culture) because members of this demographic group provide inexpensive outsourced and off-shore labor for American companies concerned about delivering ever-faster services at ever-lower costs.[16] But in Friedman's vision of a globalized hyper-productive, hyper-connected, and hyper-competitive world, the true face of gaming culture was revealed: "If you are just a little too slow or too costly—in a world where the walls around your business have been removed and competition can now come from anywhere—you will be left as roadkill before you know what hit you."[17] It is a world in which "the focus of creativity, the highest achievement ... is apparently ... ever-newer operations-flow software, to optimize your business process.... [N]o one in the flat world seems to be doing anything of loftier significance than getting Wal-Mart's suppliers to make deliveries just a few minutes nearer to ship time or inventing a new radio-frequency identification microchip to track its inventory."[18]

Readers' advisors who fail to differentiate between ephemeral literary commodities produced mainly for the sake of corporate profits and enduring literature that provides meaningful education are doing their patrons a disservice in three ways. First, by making convenient and unchallenging reading suggestions based on the recentness, popularity, and marketing buzz of a book (or by relying on the mechanical procedures associated with the *Genreflecting* series, NoveList, or DearReader-like companies), they underestimate the intellectual abilities of their patrons. Second, they become salespeople for large publishing enterprises that are only too happy that librarians are furthering a profit-driven corporate agenda by "Giving 'Em What They Want," a slogan that could be restated as "Giving 'Em What Corporations Want 'Em to Want." Writing about the many ways in which "chick lit" "is not just bad for the reader—it is bad for the authors too," Scarlett Thomas placed genre fiction squarely within the nexus of capitalist endeavor.

> It's so thoughtful of capitalism to give us exactly what we want, isn't it? Funny that chick lit is the cheapest thing for publishers to produce, and the easiest for them to get hold of.... If you were a company that had access to three apples and a thousand bananas, you would try to get people to like bananas—especially if you had to sell all your fruit at the same price.[19]

Third, readers' advisors who suggest "light, quick, escapist" books metaphorically support the psychologically destructive forces of technological change that demand that individuals function at a faster pace in all their activities, whether at work or in their leisure hours, whether in the act of reading or in the act of doing anything else. And while such blind change often has no good reason except that it produced handsome profits for large corporations, it also created a frenetic cultural and social landscape characterized by an ever-increasing emphasis on speed, multi-tasking, quantification, and careerism. When Dear-Reader specifically invoked this frenetic landscape as a justification for its products and when many public libraries made DearReader a cornerstone of their readers' advisory service, readers' advisors embraced a world that Clive Thompson called "interrupted." Although the following description paints a troubling picture of working life, it can also be easily applied to all aspects of home and leisure life.

> Each employee spent only 11 minutes on any given project before being interrupted and whisked off to do something else. What's more, each 11-minute project was itself fragmented into even shorter three-minute tasks, like answering e-mail messages, reading a Web page or working on a spreadsheet. And each time a worker was distracted from a task, it would take, on average, 25 minutes to return to that task.[20]

As Epstein observed, "our speeded-up culture—with its FedEx, fax, email, channel surfing, cell-phoning, fast-action movies, and other elements in its relentless race against boredom—has ended in a shortened national attention span. The quickened rhythms of new technology are not rhythms congenial to the slow and time-consuming and solitary act of reading. Sustained reading, sitting quietly and enjoying the aesthetic pleasure that words elegantly deployed on the page can give, contemplating careful formulations of complex thoughts—these do not seem likely to be acts strongly characteristic of an already jumpy new century."[21] As readers' advisors suggested ephemeral fiction and nonfiction that catered to "an already jumpy new century," they also contributed to the disappearance of an atmosphere where sustained thought was possible. As DearReader-style five-minute e-mail excerpts became important components of readers' advisory, public librarians implicated their institutions in the culture of speed and the shortened, disjunctive attention spans that popular culture valorized. By emphasizing "light, quick, escapist" books that required little reflective thought and provided little intellectual challenge or meaningful educational opportunities, public libraries were no longer necessary refuges from the forces propelling the debilitating culture of speed.

But there was a real need for institutions that provided meaningful educational opportunities at the beginning of the 21st century, since colleges and universities were frequently not up to the task and since students were often prisoners of a "narrow careerist mentality."[22] As Peter Beinart explained, "[s]tudents at Harvard—and at other prestigious universities—often graduate without the kind of core knowledge that you'd expect from a good high school student. Instead, they meet Harvard's curricular requirements with a hodgepodge of arbitrary, esoteric classes that cohere into nothing at all."[23] Beinart blamed professors who taught courses only in their narrow specialties and avoided sweeping foundational courses that they considered beneath them. Ultimately, this phenomenon could be traced back to 1960s' New Left dissent, a time when colleges and universities succumbed to a philosophy of "radical egalitarianism"[24] such that "a popular romance might have more value, aesthetic and otherwise, than a Shakespearean text."[25] But this also meant that the "core educational principle" of "moral education" was abandoned to a culture of narcissism, where the reigning mantra was "Less Rembrandt, more Me. Fewer theologians, more dietitians." The possibility of obtaining a meaningful and coherent education disappeared at many colleges and universities, leaving students "to find [their] own ways to learn" about historical heroes who could serve as models and standards against which to measure themselves.[26]

Public libraries therefore have a striking opportunity to play a significant role in the North American educational system. By redefining readers' advisory so that it adheres more to its pre–1963 principles than to its post–1980 principles, it could once again become a pathway to meaningful education based on serious, sustained, and purposeful reading of enduring books.

As colleges and universities in the early 21st century became incubators of educational, economic, and social stratification, the need for public libraries to provide the meaningful educational opportunities not offered at institutions such as Harvard was even more pressing. And, as the entertainment-center philosophy of chain bookstores increasingly became the norm at all retail book outlets, including many independent booksellers, public libraries could demarcate themselves from the ideal of "consumer sovereignty" and a "consumer culture [that] emphasizes novelty: new products, new experiences, a new generation of youth on the cutting edge."[27] In short, public libraries could "imagin[e]" themselves as part of "a different world,"[28] where the imperatives of commercialism, standardization, and rationalization give way to the realization that serious, thoughtful reading of enduring literature for the purpose of meaningful education is a radical political act that rejects "active involvement" in the commodification of books.[29]

But to do so effectively, public libraries must reorient their vision away from "popular romances" toward Shakespearean texts, distancing themselves from the genre titles, best-sellers, celebrity-authored books, and prize-winning titles that, for the various interlocking reasons discussed in previous chapters, were at the center of post–1980 readers' advisory. Otherwise, despite their eloquent rhetoric about being "multidimensional public spaces" and "community front porch[es]" that function as "attraction[s]" and "instrument[s] for civic and social life,"[30] they not only solidify the impress of an entertainment-oriented con-sumer culture, but also exacerbate the educational, economic, and social stratification that was a defining feature of early 21st-century North American life because the ephemeral fiction and nonfiction that was a mainstay of their collections and readers' advisory work primarily served the entertainment-oriented requirements of economically advantaged classes.

In "Harvard-Bound? Chin Up," Brooks suggested some possibilities that would ensure that everyone received "a great education": books by Reinhold Niebuhr; Plato's *Gorgias*; courses about Ancient Greece, neuroscience, and statistics; and foreign-language courses.[31] Taking these recommendations as starting points, public libraries should reconceptualize their readers' advisory service as a separate department staffed by one, two, three, or more subject specialists who, with the aid of clerical and administrative help, would offer private individual consultations to young adults and adults interested in gaining meaningful edu-cation through serious and purposeful reading. After these consultations, reading courses on specific topics would be developed for patrons, with frequent follow-up interviews and discussions to gauge progress. Libraries would advertise this service broadly, taking pro-active steps to involve less-advantaged populations. The readers' advisory office would thus be transformed into the kind of "intelligence center" envisioned by Learned in the 1920s, with "an intelligence personnel" who would be "actively aggressive ... in discovering advan-tageous ways of preparing and presenting important material to students for the purpose of arousing their progressive interest."[32] Public libraries would again become Alvin John-son's people's universities committed to sustained adult education.

Public librarians' vision of themselves and of the meaning of professionalism would have to change dramatically. No longer could they practice what Agnes Hill in 1902 labeled "librarianship by automatic figures" or what Alvin Johnson in 1938 called "pure librarian-ship," where they simply supplied books "without regard to any influence [those books] may exert" and basked in "the humble glory of standing neutrally to serve the wise man in his pursuit of wisdom, the fool in his folly, indifferently."[33] As Johnson observed, professional-ism defined in this way was an indication of librarians' "neurosis of mechanism, common to overworked and underesteemed professions" that erected "quantitative criteria" into a "stultifying ... system."[34] In the late 20th and early 21st centuries, "librarianship by auto-matic figures" and "pure librarianship" was manifested in readers' advisory service based on BCPL's "Give 'Em What They Want" slogan, which paved the way for Saricks and Brown's appeal-elements theory, NoveList, Pearl's *Book Lust* and *More Book Lust*, DearReader, Book-Letters, NextReads, and whichbook.

Rejecting these approaches, public librarians and readers' advisors could instead become Altick's "surrogate teachers" keenly interested in helping individuals from less-advantaged backgrounds, as well as "the disadvantaged educated,"[35] reach their full potential by updat-ing Carnegie's belief in the public library as an agent of social mobility. Rather than focus-ing on entertainment-oriented genre titles, bestsellers, celebrity-authored books, and prize-winning titles—Bourdieu's commodified industrial literature and increasingly compro-mised middle-brow literature that operates under the auspices of "the empire of the econ-omy"—they could actively encourage the reading of enduring literature and, by extension, the acquisition of meaningful education. Rather than directing economically advantaged patrons toward self-validating and narcissistic books of the "Less Rembrandt, more Me" variety or the "light, quick, escapist" books that are a symbol of the culture of speed, they could lay the groundwork for a culture of the intellect based on classic fiction and nonfiction. They could thus work steadily toward what Leigh called an "enlargement" of their audience by filling the "social needs" area to which commercial media "do not minister with any adequacy."[36] In this way they could rediscover the truth of Compton's findings that the less-advantaged "read good books,"[37] including novels by Thomas Hardy; the Greek Classics; and, as Razieh insisted in *Reading Lolita*, the novels of Henry James.

As a result of the new emphasis on enduring literature as the basis for meaningful education, the way that public libraries measure their performance would have to be rethought. In 1903 Winser stated that many late 19th-century and early 20th-century public libraries focused on popular fiction because it was in their best interests as organizational entities to do so. After all, they could produce impressive annual reports and save money by hiring low-paid clerks. As Lee observed, "once circulation figures were accepted as a standard for measuring library service, many librarians discovered that, in order to increase circulation each year, they had to add more and more current fiction as a means of retaining a sizable portion of library users."[38] Winser's and Lee's comments apply to the late 1990s and early 2000s. Tangible benefits accrue to public libraries with high circulation statistics (the type of statistics that are only possible when concerted emphasis is placed on popular fiction and nonfiction) and low salary structures. When readers' advisory service is seen in terms of mechanically supplying patrons with recent pop fiction and nonfiction by using NoveList, the *Genreflecting* series, Pearl's *Book Lust* series, DearReader, BookLetters, NextReads, or whichbook.net, it is natural for library administrators to think that such service can be delivered just as efficiently by lower-salaried paraprofessionals as by higher-salaried librarians. The reliance of the BCPL on paraprofessionals to deliver a wide range of services is a stark reminder that the "Give 'Em What They Want" approach is inseparable from the intertwined notions of deprofessionalization, deskilling, and cost savings. In sum, when the collective basis of public-library collections and readers' advisory is genre titles, best-sellers, celebrity-authored books, and prize-winning titles, a set of conditions is created that increases circulation statistics while holding down labor costs. This allows library administrators to boast of streamlined and "right-sized"[39] operations that, in the late 20th and early 21st centuries, were thought to represent solid value for taxpayers.

But, as Cutter observed in 1889, circulation statistics "will not indicate that good fiction is read where bad fiction was read before; they do not indicate if the novels taken are read with a purpose or not, with the mind open or shut, if they are devoured at the rate of one a day, or as by the young people's society I knew of where *Romola* was gone through one winter and the *Tale of Two Cities* another."[40] The same point could be made using nonfiction examples. Readers' advisors should therefore lobby for new non-circulation-based ways to gauge the effect of public libraries on community life. Following suggestions made in 1949 by Berelson, library service could be measured in terms of "social, political, and psychological processes" such as "the promotion of group understanding, the clarification of the goals and values of the society, the encouragement of interest in politics, [and] the development of greater rationality in political decisions."[41] Public libraries, Berelson believed, should state their "objectives in terms of the ends of democratic society as applied to the library situation instead of using terms which refer exclusively to library operation."[42]

In short, 21st-century readers' advisors should consider modeling their work on the ideas and actions of Beatrice Winser, Adolph Peck, William Learned, Alice Farquhar,

Jennie Flexner, Alvin Johnson, and George Kyle, thus bringing about a true renaissance in readers' advisory work such that public libraries could again be thought of as institutions striving to provide meaningful educational opportunities rather than short-term entertainment or edutainment. As Farquhar stated in 1939, the "educational possibilities" inherent in readers' advisory "woke us from our lethargy" of circulation-driven and quantity-based librarianship.[43] A similar awakening from a similar lethargy needs to occur in the world of 21st-century readers' advisory if public librarians want to deploy their "species of capital" to reposition readers' advisory as a field that, in Bourdieu's terms, does not adhere to the economic logic of cultural production, but rather privileges autonomous classics for the purpose of meaningful education.

Appendix A: Assignments Used in Case Study 1, Chapter 6

Assignment 1

1. Of all the many fiction books that you have read in the last 10–12 years, select your one most favorite novel. This book *must* be a novel that is meant primarily for adults. No short story collections, no children's books, no series books, please. Also, for the purposes of this exercise, this novel should have been originally written in English, or translated into English.

2. Then, using one page of paper, jot down in point form the reasons why your chosen novel is such a favorite of yours. Why did you pick this novel as your favorite one? What does it mean to you? In other words, what are the essential characteristics of this novel that made you choose this one as your favorite novel of the past 10–12 years?

3. Now go to the NoveList database (available through the local public library) and download the descriptive information provided by this database about your chosen favorite novel.

4. Carefully read over the material that NoveList provides about your chosen novel. Typically, this material has three components: subject headings; description; one or more reviews. Note that the description for your chosen novel may not have all three components: it may only have one or two components. It all depends on NoveList. Now look at the totality of what NoveList states about your chosen novel and compare this description with what you consider to be the key aspects of your chosen novel; that is, compare the description with the reasons you consider this to be your favorite novel.

Deliverables

5. Please rate numerically the totality of the NoveList components (subject headings; description; one or more reviews) that paint a picture of your chosen novel. Assign a numeric score (on a scale of 1 to 50, where 1 is the lowest and 50 is the highest) to the totality of the NoveList components (subject headings; description; one or more reviews) of your chosen novel. When assigning your rating, consider such concrete things as plots, characters, settings, genre, topics, but also such intangible and ambiguous things as themes, feelings, tone, stylistic elements, mood, atmosphere, etc. Use the following guide: Assign a score of **45–50** if you consider NoveList did an excellent job; **40–44** if you thought NoveList did a (very) good job, but one or two things were missing; **30–39** if NoveList did an acceptable job,

with many key elements missing; **20–29** if NoveList did **not** do an adequate job and could have been improved in many fundamental ways; and **0–19** if NoveList did such a bad job that it was laughable.

In other words, assign a numeric grade to the NoveList materials about your novel based on whether the three NoveList components (subject headings; description; one or more reviews) cover what in your view are the "important aspects" of your chosen novel, whatever you think those "important aspects" may be.

6. Now write a short essay (about 1,000 words; may be point form) about how the description of your chosen novel in the online database NoveList compares with what you think are important and essential aspects of your favorite novel. If you assigned a high/mid-range/low score, why did you do so? In what ways did the NoveList components (subject headings; description; reviews, if any) capture (or fail to capture) the "important aspects" of your novel? Consider not only such aspects as plots, characters, settings, genre, and topics, but also more intangible aspects such as themes, feelings, tone, stylistic elements, mood, atmosphere, etc. Provide as many details as possible.

Please also append the actual printout of the description of your novel from the NoveList database to the back of your submission. [A point-form summary of what the entire submission should resemble was provided here; this summary has been deleted.]

Assignment 2

1. Go to the NoveList database and enter the title of the same favorite novel that you used in Assignment 1. Once you are taken to the description of this novel, press the "Find Similar Books" button on the top left-hand side of the page.

2. You will now be taken to a default "Find Similar Books" page for your chosen novel. Note that there will be a list of subject headings and that there are checkmarks beside each of these headings in two columns: "Required" and "Desired." The default is that all headings in the "Desired" column are checked. Now click off the checkmarks that appear beside headings that do not interest you, or move some checkmarks over to the "Required" column. In essence, you have three choices: leave the checkmark in the "Desired" column; move it to the "Required" column, or have no checkmark in either column. Do whatever you feel will generate a book that is as similar to your original favorite novel as possible. (The only restriction is that you cannot check any of the boxes that pertain to the fact that your book won any kind of award. Leave these boxes completely blank.) Then select the reading level "Adult—19 years old and above" (lower down on your screen). Print this "criteria selection" screen *before* you press the search button (otherwise, you might not be able to replicate your search because, if you try and move back from the page listing "similar books" to the "selection criteria" page, all your original selections will have disappeared.) Now press the search button.

3. You will now be taken to a screen that lists books that are "**most like**" (similar to) your chosen favorite novel. Ideally, the list will contain the names of books other than your original favorite one. (If it only contains the name of your original favorite novel, go back to **Step 2** and broaden your parameters; that is, don't be so specific in what you "require.") Your generated list may contain five books, or it may contain dozens or hundreds.

4. Print the first page of your "Search Results." This page should contain about eight (or so) book titles. Naturally enough, the first book listed (in almost all cases, with only a few exceptions) will be your chosen novel, since it exactly meets your selected criteria. Select

the first **four** titles after your original favorite novel that are novels (i.e., make sure that they are in fact novels and not short story collections or anthologies) *and* are *not* by the same author as your original favorite novel. Click on each of these four titles, and you will be taken to the NoveList descriptions of each of these books. Print the descriptions of each of these four books.

5. Read over each of these four descriptions, and decide which **one** of them describes the book that you would "**most like**" to read, given that you liked your original favorite novel.

Deliverables

6. Write a brief essay (about 500 words; may be point form) about why you chose one of the novels as the one that you consider to be "**most like**" your original favorite and why you rejected the other three possibilities. In other words, based on just these four descriptions, explain why you think each of the four novels is or is not similar to your original favorite novel. Be as specific as you can.

7. Now read the novel that you selected (in **Step 5**) as being "**most like**" your original favorite novel. (**Q:** What if I have already read this novel? **A:** Please read it again.) After you have read the novel, write a 1,250-word essay (may be point form) discussing whether or not this new "**most like**" novel was in fact similar to your original favorite novel. Be sure to consider not only such things as plots, characters, settings, genre, and topics, but also more intangible aspects such as themes, feelings, tone, stylistic elements, mood, atmosphere, etc. Provide as many details as possible. Did this novel satisfy you, and was it what you were expecting, having liked your original favorite novel?

At the conclusion of your essay, answer the following two questions. First, would *you* have recommended *this* novel to someone coming in to your public library who said that he/she had liked your original favorite novel and who had, more specifically, liked those aspects of the original favorite novel that conformed to your customized "selection criteria" headings on the "Find Similar Books to" screen? Why or why not? Again, when answering this question, think about such things as themes, feelings, tone, stylistic elements, mood, atmosphere, as well as anything else you deem to be important. Second, if you would *not* have recommended *this* novel, which novel would you have recommended, and why?

Please also append the following elements to the back of your essay: NoveList printout of your favorite novel; your customized "Find Similar Books to" screen ("selection criteria" screen) containing your checked headings; the first page of your search results containing the names of the four novels that you took into consideration; and each of the four NoveList descriptions of these four novels. [A point-form summary of what the entire submission should resemble was provided here; this summary has been deleted.]

Appendix B: Quality of NoveList Informational Records

Table 1 summarizes the themes and issues raised by students about the quality of the informational records of their favorite novel as contained in the NoveList database. Sixty-nine students submitted written comments, which were content analyzed and categorized as per the headings in table 1. Since student comments contained multiple themes and issues, the numbers provided here do not add to 69. Table 2 displays the relationship among student ratings, the number of subject headings in the informational record, and the number of accompanying reviews in the informational record. For detailed information about these tables, please refer to chapter 6.

Table 1

Type of comments	Times mentioned
Positive comments	
Captured essence of novel	19
Enticed reader	5
Captured reading experience/literary value	2
Captured style	
General	10
Captured language	1
Captured pacing	1
Captured tone	6
Captured mood or atmosphere	5
Negative comments	
Misleading or inaccurate	16
Misplaced emphasis	
No genre	3
Insufficient character information	11
Plot revealed	8
No attention to mood or atmosphere	13
No attention to style	
General	20
No attention to language	2
No attention to tone	11
No attention to pacing	4
Unfair treatment that discouraged readers	19

Table 2

Range of Scoresand Definition of Range	Number of student papers (n = 69) having these scores (%)	Average number of subject headings in the records looked at by these students	Average number of reviews in the records looked at by these students
45–50 (excellent)	4 (5.8)	6.0	2.0
40–44 (very good to good)	16 (23.2)	9.18	2.75
30–39 (acceptable)	27 (39.1)	7.62	2.14
20–29 (inadequate)	14 (20.3)	4.71	.92
0–19 (laughable)	8 (11.6)	4.0	.25

Appendix C: Quality of NoveList Suggestions or Recommendations

Table 1 summarizes how students felt about suggesting or recommending to library patrons the NoveList-recommended novel. Sixty-nine students submitted written comments. When categories A and B were combined, only 18.8 percent would recommend the NoveList-recommended novel to library patrons, while 57.97 percent would not recommend it (when categories D and E were combined). Table 2 breaks down their decision about recommending or not recommending the NoveList-recommended novel according to its rank in the NoveList-generated list. Table 3 summarizes their reasons for either recommending or not recommending to library patrons the NoveList-recommended novel. The categories in table 3 are based on a content analysis of students' written comments. Percentages may not add to 100 because of rounding. For detailed information about these tables, please refer to chapter 6.

Table 1

Category	Category definition	Number (%)
A	Unequivocally recommend novel	9 (13.0)
B	For the most part recommend novel	4 (5.8)
C	Ambivalent	16 (23.2)
D	For the most part not recommend novel	13 (18.8)
E	Unequivocally not recommend novel	27 (39.1)

Table 2

Choice of Alternate	Category A	Category B	Category C	Category D	Category E	Total	Category D and E as percent of total
1st choice	5	1	5	6	8	25	56
2nd choice	1	0	4	1	5	11	54.5
3rd choice	1	2	2	0	5	10	50
4th choice	1	1	3	3	7	15	66.7
Other	1	0	2	3	2	8	62.5
Total	9	4	16	13	27	69	59.97

Table 3

Type of decision about recommending the NoveList-recommended novel to others	*Times mentioned*
Positive ("I would recommend the NoveList-recommended novel because...")	
Captured essence of novel	19
Similar mood or atmosphere	3
Similar style	
General	9
Similar quality of writing	2
Similar tone	3
Similar pace	4
Paid attention to detail	2
Felt satisfied	
General	11
Felt an emotional connection	4
Similar genre	4
Similar setting	5
Enjoyed characters	8
Negative ("I would not recommend the NoveList-recommended novel because...")	
Different mood or atmosphere	19
Different style	
General	25
Different quality of writing	13
Lack of attention to detail	5
Extraneous detail	2
Different tone	25
Different pace	7
Different emphases (plot vs. character driven)	8
Different genre	5
Different setting	11
Unsatisfied or needs not met	
General	18
Lack of emotional connection	12
Character flaws	34
Sensitive material	4

Chapter Notes

Preface & Acknowledgments

1. Joan M. Reitz, *Dictionary for Library and Information Science* (Westport, CT: Libraries Unlimited, 2004), 592.

Chapter 1

1. See the Adult Reading Round Table home page at http://www.arrtreads.org (accessed May 1, 2006).

2. A list of the programs offered by ARRT from its founding in 1984 is available at http://www.arrtreads.org/pastprograms.htm (accessed May 1, 2006).

3. Barry Trott, "Advising Readers Online: A Look at Internet-Based Reading Recommendation Services," *Reference & User Services Quarterly* 44, no. 3 (2005): 210–215.

4. Joyce G. Saricks, *Readers' Advisory Service in the Public Library*, 3rd ed. (Chicago: American Library Association, 2005), 19; Roberta Johnson, "Origins of Fiction_L," *Reference & User Services Quarterly* 42, no. 1 (2002): 30–33.

5. Barbara Fister, "'Reading as a Contact Sport': Online Book Groups and the Social Dimension of Reading," *Reference & User Services Quarterly* 44, no. 4 (2005): 303–309.

6. A prototype of FictionFinder is available at http://fictionfinder.oclc.org (accessed May 1, 2006). More information is available at http://www.oclc.org/research/projects/frbr/fictionfinder.htm#top (accessed May 1, 2006).

7. Michael B. Gannon, *Blood, Bedlam, Bullets, and Badguys: A Reader's Guide to Adventure/Suspense Fiction* (Westport, CT: Libraries Unlimited, 2004); Gary Warren Niebuhr, *Make Mine a Mystery: A Reader's Guide to Mystery and Detective Fiction* (Westport, CT: Libraries Unlimited, 2003); Diana Tixier Herald and Bonnie Kunzel, *Strictly Science Fiction: A Guide to Reading Interests* (Westport, CT: Libraries Unlimited, 2002); John Mort, *Christian Fiction: A Guide to the Genre* (Westport, CT: Libraries Unlimited, 2002).

8. Sarah Statz Cords and Robert Burgin, *The Real Story: A Guide to Nonfiction Reading Interests* (Westport, CT: Libraries Unlimited, 2006).

9. Betty Rosenberg, *Genreflecting: A Guide to Reading Interests in Genre Fiction* (Littleton, CO: Libraries Unlimited, 1982).

10. Betty Rosenberg and Diana Tixier Herald, *Genreflecting: A Guide to Reading Interests in Genre Fiction*, 3rd ed. (Englewood, CO: Libraries Unlimited, 1991).

11. Diana Tixier Herald, *Genreflecting: A Guide to Reading Interests in Genre Fiction*, 5th ed. (Englewood, CO: Libraries Unlimited, 2000); Diana Tixier Herald (ed. Wayne A. Wiegand), *Genreflecting: A Guide to Popular Reading Interests*, 6th ed. (Westport, CT: Libraries Unlimited, 2006).

12. Joyce G. Saricks and Nancy Brown, *Readers' Advisory Service in the Public Library* (Chicago: American Library Association, 1989); Joyce G. Saricks and Nancy Brown, *Readers' Advisory Service in the Public Library*, 2nd ed. (Chicago: American Library Association, 1997); Joyce G. Saricks, *Readers' Advisory Service in the Public Library*, 3rd ed. (Chicago: American Library Association, 2005); Joyce G. Saricks, *The Readers' Advisory Guide to Genre Fiction* (Chicago: American Library Association, 2001).

13. Becky Siegel Spratford and Tammy Hennigh Clausen, *The Horror Readers' Advisory: The Librarian's Guide to Vampires, Killer Tomatoes, and Haunted Houses* (Chicago: American Library Association, 2004); Ann Bouricius, *The Romance Readers' Advisory: The Librarian's Guide to Love in the Stacks* (Chicago: American Library Association, 2000).

14. Kathleen de la Peña McCook and Gary O. Rolstad, eds., *Developing Readers' Advisory Services: Concepts and Commitments* (New York: Neal-Schuman, 1993); Kenneth D. Shearer, ed., *Guiding the Reader to the Next Book* (New York: Neal-Schuman, 1996).

15. Kenneth D. Shearer and Robert Burgin, eds., *The Readers' Advisor's Companion* (Englewood, CO: Libraries Unlimited, 2001); Robert Burgin, ed., *Nonfiction Readers' Advisory* (Westport, CT: Libraries Unlimited, 2004).

16. Nancy Pearl, *Book Lust: Recommended Reading for Every Mood, Moment, and Reason* (Seattle, WA: Sasquatch Books, 2003); Nancy Pearl, *More Book Lust: Recommended Reading for Every Mood, Moment, and Reason* (Seattle, WA: Sasquatch Books, 2005).

17. Mary K. Chelton, ed. "Readers' Advisory," *Reference & User Services Quarterly* 40, no. 2 (2000): 135.

18. Juris Dilevko and Keren Dali, "Electronic Databases for Readers' Advisory Services and Intellectual Access to Translated Fiction Not Originally Written in English," *Library Resources & Technical Services* 47, no. 3 (2003): 80–95.

19. Nora Rawlinson, "Give 'Em What They Want!" *Library Journal* 106, no. 20 (1981): 2188–2196. See also: The Baltimore County Public Library's Blue Ribbon Committee, *Give 'Em What They Want! Managing the Public's Library* (Chicago: American Library Association, 1992).

20. Rawlinson, "Give 'Em What They Want!" 2188.

21. Hans Robert Jauss, "Theory of Genres and Medieval Literature," in *Toward an Aesthetic of Reception*, trans. Timothy Bahti (Minneapolis: University of Minnesota Press, 1982), 76–109.

22. John G. Cawelti, *Adventure, Mystery, and Romance: Formula Stories as Art and Popular Culture* (Chicago: University of Chicago Press, 1976).

23. Esther Jane Carrier, *Fiction in Public Libraries, 1876–1900* (New York: Scarecrow Press, 1965); Esther Jane Carrier, *Fiction in Public Libraries, 1900-1950* (Littleton, CO: Libraries Unlimited, 1985).

24. Christine Pawley, *Reading on the Middle Border: The Culture of Print in Late-Nineteenth-Century Osage, Iowa* (Amherst: University of Massachusetts Press, 2001), 92.

25. Sharon L. Baker and Karen L. Wallace, *The Responsive Public Library: How To Develop and Market a Winning Collection*, 2nd ed. (Englewood, CO: Libraries Unlimited, 2002).

26. Three of these articles are: Catherine Sheldrick Ross, Readers' Advisory Service: New Directions, *RQ* 30, no. 4 (1991): 503–518; Catherine Sheldrick Ross, "'If They Read Nancy Drew, So What?' Series Book Readers Talk Back," *Library & Information Science Research* 17, no. 3 (1995): 201–236; Catherine Sheldrick Ross, "Finding without Seeking: The Information Encounter in the Context of Reading for Pleasure," *Information Processing and Management* 35, no. 6 (1999): 793–795. Many of her articles form the basis of Catherine Sheldrick Ross, Lynne (E. F.) McKechnie, and Paulette M. Rothbauer, *Reading Matters: What the Research Reveals about Reading, Libraries, and Community* (Westport, CT: Libraries Unlimited, 2005).

27. Janice A. Radway, *Reading the Romance: Women, Patriarchy, and Popular Literature* (Chapel Hill: University of North Carolina Press, 1984).

28. Pierre Bourdieu and Loïc J. D. Wacquant, *An Invitation to Reflexive Sociology* (Chicago: University of Chicago Press, 1992), 94–139.

29. Pierre Bourdieu, *The Rules of Art: Genesis and Structure of the Literary Field*, trans. Susan Emanuel (Cambridge, UK: Polity Press, 1996), 142.

30. Michael H. Harris, "State, Class, and Cultural Reproduction: Toward a Theory of Library Service in the United States," *Advances in Librarianship* 14 (1986): 235.

31. An early use of this phrase is by Louis R. Wilson, *The Geography of Reading: A Study of the Distribution and Status of Libraries in the United States* (Chicago: University of Chicago Press, 1938).

32. Bourdieu, *The Rules of Art*, 142.

33. Ibid., 142, 147, 345.

34. Ibid., 142. Original emphases.

35. Ibid. Original emphasis.

36. Ibid., 147.

37. Ibid., 142.

38. Ibid., 142–143.

39. Ibid., 147.

40. Ibid., 141–142.

41. Ibid., 143–144.

42. Ibid., 347.

43. Ibid., 345.

44. Ibid., 347.

45. Pierre Bourdieu, *Distinction: A Social Critique of the Judgement of Taste*, trans. Richard Nice (Cambridge, MA: Harvard University Press, 1984), 323.

46. Pierre Bourdieu, "The Market of Symbolic Goods," in *The Field of Cultural Production: Essays on Art and Literature*, edited and introduced by Randal Johnson, 126, 128 (Cambridge, UK: Polity Press, 1993).

47. Ibid., 126.

48. Bourdieu, *Distinction*, 323.

49. Quoted in Bourdieu, "The Market of Symbolic Goods," 126.

50. Bourdieu, *Distinction*, 323.

51. Joe Moran, *Star Authors: Literary Celebrity in America* (London: Pluto Press, 2000), 9.

52. Bourdieu, *The Rules of Art*, 347.

53. Quoted in Stéphane Baillargeon, "La Fièvre de l'Hyperfestif," *Le Devoir*, 25 June 2005, sec. A, pp. 1, 10. The quotation is our translation from the original French in the cited article.

54. Moran, *Star Authors*, 39.

55. Ibid., 39–40.

56. Lorne Manly, "The Goat at Saks and Other Marketing Tales," *New York Times*, sec. C, pp. 1, 4.

57. Quoted in Rob Walker, "Stranger than Fiction," *New York Times Magazine*, 1 May 2005, sec. 6, p. 30.

58. Ibid.

59. Ibid.

60. Don Gillmor, "Anatomy of a Bestseller," *Toronto Life* 37, no. 9 (2003): 86–92.

61. Rachel Donadio, "She'd Be Great on TV," *New York Times Book Review*, 26 June 2005, sec. 7, p. 27.

62. Ibid.

63. Julie Bosman, "A Match Made in Product Placement Heaven," *New York Times*, 31 May 2006, sec. C, p. 3.

64. Andrew Adam Newman, "Placing Products, Advertisers Find Room at the Inn," *New York Times*, 5 September 2005, sec. C, p. 5.

65. Ibid.

66. Bosman, "A Match," 3.

67. Newman, "Placing Products," 5.

68. Randy Kennedy, "Cash Up Front," *New York Times Book Review*, 5 June 2005, sec. 7, pp. 14–15.

69. Ibid., 15

70. Ibid.

71. Doreen Carvajal, "For Sale: On-Line Bookstore's Recommendations," *New York Times*, 8 February 1999, sec. A, pp. 1, 21; Doreen Carvajal, "Amazon.com Plans to Revise Its Ad Program," *New York Times*, 10 February 1999, sec. C, p. 1.

72. "Paid Placements." Available from: http://www.amazon.com/exec/obidos/subst/misc/co-op/small-vendor-info.html/ref=gw1_mm_5/103-6351599-5280621 (accessed April 25, 2006).

73. Steven Zeitchik and Jim Milliot, "The Strangest Program You've Never Heard Of," *Publishers Weekly* 252, no. 14 (2005): 5–6.

74. Kennedy, "Cash Up Front," 15.

75. Brian Montopoli, "A Publisher Borrows a Page from the Movies," *New York Times*, 27 June 2005, sec. C, p. 4.

76. Edward Wyatt, "Michael Crichton? He's Just the Author," *New York Times*, 6 February 2005, sec. 3, pp. 1, 4.

77. Ibid., 1.

78. Tad Friend, "The Parachute Artist," *The New Yorker* 81, no. 9 (April 18, 2005): 78–91. Available from ProQuest.

79. "Move Over, Buffy: 17th Street Productions Takes on Hollywood," *Publishing Trends* (December 2000). Available from: http://www.publishingtrends.com/copy/0012/0012buffy.htm (accessed March 12, 2006). For a brief overview of book packagers, see Jenna Glatzer, "Book Packaging: Under-explored Terrain for Freelancers." Available from: http://www.absolutewrite.com/site/book_packaging.htm (accessed March 12, 2006).

80. "Move Over, Buffy."

81. Alloy's web site is available from: http://www.alloy.com (accessed March 13, 2006).

82. "Move Over, Buffy."

83. Available from: http://www.alloy.com (accessed March 13, 2006).

84. "Move Over, Buffy."

85. Motoko Rich and Dinita Smith, "First, Plot and Character. Then, Find an Author," *New York Times*, 27 April 2006, sec. A, p. 1.

86. Ibid.

87. "Move Over, Buffy."

88. Rich and Smith, "First," 1.

89. Naomi Wolf, "Wild Things," *New York Times Book Review*, 12 March 2006, sec. 7, p. 22.

90. Ibid.

91. Ibid.

92. Manly, "The Goat at Saks," 4.

93. Martin Arnold, "Placed Products, and Their Cost," *New York Times*, 13 September 2001, sec. E, p. 3.

94. Ibid.

95. Ibid.

96. Danny Hakim, "Would You Base the Purchase of a Car on the Prose of a Chick-lit Novelist? Ford Hopes So," *New York Times*, 23 March 2004, sec. C, p. 2.

97. Ibid.

98. Ibid.

99. Manly, "The Goat at Saks," 4.

100. Ibid.

101. Ibid.

102. Ibid.

103. Motoko Rich, "Product Placement Deals Make Leap from Film to Books," *New York Times*, 12 June 2006, sec. C, pp. 1, 5.

104. Ibid.

105. "Harlequin Enterprises and NASCAR Announce Licensing Agreement." Available from: www.newswire.ca/en/releases/archive/November2005/02/c9326.html (accessed November 2, 2005).

106. Viv Bernstein, "Eau de Nascar: Licensing and the Smell of Money," *New York Times*, 12 March 2006, sec. 8, p. 5.

107. Ibid.

108. "In the Groove by Pamela Britton." Available from: http://store.eharlequin.com/t2_book_detail.jhtml?PRO-DID=11324&_requestid=816 (accessed March 12, 2006).

109. Bernstein, "Eau de Nascar."

110. Sharon Waxman, "A Small Step at Starbucks from Mocha to Movies," *New York Times*, 1 May 2006, sec. C., p. 1, 2.

111. Ibid.

112. Ibid.

113. Quoted in Ibid.

114. Edward Wyatt, "For This Author, Writing is Only the Beginning," *New York Times*, 22 June 2005, sec. E, pp. 1, 10.

115. Ibid., 10.

116. Ibid.

117. Ibid.

118. Arnold, "Placed Products," 3.

119. Ibid.

120. Edward Wyatt, "Attention, Shoppers: Sale on Fresh Books in Aisle 3," *New York Times*, 28 April 2005, sec. E, pp. 1, 10.

121. Ibid., 10.

122. Bourdieu, *The Rules of Art*, 345.

123. Quoted in Bourdieu, *The Rules of Art*, 345.

124. Ian Parker, "Absolute Powerpoint: Can a Software Package Edit Our Thoughts," *The New Yorker* 77, no. 13 (May 28, 2001): 77.

125. Donadio, "She'd Be Great," 27.

126. Bourdieu, *The Rules of Art*, 142.

127. André Schiffrin, *The Business of Books: How International Conglomerates Took over Publishing and Changed the Way We Read* (London: Verso, 2000), 118–119.

128. Ibid., 105–106.

129. Ibid., 106. Schiffrin adopts this phrase from the Spanish newspaper *El País*.

130. Moran, *Star Authors*, 40.

131. John W. Aldridge, *Talents and Technicians: Literary Chic and the New Assembly-Line Fiction* (New York: Charles Scribner's Sons, 1992), 7. Moran also refers to Aldridge in a similar context.

132. Moran, *Star Authors*, 41. Moran quotes George Garrett, "'Once More unto the Breach, Dear Friends, Once More': The Publishing Scene and American Literary Art," *Review of Contemporary Fiction* 8, no. 3 (1988): 106. For some readers, this essay will be most readily accessible on the ProQuest database in its reprinted version, contained in *Review of Contemporary Fiction* 19, no. 3 (1999): 107–116.

133. Moran, *Star Authors*, 41.

134. Aldridge, *Talents and Technicians*, 23.

135. Ibid., 15.

136. Moran, *Star Authors*, 49.

137. Ibid., 41.

138. Ibid. Moran quotes Andrew Wernick, *Promotional Culture: Advertising, Ideology and Symbolic Expression* (London: Sage, 1991), 106.

139. Moran, *Star Authors*, 41.

140. Aldridge, *Talents and Technicians*, 25.

141. Leo Baudry, *Frenzy of Renown: Fame and Its History* (New York: Oxford University Press, 1986).

142. Ibid., 8. Also quoted in Moran, *Star Authors*, 61.

143. Andrew Wernick, *Promotional Culture: Advertising, Ideology and Symbolic Expression* (London: Sage, 1991).

144. Pierre Bourdieu, "The Production of Belief: Contribution to an Economy of Symbolic Goods," in *The Field of Cultural Production: Essays on Art and Literature*, ed. Randal Johnson, (Cambridge, UK: Polity Press, 1993), 76–77.

145. Rachel Donadio, "Promotional Intelligence," *New York Times Book Review*, 21 May 2006, sec. 7, p. 31.

146. Ibid. Statistics about book sales are taken from Donadio's article and are based on Nielsen Bookscan figures.

147. Bourdieu, *Distinction*, 323.

148. James F. English, *The Economy of Prestige: Prizes, Awards, and the Circulation of Value* (Cambridge, MA: Harvard University Press, 2005), 26, 78, 77.

149. Ibid., 36.

150. Ibid., 330. See Appendix B in *The Economy of Prestige* for detailed statistics (pp. 329–333).

151. Ibid., 20–21, 323–328.

152. Ibid., 334, 331.

153. Ibid., 76.

154. Ibid., 17, 21.

155. Ibid., 256.

156. Ibid., 91.

157. Ibid., 119, 121.

158. Ibid., 119, 131.

159. Ibid., 137–138.

160. Ibid., 146.

161. Ibid., 121–154.

162. Ibid., 334.

163. Ibid.

164. Ibid., 147.

165. Ibid., 281–282.

166. Ibid., 208. Original emphasis.

167. Robert H. Frank and Philip J. Cook, *The Winner-Take-All Society: How More and More Americans Compete for Ever Fewer and Bigger Prizes, Encouraging Economic Waste, Income Inequality, and an Impoverished Cultural Life* (New York: Free Press, 1995).

168. See Rebecca Caldwell, "CBC Fishes 1928 Novel out of Obscurity," *The Globe and Mail*, 26 February 2005, sec. R, p. 11. One is also struck by the choice of Sophocles's play "Antigone" by the city of Ithaca, New York, as its 2003 choice in the "One Book" reading program, and by its subsequent choice of Kafka's *The Trial* in 2004.

169. English also refers to *The Winner-Take-All Society*. Our reference to this book derives from English's reference.

170. Sarah Boxer, "Literary Sport: The Roar of the Crowd, the Review of the Books," *New York Times*, 17 February 2005, sec. E, pp. 1, 5.

171. Seattle Public Library, "Seattle Reads." Available from: http://www.spl.org (accessed November 25, 2005).

172. A complete list of these projects is available at the web site of the National Library of Congress, The Center for the Book, "One Book Reading Promotion Projects." Available from: http://www.loc.gov/loc/cfbook/one-book.html (accessed December 17, 2005).

173. The entire list of Oprah's Book Club books is available from: http://www.oprah.com/obc/pastbooks (accessed December 21, 2005).

174. English, *The Economy of Prestige*, 34–35.

175. All quotations in the remainder of this paragraph are from Gavin McNett, "Reaching to the Converted: Oprah's Book Club Introduces Readers to People They Already Know—Themselves," *Salon*, 12 November 1999. Available from: http://www.salon.com/books/feature/1999/11/12/oprahcon/index.html (accessed May 8, 2005).

176. Laura J. Miller, *Reluctant Capitalists: Bookselling and the Culture of Consumption* (Chicago: University of Chicago Press, 2006), 53, 52.

177. Ibid., 52.
178. Ibid., 54.
179. Ibid., 54, 66.
180. Ibid., 67, 57, 215, 225.
181. Ibid., 215.
182. Ibid., 57, 58.
183. Ibid., 215, 57, 58, 62.
184. Ibid., 63.
185. Ibid., 62.
186. Ibid., 66.
187. Ibid., 67.
188. Ibid., 54, 69.
189. Ibid., 69, 54, 74.
190. Ibid., 78.
191. Ibid., 79, 74.
192. Donadio, "Promotional Intelligence," 31.
193. Miller, *Reluctant Capitalists*, 79.
194. Ibid., 81.
195. Ibid., 96.
196. Donadio, "Promotional Intelligence," 31.
197. Miller, *Reluctant Capitalists*, 124, 135, 124.
198. Ibid., 131.
199. All information and quotes about Indigo Books are drawn from: Dana Flavelle, "Next Chapter for Indigo: More Gifts," *Toronto Star*, 9 June 2004, sec. E, p. 1; Nancy Carr, "Indigo Sees Itself as Purveyor of Lifestyle," *Toronto Star*, 15 September 2004, sec. E, p. 2; Shirley Won, "Indigo Targets Kids with 'Edutainment,'" *The Globe and Mail*, 30 September 2005, sec. B, p. 3. See also: http://www.chapters.indigo.ca/gifts (accessed May 1, 2006).

200. Miller, *Reluctant Capitalists*, 124.
201. Ibid., 135, 138.
202. Ibid., 135.
203. Ibid., 217, 216, 135.
204. Bourdieu, *The Rules of Art*, 344.
205. Ibid., 146–147.
206. Ibid., 344–345.
207. Ibid., 348, 146–147.
208. Ibid., 347.
209. Ibid., 147.
210. See Judi McCallum and Debbie Walker, "'A 'Wow!' Library": FIS Grads Plan Markham's Library for the 21st Century," *Informed* 57 (December 2005): 9. This article boasts about "learn[ing] from the success of the superbookstores" by "us[ing] merchandising retail-type displays to market the collection to our customers and to provide retail-type comfort to encourage customers to stay, browse, learn and borrow."
211. Miller, *Reluctant Capitalists*, 61.
212. Ibid., 57.
213. Bourdieu, *The Rules of Art*, 340.
214. Statistics cited in Miller, *Reluctant Capitalists* (p. 251, endnote 85).
215. Alan Riding, "Pierre Bourdieu, 71, French Thinker and Globalization Critic [Obituary]," *New York Times*, 25 January 2002, sec. A, p. 21.
216. If we define small and mid-sized public libraries as those with legal service area populations (LSAPs) of less than 25,000, then 7,242 of the 9,211 pubic libraries (78.6 percent) in the United States were small or mid-sized in 2003. If we define small public libraries as those with LSAPs of less than 10,000, then 5,470 of the 9,211 public libraries

(59.4 percent) in the United States were small in 2003. Viewed from another perspective, 68.7 percent of the public libraries in the United States had print material collections—defined as book and serial volumes—of less than 50,000 volumes in 2003. Viewed from still another perspective, each of the 1,032 public libraries in the United States with an LSAP of fewer than 1,000 people spent on average $3,893.04 for collection development (books, serials, etc.); each of the 1,649 public libraries with an LSAP between 1,000 and 2,499 people spent on average $7,696.66; each of the 1,326 public libraries with an LSAP of between 2,500 and 4,999 people spent on average $14,844.08; each of the 1,463 public libraries with an LSAP of between 5,000 and 9,999 people spent on average $30,825.37; and each of the 1,772 public libraries with an LSAP of between 10,000 and 24,999 people spent on average $67,584.11. All statistics taken from: National Center for Education Statistics, *Public Libraries in the United States: Fiscal Year 2003* [NCS 2005-363] (September 2005), Table 1A (p. 14), Table 12A (p. 61), Table 18A (p. 85). Available from: http://nces.ed.gov/pubsearch/pubsinfo.asp?pubid=2005363 (accessed December 22, 2005). Calculations were required to derive these figures from Table 18A of *Public Libraries in the United States: Fiscal Year 2003*. In each case, multiply the total expenditures (Column 3) by the percentage of expenditures spent on collections (Column 5). Then divide this figure by the number of public libraries in the appropriate category (Column 2).

217. For another perspective on the way in which libraries and museums are participating in edutainment, see Juris Dilevko and Lisa Gottlieb, *The Evolution of Library and Museum Partnerships: Historical Antecedents, Contemporary Manifestations, and Future Directions* (Westport, CT: Libraries Unlimited, 2004).

218. Edward Rothstein, "Strumming the Mystic Chords of Memory," *New York Times*, 19 April 2005, sec. E., pp. 1, 7.

219. Rothstein uses a similar metaphor at the conclusion of his article: "But it is telling that by the end of the presentation "Ghosts of the Library," the historian ends up turning into a ghost himself, and disappears into thin air."

Chapter 2

1. Joyce G. Saricks, *Readers' Advisory Service in the Public Library*, 3rd ed. (Chicago: American Library Association, 2005); Bill Crowley, "A History of Readers' Advisory Service in the Public Library," in *Nonfiction Readers' Advisory*, ed. Robert Burgin, 3–29 (Westport, CT: Libraries Unlimited, 2004).

2. Saricks, *Readers' Advisory Service*, 3rd ed., 1.
3. Ibid., 2.
4. Ibid., 4.
5. Ibid.
6. Ibid., 8.
7. Ibid., 6, 8.
8. Ibid., 6.
9. Ibid., 12. Original emphasis.
10. Bill Crowley, "Rediscovering the History of Readers Advisory Service," *Public Libraries* 44, no. 1 (2005): 38.
11. Crowley, "A History of Readers' Advisory Service in the Public Library," 6.
12. Ibid.
13. Ibid.
14. Mortimer J. Adler, *A Second Look in the Rearview Mirror: Further Autobiographical Reflections of a Philosopher at Large* (New York: Macmillan, 1992), 141–168; Alan Bloom, *The Closing of the American Mind* (New York: Simon and Schuster, 1987), 336–347. See also Jay Satterfield's catalog text for the exhibition entitled "The Great Ideas: The University of Chicago and the Idea of Liberal Education" [An

Exhibition in the Department of Special Collections, The University of Chicago Library, May 1, 2002—September 6, 2002]. Available: http://www.lib.uchicago.edu/e/spcl/excat/ideasint.html (accessed November 17, 2005).

15. Adler, *A Second Look*, 142.

16. Institutions with great-books programs include: St. John's College (Annapolis, Maryland, and Santa Fe, New Mexico); Boston University; Brock University (St. Catharines, Ontario); East Carolina University (Greenville, North Carolina); Malaspina University-College (Nanaimo, British Columbia); Mercer University (Macon, Georgia); Thomas Aquinas College (Santa Paula, California); and The University of Chicago, Graham School of General Studies, The Basic Program of Liberal Education for Adults. Web sites for these programs are available at the following web addresses, all accessed between November 10–17, 2005: Boston University (http://www.bu.edu/core/about/books.htm); Brock University (http://www.brocku.ca/great-books/); East Carolina University (http://www.ecu.edu/greatbooks/intro.htm); Malaspina University-College (http://www.mala.bc.ca/~mcneil/target.htm); Mercer University (http://www.mercer.edu/gbk/program.htm); St. John's College (http://www.sjcsf.edu/asp/main.aspx?page=1003); Thomas Aquinas College (http://www.thomasaquinas.edu/curriculum/index.htm); and The University of Chicago's Graham School (http://grahamschool.uchicago.edu/pdf/BP%20Reading%20List%20F05.pdf).

17. Quoted from the East Carolina University "Great Books—Introduction" website; address given in a previous endnote.

18. Quoted from the Thomas Aquinas College "Great Books—Curriculum" website; address given in a previous endnote.

19. Adler, *A Second Look*, 145.

20. Ibid.

21. Samuel G. Freedman, "The Achievement Gap in Elite Schools," *New York Times*, 28 September 2005, sec. C, p. 21.

22. Figures taken from "About Evanston: Facts, Figures, & Demographics." Available from: http://www.cityofevanston.org/about/demographics.shtml (accessed October 22, 2005) and the U.S. Census Bureau, Census 2000, "Table DP-1: Profile of General Demographic Characteristics: 2000: Geographic area: Evanston city, Illinois."

23. Figures taken from: ETHS School Improvement Plan 2004–06. Available from: http://www.eths.k12.il.us/eval/SIP_04_06.htm (accessed October 22, 2005).

24. Freedman, "The Achievement Gap," C21.

25. Transcript of "George W. Bush's Speech to the NAACP." Available from: http://www.washingtonpost.com/wp-srv/onpolitics/elections/bushtext071000.htm (accessed February 24, 2006).

26. Steven R. Weisman, "On Trip to South, Rice Uses an Atypical Topic: Herself," *New York Times*, 24 October 2005, sec. A, p. 15.

27. Other statistics continue the story: only 4 percent of adults who graduated from high school were proficient in 2003 (down from 5 percent in 1992); only 19 percent of adults with an associate's or 2-year degree were proficient in 2003 (down from 23 percent in 1992); and only 41 percent of adults with a graduate degree were proficient in 2003 (down from 51 percent in 1992). All figures and quotations taken from: United States Department of Education, National Center for Education Statistics, National Assessment of Adult Literacy (NAAL), "A First Look at the Literacy of America's Adults in the 21st Century," pp. 3, 11, 15. Available from: http://nces.ed.gov/NAAL/PDF/2006470_1.PDF (accessed December 17, 2005).

28. Quoted in Sam Dillon, "Literacy Falls for Graduates from College, Testing Finds," *New York Times*, 16 December 2005, sec. A, p. 34.

29. National Endowment for the Arts, *Reading at Risk: A Survey of Literary Reading in America* [Research Division Report #46], ix–xii. Available from: http://www.nea.gov/pub/ReadingAtRisk.pdf (accessed June 21, 2005).

30. Bowman, "Why Is Reading at Risk?"

31. Quoted from the Thomas Aquinas College "Great Books—Curriculum" website; address given in a previous endnote.

32. Herbert J. Gans, *Popular Culture and High Culture: An Analysis and Evaluation of Taste* (New York: Basic Books, 1974), vii.

33. Rosenberg, *Genreflecting*, 5.

34. Ibid., 15.

35. Pearl, *More Book Lust*, ix.

36. Joseph Epstein, "Is Reading Really at Risk?" *The Weekly Standard* 9, no. 46 (August 16–23, 2004): 20.

37. Ibid., 21.

38. Ibid., 21–22.

39. David Brooks, "Joe Strauss to Joe Six-Pack," *New York Times*, 16 June 2005, sec. A, p. 27.

40. Ibid.

41. Michiko Kakutani, "Bending the Truth in a Million Little Ways," *New York Times*, 17 January 2006, sec. E, p. 1.

42. Christopher Lasch, *The Culture of Narcissism: American Life in an Age of Diminishing Expectations* (New York: W. W. Norton, 1979).

43. Ibid., 47.

44. Ibid., 21.

45. Diantha Schull, "The Civic Library: A Model for 21st Century Participation," *Advances in Librarianship* 28 (2004): 58. Schull quotes Fred Kent and Phil Myrick of the Project for Public Spaces movement. Kent and Myrick's words are originally found in Marylaine Block, "How to Become a Great Public Space," *American Libraries* 34, no. 4 (2003): 72–74, 76.

46. Sharon L. Baker and Karen L. Wallace, *The Responsive Public Library: How to Develop and Market a Winning Collection*, 2nd ed. (Englewood, CO: Libraries Unlimited, 2002).

47. Ibid., 48.

48. Ibid., 79, 166, among others.

49. Ibid., 79.

50. Ibid., 266.

51. Ibid., 79.

52. Ibid., 254.

53. Ibid., 12, 50, 80–81, 197, 206.

54. Ibid., 197–221.

55. Ibid., 254.

56. Judith McPheron, "A Critique of the Progressive Public Library Movement in America," in *Library Lit. 8—The Best of 1977*, ed. Bill Katz, 291 (Metuchen, NJ: Scarecrow Press, 1978).

57. Gordon Stevenson, "Popular Culture and the Public Library," *Advances in Librarianship* 7 (1977): 223.

58. McPheron, "A Critique of the Progressive Public Library Movement in America," 288.

59. Ibid., 292. McPheron quotes Susan Sontag, "Women, The Arts and the Politics of Culture," *Salmagundi* (Fall 1975-Winter 1976): 47.

60. Scarlett Thomas, "The Great Chick Lit Conspiracy," *Independent on Sunday* (London), 4 August 2002, pp. 1, 2.

61. Amy Johnson Frykholm, *Rapture Culture: Left Behind in Evangelical America* (New York: Oxford University Press, 2004), 8.

62. Jesse H. Shera, *Foundations of the Public Library: The Origins of the Public Library Movement in New England 1629-1855* (Hamden, CT: Shoe String Press, 1965), 162–164.

63. Sidney Ditzion, *Arsenals of a Democratic Culture: A Social History of the American Public Library Movement in New England and the Middle States from 1850 to 1900* (Chicago: American Library Association, 1947), 96, 181.

64. Quoted in Walter Muir Whitehill, *Boston Public Library: A Centennial History* (Cambridge, MA: Harvard University Press, 1956), 23. Also quoted in Shera, *Foundations of the Public Library*, 225. The words are those of George Ticknor in a letter to Edward Everett in 1851.

65. Quoted in Shera, *Foundations of the Public Library*, 225. The words are those of George Ticknor in a letter to Mayor Bigelow in 1850.

66. "Board of Trustees—Former Trustees: George Ticknor." Available from: http://www.bpl.org/general/trustees/ticknor.htm (accessed February 28, 2006).

67. Shera, *Foundations of the Public Library*, 269, 272. As an appendix to his book, Shera includes the "Report of the Trustees of the Public Library of the City of Boston, July, 1852." The quotations in this sentence and the following sentence are from this appended Report.

68. Ibid., 274–275.

69. "Report of the Examining Committee," *Twenty-third Annual Report of the Trustees of the Public Library* (City of Boston, City Document No. 89, 1875), 17.

70. J. P. Quincy, "Free Libraries," in *Public Libraries in the United States of America: Their History, Condition, and Management: Part I* (Washington, DC: Government Printing Office; reprinted by the University of Illinois Graduate School of Library Science Monograph Series Number 4), 395.

71. Shera, *Foundations of the Public Library*, 149–151.

72. Wayne A. Wiegand, *The Politics of an Emerging Profession: The American Library Association, 1876–1917* (New York: Greenwood Press, 1986). The chapter titles of this book reflect the three component parts of the new ALA motto.

73. Wayne A. Wiegand, "Tunnel Vision and Blind Spots: What the Past Tells Us about the Present: Reflections on the Twentieth-century History of American Librarianship," *Library Quarterly* 69, no. 1 (1999): 4.

74. Wiegand, *The Politics of an Emerging Profession*, 43.

75. Quoted in Robert Ellis Lee, *Continuing Education for Adults through the American Public Library, 1833–1964* (Chicago: American Library Association, 1966), 40.

76. Ibid., 44.

77. Ibid., 44, 46.

78. William S. Learned, *The American Public Library and the Diffusion of Knowledge* (New York: Harcourt, Brace and Company, 1924), 12, 13.

79. Ibid., 15.

80. Alvin S. Johnson, *The Public Library—A People's University* (New York: American Association for Adult Education, 1938), 24.

81. Ibid., 25.

82. Ibid., 27.

83. Carrier, *Fiction in Public Libraries, 1900–1950*, 295.

84. Lee, *Continuing Education for Adults*, 58.

85. Lynn E. Birge, *Serving Adult Learners: A Public Library Tradition* (Chicago: American Library Association, 1981), 121–27.

86. Ibid., 128. Birge quotes Toro's remarks in: "'People's University' Set for Public Libraries," *Library Journal* 98, no. 2 (1973): 113–114.

87. Ibid., 132. Birge quotes Toro's statements in: Jose Orlando Toro, "Office of Library Independent Study and Guidance Projects, College Examination Board, Advisory Council Meeting, January 31, 1975, Tulsa City-County Library, Report from the Director," pp. 16–17 (mimeograph).

88. "Hippyland." "Hippyland Glossary F to H." Available from: http://www.hippy.com/php/article-18.html (accessed November 3, 2005).

89. D. W. Davies, "Libraries as Social & Entertainment Centers," in *Public Librarianship: A Reader*, ed. Jane Robbins-Carter, 109 (Littleton, CO: Libraries Unlimited, 1982).

90. Topic lists and titles are taken from the following sources: *Catalogue and Rules of the Library & Reading Room of the Québec Mechanics' Institute* (Québec, QC: W. Cowan & Son, 1841); *Constitution, Rules and Bye Laws of the Halifax Mechanics' Library* (Halifax, NS: J. H. Crosskill, 1846). Both items are available on microform through the Canadian Institute for Historical Microproductions (CIHM) as CIHM 47715 and CIHM 35997, respectively.

91. Davies, "Libraries as Social & Entertainment Centers," 116, 119, 125.

92. Ibid., 117.

93. Ibid.

94. Susan Stellin, "Library Science, Home Depot Style," *New York Times*, 4 November 2004, sec. F, p. 10. This article describes the Berkeley Tool Lending Library, which is a branch of the Berkeley library system. Overall, the library has some 5,000 tools, including "routers, belt sanders, and reciprocating saws, levels, ladders, soldering irons and a cement mixer." The article also mentions that other tool libraries exist in Oakland, California; San Francisco, California; Portland, Oregon; and Grosse Pointe, Michigan.

95. Michael H. Harris, "The Purpose of the American Public Library: A Revisionist Interpretation of History," *Library Journal* 98, no. 16 (1973): 2509–2514; Michael H. Harris and Gerard Spiegler, "Everett, Ticknor and the Common Man: The Fear of Societal Instability as the Motivation for the Founding of the Boston Public Library," *Libri* 24, no. 4 (1974): 249–275.

96. Dee Garrison, *Apostles of Culture: The Public Librarian and American Society, 1876–1920* (New York: Free Press, 1979). See also Dee Garrison, "The Tender Technicians: The Feminization of Public Librarianship, 1876–1905," *Journal of Social History* 6, no. 2 (1972/1973): 131–159. Her dissertation is available as: Lora Doris Garrison, "Cultural Missionaries: A Study of American Public Library Leaders, 1876–1910" (University of California, Irvine; 1973).

97. Garrison, *Apostles of Culture*, xi.

98. Ibid., xiii.

99. Ibid., 36, 45.

100. Harris, "The Purpose of the American Public Library," 2510, 2511.

101. Harris and Spiegler, "Everett, Ticknor and the Common Man," 252.

102. Ibid., 253, 256.

103. Ibid., 258.

104. Harris, "The Purpose of the American Public Library," 2510, 2511.

105. Ibid., 2511.

106. Ibid., 2512.

107. Ibid.

108. Quoted in Harris, "The Purpose of the American Public Library," 2513.

109. Harris and Spiegler, "Everett, Ticknor and the Common Man," 264.

110. Quoted in Richard Harwell and Roger Michener, "As Public as the Town Pump," *Library Journal* 99, no. 7 (1974): 962.

111. Ibid., 962. Harwell and Michener quote Edward Shils, "Intellectuals, Tradition, and the Traditions of Intellectuals: Some Preliminary Considerations," *Daedalus* (Spring 1972): 31.

112. Francis Miksa, "The Interpretation of American Public Library History," in *Public Librarianship: A Reader*, ed. Jane Robbins-Carter, 79 (Littleton, CO: Libraries Unlimited, 1982).

113. Ibid., 78.

114. Ibid., 85.

115. Harwell and Michener, 961.

116. Ibid., 960.

117. James Piereson, "The Left University," *The Weekly Standard* 11, no. 3 (October 3, 2005): 21–30.

118. Ibid., 28.

119. Ibid.

120. Ibid., 30.

121. Davies, "Libraries as Social & Entertainment Centers," 115.

122. Mark Hamilton Lytle, *America's Uncivil Wars: The Sixties Era from Elvis to the Fall of Richard Nixon* (New York: Oxford University Press, 2006), 5, 6.

123. Ibid., 5. Words in single quotes are Lytle quoting Baltzell.

124. Ibid. Words in single quotes are Lytle quoting Baltzell.

125. Ibid., 6.

126. Ibid., 6, 26, 29, 32, 39.

127. Alan Nadel, *Containment Culture: American Narratives, Postmodernism, and the Atomic Age* (Durham, NC: Duke University Press, 1995), 4, 5.

128. Vincent B. Leitch, *American Literary Criticism from the Thirties to the Eighties* (New York: Columbia University Press, 1988), 374.

129. Quoted in Leitch, *American Literary Criticism*, 374.

130. Ibid.

131. Ibid., 404–405.

132. Ibid., 405.

133. Gans, *Popular Culture and High Culture*, vii, 69.

134. Ibid., 69–70.

135. Ibid., 70.

136. Ibid., 71–103, 108–109.

137. Ibid., 70. Original emphasis.

138. Ibid., 125.

139. Ibid., 127–128.

140. Ibid., 3–4.

141. John Fiske, *Understanding Popular Culture* (Boston, MA: Unwin Hyman, 1989), 28.

142. Ibid.

143. Ibid., 161.

144. Stuart Hall, "Notes on Deconstructing 'the Popular,'" in *Cultural Theory and Popular Culture: A Reader*, ed. John Storey, 465–466 (New York: Harvester Wheatsheaf, 1994).

145. Fiske, *Understanding Popular Culture*, 161.

146. Clifford Geertz, "Thick Description: Toward an Interpretive Theory of Culture," in *The Interpretation of Cultures: Selected Essays* (New York: Basic Books, 1973), 5.

147. Clifford Geertz, *Available Light: Anthropological Reflections on Philosophical Topics* (Princeton, NJ: Princeton University Press, 2001), 16.

148. Ibid.

149. Ien Ang, "Culture and Communication: Towards an Ethnographic Critique of Media Consumption in the Transnational Media System," *European Journal of Communication* 5, no. 2/3 (2000): 242.

150. Leitch, *American Literary Criticism*, 212–213.

151. Wiegand, "Tunnel Vision," 13, 18, 19. Original emphases.

152. Wayne A. Wiegand, "Where Stories Aren't Important: An Alternative Perspective on Library and Information Science Education," in *Alternative Library Literature, 2000/2001: A Biennial Anthology*, eds. Sanford Berman and James P. Danky, 155 (Jefferson, NC: McFarland, 2002).

153. Frank W. Hoffman, *Popular Culture and Libraries* (Hamden, CT: Shoe String Press, 1984).

154. Quoted in Hoffman, *Popular Culture and Libraries*, 14.

155. Gans, *Popular Culture and High Culture*, 132.

156. Ibid., 129.

157. Ibid., 128.

158. Ibid.

159. The discussion of traditional conservatism relies heavily on Lytle, Andrew, and Hodgson.

160. Lytle, *America's Uncivil Wars*, 89.

161. Ibid. Lytle quotes Bell.

162. John A. Andrew III, *The Other Side of the Sixties: Young Americans for Freedom and the Rise of Conservative Politics* (New Brunswick, NJ: Rutgers University Press, 1997), 13. Andrew quotes Weaver.

163. Ibid.

164. Godfrey Hodgson, *The World Turned Right Side Up: A History of the Conservative Ascendancy in America* (Boston: Houghton Mifflin, 1996), 17. Hodgson quotes Burke.

165. Lytle, *America's Uncivil Wars*, 89.

166. For an in-depth discussion of these differences, see Rebecca E. Klatch, *A Generation Divided: The New Left, The New Right, and the 1960s* (Berkeley: University of California Press, 1999).

167. Janice A. Radway, *Reading the Romance: Women, Patriarchy, and Popular Literature* (Chapel Hill: University of North Carolina Press, 1984).

168. Ibid., 23.

169. Ibid., 17–18.

170. Ibid., 15, 17.

171. Ibid., 221–222.

172. Ibid., 221.

173. Ibid., 15–16.

174. Ibid., 217.

175. Ibid., 222.

176. Ang, Culture and Communication," 246. Text within single quotes represents Ang quoting Morris. Morris's 1988 article is entitled "Banality in Cultural Studies," *Block* 14:15–25. Original emphasis.

177. Ibid., 247.

178. Ibid. Original emphasis.

179. Guy Debord, *Society of the Spectacle* (Detroit, MI: Black and Red, 1983), par. 12.

180. Nick Chiles, "Their Eyes Were Reading Smut," *New York Times*, 4 January 2006, sec. A, p. 21.

181. Corey Kilgannon, "Street Lit with Publishing Cred: Relentless Aaron's Journey from Prison to Four-Book Deal," *New York Times*, 14 February 2006, sec. E. pp. 1, 7.

182. Chiles, "Their Eyes Were Reading Smut," 21.

183. Ibid.

184. Ibid.

185. Epstein, "Is Reading Really at Risk?" 23.

186. Camille Paglia, "An Open Letter to the Students at Harvard," in *Vamps & Tramps: New Essays* (New York: Vintage Books, 1994), 120.

187. Ibid.

188. Ibid.

189. Paglia, "The Nursery-School Campus: The Corrupting of the Humanities in the U.S.," in *Vamps & Tramps: New Essays* (New York: Vintage Books, 1994), 101.

190. Ibid., 98.

191. Ibid.

192. Ibid., 100.

193. Paglia, "An Open Letter," 120.

194. Ibid.

195. Ibid.

196. Bloom, *The Closing of the American Mind*, 319–320.

197. Jesse H. Shera, *The Foundations of Education for Librarianship* (New York: Becker and Hayes, 1972), 295–296.

198. Lowell Martin, "The American Public Library as a Social Institution," in Barbara McCrimmon (selector and introducer), *American Library Philosophy: An Anthology*, 95 (Hamden, CT: Shoe String Press, 1975).

199. Ibid.

200. Michael Lorenzen, "Deconstructing the Philanthropic Library: The Sociological Reasons behind Andrew Carnegie's Millions to Libraries." Available at: http://michaellorenzen.com/carnegie.html (accessed November 2, 2005).

201. Peter Mickelson, "American Society and the Public Library in the Thought of Andrew Carnegie," *The Journal of Library History* 10, no. 2 (1975): 121.

202. Quoted in Mickelson, 127.
203. Ibid.
204. George S. Bobinski, *Carnegie Libraries: Their History and Impact on American Public Library Development* (Chicago: American Library Association, 1969), 9–10.
205. Andrew Carnegie, *Autobiography of Andrew Carnegie* (Boston: Houghton Mifflin, 1920), 43.
206. Ibid., 44–45.
207. For references to the chapter and article by Crowley, see endnotes 1 and 10 of this chapter.
208. Brendan Luyt, "Regulating Readers: The Social Origins of the Readers' Advisor in the United States," *Library Quarterly* 71, no. 4 (2001): 443–466.
209. For the reference to Saricks's chapter, see endnote 1 of this chapter.
210. Melanie A. Kimball, "A Brief History of Readers' Advisory," in Diana Tixier Herald (ed. Wayne A. Wiegand), *Genreflecting: A Guide to Popular Reading Interests*, 6th ed., 15–23 (Westport, CT: Libraries Unlimited, 2006).
211. Catherine Sheldrick Ross, "Advising Readers" (A subsection of "Adult Readers" [Chapter 4, pp. 133–245]), in Catherine Sheldrick Ross, Lynne (E.F.) McKechnie, and Paulette Rothbauer, *Reading Matters: What the Research Reveals about Reading, Libraries, and Community* (Westport, CT: Libraries Unlimited, 2006), 209–213.
212. Kimball, "A Brief History," 15, 18.
213. Quoted in Crowley, "A History of Readers' Advisory in the Public Library," 11. Also quoted in Crowley, "Rediscovering the History," 37. Crowley adds the words "or her" after Perkins's use of "him." In the first mentioned essay in this footnote, the "or her" is in parentheses; in the second essay, the "or her" is in square brackets. For the original quote, see: F. B. Perkins, "How to Make Town Libraries Successful," in *Public Libraries in the United States of America: Their History, Condition, and Management* (Washington, DC: Government Printing Office, 1876), 428–429.
214. Ross, "Advising Readers," 210.
215. Ibid., 211, 210.
216. Crowley, "Rediscovering the History," 41.
217. Luyt, 446–447.
218. Ibid., 447.
219. Ibid., 455.
220. Ibid., 464.
221. Ibid.
222. Ibid., 449.
223. Ibid., 459.
224. Azar Nafisi, *Reading Lolita in Tehran: A Memoir in Books* (New York: Random House, 2003), 221.
225. Ibid., 221–222.
226. Jonathan Rose, *The Intellectual Life of the British Working Classes* (New Haven, CT: Yale University Press, 2001).
227. Ibid., 129.
228. Ibid., 116.
229. Quoted in Rose, *The Intellectual Life of the British Working Classes*, 128. Rose quotes C. H. Rolph.
230. Ibid., 129.
231. Quoted in Rose, *The Intellectual Life of the British Working Classes*, 129–130.
232. Ibid., 129.
233. Elizabeth McHenry, *Forgotten Readers: Recovering the Lost History of African American Literary Societies* (Durham, NC: Duke University Press, 2002).
234. Ibid., 41.
235. Ibid., 51.
236. Ibid., 166.
237. Ibid., 172. McHenry quotes Reverend Frank F. Hall's speech "The Companionship of Books," delivered in January 1902 to the Boston Literary and Historical Association.
238. Ibid., 166, 173.
239. Ibid., 167.
240. Ibid., 174.
241. Ibid., 56–57.
242. Ibid.
243. Ibid., 225.
244. Ibid., 225, 227.
245. Ibid., 227.
246. Ibid., 217–218.
247. Ibid., 232. McHenry quotes Sarah E. Tanner, "principal of New Jersey's Bordentown Industrial School." Original emphasis.
248. Ibid.
249. Ibid., 236.
250. Ibid., 233.
251. Ibid., 249.
252. Neil Postman, *Amusing Ourselves to Death: Public Discourse in the Age of Show Business* (New York: Viking, 1985), vii–viii.
253. Wiegand, "Where Stories Aren't Important," 155.
254. Ted Balcom, "Rediscovering Readers' Advisory— and Its Rewards," *Illinois Libraries* 70, no. 9 (1988): 583.
255. McPheron, "A Critique of the Progressive Public Library Movement in America," 287.
256. Ibid., 292.
257. Nafisi, *Reading Lolita in Tehran*, 221.
258. Stephen Akey, "McLibraries," *The New Republic* 202, no. 9 (1990): 12.
259. Ibid.
260. Ibid.
261. Jerry Spiegler, "BCPL: Road to Extinction" [Letter to the Editor], *Library Journal* 105, no. 1 (1980): 2.
262. Ibid.
263. Wiegand, "Where Stories Aren't Important," 155.
264. McPheron, "A Critique of the Progressive Public Library Movement in America," 291.
265. Ibid., 291.
266. Ibid., 289.
267. Ibid., 291.
268. Ibid., 288.
269. Ibid., 291.
270. Ibid., 292.
271. Ibid., 288.
272. David Von Drehle, "Fighting Words," *The Washington Post Magazine*, 17 July 2005, sec. W, pp. 12–19.

Chapter 3

1. Crowley, "Rediscovering the History," 38–39.
2. Ibid., 37–38.
3. Abigail A. Van Slyck, *Free to All: Carnegie Libraries & American Culture, 1890–1920* (Chicago: University of Chicago Press, 1995), 166–167.
4. Samuel S. Green, "Personal Relations between Librarians and Readers," *Library Journal* 1, no. 2 (1876): 74–81.
5. Ibid., 79.
6. Ibid., 74.
7. Ibid.
8. Ibid., 79.
9. Ibid., 74.
10. Ibid., 81.
11. Ibid., 79–80.
12. Ibid., 79.
13. Samuel S. Green, "Second Session: Novel-Reading," *Library Journal* 1, no. 2 (1876): 99.
14. Ibid.
15. Ibid.
16. Justin Winsor, "Reading in Popular Libraries," in *Public Libraries in the United States of America: Part I: 1876 Report*, eds. S. R. Warren and S. N. Clark, 432 (reprinted

by the University of Illinois Graduate School of Library Science, 1966).

17. Ibid., 432.
18. Ibid.
19. Ibid.
20. Ibid., 433.
21. Ibid., 432.
22. Ibid., 433.
23. Ibid., 432–433.
24. Ibid., 433.
25. Ibid.
26. W. E. Foster, "On Aimless Reading and Its Correction," *Library Journal* 4, no. 3 (1879): 78–80.
27. Ibid., 78.
28. Ibid.
29. Ibid.
30. Ibid., 79.
31. Ibid.
32. Ibid.
33. Samuel S. Green, "Sensational Fiction in Public Libraries," *Library Journal* 4, no. 9/10 (1879): 352.
34. Foster, "On Aimless Reading," 79.
35. Ibid., 80.
36. Ibid.
37. Ibid.
38. Ibid.
39. Frederick M. Crunden, "Report on Aids and Guides, August, '83, to June, '85," *Library Journal* 11, no. 8/9 (1886): 316.
40. Ibid.
41. Ibid.
42. Margery Doud, "The Readers' Advisory Service of the St. Louis Public Library," in *St. Louis Public Library Annual Report 1928–1929* (St. Louis, MO: 1929), 20.
43. Foster, "On Aimless Reading," 80.
44. Samuel S. Green, "Aids and Guides for Readers," *Library Journal* 7, no. 7/8 (1882): 144.
45. Ibid.
46. W. E. Foster, "Report on Aids and Guides to Readers: 1883," *Library Journal* 8, no. 9/10 (1883): 244.
47. Crunden, "Report on Aids and Guides," 319.
48. Crunden, "Report on Aids and Guides," 310.
49. Joan M. Reitz, *Online Dictionary for Library and Information Science* (Westport, CT: Libraries Unlimited, 2004). Available from: http://lu.com.odlis (accessed December 31, 2005).
50. Charles A. Cutter, "Common Sense in Libraries," *Library Journal* 14, no. 5/6 (1889): 151.
51. Ibid.
52. Ibid.
53. Ibid.
54. Ibid.
55. The article was originally delivered as a speech at the ALA conference in St. Louis in 1889.
56. Cutter, "Common Sense in Libraries," 151.
57. Ibid. Original emphasis.
58. Ibid.
59. Ibid.
60. For an overview of the history of the St. Louis Public Library in its various incarnations, see Budd L. Gambee, "Crunden, Frederick Morgan (1847–1911)," in *Dictionary of American Library Biography*, ed. Bohdan S. Wynar, 103–105 (Littleton, CO: Libraries Unlimited, 1978).
61. Frederick M. Crunden, "The Most Popular Books," *Library Journal* 16, no. 9 (1891): 277–278.
62. Ibid., 278.
63. Charles A. Cutter, "Should Libraries Buy Only the Best Books or the Best Books that People Will Read?" *Library Journal* 26, no. 2 (1901): 70–72. This article also appears in Francis L. Miksa, ed., *Charles Ammi Cutter: Library Systematizer* (Littleton, CO: Libraries Unlimited, 1977): 118–120.

64. Cutter, "Should Libraries Buy," 72.
65. Ibid. Original emphasis.
66. Ibid., 71.
67. Ibid.
68. Ibid., 72.
69. Ibid.
70. Ibid.
71. A. L. Peck, "What May a Librarian Do to Influence the Reading of a Community?" *Library Journal* 22, no. 2 (1897): 77–80.
72. Ibid., 77.
73. Ibid., 78.
74. Ibid.
75. Ibid.
76. Ibid.
77. Ibid.
78. W. E. Foster, "Methods of Securing the Interest of a Community," *Library Journal* 5, no. 9/10 (1880): 247.
79. Ibid.
80. Ibid.
81. Peck, "What May a Librarian Do," 79.
82. Ibid.
83. Beatrice Winser, "Encouragement of Serious Reading by Public Libraries," *Library Journal* 28, no. 5 (1903): 238.
84. Foster, "Methods of Securing the Interest," 246–247.
85. Ibid., 246.
86. Ibid., 247.
87. Peck, "What May a Librarian Do," 79.
88. Ibid., 80.
89. Ibid.
90. W. E. Foster, "The School and the Library: Their Mutual Relation," *Library Journal* 4, no. 9/10 (1879): 319–325.
91. Ibid., 320.
92. Ibid., 321.
93. Ibid., 322.
94. Ibid. Original emphasis.
95. Ibid.
96. Crunden, "Report on Aids and Guides," 311.
97. James M. Hubbard, "How to Use a Public Library," *Library Journal* 9, no. 2 (1884): 25–29. No identification is provided about Hubbard in this article, except that the article is "[t]he substance of two addresses delivered in Pittsfield, Mass."
98. Ibid., 28.
99. Ibid.
100. Ibid.
101. C. Knowles Bolton, "Better Circulation in Small Libraries—The 'Two-Book' System," *Library Journal* 19, no. 5 (1894): 161–162.
102. E. A. Birge, "The Effect of the 'Two-Book System' on Circulation," *Library Journal* 23, no. 3 (1898): 93.
103. Ibid.
104. Ibid.
105. Ibid., 98.
106. Ida Rosenberg, "Directing the Taste of Casual Readers," *Public Libraries* 13, no. 7 (1908): 295–299.
107. "Are the Classics Read?" *Library Journal* 38, no. 3 (1912): 145–146.
108. Josephine Adams Rathbone, "The Classification of Fiction," *Library Journal* 27, no. 3 (1902): 121, 122.
109. Ibid., 122.
110. Ibid., 123.
111. Frances L. Rathbone, "A Successful Experiment in Directing the Reading of Fiction," *Library Journal* 32, no. 9 (1907): 406–408.
112. William Alanson Borden, "On Classifying Fiction," *Library Journal* 34, no. 6 (1909): 264–265.
113. Ibid., 264.

114. Ibid.

115. Ibid., 264–265.

116. Maude R. Henderson, "The Librarian as a Host," *Public Libraries* 1, no. 5 (1896): 187–189.

117. Ibid., 189.

118. Ibid.

119. Frederick M. Crunden, "The Library as a Factor in the Intellectual Life of St. Louis," *Library Journal* 15, no. 5 (1890): 138.

120. Ibid.

121. A. L. Peck, "Workingmen's Clubs and the Public Library," *Library Journal* 23, no. 11 (1898): 612–614.

122. Ibid., 613.

123. Ibid.

124. Ibid.

125. Ibid.

126. Ibid.

127. Alice B. Kroeger, "The Encouragement of Serious Reading: Survey of the Field," *Library Journal* 28, no. 5 (1903): 224.

128. "'Topic Blanks' at Cincinnati Public Library," *Library Journal* 28, no. 5 (1903): 239.

129. Ibid.

130. Kroeger, "Encouragement of Serious Reading," 224.

131. Mary Frances Isom, "The Library a Civic Center," *Public Libraries* 19, no. 2 (1914): 94.

132. Green, "Sensational Fiction," 346.

133. William Kite, "Fiction in Public Libraries," *Library Journal* 1, no. 8 (1877): 279.

134. Ibid., 278.

135. Ibid.

136. Ibid. Kite quotes George Ticknor.

137. Ibid., 278–279.

138. Ibid., 277.

139. Noah Porter, *Books and Reading, or What Books Shall I Read and How Shall I Read Them?* (Freeport, NY: Books For Libraries Press, 1972 [reprint of the 1881 ed.]), 224, 231, 233–237.

140. Ibid., 76.

141. Ibid., 75.

142. Ibid., 231.

143. Ibid.

144. Ibid.

145. Ibid., 224.

146. Ibid.

147. Ibid., 237.

148. Ibid., 234.

149. Ibid., 237.

150. Green, "Sensational Fiction," 346.

151. Ibid., 352.

152. Ibid., 353.

153. Ibid., 352.

154. Ibid.

155. Ibid.

156. Winser, "Encouragement of Serious Reading," 237–238.

157. Ibid., 237.

158. Ibid.

159. Ibid., 238.

160. Ibid.

161. Ibid.

162. Agnes Hill, "The Public Library and the People," *Library Journal* 27, no. 1 (1902): 11–15.

163. Ibid., 13.

164. Ibid.

165. Ibid.

166. Ibid., 15.

167. Ibid.

168. Ibid., 14.

169. Lee, *Continuing Education for Adults*, 36. Original emphasis.

170. Tessa L. Kelso, "Some Economical Features of Public Libraries," *The Arena* 7, no. 6 (1893): 709–713.

171. Ibid., 710.

172. Ibid., 709–710.

173. Ibid., 712.

174. Ibid.

175. Lindsay Swift, "Paternalism in Public Libraries," *Library Journal* 24, no. 11 (1899): 609–618.

176. Ibid., 613.

177. Ibid., 615.

178. Ibid., 618.

179. Ibid.

180. Ibid.

181. Ibid.

182. Ruth Bordin, *Woman and Temperance: The Quest for Power and Liberty, 1873–1900* (Philadelphia, PA: Temple University Press, 1981), 13–14.

183. Alison M. Parker, *Purifying America: Women, Cultural Reform, and Pro-Censorship Activism, 1873–1933* (Urbana: University of Illinois Press, 1997), 5–6. Parker's book compares and contrasts the pro-censorship efforts of the WCTU and the ALA. Our idea to juxtaposition the WCTU and ALA is derived from her.

184. Bordin, *Woman and Temperance*, 12.

185. The information in this paragraph follows Parker, *Purifying America*, 50–74.

186. Parker, *Purifying America*, 52. Parker quotes Mary Allen West, editor of the WCTU's official publication *Union Signal*.

187. Ibid., 54.

188. Quoted in Parker, *Purifying America*, 54.

189. Ibid., 55.

190. Ibid.

191. Quoted in Parker, *Purifying America*, 55.

192. Ibid., 229. Original emphasis.

193. Swift, "Paternalism in Public Libraries," 618.

194. Melvil Dewey, "Advice to a Librarian," *Public Libraries* 2, no. 6 (1897): 266–267.

195. Jesse H. Shera, *The Foundations of Education for Librarianship*, 233.

196. Ibid., 233–234.

197. See Sarah K. Vann, *Training for Librarianship before 1923: Education for Librarianship Prior to the Publication of Williamson's Report on Training for Library Service* (Chicago: American Library Association, 1961); Carl M. White, *A Historical Introduction to Library Education: Problems and Progress to 1951* (Metuchen, NJ: Scarecrow Press, 1976).

198. Dewey, "Advice," 266.

199. Ibid., 267.

200. Ibid.

201. Ibid., 266.

202. Van Slyck, *Free to All*, 161–162.

203. Ibid., 161.

204. Quoted in Van Slyck, *Free to All*, 162.

205. Frederick Winslow Taylor, *The Principles of Scientific Management* (New York: Harper & Brothers, 1911).

206. Van Slyck, *Free to All*, 170.

207. Ibid., 170–171.

208. Ibid., 171.

209. Ibid.

210. Almira L. Hayward, "The Training of a Librarian," *Library Journal* 17, no. 12 (1892): 480.

211. Ibid.

212. Virginia E. Graeff, "The Gentle Librarian: A Transcript from Experience," *Library Journal* 30, no. 12 (1905): 922.

213. Green, "Sensational Fiction," 352.

214. Ibid.

215. Green, "Aids and Guides," 143–144.

216. "Report of the Examining Committee," *Twenty-sixth Annual Report of the Trustees of the Public Library 1878* (City of Boston, City Document No. 61, 1878), 13.

217. Ibid.

218. "Librarian's Report," *Twenty-eighth Annual Report of the Trustees of the Public Library 1880* (City of Boston, City Document No. 94, 1880), 18.

219. "Report of the Examining Committee," *Fifteenth Annual Report of the Trustees of the Public Library 1867* (City of Boston, City Document No. 114, 1867), 35.

220. Ibid., 21.

221. Ibid.

222. Ibid., 41–42.

223. "Appendixes to the Librarian's Report," *Twenty-eighth Annual Report of the Trustees of the Public Library 1880* (City of Boston, City Document No. 94, 1880), 55. Compare the list of employees and their titles in the *Twenty-eighth Annual Report* with the list of employees and their titles in the *Twenty-sixth Annual Report*, pp. 59–60.

224. "Appendixes to the Librarian's Report," *Thirtieth Annual Report of the Trustees of the Public Library 1882* (City of Boston, City Document No. 92, 1880), 63.

225. All comparative information about job titles and number of employees taken from: "Appendixes to the Librarian's Report," *Twenty-eighth Annual Report of the Trustees of the Public Library 1880* (City of Boston, City Document No. 94, 1880), 55–56; "Appendixes to the Librarian's Report," *Twenty-sixth Annual Report of the Trustees of the Public Library 1878* (City of Boston, City Document No. 61, 1878), 59–60; *Thirtieth Annual Report of the Trustees of the Public Library 1882* (City of Boston, City Document No. 92, 1882), 63–64.

226. "Librarian's Report," *Twenty-eighth Annual Report of the Trustees of the Public Library 1880* (City of Boston, City Document No. 94, 1880), 18.

227. "Librarian's Report," *Thirtieth Annual Report of the Trustees of the Public Library 1882* (City of Boston, City Document No. 92, 1880), 24–25.

228. "Librarian's Report," *Twenty-ninth Annual Report of the Trustees of the Public Library 1881* (City of Boston, City Document No. 97, 1881), 41.

229. "Librarian's Report," *Twenty-eighth Annual Report of the Trustees of the Public Library 1880* (City of Boston, City Document No. 94, 1880), 18.

230. Ibid.

231. "Librarian's Report," *Twenty-ninth Annual Report of the Trustees of the Public Library 1881* (City of Boston, City Document No. 97, 1881), 42.

232. Foster, "Report on Aids and Guides to Readers: 1883," 243.

233. "Fiction at the Boston Public Library" [reprint], *Library Journal* 6, no. 7 (1881): 204–205.

234. Ibid., 204.

235. Ibid., 205.

236. Ibid.

237. "Librarian's Report," *Thirtieth Annual Report of the Trustees of the Public Library 1882* (City of Boston, City Document No. 92, 1882), 25.

238. Ibid. Original emphases.

239. Ibid.

240. Ibid., 26.

241. "Report of the Examining Committee," *Twenty-ninth Annual Report of the Trustees of the Public Library 1881* (City of Boston, City Document No. 97, 1881), 20.

242. "Librarian's Report," *Thirtieth Annual Report of the Trustees of the Public Library 1882* (City of Boston, City Document No. 92, 1882), 15.

243. "Librarian's Report," *Twenty-ninth Annual Report of the Trustees of the Public Library 1881* (City of Boston, City Document No. 97, 1881), 42.

244. "Appendixes to the Librarian's Report," *Thirtieth Annual Report of the Trustees of the Public Library 1882* (City of Boston, City Document No. 92, 1880), 56.

245. "Librarian's Report," *Thirtieth Annual Report of the*

Trustees of the Public Library 1882 (City of Boston, City Document No. 92, 1880), 25.

246. "Section A," *Twenty-ninth Annual Report of the Trustees of the Public Library 1881* (City of Boston, City Document No. 97, 1881), 10.

247. Ibid., 10.

248. Ibid., 9.

249. Ibid., 11.

250. Doud, "The Readers' Advisory Service of the St. Louis Public Library," 5. Doud quotes Arthur E. Bostwick, who succeeded Crunden.

251. Frederick M. Crunden, "How Things are Done in One American Library: The New Novel Problem and Its Solution," *The Library* 1 (2nd. series, 1900): 92–100; Frederick M. Crunden, "How Things are Done in One American Library: Board and Staff Organization and Finances," *The Library* 1 (2nd. series, 1900): 147–152; Frederick M. Crunden, "How Things are Done in One American Library: Selection, Purchase, and Cataloguing of Books," *The Library* 1 (2nd. series, 1900): 290–298; Frederick M. Crunden, "How Things are Done in One American Library: Registration and Circulation," *The Library* 1 (2nd. series, 1900): 384–406; Frederick M. Crunden, "How Things are Done in One American Library: Juvenile Department, [etc.]," *The Library* 2 (2nd. series, 1900): 20–43.

252. Crunden, "How Things are Done in One American Library: Board and Staff Organization and Finances," 150.

253. Crunden, "How Things are Done in One American Library: Registration and Circulation," 394–395.

254. "The St. Louis Public Library," *Public Libraries* 5, no. 4 (1900): 171.

255. Ibid.

256. Ibid.

257. Ibid.

258. Doud, "The Readers' Advisory Service of the St. Louis Public Library," 5.

259. Ibid., 5–6.

260. George F. Bowerman, "The Public Library of the District of Columbia as an Organ of Social Advance," *Charities and the Commons* 16, no. 2 (1906): 108.

261. Rachel Rhoades, "The Work of a Library Information Desk," *Library Journal* 39, no. 5 (1914): 350–353.

262. Ibid., 351.

263. Ibid., 352.

264. Ibid.

265. Ibid., 353.

266. Max Cohen, "The Librarian an Educator, and not a Cheap-John," *Library Journal* 13, no. 12 (1888): 366–367.

267. Ibid., 366.

268. For good descriptions of librarians' involvement with social reform, see Rosemary Ruhig Du Mont, *Reform and Reaction: The Big City Public Library in American Life* (Westport, CT: Greenwood Press, 1977), 31–49, 95–106. The settlement-house movement in its relation to librarianship is also described in Garrison, *Apostles of Culture*, 196–225. We have learned much from these books and are very much indebted to both of them.

269. John Whiteclay Chambers II, *The Tyranny of Change: America in the Progressive Era, 1890–1920*, 2nd ed. (New York: St. Martin's Press, 2000), 151.

270. Marvin Olasky, *The Tragedy of American Compassion* (Washington, DC: Regnery Publishing, 1992), 50–51, 124–125.

271. "About Jane Addams," *Jane Addams Hull-House Museum*. Available from: http://wall.aa.uic.edu/62730/artifact/HullHouse.asp (accessed January 3, 2006).

272. Ibid.

273. Ibid.

274. Olasky, *The Tragedy of American Compassion*, 124, 125, 121, 125, 124. All quotes in this sentence are Olasky's except

on

"cultivated young people," which he quotes from Addams (p. 125).

275. Cora Stewart, "Libraries in Relation to Settlement Work," *Library Journal* 31, no. 8 (1906): C82.
276. Ibid., C83-C84.
277. Ibid., C85.
278. Ibid.
279. "The Public Library and Allied Agencies," *Library Journal* 30, no. 8 (1905): 459–472.
280. Ibid., 460.
281. Ibid., 461.
282. Ibid., 467.
283. "The Library as a Social Center," *Public Libraries* 21, no. 7 (1916): 315–316.
284. "The Library as a Social Center," 315.
285. Hiller C. Wellman, "President's Address," *Library Journal* 40, no. 7 (1915): 469.
286. Ibid., 469.
287. A. W. Lupton, "Social Activities of the Library," *Library Journal* 39, no. 6 (1914): 441–443.
288. Jane Addams, *Twenty Years at Hull-House with Autobiographical Notes* (New York: The Macmillan Company, 1910), 452.
289. Ibid., 435.
290. Ibid.
291. Wellman, "President's Address," 469–471. Original emphasis.
292. Ibid., 471.
293. The quote is from John Ruskin. It is contained in John Nolen, "Aid from University Extension Methods," *Library Journal* 28, no. 5 (1903): 226.
294. Quoted in Nolen, "Aid from University Extension Methods," 227.
295. Samuel H. Ranck, "The Relation of the Public Library to Technical Education," *Library Journal* 36, no. 6 (1911): 278–285.
296. Ibid., 282.
297. Frank P. Hill, "Fiction in Libraries," *Library Journal* 15, no. 11 (1890): 325. Also quoted in Lee, *Continuing Education for Adults*, 26.
298. Arthur E. Bostwick, "The Purchase of Current Fiction," *Library Journal* 28, no. 7 (1903): C31-C33.
299. Ibid., C31.
300. Ibid.
301. R. [Anonymous], "The Predominance of Fiction in Public Libraries, *Library Journal* 30, no. 8 (1905): 473.
302. Ibid., 473.
303. Edwin E. Slosson, "How the Public Library Looks to a Journalist," *Library Journal* 40, no. 11 (1915): 786–790.
304. Ibid., 790.
305. Ibid.
306. Ibid., 788–789.
307. Ibid., 790.

Chapter 4

1. Theodore Wesley Koch, *War Service of the American Library Association* (Washington, DC: American Library Association War Service, Library of Congress, 1918), 4. A more complete account is provided in Theodore Wesley Koch, *Books in the War: The Romance of Library War Service* (Boston: Houghton Mifflin Company, 1919). In this latter volume, the description of the Library War Service Program in the United States is on pp. 5–60; in Siberia, pp. 73–80; and in France, pp. 86–107.
2. Koch, *War Service*, 5.
3. Ibid., 8.
4. Lee, *Continuing Education for Adults*, 43. Figures taken from Koch, *Books in the War*.
5. Koch, *War Service*, 22.

6. Koch, *Books in the War*, 27–28.
7. Koch, *War Service*, 18–19. Pictures showing activity in camp libraries in the United States are on unpaginated plates between the following sets of pages in *War Service*: pp. 4–5; pp. 8–9; pp. 12–13; and pp. 20–21. Pictures showing activity in camp libraries in the United States are on unpaginated plates between the following sets of pages in *Books in the War*: pp. 4–5; pp. 8–9; pp. 16–17; pp. 24–25; pp. 28–29; pp. 36–37; pp. 44–45; and pp. 48–49.
8. Koch, *Books in the War*, 17.
9. This caption and picture appear opposite p. 21 in *War Service*.
10. *War Service*, 19, 22; *Books in the War*, 24, 28, 30–31.
11. Koch, *Books in the War*, 42.
12. Ibid., 367.
13. Ibid., 366, 368.
14. Katherine J. Harig, *Libraries, the Military, & Civilian Life* (Hamden, CT: Library Professional Publications, 1989), 6. Original emphasis.
15. Ibid., 4.
16. Koch, *Books in the War*, 40.
17. Quoted in Koch, *Books in the War*, 41.
18. Quoted in Ibid.
19. Harig, *Libraries, the Military, & Civilian Life*, 2.
20. Lee, *Continuing Education for Adults*, 44.
21. Quoted in Harig, *Libraries, the Military, & Civilian Life*, 6–7.
22. Edward L. Munson, "Libraries and Reading as an Aid to Morale," *ALA Bulletin* 13, no. 3 (1919): 185.
23. Koch, *Books in the War*, 354.
24. Ibid., 355. The quote is from the unpaginated plate opposite p. 355.
25. Paul M. Paine, "The Library's Task in Reconstruction," *ALA Bulletin* 13, no. 3 (1919): 118.
26. Ibid., 118–119.
27. A comprehensive account of the Enlarged Program is Arthur P. Young, "Aftermath of a Crusade: World War I and the Enlarged Program of the American Library Association," in *Library Lit. 11—The Best of 1980*, ed. Bill Katz, 70–84 (Metuchen, NJ: Scarecrow Press, 1981). The article is reprinted from *Library Quarterly* 50, no. 2 (1980): 191–207. Our account is based on Young's work.
28. Ibid., 75. Young quotes the "Preliminary Report of Committee on Enlarged Program for American Library Service," *Library Journal* 44, no. 10 (1919): 645–653.
29. Young, "Aftermath," 80.
30. Ibid., 75.
31. Ibid., 80.
32. Ibid., 81.
33. Ibid., 82, 83.
34. Ibid., 83.
35. A. Ruth Rutzen, "The Readers' Advisory Corps in the Large City Public Library: In a Large Open-Shelf Room," in *Helping Adults to Learn: The Library in Action*, ed. John Chancellor, 27–32 (Chicago: American Library Association, 1939); Commission on the Library and Adult Education, *Libraries and Adult Education: Report of a Study Made by the American Library Association* (Chicago: American Library Association, 1926), 233–238.
36. With the exception of the date for the Omaha Public Library (OPL), all dates are contained in *Libraries and Adult Education*, 221–246. The date for the opening of the readers' advisory service at the OPL is contained in *Libraries (A Continuation of Public Libraries)* 33, no. 6 (1928): 292–293.
37. In *Continuing Education for Adults*, Lee states that "[b]etween 1922 and 1925, readers' advisory services were instituted in seven urban public libraries" (p. 57). His list includes the public libraries in Detroit, Cleveland, Chicago, Milwaukee, Indianapolis, and Cincinnati. As his seventh library, he adds the Portland (Oregon) Public Library (PPL). His list does not include the Omaha (Nebraska) Public

Library (OPL). We include the OPL based on a statement in "Individualizing Library Service," *Libraries (A Continuation of Public Libraries)* 33, no. 6 (1928): 292–293. The quotation reads: "In September, 1925, the Omaha public library established a Reader's Advisory service, which is an independent unit functioning in the circulation department. The reader's assistant, as she is called, meets the readers with the help of a small staff of part-time workers.... We are experimenting yet with our organization." Lillian C. Gates, the person primarily responsible for assisting readers at the OPL, describes her job in the following way: "Students, young and old, come to us for contemporary philosophy, poetry, psychology, and science. For encouragement we often give them prepared lists, but a telephone call or a short book conversation seems to us more effective" (p. 293). On the other hand, readers' advisory service at the PPL did not start until 1926: "The service of the Library Adviser in Adult Education was first announced in September, 1925, but owing to illness the work was not actually offered to the public until January 1, 1926" (*Libraries and Adult Education*, p. 246). Thus, the PPL service was instituted, but not offered. Lee's statement therefore should read either that readers' advisory service had been instituted at eight urban public libraries between 1922 and 1925, or that readers' advisory service was offered to the public at seven urban public libraries between 1922 and 1925. Yet another possibility exists. Lee may have thought that Omaha was not sufficiently large to count as an urban area by his criteria, or that the readers' advisory service offered at the OPL was not, from an organizational perspective, at the level of the other large urban public libraries that he mentions. In this case, his statement that seven urban public libraries had instituted readers' advisory service between 1922 and 1925 is accurate.

38. Rutzen, "The Readers' Advisory Corps in the Large City Public Library," 28. Also quoted in Lee, *Continuing Education for Adults*, 57–58.

39. "Individualizing Library Service," *Libraries (A Continuation of Public Libraries)* 33, no. 6 (1928): 286.

40. Ibid., 286–287.

41. Mabel Booton, "A Close View of Advisory Service: In a Large Library," in *Helping Adults to Learn: The Library in Action*, ed. John Chancellor, 28 (Chicago: American Library Association, 1939).

42. Ibid., 16.

43. Ibid.

44. Lucia H. Sanderson, "A Many-sided Adult Education Program: In a Large Library," in *Helping Adults to Learn: The Library in Action*, ed. John Chancellor, 160 (Chicago: American Library Association, 1939).

45. Ibid., 161.

46. Booton, "A Close View," 9.

47. Ibid., 9.

48. Ibid., 10.

49. Ibid.

50. Ibid.

51. Ibid., 11.

52. Ibid.

53. Ibid.

54. Ibid., 11, 12.

55. Ibid., 12.

56. Ibid., 9, 10.

57. Ibid., 12.

58. Ibid.

59. Ibid., 13.

60. Ibid., 15.

61. Ibid.

62. Ibid., 13–14.

63. Ibid., 14.

64. Ibid., 17.

65. Ibid.

66. Ibid., 15.

67. Sanderson, "A Many-sided Adult Education Program," 162.

68. Ibid.

69. *Libraries and Adult Education*, 233–238.

70. Alice M. Farquhar, "The Organization Plan for Adult Education in a Public Library," in *Helping Adults to Learn: The Library in Action*, ed. John Chancellor, 182 (Chicago: American Library Association, 1939).

71. Quoted in *Libraries and Adult Education*, 221.

72. Ibid., 222, 221.

73. Ibid., 221.

74. Ibid., 222.

75. Carleton Bruns Joeckel and Leon Carnovsky, *A Metropolitan Library in Action: A Survey of the Chicago Public Library* (Chicago: University of Chicago Press, 1940), 347.

76. *Libraries and Adult Education*, 225.

77. Joeckel and Carnovsky, *A Metropolitan Library*, 347.

78. Ibid., 351.

79. Ibid., 348–349.

80. Ibid., 350.

81. Ibid.

82. Ibid., 360.

83. Ibid., 359–360. Original emphasis.

84. *Libraries and Adult Education*, 228.

85. Ibid., 232.

86. "Those Who Follow Reading Courses," *Adult Education and the Library* 3, no. 2 (1928): 36.

87. Ibid., 37.

88. Ibid., 36, 35.

89. Ibid., 39–42.

90. *Libraries and Adult Education*, 244, 241.

91. William S. Learned, *The American Public Library and the Diffusion of Knowledge* (New York: Harcourt, Brace and Company, 1924).

92. Ibid., 12–13.

93. Ibid., 14.

94. Ibid.

95. Ibid.

96. Ibid.

97. Ibid., 15. Learned's exact words with regard to the number of librarians needed is "a score," which is an expression rarely used in the 21st century and means "twenty."

98. Ibid., 16.

99. Ibid., 15–16.

100. Ibid., 17.

101. Ibid., 27.

102. Ibid., 38.

103. Ibid., 39.

104. Ibid., 38.

105. Judson T. Jennings, "Sticking to Our Last," *Library Journal* 49, no. 13 (1924): 617.

106. Ibid.

107. Ibid.

108. Ibid.

109. Ibid.

110. Ibid., 614–615.

111. Ibid., 615.

112. Ibid., 614.

113. Ibid., 618.

114. Lee, *Continuing Education for Adults*, 47.

115. Ibid., 48–49.

116. "Headnote," *Adult Education and the Library* 1, no. 2 (1924): 3.

117. *Adult Education and the Library* was published as a quarterly between 1927 and 1930.

118. Commission on the Library and Adult Education, *Libraries and Adult Education: Report of a Study Made by the American Library Association* (Chicago: American Library Association, 1926).

119. Ibid., 9, 37.

120. Ibid., 37.
121. Lee, *Continuing Education for Adults*, 62.
122. Commission on the Library and Adult Education, *Libraries and Adult Education*, 9.
123. Ibid., 28.
124. Ibid.
125. Ibid.
126. Ibid., 29.
127. Ibid., 32.
128. Ibid., 33.
129. Lee, *Continuing Education for Adults*, 50.
130. Sixty-eight titles were projected, but only 66 titles were published: volume 53 (*Investment*) and volume 58 (*Aviation*) were not published. The titles of these two missing volumes were derived from the "in preparation" lists contained in some of the earlier volumes; these "in preparation" lists were then matched with the final publication list as contained in volume 68. *Investment* and *Aviation* were missing from this final list. However, Lee, in *Continuing Education for Adults*, states that "sixty-seven of these courses were issued" (p. 50). Lee's figure has been accepted by many other writers. Our figure of 66 is based on the following. First, we assume that volume 68 (Alain Locke's *The Negro in America*) was the last volume issued. Second, in the opening pages of volume 68, all previously issued volumes are listed in order, with the exception of volume 53 and 58. The ALA Archives Holdings Database (Record Series number 29/3/10) also lists 66 titles for the RWAP series (http://web.library.uiuc.edu/ahx/alasfa/2903010a.pdf [accessed January 20, 2006]).The 66 published titles that were physically examined are as follows: Vernon Kellogg, *Biology* (v. 1, 1925); W. N. C. Carlton, *English Literature* (v. 2, 1925); Ambrose W. Vernon, *Ten Pivotal Figures of History* (v. 3, 1925); Dallas Lore Sharp, *Some Great American Books* (v. 4, 1925); Walton H. Hamilton, *Economics* (v. 5, 1929); Jesse Lee Bennett, *Frontiers of Knowledge* (v. 6, 1925); Daniel Gregory Mason, *Ears to Hear: A Guide for Music Lovers* (v. 7, 1925); Howard W. Odum, *Sociology and Social Problems* (v. 8, 1925); Edwin E. Slosson, *The Physical Sciences* (v. 9, 1926); William Allen White and Walter E. Myer, *Conflicts in American Public Opinion* (v. 10, 1925); Everett Dean Martin, *Psychology and Its Use* (v. 11, 1926); Alexander Meiklejohn, *Philosophy* (v. 12, 1926); M. V. O'Shea, *Our Children* (v. 13, 1926); Wilfred T. Grenfell, *Religion in Everyday Life* (v. 14, 1926); Rufus M. Jones, *The Life of Christ* (v. 15, 1926); Frankwood E. Williams, *Mental Hygiene* (v. 16, 1929); Lorado Taft, *The Appreciation of Sculpture* (v. 17, 1927); Herbert Adams Gibbons, *The Europe of Our Day* (v. 18, 1927); Marguerite Wilkinson, *The Poetry of Our Own Times* (v. 19, 1926); Frederic L. Paxson, *The United States in Recent Times* (v. 20, 1926); Henry Turner Bailey, *Pleasure from Pictures* (v. 21, 1926); William F. Russell, *American Education* (v. 22, 1926); Lewis Mumford, *Architecture* (v. 23, 1926); Samuel McChord Crothers, *The Modern Essay* (v. 24, 1926); John Palmer Gavit, *Americans from Abroad* (v. 25, 1926); William Stearn Davis, *The French Revolution as Told in Fiction* (v. 26, 1927); Raymond Moley, *The Practice of Politics* (v. 27, 1927); Barrett H. Clark, *The Modern Drama* (v. 28, 1927); Hamlin Garland, *The Westward March of American Settlement* (v. 29, 1927); Harlow Shapley, *The Stars* (v. 30, 1927); Claude G. Bowers, *The Founders of the Republic* (v. 31, 1927); Paul Scott Mowrer, *The Foreign Relations of the United States* (v. 32, 1927); William Lyon Phelps, *Twentieth Century American Novels* (v. 33, 1927); Walter Prichard Eaton, *A Study of English Drama on the Stage* (v. 34, 1927); Virginia C. Bacon, *Good English* (v. 35, 1928); Sydney B. Mitchell, *Adventures in Flower Gardening* (v. 36, 1928); Irving Babbitt, *French Literature* (v. 37, 1928); Bird T. Baldwin, *The Young Child* (v. 38, 1928); Dudley Crafts Watson, *Interior Decoration* (v. 39, 1932); J. Russell Smith, *Geography and Our Need of It* (v. 40, 1928); Arthur E. Bostwick, *Pivotal Figures of Science* (v. 41, 1928); Albert Bushnell Hart, *George Washington* (v. 42, 1927);

George Grant MacCurdy, *Prehistoric Man* (v. 43, 1928); J. B. Condliffe, *The Pacific Area in International Relations* (v. 44, 1931); George H. Locke, *English History* (v. 45, 1930); Fitzhugh Green, *The Romance of Modern Exploration* (v. 46, 1929); Morris Fishbein, *The Human Body and Its Care* (v. 47, 1929); John A. Fitch, *Capital and Labor* (v. 48, 1929); Willard Grosvenor Bleyer, *Journalism* (v. 49, 1929); Helen W. Atwater, *Home Economics: The Art and Science of Homemaking* (v. 50, 1929); Earnest Elmo Calkins, *Advertising* (v. 51, 1929); John Alford Stevenson, *Salesmanship* (v. 52, 1929); Hanna Astrup Larsen, *Scandinavian Literature* (v. 54, 1930); Philip N. Youtz, *American Life in Architecture* (v. 55, 1932); Waldemar Kaempffert, *Invention and Society* (v. 56, 1930); J. Arthur Thomson, *Evolution* (v. 57, 1931); Felix E. Schelling, *Shakespeare* (v. 59, 1930); Isaiah Bowman, *International Relations* (v. 60, 1930); Avrahm Yarmolinsky, *Russian Literature* (v. 61, 1931); Clarence Poe, *Farm Life: Problems and Opportunities* (v. 62, 1931); M. A. DeWolfe Howe, *Representative Twentieth-Century Americans* (v. 63, 1930); Blanche Colton Williams, *Short Story Writing* (v. 64, 1930); James G. McDonald, *Latin America* (v. 65, 1931); Aaron Director, *Unemployment* (v. 66, 1932); *Russia: The Soviet Way* (v. 67, 1933); and Alain Locke, *The Negro in America* (v. 68, 1933).
131. Lee, *Continuing Education for Adults*, 50.
132. Ibid. Lee states that between 8–12 books were recommended (p. 50). *Libraries and Adult Education* states that the number of recommended readings was "usually ... six or eight books likely to be found in the average library" (p. 249). Our figure is based on the following data: two volumes recommended four books; seven volumes recommended five books; 24 volumes recommended six books; 17 volumes recommended seven books; six volumes recommended eight books; three volumes recommended nine books; four volumes recommended 10 books; and three volumes recommended more than 10 books. Our statement that the volumes typically contained 6–10 books is therefore accurate: 81.8 percent of the volumes contained 6–10 books.
133. George Locke, *English History* (Chicago: American Library Association, 1930), 53–54.
134. Alexander Meiklejohn, *Philosophy* (Chicago: American Library Association, 1926), 52.
135. Most of the volumes started on p. 9, but eight volumes started on p. 11 (*The Westward March of American Settlement*; *Adventures in Flower Gardening*; *French Literature*; *The Young Child*; *Prehistoric Man*; *The Human Body and Its Care*; *Capital and Labor*; and *Journalism*) and one volume started on p. 13 (*Pivotal Figures of Science*).
136. W. N. C. Carlton, *English Literature* (Chicago: American Library Association, 1925); William F. Russell, *American Education* (Chicago: American Library Association, 1926).
137. Vernon Kellogg, *Biology* (Chicago: American Library Association, 1925), 5.
138. The six volumes written by librarians were as follows. W. N. C. Carlton, identified as a librarian at Trinity College, Hartford; the Newberry Library, Chicago; the American Library in Paris; and Williams College, wrote *English Literature* (vol. 2). Virginia E. Bacon, identified as a readers' advisor at the Portland (Oregon) Public Library, wrote *Good English* (vol. 35). Sydney B. Mitchell, identified as the director of the School of Librarianship at the University of California in Berkeley, wrote *Adventures in Flower Gardening* (vol. 36). Arthur E. Bostwick, identified as the head of the St. Louis Public Library and a former ALA president, wrote *Pivotal Figures of Science* (v. 41). George H. Locke, identified as the chief librarian of the Toronto Public Library and a former president of the ALA, wrote *English History* (v. 45). Avrahm Yarmolinksy, identified as the chief of the Slavonic Division of the New York Public Library, wrote *Russian Literature* (v. 61). Thus, only 9.1 percent of the vol-

umes in the RWAP series were written by librarians. All information in this footnote is drawn from the authorial headnotes appearing at the beginning of each volume.

139. Kellogg, *Biology*, 7.

140. Meiklejohn, *Philosophy*, 37, 8.

141. "Alain Locke," *Contemporary Black Biography*, Volume 10 (Detroit, MI: Gale Research, 1995). Reproduced in *Biography Resource Center* (Farmington Hills, MI: Thomson Gale). Available from: http://galenet.galegroup.com/servlet/BioRC (accessed January 21, 2006).

142. Alain Locke, *The Negro in America* (Chicago: American Library Association, 1933), 7.

143. Wilfred T. Grenfell, *Religion in Everyday Life* (Chicago: American Library Association, 1926), 7–8.

144. Ibid., 14–15.

145. Hanna Astrup Larsen, *Scandinavian Literature* (Chicago: American Library Association, 1930), 45–46.

146. Locke, *The Negro in America*, 61–64.

147. Philip N. Youtz, *American Life in Architecture* (Chicago: American Library Association, 1932), 43–45.

148. Robert C. Brooks, *Russia: The Soviet Way* (Chicago: American Library Association, 1933), 41–44.

149. These ten titles are: *Interior Decoration*; *The Pacific Area in International Relations*; *American Life in Architecture*; *Evolution*; *Russian Literature*; *Farm Life: Problems and Opportunities*; *Latin America*; *Unemployment*; *Russia: The Soviet Way*; and *The Negro in America*.

150. J. Russell Smith, *Geography and Our Need of It* (Chicago: American Library Association, 1928), 23–24.

151. Locke, *The Negro in America*, 10–11, 17.

152. Avrahm Yarmolinsky, *Russian Literature* (Chicago: American Library Association, 1931), 15.

153. Lewis Mumford, *Architecture* (Chicago: American Library Association, 1926), 23, 27–28.

154. Youtz, *American Life in Architecture*, 16.

155. Ibid., 14–15.

156. Clarence Poe, *Farm Life: Problems and Opportunities* (Chicago: American Library Association, 1931), 20.

157. Ibid., 11.

158. Ibid., 15. Poe quotes George H. Stevenson.

159. Ibid., 19.

160. Ibid., 26–27.

161. Hamlin Garland, *The Westward March of American Settlement* (Chicago: American Library Association, 1927), 19, 18.

162. Ibid., 22

163. Ibid., 23–24.

164. Margaret E. Monroe, *Library Adult Education: The Biography of an Idea* (New York: Scarecrow Press, 1963), 35–40.

165. Quoted in Lee, *Continuing Education for Adults*, 68.

166. Monroe, *Library Adult Education*, 35–36.

167. "ALA Activities Committee Report," *ALA Bulletin* 24, no. 12 (1930): 607–680.

168. Ibid., 617–618.

169. Ibid., 618.

170. F. K. W. Drury, "Six Years' Activity in Adult Education," *ALA Bulletin* 25, no. 1 (1931): 31–37.

171. Monroe, *Library Adult Education*, 39.

172. E. F. Stevens, "Adult Erudition," *Libraries (A Continuation of Public Libraries)* 34, no. 6 (1934): 250–254. Important parts of this article are quoted in Lee, *Continuing Education for Adults*, 50.

173. Quoted in Lee, *Continuing Education for Adults*, 50.

174. Ibid.

175. Ibid.

176. Ibid.

177. Stevens, "Adult Education," 252.

178. Ibid., 254.

179. Ibid.

180. Ibid., 252.

181. Margaret Egan, "An Experiment in Advisory Service and Graded Reading in the C.C.C. Camps," *Library Quarterly* 7, no. 4 (1937): 471.

182. The participants in the Cincinnati experiment were from three backgrounds: "white and predominantly ... urban"; "negro"; and "white ... from rural or mountain localities" (pp. 471–472).

183. Some questions requested demographic information about date of birth, national background, and educational attainments, but other questions asked about previously read books and preferred leisure-time activities. The questionnaire concluded by asking "If you could ask one question, and be sure of receiving the correct answer, what would you ask?" (p. 474).

184. Egan, "An Experiment," 476.

185. Ibid., 476–477. Percentage calculated based on data provided in Table 1: Book Reports by Type of Book.

186. Ibid., 477.

187. Viarda Clark Brubeck, "A Close View of Advisory Service: In a Small Public Library," in *Helping Adults to Learn: The Library in Action*, ed. John Chancellor, 3–9 (Chicago: American Library Association, 1939).

188. Ibid., 7.

189. Ibid.

190. Ibid., 7–8.

191. Ibid., 8–9.

192. Ibid., 4. Original emphasis.

193. The summary of library education in this paragraph follows Jesse H. Shera, *The Foundations of Education for Librarianship* (New York: Becker and Hayes, 1972). Supplementary information was derived from Sarah K. Vann, *Training for Librarianship before 1923: Education for Librarianship Prior to the Publication of Williamson's Report on Training for Library Service* (Chicago: American Library Association, 1961), as well as L. Houser and Alvin M. Schrader, *The Search for a Scientific Profession: Library Science Education in the U.S. and Canada* (Metuchen, NJ: Scarecrow Press, 1978).

194. Quoted in Vann, *Training for Librarianship*, 158. Also quoted in Houser and Schrader, *The Search for a Scientific Profession*, 34.

195. "Definitions: Flexner Report," Medicinenet.com. Available from: http://www.medterms.com/script/main/art.asp?articlekey=8727 (accessed January 4, 2006).

196. Alvin S. Johnson, *A Report to Carnegie Corporation of New York on the Policy of Donations to Free Public Libraries* (New York: Carnegie Corporation, 1915), 1.

197. Ibid., 49.

198. Ibid., 47, 49.

199. Shera, *The Foundations of Education for Librarianship*, 237–239.

200. John V. Richardson Jr., *The Spirit of Inquiry: The Graduate Library School at Chicago, 1921–51* (Chicago: American Library Association, 1982), 9.

201. Shera, *The Foundations of Education for Librarianship*, 238. The first two quotations in this sentence are Williamson's words quoted by Shera. The last two quotations in this sentence are Shera's summary of Williamson's report.

202. Learned, *The American Public Library*, 79, 78.

203. Richardson Jr., *The Spirit of Inquiry*, 9–10. The first quotation in this sentence uses Richardson's words. The second quotation in this sentence represents the words of Frederick P. Keppel, president of the Carnegie Corporation of New York, in a letter to Carl Milam, the Executive Secretary of the ALA (as quoted by Richardson Jr.).

204. Richardson Jr., *The Spirit of Inquiry*, 12. The actual amount granted by the Carnegie Corporation is reported as $1,385,000 (Richardson Jr., *The Spirit of Inquiry*, 36).

205. Ibid., 14–22.

206. Ibid., 22–44.

207. Stephen Karetzky's *Reading Research and Librarian-*

ship: *A History and Analysis* (Westport, CT: Greenwood Press, 1976) was a crucial document for alerting us to the importance of the reading research conducted at the Graduate Library School of the University of Chicago, as well as the responses to it.

208. Quoted in Richardson Jr., *The Spirit of Inquiry*, 62.

209. Douglas Waples, "The Graduate Library School at Chicago," *Library Quarterly* 1, no. 1 (1931): 26–36.

210. C. C. Williamson, "The Place of Research in Library Service," *Library Quarterly* 1, no. 1 (1931): 1–17.

211. Ibid., 3.

212. Ibid.

213. Ibid., 8.

214. Ibid., 8–9. Williamson quotes John Dewey from *How We Think*.

215. Ibid., 9.

216. Ibid., 8.

217. Ibid., 14.

218. Richardson Jr., *The Spirit of Inquiry*, 52–54.

219. Quoted in Richardson Jr., *The Spirit of Inquiry*, 54.

220. Douglas Waples, "Propaganda and Leisure Reading: A Method by Which to Identify and Offset Propaganda in Students' Leisure Reading," *Journal of Higher Education* 1, no. 2 (1930): 73–77.

221. Ibid., 74.

222. Ibid., 76.

223. Ibid., 73.

224. Ibid., 77.

225. Douglas Waples and Ralph W. Tyler, *What People Want to Read About: A Study of Groups Interests and A Survey of Problems in Adult Reading* (Chicago: American Library Association and the University of Chicago Press, 1932).

226. Ibid., xix.

227. Ibid., xxvi–xxvii.

228. Ibid., xxvii.

229. Ibid., xxviii.

230. Ibid., xxix.

231. Ibid., 10.

232. Ibid., 11.

233. Ibid., 224–246.

234. Ibid., 236–238.

235. Ibid., 239.

236. Ibid., 306–308.

237. Ibid., 14.

238. Ibid., 224.

239. Ibid., 19.

240. Ibid., 20.

241. Ibid., 60.

242. Ibid., 61.

243. Ibid., 82–84.

244. Douglas Waples, "The Relation of Subject Interests to Actual Reading," *Library Quarterly* 2, no. 1 (1932): 69.

245. Waples and Tyler, *What People Want to Read About*, 31.

246. Hill, "The Public Library and the People," 15.

247. Douglas Waples, "Community Studies in Reading: I. Reading in the Lower East Side," *Library Quarterly* 3, no. 1 (1933): 1–20; Leon Carnovsky, "Community Studies in Reading: II. Hinsdale, A Suburb of Chicago," *Library Quarterly* 5, no. 1 (1935): 1–30; Helen A. Ridgway, "Community Studies in Reading: III. Reading Habits of Adult Non-Users of the Public Library," *Library Quarterly* 6, no. 1 (1936): 1–33; and Laurel Krieg, "Community Studies in Reading: IV. A Middle-Western Manufacturing Community," *Library Quarterly* 9, no. 1 (1939): 72–86.

248. Waples, "Community Studies in Reading: Reading in the Lower East Side," 16.

249. Carnovsky, "Community Studies in Reading: Hinsdale, A Suburb of Chicago," 30.

250. Krieg, "Community Studies in Reading: A Middle-Western Manufacturing Community," 86.

251. Jeannette Howard Foster, "An Approach to Fiction through the Characteristics of Its Readers," *Library Quarterly* 6, no. 2 (1936): 124–174.

252. Ibid., 126.

253. Ibid., 162.

254. Ibid.

255. Ibid.

256. Ibid., 155–156.

257. Hazel I. Medway, "Understanding the Reader," in *Helping the Reader toward Self-Education*, eds. John Chancellor, Miriam D. Tompkins, and Hazel I. Medway, 55–70 (Chicago: American Library Association, 1938).

258. James Howard Wellard, *Book Selection: Its Principles and Practice* (London, England: Grafton & Co., 1937), 93.

259. Ibid., 123.

260. Ibid., 92, 164. Original emphasis.

261. Ibid., 95.

262. Ibid., 123, 164.

263. Ibid., 174.

264. Ibid., 130.

265. Carnegie Corporation of New York, *Report of the President & of the Treasurer* (New York: Carnegie Corporation, 1929), 12–13.

266. Ibid., 13.

267. Ibid.

268. Shera, in *The Foundations of Education for Librarianship* (p. 249), first drew our attention to Flexner's *Universities: American, English, German*. Flexner, in turn, quoted from Keppel's comments in *Report of the President & of the Treasurer*.

269. Abraham Flexner, *Universities: American, English, German* (New York: Oxford University Press, 1930), 172–175.

270. For a concise overview of the differences between the philosophical approaches of Waples and Butler, see Charles I. Terbille, "Competing Models of Library Science: Waples-Berelson and Butler," *Libraries and Culture* 27, no. 3 (1992): 296–319.

271. Quoted in John V. Richardson Jr., *The Gospel of Scholarship: Pierce Butler and a Critique of American Librarianship* (Metuchen, NJ: Scarecrow Press, 1992), 87. This book should be consulted in its entirety for an account of the simmering differences between Butler and Waples.

272. Richardson Jr., *The Gospel of Scholarship*, 86.

273. Richardson Jr., *The Spirit of Inquiry*, 63–70.

274. Doud, "The Readers' Advisory Service of the St. Louis Public Library," 20–21.

275. Ibid., 21.

276. William S. Gray and Ruth Munroe, *The Reading Interests and Habits of Adults: A Preliminary Report* (New York: The Macmillan Company, 1930), 103.

277. Ibid., 103.

278. Ibid., 210–257.

279. Ibid., 213–214.

280. Ibid., 213.

281. Ibid., 220.

282. Ibid., 221.

283. Ibid., 222.

284. Ibid., 223.

285. Ibid., 223–224.

286. James I. Wyer, *Reference Work: A Textbook for Students of Library Work* (Chicago: American Library Association, 1930), 180.

287. Charles H. Compton, *Who Reads What? Essays on the Readers of Mark Twain, Hardy, Sandburg, Shaw, William James, the Greek Classics* (New York: H. W. Wilson Company, 1934). A synopsis of this work is contained in Charles H. Compton, "The Outlook for Adult Education in the Library," *Adult Education and the Library* 3, no. 3 (1928): 59–71.

288. Paxton P. Price, "Compton, Charles Herrick (1880–1966)," in *Dictionary of American Library Biography*, ed. Bohdan S. Wynar, 91–94 (Littleton, CO: Libraries Unlimited, 1978).

289. Compton, "The Outlook," 65.

290. Ibid.

291. Ibid., 66.

292. Compton, *Who Reads What?* 35–52.

293. Ibid., 35.

294. Carnovsky, "Community Studies in Reading: II. Hinsdale, A Suburb of Chicago," 1.

295. C. Seymour Thompson, "Do We Want a Library Science?" *Library Journal* 56, no. 13 (1931): 581–587. Waples replied to Thompson in Douglas Waples, "Do We Want a Library Science? A Reply," *Library Journal* 56, no. 16 (1931): 743–746. Thompson replied to Waples's reply in C. Seymour Thompson, "Comment on the Reply," *Library Journal* 56, no. 16 (1931): 746–747.

296. Quoted in Richardson Jr., *The Spirit of Inquiry*, 92.

297. Thompson, "Do We Want a Library Science?" 587.

298. Ibid., 585.

299. Ibid.

300. Ibid., 586.

301. Ibid., 586, 583. Original emphasis.

302. Helen E. Haines, *Living with Books: The Art of Book Selection* (New York: Columbia University Press, 1935); Helen E. Haines, "Technics or Humanization in Librarianship? *Library Journal* 63, no. 15 (1938): 619–627.

303. Althea Warren, "Foreword," in Helen E. Haines *Living with Books: The Art of Book Selection*, 2nd ed. (New York: Columbia University Press, 1950), vii–x.

304. Haines, *Living with Books*, 4. Haines quotes John Morley.

305. Ibid., 7.

306. Ibid., 5.

307. Ibid., 29–30.

308. Ibid., 4.

309. Ibid., 430–432.

310. Ibid., 430–431.

311. Ibid., 432.

312. Haines, "Technics or Humanization," 620.

313. Ibid., 622.

314. Ibid.

315. Ibid., 623, 622.

316. Margaret E. Monroe, "Flexner, Jennie Maas (1882–1944)," in *Dictionary of American Library Biography*, ed. Bohdan S. Wynar, 179–182 (Littleton, CO: Libraries Unlimited, 1978).

317. Mildred V. D. Matthews, "Readers' Services: Role as Adult Educators," *Library Journal* 79, no. 3 (1954): 174.

318. Jennie M. Flexner and Sigrid A. Edge, *A Readers' Advisory Service* (New York: American Association for Adult Education, 1934); Jennie M. Flexner and Byron C. Hopkins, *Readers' Advisers at Work: A Survey of Development in the New York Public Library* (New York: American Association for Adult Education, 1941). The quote is from Flexner and Edge, *A Readers' Advisory Service*, 57.

319. Flexner and Edge, *A Readers' Advisory Service*, 55.

320. Ibid., 2, 6.

321. Flexner and Hopkins, *Readers' Advisers at Work*, 34.

322. Ibid., *Readers' Advisers at Work*, 12–13, 24–33.

323. Ibid., 32.

324. Ibid., 28.

325. "Individualizing Library Service," *Libraries (A Continuation of Public Libraries)* 33, no. 6 (1928): 293.

326. Flexner and Hopkins, *Readers' Advisers at Work*, 8, 12, 15.

327. Ibid., 36.

328. Ibid., 38.

329. Ibid., 36.

330. Ibid., 55.

331. Helen L. Butler, "An Inquiry into the Statement of Motives by Readers," *Library Quarterly* 10, no. 1 (1940): 44–45.

332. Ibid., 45.

333. Flexner and Edge, *A Readers' Advisory Service*, 50–51.

334. Ibid., 51.

335. Ibid., 53–54.

336. Ibid., 53.

337. The list of books recommended by the NYPL readers' advisory service that readers considered to be "most satisfactory" is contained in Flexner and Edge, *A Readers' Advisory Service*, 48–49.

338. Robert S. Lynd and Helen Merrell Lynd, *Middletown: A Study in American Culture* (New York: Harcourt, Brace and Company, 1929), 235.

339. Calculations based on data provided in Table 13: Reasons for Reading (1933–1939) in Flexner and Hopkins, *Readers' Advisers at Work*, 49.

340. Alvin S. Johnson, *The Public Library—A People's University* (New York: American Association for Adult Education, 1938).

341. Thorstein Veblen, *The Higher Learning in America: A Memorandum on the Conduct of Universities by Business Men* (New York: Hill and Wang, 1967), 165.

342. "Economics at the New School for Social Research." Available from: http://cepa.newschool.edu/het/schools/newsch.htm (accessed January 17, 2006).

343. Monroe, *Library Adult Education*, 40–43.

344. Ibid., 42.

345. John Chancellor, "The Smaller Library and Adult Education," in *Helping Adults to Learn: The Library in Action*, ed. John Chancellor, 198 (Chicago: American Library Association, 1939).

346. Ibid., 205.

347. Monroe, *Library Adult Education*, 42.

348. Johnson, *The Public Library—A People's University*, 1, 4–5.

349. Ibid., 2.

350. Ibid., 5.

351. Ibid., 20.

352. Ibid.

353. Ibid., 38.

354. Ibid., 41.

355. Ibid., 32, 41.

356. Ibid., 33

357. Ibid., 33, 35.

358. Ibid., 32.

359. Ibid., 34.

360. Ibid.

361. Ibid.

362. Ibid., 34–35.

363. Ibid., 35.

364. Ibid., 78–79.

365. Ibid., 73–74.

366. Ibid., 74.

367. Ibid.

368. Ibid., 44.

369. Ibid., 47–54.

370. Ibid., 70.

371. Ibid., 65.

372. Veblen, *The Higher Learning in America*, 163.

373. Ibid., 166.

374. Johnson, *The Public Library—A People's University*, 70.

375. "A National Plan for Libraries, *ALA Bulletin* 33, no. 2 (1939): 140.

376. Ibid.

377. Ibid., 141.

378. Ibid. Also quoted in Lee, *Continuing Education for Adults*, 69.

379. "A National Plan for Libraries," 141. Also quoted in Lee, *Continuing Education for Adults*, 69.

380. Douglas Waples, "People and Libraries," in *Current Issues in Library Administration: Papers Presented before The Library Institute at the University of Chicago, August 1–12, 1938*, ed. Carleton Bruns Joeckel, 355–370 (Chicago: University of Chicago Press, 1939).

381. Alice I. Bryan, "The Psychology of the Reader," *Library Journal* 64, no. 1 (1939): 7–12; Alice I. Bryan, "Personality Adjustment through Reading," *Library Journal* 64, no. 14 (1939): 573–576; and Alice I. Bryan, "The Reader as a Person," *Library Journal* 65, no. 4 (1940): 137–141. Bryan also wrote "Can There Be a Science of Bibliotherapy?" *Library Journal* 64, no. 18 (1939): 773–776. Here she argued that it would be possible to develop "a science of bibliotherapy" if "carefully controlled case studies of the effects of reading certain types of materials upon hundreds of unselected patients convalescing from particular types of illness" were conducted (p. 774). Of course, it would be necessary to keep in mind the numerous "variables that might have a bearing upon the results" (p. 774). If and when bibliotherapy became a science, it should therefore be broadly defined as "the prescription of reading materials which will help to develop emotional maturity and nourish and sustain mental health" (pp. 774–775).

382. Richardson Jr., *The Gospel of Scholarship*, 94.

383. Karetzky, *Reading Research and Librarianship*, 110.

384. Ibid., 114. See also Douglas Waples, *People and Print: Social Aspects of Reading in the Depression* (Chicago: University of Chicago Press, 1937), 119–125, 197.

385. Waples, "People and Libraries," 370.

386. Ibid., 358.

387. Ibid., 363, 360.

388. Ibid., 367.

389. Ibid., 370.

390. Our account of the development of bibliotherapy is heavily dependant on the sources listed in the following endnotes.

391. Mary Niles Maack, "Bryan, Alice I. (1902–1992)," in *Dictionary of American Library Biography, Second Supplement* ed. Donald G. Davis Jr., 43–47 (Westport, CT: Libraries Unlimited, 2003).

392. Rhea Joyce Rubin, "Preface," in *Bibliotherapy Sourcebook*, ed. Rhea Joyce Rubin (Phoenix, AZ: Oryx Press, 1978), xi.

393. Rhea Joyce Rubin, *Using Bibliotherapy: A Guide to Theory and Practice* (Phoenix, AZ: Oryx Press, 1978), 14.

394. Eleanor Frances Brown, *Bibliotherapy and Its Widening Applications* (Metuchen, NJ: Scarecrow Press, 1975), 13.

395. Rubin, "Preface," xi.

396. Ibid.

397. Quoted in Brown, *Bibliotherapy and Its Widening Applications*, 13.

398. Brown, *Bibliotherapy and Its Widening Application*, 15.

399. Ibid.

400. Rubin, "Preface," xii.

401. Brown, *Bibliotherapy and Its Widening Application*, 17.

402. Ibid.

403. Rubin, *Using Bibliotherapy*, 14.

404. Rubin, "Preface," xii.

405. Rubin, *Using Bibliotherapy*, 3–4, 7.

406. Ibid., 5.

407. Quoted in Rubin, *Using Bibliotherapy*, 5.

408. Ibid.

409. Bryan, "The Reader as a Person," 137–138.

410. Ibid., 137.

411. Ibid., 137–138.

412. Ibid., 138.

413. Ibid.

414. Ibid., 139.

415. Ibid., 140.

416. Ibid., 141.

417. Bryan, "The Psychology of the Reader," 9.

418. Ibid.

419. Ibid., 11.

420. Ibid., 10.

421. Ibid.

422. Bryan, "Personality Adjustment through Reading," 574.

423. Ibid., 575.

424. Ibid.

425. Ibid.

426. Ibid.

427. Ibid., 576.

428. Ibid.

429. Ibid.

430. Ibid.

431. Cyril O. Houle, "Chicago Public Library Staff Studies Adult Education," *Library Journal* 71, no. 1 (1946): 23–27, 47.

432. Ibid., 24–25.

433. Ibid., 25.

434. Quoted in Houle, "Chicago Public Library Staff," 25.

435. Ibid., 26–27.

436. Ibid., 27.

437. Lowell Martin specifically attributes the rise of guided group-reading to Houle. See Lowell Martin, "Guided Group Reading as a Library Service: The Chicago Project," *Library Journal* 71, no. 10 (1946): 736.

438. Lowell Martin, "Guided Group Reading as a Library Service: The Chicago Project," *Library Journal* 71, no. 10 (1946): 738–739.

439. John Powell, "One Step Nearer Leadership: Guided Group Reading as a Library Service," *Library Journal* 71, no. 7 (1946): 444.

440. Powell, "One Step Nearer Leadership" 443–449; Martin, "Guided Group Reading as a Library Service," 734–739.'.

441. Haines, *Living with Books*, 2nd ed., 34–35.

442. John P. Barden, "The Great Books and the Good Life," *Wilson Library Bulletin* 22, no. 4 (1947): 313.

443. Powell, "One Step Nearer Leadership," 444.

444. Ibid., 447.

445. A complete list of the "Great Books" reading program is contained in John P. Barden, "The Great Books and the Good Life," *Wilson Library Bulletin* 22, no. 4 (1947): 313–316.

446. Powell, "One Step Nearer Leadership," 445.

447. Ibid.

448. Robert M. Hutchins, "The Public Library: Its Place in Education," *Library Quarterly* 20, no. 3 (1950): 184.

449. Powell, "One Step Nearer Leadership," 444.

450. Hutchins, "The Public Library: Its Place in Education," 183.

451. Powell, "One Step Nearer Leadership," 443–444.

452. Hutchins, "The Public Library," 184.

453. Ibid., 180.

454. Barden, "The Great Books," 315.

455. The phrase "shared inquiry" is drawn from The Great Books Foundation web site and the page entitled "Shared Inquiry: The Shared Inquiry Method of Learning." Available from: http://www.greatbooks.org (accessed February 3, 2006).

456. John P. Barden, "The Great Books and the Good Life," *Wilson Library Bulletin* 22, no. 4 (1947): 314.

457. Hutchins, "The Public Library," 182.

458. Oscar A. Silverman, "Why Read the Great Books?" *Wilson Library Bulletin* 22, no. 4 (1947): 317, 330.

459. Martin, "Guided Group Reading as a Library Service," 739.

460. Quoted in Monroe, *Library Adult Education*, 51.

461. Lee, *Continuing Education for Adults*, 74–75. Lee quotes important extracts from the *Post-War Standards for Public Libraries*. We use Lee's extracts in our account.

462. Lee, *Continuing Education for Adults*, 75.

463. Margery Doud, "The Veteran via the Public Library: A Symposium: Readers' Advisory Service," *Catholic Library World* 18, no. 5 (1947): 139.

464. Ibid., 139.

465. Ibid., 140.

466. Mary U. Rothrock, "On Some Library Questions of Our Time," *ALA Bulletin* 41, no. 7 (1947): 243.

467. Ibid.

468. Carleton Bruns Joeckel and Amy Winslow, *A National Plan for Public Library Service: Prepared for the Committee on Postwar Planning of the American Library Association* (Chicago: American Library Association, 1948), 3, 10.

469. Bernard Berelson with the assistance of Lester Asheim, *The Library's Public* (New York: Columbia University Press, 1949), 77.

470. Bernard Berelson, "Reply to the Discussants," in *A Forum on the Public Library Inquiry: The Conference at the University of Chicago Graduate Library School, August 8–13, 1949*, ed. Lester Asheim, 64 (New York: Columbia University Press, 1950).

471. Ibid.

472. "A.L.A.'s 'Great Issues' Program," *ALA Bulletin* 42, no. 1 (1948): 81; Ruth Rutzen, "The Marshall Plan—Pro and Con," *ALA Bulletin* 42, no. 1 (1948): 10–14; Grace Thomas Stevenson, "ALA's New Project," *ALA Bulletin* 45, no. 9 (1951): 301–303.

473. Rutzen, "The Marshall Plan," 11.

474. "A.L.A.'s 'Great Issues' Program," 81.

475. Stevenson, "ALA's New Project," 303.

476. Ibid.

477. Lester Asheim, "Response to the Great Issues Program," *ALA Bulletin* 44, no. 7 (1950): 285–289.

478. Lee, *Continuing Education for Adults*, 86.

479. Ibid.

480. "The American Heritage Project at Work," *Wilson Library Bulletin* 27, no. 6 (1953): 436.

481. Alice I. Bryan, "Leigh, Robert Devore" (1890–1961)," in *Dictionary of American Library Biography*, ed. Bohdan S. Wynar, 310–313 (Littleton, CO: Libraries Unlimited, 1978).

482. Robert D. Leigh, *The Public Library in the United States: The General Report of the Public Library Inquiry* (New York: Columbia University Press, 1950), 16–24, 48.

483. *A Forum on the Public Library Inquiry*, 276. Also quoted in Lee, *Continuing Education for Adults*, 78.

484. Robert D. Leigh, *The Public Library in the United States* (New York: Columbia University Press, 1950), 34–37.

485. Ibid., 224.

486. Ibid., 223.

487. Ibid., 17.

488. Ibid., 18.

489. Ibid., 48, 50.

490. Ibid., 17.

491. Lester Asheim, *Training Needs of Librarians Doing Adult Education Work: A Report of the Allerton Park Conference, November 14–16, 1954* (Chicago: American Library Association, 1955), i.

492. Ibid., ii, 8–9.

493. Ibid., 9.

494. Ibid.

495. Quoted in Marion E. Hawes, "The Role of the Large Public Library in Adult Education," *Library Trends* 8, no. 1 (1959): 21.

496. Hawes, "The Role of the Large Public Library," 22–23.

497. Lee, *Continuing Education for Adults*, 109.

498. Grace Thomas Stevenson, "The Role of the Public Library in Adult Reading," in *Adult Reading: The Fifty-fifth Yearbook of the National Society for the Study of Education Part II*, ed., Nelson B. Henry, 124 (Chicago: University of Chicago Press, 1956).

499. Ralph A. Ulveling, "The Public Library—An Educational Institution?" *Library Resources & Technical Services* 3, no. 1 (1959): 12–20.

500. Ibid., 16.

501. Ibid.

502. Hawes, "The Role of the Large Public Library," 23.

503. Ibid., 22.

504. Lee, *Continuing Education for Adults*, 109.

505. Ibid.

506. Stevenson, "The Role of the Public Library," 125.

507. Monroe, *Library Adult Education*, 61.

508. Helen Hugenor Lyman, "Discussion Groups and World Understanding," *ALA Bulletin* 46, no. 2 (1952): 44.

509. Ibid.

510. Helen Lyman Smith, *Adult Education Activities in Public Libraries* (Chicago: American Library Association, 1954), 31.

511. Grace Thomas Stevenson, "Recent Developments in the Methods by which People are Encouraged to Use Public Libraries and Improve their Personal Interests through Books in the United States of America," *Libri* 13, no. 3/4 (1963): 286.

512. Ibid.

513. Lee, *Continuing Education for Adults*, 90–91.

514. Ibid., 90.

515. Andrew M. Hansen, "RASD: Serving Those Who Serve the Public." Available from: http://www.ala.org/ala/rusa/rusapubs/rusq/specialfeatures/rasdhistory/rasdhistory1.htm (accessed February 8, 2006).

516. The ten volumes were: William O. Douglas, *Freedom of the Mind* (1962; 44 pages); Ralph Eugene Lapp, *Space Science* (1962; 52 pages); Bartlett H. Hayes Jr., *The Contemporary Arts* (1962; 20 pages); Robert L. Heilbroner, *The World of Economics* (1963; 30 pages); Marston Bates, *Expanding Population in a Shrinking World* (1963; 32 pages); John Gassner, *The World of Contemporary Drama* (1965; 32 pages); Lorus Johnson Milne and Margery Joan Greene Milne, *Biological Frontiers* (1966; 28 pages); Walter Rochs Goldschmidt, *Cultural Anthropology* (1967; 40 pages); Sidney Hook, *Contemporary Philosophy* (1968, 44 pages); and Harold Dwight Lasswell, *Man and His Government* (1968, 28 pages).

517. Wording taken from the inside front cover of Marston Bates, *Expanding Population in a Shrinking World* (Chicago, American Library Association, 1963).

518. Ibid.

519. William O. Douglas, *Freedom of the Mind* (Chicago: American Library Association, 1962), 2.

520. Ibid., 43.

521. Robert L. Heilbroner, *The World of Economics* (Chicago: American Library Association, 1963), 3.

522. Ibid., 31–32.

523. Bartlett H. Hayes Jr., *The Contemporary Arts* (Chicago: American Library Association, 1962), 15.

524. Ibid., 16.

525. Helen Huguenor Lyman, *Reader's Guidance Service in a Small Public Library* (Chicago: American Library Association, 1962), 1–2.

526. Ibid., 2.

527. Ibid.

528. Ibid.

Chapter 5

1. Leigh, *The Public Library in the United States*, 19.

2. Ibid., 47.

3. Ibid.

4. Ibid., 47, 49.

5. Ibid., 50.

6. Ibid.

7. Ibid., 50, 48.

8. Ibid., 47.

9. Ibid., 50.

10. Ibid., 47.

11. Ibid., 48.

12. Ibid., 18.

13. Ibid., 224.

14. *A Forum on the Public Library Inquiry*, 255.

15. The story of the expansion of universities and colleges, as well as university and college libraries, in the United States after World War II is told by Charles B. Osburn, *Academic Research and Library Resources: Changing Patterns in America* (Westport, CT: Greenwood Press, 1979), 4–38. This account of the postwar expansion of universities and colleges draws heavily on Osburn.

16. "The GI Bill from Roosevelt to Montgomery." Available from: http://www.gibill.va.gov/education/GI_Bill.htm (accessed December 8, 2005).

17. Ibid.

18. Theodore J. Marchese, "U.S. Higher Education in the Postwar Era: Expansion and Growth," *U.S. Society & Values* 2, no. 4 (1997). Available from: http://usinfo.state.gov/journals/itsv/1297/ijse/marchese.htm (accessed February 23, 2006).

19. Osburn, *Academic Research and Library Resources*, 4–38.

20. Marchese, "U.S. Higher Education."

21. Ibid.

22. Ibid.

23. Lasch, *The Culture of Narcissism*, 71–99.

24. Lee Regan, "Status of Reader's Advisory Service," *RQ* 12, no. 3 (1973): 230.

25. Helen Huguenor Lyman, "The Art of Reading Guidance," in *Reading Guidance Institute June 29–July 2, 1965* (Madison: The University of Wisconsin Library School and University Extension Division, Department of Library Science), 70. The *Reading Guidance Institute June 29–July 2, 1965* is a collection of mimeographed papers and supplementary handout-type materials that was likely given to each of the Institute's participants. According to WORLDCAT, this collection is available only from the University of Wisconsin or University of Pittsburgh library systems. Page numbers refer to the consecutively numbered copy held by the University of Pittsburgh.

26. Lyman, "The Art of Reading Guidance," 71.

27. Ibid., 72.

28. Ibid., 73.

29. Ibid., 76.

30. Margaret E. Monroe, "Reading Guidance as a Fundamental Library Service," in *Reading Guidance Institute June 29–July 2, 1965* (Madison: The University of Wisconsin Library School and University Extension Division, Department of Library Science), 27.

31. Ibid., 19–20.

32. Richard D. Altick, "Education, the Common Reader, and the Future," *ALA Bulletin* 60, no. 3 (1966): 275–276.

33. Ibid., 276.

34. Ibid., 278.

35. Ibid.

36. Ibid., 279.

37. Ibid., 280.

38. Ibid., 279.

39. Ibid.

40. Ibid., 280.

41. Ibid., 281.

42. Ibid., 282.

43. Lynn E. Birge, *Serving Adult Learners: A Public Library Tradition* (Chicago: American Library Association, 1981), 73.

44. Regan, "Status of Reader's Advisory Service," 230.

45. Ibid., 231–232.

46. Ibid., 232.

47. Eleanor Frances Brown, *Bibliotherapy and Its Widening Applications* (Metuchen, NJ: Scarecrow Press, 1975); Rhea Joyce Rubin, *Using Bibliotherapy: A Guide to Theory and Practice* (Phoenix, AZ: Oryx Press, 1978); Rhea Joyce Rubin, ed., *Bibliotherapy Sourcebook* (Phoenix, AZ: Oryx Press, 1978).

48. Ruth M. Tews, ed. *Bibliotherapy*. Special Issue of *Library Trends* 11, no. 2 (1962). In addition to Tews's introduction, this special issue contains 11 articles. Eight of the articles are about institutional bibliotherapy: Margaret M. Kinney, "The Bibliotherapy Program: Requirements for Training"; Artemisia J. Junier, "Bibliotherapy: Projects and Studies with the Mentally Ill Patient"; Mildred T. Moody, "Bibliotherapy: Modern Concepts in General Hospitals and Other Institutions"; Edwin F. Alston, "Bibliotherapy and Psychotherapy"; John S. Pearson, "Bibliotherapy and the Clinical Psychologist"; Margaret C. Hannigan, "The Librarian in Bibliotherapy: Pharmacist or Bibliotherapist?"; Dorothy Mereness, "Bibliotherapy: Its Use in Nursing Therapy"; and Inez Huntting, "The Role of the Occupational Therapist as Related To Bibliotherapy."

49. Orrilla T. Blackshear, "A Bibliotherapy Workshop," *Wisconsin Library Bulletin* 60, no. 5 (1964): 296–298.

50. Margaret C. Hannigan's "Counseling and Bibliotherapy for the General Reader," in *Reading Guidance Institute June 29–July 2, 1965* (Madison: The University of Wisconsin Library School and University Extension Division, Department of Library Science), 59–65.

51. Evalene P. Jackson, "Bibliotherapy and Reading Guidance: A Tentative Approach to Theory," *Library Trends* 11, no. 2 (1962): 118–126.

52. Ibid., 118–119.

53. Two chapters of this dissertation are reprinted as follows: Caroline Shrodes, "Application of Dynamic Personality Theory to the Dynamics of the Aesthetic Experience," in *Bibliotherapy Sourcebook*, ed. Rhea Joyce Rubin, 77–95 (Phoenix, AZ: Oryx Press, 1978); Caroline Shrodes, "Implications for Psychotherapy," in *Bibliotherapy Sourcebook*, ed. Rhea Joyce Rubin, 96–122 (Phoenix, AZ: Oryx Press, 1978).

54. Shrodes, "Application of Dynamic Personality Theory," 78.

55. Rubin, *Using Bibliotherapy*, 37.

56. Shrodes, "Implications," 115.

57. Ibid.

58. Rubin, *Using Bibliotherapy*, 67.

59. References to these novels and plays are found in: Shrodes, "Application of Dynamic Personality Theory," 77–95; Shrodes, "Implications," 96–122.

60. Jackson, "Bibliotherapy and Reading Guidance," 125.

61. Bryan, "The Psychology of the Reader," 12.

62. Jackson, "Bibliotherapy and Reading Guidance," 124.

63. Blackshear, "A Bibliotherapy Workshop," 296–298; Hannigan, "Counseling and Bibliotherapy for the General Reader," 64–65; Brown, *Bibliotherapy and Its Widening Applications*, 225–241.

64. Our account of the non-traditional education movement follows Birge, *Serving Adult Learners*, 118–135.

65. Commission on Non-Traditional Study, *Diversity by Design* (San Francisco, CA: Jossey-Bass, 1973).

66. Quoted in Birge, *Serving Adult Learners*, 119.

67. Commission on Non-Traditional Study, *Diversity by Design*, 5.

68. Ibid., 82, 79.

69. Ibid., 83.

70. Ibid.

71. Ibid., 84.

72. Ibid., 85.

73. Birge, *Serving Adult Learners*, 121.

74. Ibid.

75. Ibid., 122.

76. Quoted in Birge, *Serving Adult Learners*, 122.

77. Quoted in Birge, *Serving Adult Learners*, 132, 128.

78. Ibid., 128.

79. Ibid., 129.

80. Jane A. Reilly, *The Public Librarian as Adult Learners' Advisor: An Innovation in Human Services* (Westport, CT: Greenwood Press, 1981), 21. Reilly makes extensive use of

Sister Marie Schuster, *The Library-Centered Approach to Learning* (Palm Springs, CA: ETC Publications, 1977).

81. Reilly, *The Public Librarian*, 21.

82. Ibid., 128.

83. Ibid., 56.

84. Gerald R. Shields, "Another Hornblowing Bandwagon," *Library Journal* 100, no. 10 (1975): 927. Birge also quotes Shields's remarks.

85. Shields, "Another Hornblowing Bandwagon," 927.

86. Birge, *Serving Adult Learners*, 127.

87. Ibid., 133.

88. Nancy Pearl, "Gave 'Em What They Wanted," *Library Journal* 121, no. 14 (1996): 136–138.

89. Ibid., 136.

90. Ibid., 138.

91. Hill, "The Public Library and the People," 15.

92. Johnson, *The Public Library–A People's University*, 2.

93. Ibid., 136.

94. Ibid., 138.

95. Ibid.

96. Ibid.

97. Ibid, 137.

98. Ibid., 138.

99. May Shortt, "Advisers Anonymous, Arise!" *Ontario Library Review* 49, no. 2 (1965): 82.

100. Ibid.

101. Ibid.

102. Ibid.

103. Ibid.

104. Annelise Mark Pejtersen, "Fiction and Library Classification," *Scandinavian Public Library Quarterly* 11, no. 1 (1978): 5.

105. Sharon L. Baker and Gay W. Shepherd, "Fiction Classification Schemes: The Principles behind Them and Their Success," *RQ* 27, no. 2 (1987): 249.

106. Pejtersen, "Fiction and Library Classification," 5.

107. Pejtersen, "Fiction and Library Classification," 5–12; Annelise Mark Pejtersen and Jutta Austin, "Fiction Retrieval: Experimental Design and Evaluation of a Search System Based on Users' Value Criteria (Part 1)," *Journal of Documentation* 39, no. 4 (1983): 230–246; Annelise Mark Pejtersen and Jutta Austin, "Fiction Retrieval: Experimental Design and Evaluation of a Search System Based on Users' Value Criteria (Part 2)," *Journal of Documentation* 40, no. 1 (1984): 25–35.

108. Sharon L. Baker, "Will Fiction Classification Schemes Increase Use?" *RQ* 27, no. 3 (1988): 366–376.

109. Ibid., 369. Original emphasis.

110. Ibid., 374.

111. Jeffrey Cannell and Eileen McCluskey, "Genrefication: Fiction Classification and Increased Circulation," in *Guiding the Reader to the Next Book*, ed. Kenneth D. Shearer, 159–165 (New York: Neal-Schuman, 1996).

112. Ibid., 163.

113. Gail Harrell, "Use of Fiction Categories in Major American Public Libraries," in *Guiding the Reader to the Next Book*, ed. Kenneth D. Shearer, 149–157 (New York: Neal-Schuman, 1996).

114. Betty Rosenberg, *Genreflecting: A Guide to Reading Interests in Genre Fiction* (Littleton, CO: Libraries Unlimited, 1982), 5, 15.

115. Ibid., 15.

116. Ibid., 16. Original emphasis.

117. Ibid.

118. Information about Wilson is drawn from the following sources: Louis Menand, "Edmund Wilson," *The Johns Hopkins Guide to Literary Theory and Criticism*, 1st ed. Available from: http://litguide.press.jhu.edu/cgi-bin/view.cgi?eid=295&query=wilson%2C%20Edmund (accessed March 23, 2006). "Edmund Wilson," *The New York Review of Books*. Available from: http://www.nybooks.com/authors/2917 (accessed March 23, 2006). In addition to calling Wilson "the preeminent American man of letters of the twentieth century," *The New York Review of Books* wrote as follows: "Over his long career, he wrote for *Vanity Fair*, helped edit *The New Republic*, served as chief book critic for *The New Yorker*, and was a frequent contributor to *The New York Review of Books*. Wilson was the author of more than twenty books, including *Axel's Castle*, *Patriotic Gore*, and a work of fiction, *Memoirs of Hecate County*." Wilson's other landmark works were *The Triple Thinkers* (1938) and *The Wound and the Bow* (1941), which contained seminal essays about Dickens, Flaubert, Henry James, Kipling, Pushkin, and Edith Wharton, among others. A good overview of Wilson's work is contained in Louis Menand, "Edmund Wilson and American Culture," *The New Yorker* 81, no. 23 (2005): 82–88. Menand refers to Wilson's role in the conception of *The Library of America* series. The definitive biography of Wilson is Lewis M. Dabney, *Edmund Wilson: A Life in Literature* (New York: Farrar, Straus, & Giroux, 2005).

119. Johnson, *The Public Library–A People's University*, 33.

120. Diana Tixier Herald, *Genreflecting: A Guide to Reading Interests in Genre Fiction*, 5th ed. (Englewood, CO: Libraries Unlimited, 2000).

121. Ibid., 423–448.

122. Ibid., 250–255.

123. Ibid., 205–209.

124. Ibid., v–viii.

125. Ibid., 302–306.

126. Ibid., 176–180.

127. Ibid., 384–389.

128. Anthony J. Fonseca and June Michele Pulliam, *Hooked on Horror: A Guide to Reading Interests in Horror Fiction*, 2nd ed. (Westport, CT: Libraries Unlimited, 2002), v–vii.

129. John Mort, *Christian Fiction: A Guide to the Genre* (Westport, CT: Libraries Unlimited, 2002), v–vii.

130. Diana Tixier Herald, *Fluent in Fantasy: A Guide to Reading Interests* (Englewood, CO: Libraries Unlimited, 1999), v–vii.

131. Sarah L. Johnson, *Historical Fiction: A Guide to the Genre* (Westport, CT: Libraries Unlimited, 2005), v–xiii.

132. This figure was accurate when the NoveList database was accessed on December 15, 2005.

133. English, *The Economy of Prestige*, 36.

134. Rosenberg, *Genreflecting*, 17.

135. Ibid.

136. "Retirees Combine 70 Years of Service," *Discoveries: Downers Grove Public Library* 18, no. 3 (2004), 1. Available from: http://www.downersgrovelibrary.org/Discoveries-/may-june04disc.pdf (accessed March 25, 2006). Information about Downers Grove may be found at: http://edc.downers.us/facts/index.htm (accessed March 25, 2006).

137. Saricks and Brown, *Readers' Advisory Service*, 51, 55.

138. Saricks and Brown, *Readers' Advisory Service*, 2nd ed., 35–36.

139. Ibid., 36.

140. Ibid., 37–38.

141. Ibid., 39.

142. Ibid., 43.

143. Ibid., 47, 50. The first three questions pertain to story line. The last three questions pertain to frame. In the 3rd edition of *Readers' Advisory Service*, Saricks adds a fourth question under story line: "Does the story take place on more than one level?" (p. 57).

144. Saricks, *Readers' Advisory Service*, 3rd ed., 65–66.

145. Joyce G. Saricks, *The Readers' Advisory Guide to Genre Fiction* (Chicago: American Library Association, 2001).

146. Nancy Pearl (with assistance from Martha Knappe and Chris Higashi), *Now Read This: A Guide to Mainstream Fiction, 1978-1998* (Englewood, CO: Libraries Unlimited, 1999); Nancy Pearl, *Now Read This II: A Guide to Mainstream*

Fiction, 1990–2001 (Englewood, CO: Libraries Unlimited, 2002).

147. Saricks and Brown, *Readers' Advisory Service*, 2nd ed., 38.

148. Saricks, *Readers' Advisory Service*, 3rd ed., 75–76.

149. Ibid., 65. Original emphasis.

150. Ibid., 75, 84.

151. Ibid., 75.

152. Ibid.

153. Ibid., 157–158.

154. Diantha Schull, "The Civic Library: A Model for 21st Century Participation," *Advances in Librarianship* 28: 58. Schull quotes Fred Kent and Phil Myrick of the Project for Public Spaces movement. Kent and Myrick's words are originally found in Marylaine Block, "How to Become a Great Public Space," *American Libraries* 34, no. 4 (2003): 72–74, 76.

155. Saricks, *Readers' Advisory Service*, 3rd ed., 130–131.

156. Ibid., 131.

157. Ibid., 127.

158. Ibid., 133–134, 188.

159. Ibid., 181–187.

160. Ibid., 173.

161. Ibid., 84.

162. Ibid.

163. Ibid., 85.

164. Ibid.

165. Ibid., 84, 91–92.

166. Ibid., 88.

167. Agnes Hill, "The Public Library and the People," *Library Journal* 27, no. 1 (1902): 11–15.

168. Saricks and Brown, *Readers' Advisory Service*, 2nd ed., 38–51.

169. David Brooks, *Bobos in Paradise: The New Upper Class and How They Got There* (New York: Simon & Schuster, 2000), 98.

170. Ibid., 84–85.

171. Quoted in Rivkah K. Sass, "An Interview with Duncan Smith, Creator and Product Manager, NoveList," *The Charleston Adviser* (July 2004), 42–44. Available from: http://www.ebscohost.com/uploads/thisTopic-dbTopic-185.pdf (accessed March 23, 2006).

172. Ted Balcom, "The Adult Reading Round Table: Chicken Soup for Readers' Advisors," *Reference & User Services Quarterly* 41, no. 3 (2002): 238–243.

173. Ted Balcom, "Rediscovering Readers' Advisory— and Its Rewards," *Illinois Libraries* 70, no. 9 (1988): 583.

174. Ibid., 585–586.

175. Ibid., 586.

176. Ang, "Culture and Communication," 247.

177. Catherine Sheldrick Ross, "Readers' Advisory Service: New Directions," *RQ* 30, no. 4 (1991): 503–518.

178. Catherine Sheldrick Ross, "Finding without Seeking: The Information Encounter in the Context of Reading for Pleasure," *Information Processing and Management* 35, no. 6 (1999): 793–795.

179. Catherine Sheldrick Ross, "Making Choices: What Readers Say About Choosing Books to Read for Pleasure," *The Acquisitions Librarian* 25 (2001): 5–21; Catherine Sheldrick Ross, "What We Know from Readers about the Experience of Reading," in *The Readers' Advisor's Companion*, eds. Kenneth D. Shearer and Robert Burgin, 77–95 (Englewood, CO: Libraries Unlimited, 2001); Catherine Sheldrick Ross, "'If They Read Nancy Drew, so What?': Series Book Readers Talk Back," *Library & Information Science Research* 17, no. 3 (1995): 201–236. This last article is based on a sub-set of 142 transcribed interviews of 194 "heavy readers."

180. Ross, "Finding without Seeking," 785.

181. Ibid.

182. Ross, "What We Know from Readers," 80–81.

183. Ross, "Making Choices," 6, 8.

184. Ross, "What We Know from Readers," 89.

185. Ibid., 81.

186. Catherine Sheldrick Ross, Lynne (E. F.) McKechnie, and Paulette M. Rothbauer, *Reading Matters: What the Research Reveals about Reading, Libraries, and Community* (Westport, CT: Libraries Unlimited, 2005), 244.

187. Ross, "What We Know from Readers," 90–94.

188. Ibid., 89.

189. Ibid.

190. Catherine Sheldrick Ross and Mary K. Chelton, "Reader's Advisory: Matching Mood and Material," *Library Journal* 126, no. 3 (2001): 55.

191. Ross, McKechnie, and Rothbauer, *Reading Matters*, 192.

192. Ibid., 193. Original emphasis.

193. Alan T. Sorensen, "Bestseller Lists and Product Variety: The Case of Book Sales" (Research Paper No. 1878, Research Paper Series, Stanford Graduate School of Business, 2004). Available from: https://gsbapps.stanford.edu/researchpapers/library/RP1878.pdf (accessed March 26, 2006).

194. Ibid., 18.

195. Ibid.

196. Ibid., 19–20, 22.

197. Ibid., 20.

198. Quoted in David Brooks, "The Education Gap," *New York Times*, 25 September 2005, sec. 4, p. 11.

199. Ibid.

200. Ibid.

201. Michiko Kakutani, "Bending the Truth in a Million Little Ways," *New York Times*, 17 January 2006, sec. E, p. 1.

202. Quoted in Stéphane Baillargeon, "La Fièvre de l'Hyperfestif," *Le Devoir*, 25 June 2005, sec. A, pp. 1, 10. The quotation is our translation from the original French in the cited article.

203. Andrew Wernick, *Promotional Culture: Advertising, Ideology and Symbolic Expression* (London: Sage, 1991).

204. Ibid., 11.

205. Edward Wyatt, "For This Author, Writing Is Only the Beginning," *New York Times*, 22 June 2005, sec. E, pp. 1, 10.

206. Sass, "An Interview with Duncan Smith," 43.

207. Ibid.

208. Ibid.

209. Ibid.

210. Ibid.

211. Ibid., 44.

212. Ibid.

213. Duncan Smith, "Reinventing Readers' Advisory," in *The Readers' Advisor's Companion*, ed. Kenneth D. Shearer and Robert Burgin, 59–76 (Englewood, CO: Libraries Unlimited, 2001).

214. Kenneth Shearer, "The Nature of the Readers' Advisory Transaction in Adult Reading," in *Guiding the Reader to the Next Book*, ed. Kenneth D. Shearer, 1–19 (New York: Neal-Schuman, 1996).

215. Anne K. May, Elizabeth Olesh, Anne Weinlich Miltenberg, and Catherine Patricia Lackner, "A Look at Reader's Advisory Services," *Library Journal* 125, no. 15 (2000): 40–43.

216. Smith, "Reinventing Readers' Advisory," 60.

217. Ibid., 69–70.

218. Ibid., 65.

219. Ibid., 70.

220. Ibid., 72.

221. Ibid., 73.

222. Ibid., 71.

223. Duncan Smith, "Talking with Readers: A Competency Based Approach to Readers' Advisory Service," *Reference & User Services Quarterly* 40, no. 2 (2000): 135–142.

224. Ibid., 138.
225. Ibid., 140.
226. Sass, "An Interview with Duncan Smith," 42.
227. EBSCO Support, "In Book Index with Reviews (BIR), What Is the Advantage of Searchable Full-text Reviews? How Do I Find Books on Topics That Are Not Subject Headings?" Available from: http://support.epnet.com/knowledge_base (accessed March 28, 2006).
228. EBSCO Support, "How Does the Popularity Feature in Book Index with Reviews (BIR) Work?" Available from: http://support.epnet.com/knowledge_base (accessed March 28, 2006).
229. Sass, "An Interview with Duncan Smith," 42.
230. "Sorting Results in NoveList." Available from: http://novelst3.epnet.com/NovApp/novelist/nlc/InfoPages/PopularitySort.htm (accessed June 13, 2006).
231. Carol Collier Kuhlthau, *Seeking Meaning: A Process Approach to Library and Information Services* (Norwood, NJ: Ablex, 1993), 143–144.
232. Ibid., 151.
233. Ibid., 71.
234. Sharon L. Baker, "What Patrons Read and Why: The Link between Personality and Reading," in *Research Issues in Public Librarianship: Trends for the Future*, ed. Joy M. Greiner, 145 (Westport, CT: Greenwood Press, 1994).
235. Ibid., 141–142.
236. Ibid., 143.
237. Ibid.
238. Ibid., 145.
239. Stephen Mihm, "McProfiling," *The New York Times Magazine*, 12 December 2004, p. 83.
240. Ibid.
241. Richard Waters, "Screened Out: Life Online is Widening Choice but Risks a Surrender of Serendipity," *Financial Times* (London, England), 29 December 2005, p. 13.
242. Sander Spek, "Personalisation." Available from: http://www.cs.unimaas.nl/s.spek/personalisation.pdf (accessed March 29, 2006).
243. Ibid.
244. Waters, "Screened Out," 13.
245. Ibid.
246. Kate Moser, "How They Know What You Like Before You Do," *The Christian Science Monitor*, 16 February 2006, p. 13.
247. Laurie J. Flynn, "Like This? You'll Hate That. (Not All Web Recommendations are Welcome.)," *New York Times*, 23 January 2006, sec. C, p. 1, 4.
248. Moser, "How They Know," 13.
249. Ibid.
250. Galant, "They've Got Your Number," 7.
251. "Claritas: Adding Intelligence to Information." Available at: http://www.claritas.com/claritas/Default.jsp and http://www.claritas.com/claritas/Default.jsp?ci=3&si=4&pn=prizmne_segments (accessed April 27, 2006); Bruce Weber, "Building a Better Pigeonhole," *New York Times Book Review*, 27 February 2000, sec. 7, p. 33; Debra Galant, "They've Got Your Number," *New York Times*, 30 March 1997, sec. 13NJ, pp. 1, 7. The figure of 66 clusters or segments was accurate as at April 30, 2006.
252. Patrick Brethour, "Sorry, Your Coefficients Aren't Right for the Job," *The Globe and Mail*, 7 March 2006, sec. B, p. 1, 3.
253. Jon Katz, "'Orwellian Technology No Match for Today's Invasive Corporate Technology, Assault on Privacy." Available from: http://www.freedomforum.org (accessed March 30, 2006).
254. Waters, "Screened Out," 13.
255. Ibid.
256. Ibid.
257. Quoted in Ibid.

258. Smith, "Reinventing Readers' Advisory," 73.
259. Altick, "Education, the Common Reader, and the Future," 278.
260. Ibid., 278, 282.
261. Nancy Pearl and Craig Buthod, "Upgrading the 'McLibrary,'" *Library Journal* 117, no. 17 (1992): 37.
262. Ibid.
263. Quoted in Pearl and Buthod, "Upgrading," 37–38.
264. Ibid., 38.
265. Ibid.
266. Ibid.
267. Nancy Pearl, *Book Lust: Recommended Reading for Every Mood, Moment, and Reason* (Seattle, WA: Sasquatch Books, 2003), vii; Nancy Pearl, *More Book Lust: Recommended Reading for Every Mood, Moment, and Reason* (Seattle, WA: Sasquatch Books, 2005), vii–viii.
268. Pearl, *Book Lust*, vii; Pearl, *More Book Lust*, vii–viii.
269. Each of the four following quotations is taken from Pearl, *More Book Lust*, i.
270. See *American Libraries* 34, no. 9 (2003): 31.
271. Will Manley, "Book Lust: A Celebration of the Written Word," *American Libraries* 35, no. 2 (2004): 72. The blurb quote in *More Book Lust* does not exactly replicate the original. It has been corrected here to reflect the original.
272. "Lust for Reading," *American Libraries* 36, no. 5 (2005): 33–34.
273. Manley, "Book Lust," 72.
274. Pearl, *More Book Lust*, xii–xiii.
275. Kakutani, "Bending the Truth," 1.
276. Pearl, *More Book Lust*, xii.
277. Brian Fawcett, "Dooney's Café," *Books in Canada* 35, no. 2 (2006): 10.
278. Ibid., ix–x.
279. Pearl, *Book Lust*, 88.
280. Ibid., 161.
281. Ibid., 226.
282. Ibid., 40.
283. Ibid., 81.
284. Ibid., 59.
285. Pearl, *More Book Lust*, 237.
286. Pearl, *Book Lust*, xii.
287. Altick, "Education, the Common Reader, and the Future," 280.
288. "R. R. Bowker Partners with H. W. Wilson to Deliver Bowker's Book Analysis System for School and Public Libraries," Available from: http://home.businesswire.com (accessed June 6, 2005). News release dated May 17, 2005.
289. Ibid.
290. Juris Dilevko and Lisa Gottlieb, "The Politics of Standard Selection Guides: The Case of the *Public Library Catalog*," *Library Quarterly* 73, no. 3 (2003): 299.
291. Saricks, *Readers' Advisory Service*, 3rd ed., 27.
292. Thomas J. Hennen Jr., "HAPLR 100 for 2005: Top Ten Libraries in Each Population Category." Available from: http://www.haplr-index.com/HAPLR100.htm (accessed April 30, 2006).
293. All information about the Columbus (Ohio) Metropolitan Library is taken from: http://www.cml.lib.oh.us/ (accessed April 30, 2006).
294. Halifax Public Libraries, "Join Our Online Book Club." Available from: http://www.halifaxpubliclibraries.ca/readerscafe/bookclub.html (accessed April 30, 2006).
295. Johnson County Library, "Fiction Booklists." Available from: http://www.jocolibrary.org/index.asp?DisplayPageID=1754 (accessed March 22, 2006).
296. Waterboro Public Library," "Mostly Fiction: Booklists!" Available from: http://www.waterborolibrary.org/bklista.htm (accessed March 22, 2006).
297. Barry Trott, "Advising Readers Online: A Look at Internet-based Reading Recommendation Services," *Reference & User Services Quarterly* 44, no. 3 (2005): 211.

298. Saricks, *Readers' Advisory Service*, 3rd ed., 27.

299. Trott, "Advising Readers Online," 212. ReadThisNow is available at: http://www.readthisnow.org (accessed March 30, 2006).

300. Saricks, *Readers' Advisory Service*, 3rd ed., 27.

301. Quoted in Trott, "Advising Readers Online," 212.

302. Trott, "Advising Readers Online," 212.

303. Ibid., 214.

304. Ibid., 215.

305. Ibid., 214.

306. Ibid., 213.

307. Lincoln City Libraries, "PEARLs: Personalized Adult Reading Lists." Available from: http://www.lcl.lib.ne.us/depts/bookguide/pearls.htm (accessed March 31, 2006).

308. All multiple-choice wording quoted here is taken directly from: Williamsburg Regional Library, "Looking for a Good Book?" Available from: http://www.wrl.org/bookweb/RA/index.html (accessed March 31, 2006).

309. Trott, "Advising Readers Online," 214.

310. The classic study about deskilling in librarianship remains Roma M. Harris, *The Erosion of a Woman's Profession* (Norwood, NJ: Ablex Publishing, 1992). For the deskilling of cataloging, see Ruth Hafter, *Academic Librarians and Cataloging Networks: Visibility, Quality Control, and Professional Status* (Westport, CT: Greenwood Press, 1986). A good overview of the issues surrounding outsourcing is Claire-Lise Bénaud and Sever Bordeianu, *Outsourcing Library Operations in Academic Libraries: An Overview of Issues and Outcomes* (Englewood, CO: Libraries Unlimited, 1998). For the deskilling and outsourcing of library data entry work, see Steven Ellis, "Data Entry and the Economy of Offshore Information Production," *Library Resources & Technical Services* 41, no. 2 (1997): 112–122. For the deskilling of collection development through approval plans, see, for example, Charles Willett, "Consider the Source: A Case against Outsourcing Material Selection in Academic Libraries," *Collection Building* 17, no. 1 (1998): 91–95; Rebecca Knuth and Donna G. Bair-Mundy, "Revolt over Outsourcing: Hawaii's Librarians Speak out about Contracted Selection," *Collection Management* 23, no.1/2 (1998), 81–112. For deskilling in reference work, see especially chapters 1 and 8 of Juris Dilevko and Lisa Gottlieb, *Reading and the Reference Librarian: The Importance to Library Service of Staff Reading Habits* (Jefferson, NC: McFarland & Co., 2004).

311. Roma M. Harris and Victoria Marshall, "Reorganizing Canadian Libraries: A Giant Step Back from the Front," *Library Trends* 46, no. 3 (1998): 570.

312. Ibid., 570–571.

313. For a different viewpoint about these services, see Raya Kuzyk, "A Reader at Every Shelf," *Library Journal* 131, no. 3 (2006): 32–35.

314. All quotes used to describe DearReader are derived from the wide array of main and subsidiary web pages located at http://www.dearreader.com/ (accessed April 30, 2006).

315. In early 2006, the 11 "daily book clubs" offered by DearReader were: Nonfiction, Fiction, Mystery, Romance, Teen, Prepublication, Audio, Horror, Good News, Business, and Science Fiction (http://www.dearreader.com/service/book_clubs.html). DearReader also offered a "Classics" club, but this was a monthly club: "Every Tuesday on the second week of the month you'll receive an email and you'll be able to read the first two or three chapters from the featured Classic title." The frequency with which DearReader offered readers genre titles and bestsellers, on the one hand, and classics, on the other, spoke volumes about its priorities. For insight into the type of books offered by DearReader, click on "Advance Notice," which appears at http://www.dearreader.com/service/. Upcoming books that form part of DearReaders's 11 daily book clubs are listed here. Most of the selections are genre titles and heavily promoted bestsellers.

316. Kuzyk, "A Reader at Every Shelf," 35.

317. All quotes used to describe BookLetters are derived from the wide array of main and subsidiary web pages located at http://www.bookletters.com/ (accessed April 30, 2006).

318. All quotes used to describe NextReads are derived from the wide array of main and subsidiary web pages located at http://www.nextreads.com/ (accessed April 30, 2006).

319. All quotes used to describe whichbook are derived from the wide array of main and subsidiary web pages located at http://www.whichbook.net (accessed April 30, 2006).

320. Kuzyk, "A Reader at Every Shelf," 33.

321. See http://www.reader2reader.net/ (accessed April 30, 2006).

322. Bourdieu, *The Rules of Art*, 342.

323. Wernick, *Promotional Culture*.

324. Bourdieu, *The Rules of Art*, 344–345.

Chapter 6

1. Two students selected Rohinton Mistry's *A Fine Balance*, and another two students selected Jane Austen's *Pride and Prejudice*.

2. *The Concise Oxford Dictionary of Literary Terms*. Christopher Baldick. Oxford University Press, 1996. *Oxford Reference Online*. Oxford University Press. University of Toronto Libraries. Available from: http://www.oxfordreference.com.myaccess.library.utoronto.ca (accessed August 21, 2004); M. H. Abrams, *A Glossary of Literary Terms*, 7th ed. (Fort Worth: Harcourt Brace College Publishers, 1999).

3. Malcolm Gladwell, "How the Information Age Could Blow away the Blockbuster," *The New Yorker* 75, no. 29 (October 4, 1999): 48–55.

4. Ibid., 50.

5. Ibid.

6. Pat Holt, "That Bookstore in Blytheville: A Talk with Mary Gay Shipley—Part 1." Available from: http://www.holtuncensored.com/members/column321.html (accessed November 21, 2003).

7. Gladwell, "How the Information Age," 51, 54.

8. Ibid., 44–45.

9. Pearl, *More Book Lust*, 91–92.

10. Pearl, *Book Lust*, 23, 26–27.

11. Pearl, *Book Lust*, 238–239; Pearl, *More Book Lust*, 178–180.

12. Ibid., 126–127, 154.

13. Peter Stansky, "Failure, Success, Failure," *New York Times Book Review*, 13 June 1982, sec. 7, p. 12.

14. Quoted in Pearl, *Book Lust*, 45. Pearl quotes Roy Jenkins.

15. John Ramsden, *Man of the Century: Winston Churchill and His Legend since 1945* (London: HarperCollins, 2002), 209.

16. Ibid., 542.

17. Ibid., 545.

18. Michiko Kakutani, "Review of *The Last Lion: Winston Spencer Churchill: Visions of Glory*," *New York Times*, 25 May 1983, sec. C, p. 26.

19. Ramsden, *Man of the Century*, 587.

20. Gerard Degroot, "Review of *Man of the Century: Winston Churchill and his Legend since 1945*: Legend of His Own Making," *Scotland on Sunday*, 24 November 2002, p. 6.

21. Quoted in Degroot, 6. Degroot quotes Lord Plumb.

22. Michael F. Hopkins, "Churchill and the Making of His Legend," *Contemporary Review* 283, no. 1650 (2003): 47–48.

23. Degroot, 6.

24. John Ramsden, *Man of the Century: Winston Churchill and his Legend since 1945* (London: HarperCollins, 2002); Clive Ponting, *Churchill* (London: Sinclair-Stevenson, 1994); and John Charmley's *Churchill: The End of Glory* (London: Hodder & Stoughton, 1993).

25. Degroot, 6.

26. Ibid.

27. Hopkins, 48.

28. John Newsinger, "Churchill: Myth and Imperialist History," *Monthly Review* 46, no. 8 (1995): 56–64.

29. Richard Brooks, "Biographies See Churchill as Far Less Than Saintly: One Calls Him a Racist, the Other an Appeaser," *State Journal Register*, 20 March 1994, p. 51.

30. Louis D. Rubin Jr., "Did Churchill Ruin 'the Great Work of Time'? Thoughts on the New British Revisionism," *Virginia Quarterly Review* 70, no. 1 (1994): 59–78.

31. Roger Adelson and Jonathan Sikorsky, "Review Essay: Churchill in the 1990s," *Historian* 58, no. 1 (1995): 119–23.

32. Barry Gewen, "Forget the Founding Fathers," *New York Times Book Review*, 5 March 2005, sec 7, pp. 30–33.

33. Pearl cross-references David McCollough's *John Adams* in "Founding Fathers," referring readers to "Presidential Biographies" in *Book Lust*.

34. Gewen, 30–33.

35. Ibid.

36. Ibid.

37. Ibid.

38. Woody Holton, *Forced Founders: Indians, Debtors, Slaves, and the Making of the American Revolution in Virginia* (Chapel Hill: University of North Carolina, 1999).

39. Terri L. Synder, "Review of *Forced Founders: Indians, Debtors, Slaves, and the Making of the American Revolution in Virginia*," *The Virginia Magazine of History and Biography* 108, no. 3 (2000): 310–312.

40. Ibid.

41. Robert Gross, "Origins of the American Revolution," *Virginia Quarterly Review* 77, no. 1 (2001): 149–159.

42. Ibid.

43. Brendan McConville, *These Daring Disturbers of the Public Peace: The Struggle for Property and Power in Early New Jersey* (Ithaca, NY: Cornell University Press, 1999).

44. Terry Bouton, "Whose Original Intent? Expanding the Concept of the Founders," *Law and History Review* 19, no. 3 (2001): 661–71.

45. Ibid.

46. Bruce E. Johansen, *Forgotten Founders: How the American Indian Helped Shape Democracy* (Boston: The Harvard Common Press, 1982).

47. Mary Frances Stotler, "Forgotten Founders." Available from: http://web.syr.edu/~mfstotle/johansen.html (accessed March 11, 2006).

48. Gary B. Nash, *The Urban Crucible: Social Change, Political Consciousness, and the Origins of the American Revolution* (Cambridge, MA: Harvard University Press, 1979); Gary B. Nash, *Race, Class, and Politics: Essays on American Colonial and Revolutionary Society* (Urbana: University of Illinois Press, 1986).

49. Carla Gardina Pestana and Sharon V. Salinger, "Introduction: Inequality in Early America," in *Inequality in Early America*, eds. Carla Gardina Pestana and Sharon V. Salinger, 11 (Hanover, NH: University Press of New England, 1999).

50. Raymond A. Mohl, "Review of *The Urban Crucible: Social Change, Political Consciousness, and the Origins of the American Revolution*," *The Journal of American History* 67, no. 2 (1980): 390–391.

51. Nash, *The Urban Crucible*, 384.

52. Mohl, 390–391.

53. Nash, *Race, Class, and Politics*, 212, 235.

54. Elizabeth Cook-Lynn, "The American Indian Fiction Writers: Cosmopolitanism, Nationalism, the Third World, and First Nation Sovereignty," in *Why I Can't Read Wallace Stegner and Other Essays: A Tribal Voice* (Madison: University of Wisconsin Press, 1996), 86.

55. Elizabeth Cook-Lynn, "American Indian Intellectualism and the New Indian Story," *American Indian Quarterly* 20, no. 1 (1996): 57–76.

56. Ibid., 66.

57. Cook-Lynn, "The American Indian Fiction Writers," 80.

58. Cook-Lynn, "American Indian Intellectualism," 67.

59. Susan Bernardin, "The Authenticity Game: 'Getting Real' in Contemporary American Literature," in *True West: Authenticity and the American West*, eds. William R. Handley and Nathaniel Lewis, 155–175 (Lincoln: University of Nebraska Press, 2004). Bernardin quotes Gloria Bird and Louis Owens.

60. Cook-Lynn, "American Indian Intellectualism," 67.

61. Cook-Lynn, "The American Indian Fiction Writers," 85.

62. Cook-Lynn, "American Indian Intellectualism," 68.

63. Ibid., 69.

64. Cook-Lynn, "The American Indian Fiction Writers," 85, 84.

65. Ibid., 86.

66. Kenneth M. Roemer, "Silko's Arroyos as Mainstream: Processes and Implications of Canonical Identity," *Modern Fiction Studies* 45, no. 1 (1999): 27.

67. For a good overview of the negative critical reception accorded *Almanac of the Dead*, see Joni Adamson, *American Indian Literature, Environmental Justice, and Ecocriticism: The Middle Place* (Tucson: University of Arizona Press, 2001), 128–135.

68. Adamson, *American Indian Literature*, 129.

69. Bridget O'Meara, "The Ecological Politics of Leslie Silko's *Almanac of the Dead*," *Wicazo Sa Review: A Journal of Native American Studies* 15, no. 2 (2000): 71.

70. Adamson, *American Indian Literature*, 133.

71. Pearl, *Book Lust*, 23.

72. Cook-Lynn, "The American Indian Fiction Writers," 90–91.

73. Cook-Lynn, "American Indian Intellectualism," 69.

74. Jeffrey Paul Chan, Frank Chin, Lawson Fusao Inada, and Shawn Wong, "Introduction," in *The Big Aiiieeeee! An Anthology of Chinese American and Japanese American Literature*, eds. Jeffrey Paul Chan, Frank Chin, Lawson Fusao Inada, and Shawn Wong, xi-xii (New York: Meridian, 1991).

75. Frank Chin, "Come All Ye Asian American Writers of the Real and the Fake," in *The Big Aiiieeeee! An Anthology of Chinese American and Japanese American Literature*, eds. Jeffrey Paul Chan, Frank Chin, Lawson Fusao Inada, and Shawn Wong, 3 (New York: Meridian, 1991).

76. Chan, Chin, Inada, and Wong, "Introduction," xv-xvi.

77. Ibid., xii-xiii.

78. Laura Miller, "A Change in the Weather," *New York Times Book Review*, 30 November 2003, sec. 7, p. 31.

79. Ibid.

80. Ibid.

81. Ibid.

82. Michiko Kakutani, "Taking on Wildness in Nature or People," *New York Times*, 17 February 2003, sec. E, pp. 1, 12.

83. Ron Charles, "Tune In, Drop Out: Trying to Make a Perfect Society Can Be Such a Drag, Man," *Christian Science Monitor*, 3 March 2003, p. 15.

84. Fred Barnes, "The Truth about Vietnam; It Was a Just War and We Had It Won," *The Weekly Standard* 5, no. 1 (September 20, 1999): 31–34.

85. Robert D. Novak, "What Happens When Reporters

Make War," *The Weekly Standard* 1, no. 18 (January 15, 1996): 36.

86. Ibid.

87. Ibid., 38.

88. James Fallows, "In Defense of an Offensive War," *New York Times Book Review*, 28 March 1982, sec. 7, p. 7.

89. Pearl, *Book Lust*, 126.

90. Edward Said, "Impossible Histories: Why the Many Islams Cannot Be Simplified," *Harper's Magazine* 305, no. 1826 (July 2002): 69–74.

91. These three titles are mentioned by Edward Said in the second last paragraph of the review essay cited in the previous endnote.

92. Edward Said, *Orientalism* [Twenty-fifth anniversary edition] (New York: Vintage Books, 2003), 316. Original emphasis.

93. Said, "Impossible Histories," 69–74.

94. Ibid.

95. Said, *Orientalism*, 318–319.

96. Ibid., 341.

97. Ibid., 4.

98. Pearl, *Book Lust*, 80–81.

99. Said, "Impossible Histories," 69–74.

100. Anonymous, "Review of *A Portrait of Egypt: A Journey through the World of Militant Islam*," *Virginia Quarterly Review* 75, no. 3 (1999): 99–101.

101. Jerome Slater, "Review of *Six Days of War: June 1967 and the Making of the Modern Middle East*," *Political Science Quarterly* 118, no. 2 (2003): 363.

102. Norman G. Finkelstein, "Abba Eban with Footnotes," *Journal of Palestine Studies* 32, no. 3 (2003): 74–89.

103. Micah L. Sifry, "Sermon from the Mount," *The Nation* 249, no. 17 (November 20, 1989): 605–607.

104. Ibid.

105. Pearl, *Book Lust*, 154.

106. Thomas Frank, "It's Globalicious! Two Servings, Half-baked, of the New Economy," *Harper's Magazine* 299, no. 1793 (October 1999): 72–75; Amitabh Pal, "The Pooh Bah of Capitalism," *The Progressive* 63, no. 7 (July 1999): 41–43.

107. Frank, "It's Globalicious!" 72.

108. Pal, "The Pooh Bah of Capitalism," 41.

109. William A. McWhirter, "Blinkers On: A Journalist Looks at Global Changes in Technology and Finance but Doesn't See the Whole Picture," *Chicago Tribune*, 18 April 1989, p. 3.

110. Jackson Lears, "The Magicians of Money," *The New Republic* 232, no. 23 (June 20, 2005): 35–44.

111. David C. Korten, "We Are the Capitalists. You Will Be Assimilated. Resistance is Futile," *Tikkun* 14, no. 4 (July/August 1999): 71–76.

112. Said, *Orientalism*, 351.

113. Pearl, *Book Lust*, xii.

114. Dilevko and Gottlieb, "The Politics of Standard Selection Guides," 299.

Chapter 7

1. All quotes about George Kyle are taken from the following two articles: Joel Currier, "Library Gets $351,000 Bequest: Longtime Clerk's Gift Is Probably the Largest Ever by a Former Employee, Officials Say," *St. Louis Post-Dispatch*, 5 May 2005, sec. B, p. 1; Associated Press, "St. Louis Library Clerk Leaves $350,000," *New York Times* [online], 9 May 2005. Accessed May 10, 2005.

2. Currier, "Library Gets $351,000 Bequest," 1.

3. Murray C. Bob, "The Case for Quality Book Selection," *Library Journal* 107, no. 16 (1982): 1707.

4. Ibid.

5. Ibid., 1708.

6. Ibid., 1708–1709.

7. Quoted in Birge, *Serving Adult Learners*, 128, 132.

8. Reilly, *The Public Librarian as Adult Learners' Advisor*, 21.

9. Steven Johnson, *Everything Bad is Good for You: How Today's Popular Culture is Actually Making us Smarter* (New York: Riverhead Books, 2005), xiii.

10. Ibid., 41.

11. Ibid., 61.

12. Ibid., 65, 63.

13. Ibid., 41.

14. John C. Beck and Mitchell Wade, *Got Game: How the Gamer Generation is Reshaping Business Forever* (Boston: Harvard Business School Press, 2004), front flap.

15. Ibid., 11–14, 77.

16. Thomas L. Friedman, *The World Is Flat: A Brief History of the Twenty-first Century* (updated and expanded edition) (New York: Farrar, Straus and Giroux, 2006), 218–222.

17. Quoted in George Scialabba, "Zippie World!" *The Nation* 280, no. 23 (June 13, 2005): 39.

18. Ibid., 40.

19. Thomas, "The Great Chick Lit Conspiracy," 2.

20. Clive Thompson, "Meet the Life Hackers," *New York Times Magazine*, 16 October 2005, p. 40.

21. Epstein, "Is Reading Really at Risk?" 21.

22. David Brooks, "Harvard-Bound? Chin Up," *New York Times*, 2 March 2006, sec. A, p. 27.

23. Peter Beinart, "Failing Grade," *The New Republic* 234, no. 8 (March 6, 2006): 6.

24. Brooks, "Harvard-Bound?" 27.

25. Leitch, *American Literary Criticism*, 405.

26. Brooks, "Harvard-Bound?" 27.

27. Miller, *Reluctant Capitalists*, 215.

28. Ibid., 214.

29. Ibid., 223–229.

30. Schull, "The Civic Library," 58.

31. Brooks, "Harvard-Bound?" 27.

32. Learned, *The American Public Library and the Diffusion of Knowledge*, 12–13, 15–16.

33. Johnson, *The Public Library—A People's University*, 1, 4–5.

34. Ibid., 5.

35. Altick, "Education, the Common Reader, and the Future," 278, 275–276.

36. Leigh, *The Public Library in the United States*, 48.

37. Compton, *Who Reads What?* 35.

38. Lee, *Continuing Education for Adults*, 43.

39. See the definition for right-sizing at http://www.wordspy.com/words/rightsizing.asp (accessed April 27, 2006).

40. Cutter, "Common Sense in Libraries," 151.

41. Berelson, "Reply to the Discussants," 64.

42. Ibid.

43. Farquhar, "The Organization Plan for Adult Education in a Public Library," 182.

Bibliography

Except where indicated otherwise, all English-language newspaper articles were accessed through LexisNexis: Total Research System, which is available by subscription at www.lexis.com. Lexis-Nexis is a division of Reed Elsevier Inc.

Abrams, M. H. *A Glossary of Literary Terms*, 7th ed. Fort Worth: Harcourt Brace College Publishers, 1999.

Addams, Jane. *Twenty Years at Hull-House with Autobiographical Notes*. New York: The Macmillan Company, 1910.

Adelson, Roger, and Jonathan Sikorsky. "Review Essay: Churchill in the 1990s." *Historian* 58, no. 1 (1995): 119–23.

Adler, Mortimer J. *A Second Look in the Rearview Mirror: Further Autobiographical Reflections of a Philosopher at Large*. New York: Macmillan, 1992.

"ALA Activities Committee Report." *ALA Bulletin* 24, no. 12 (1930): 607–680.

"A.L.A.'s 'Great Issues' Program." *ALA Bulletin* 42, no. 1 (1948): 81.

Aldridge, John W. *Talents and Technicians: Literary Chic and the New Assembly-Line Fiction*. New York: Charles Scribner's Sons, 1992.

Altick, Richard D. "Education, the Common Reader, and the Future." *ALA Bulletin* 60, no. 3 (1966): 275–282.

Andrew, John A., III. *The Other Side of the Sixties: Young Americans for Freedom and the Rise of Conservative Politics*. New Brunswick, NJ: Rutgers University Press, 1997.

Ang, Ien. "Culture and Communication: Towards an Ethnographic Critique of Media Consumption in the Transnational Media System." *European Journal of Communication* 5, no. 2/3 (2000): 239–260.

"Appendixes to the Librarian's Report." *Twenty-sixth Annual Report of the Trustees of the Public Library 1878*. City of Boston, City Document No. 61, 1878.

"Appendixes to the Librarian's Report." *Twenty-eighth Annual Report of the Trustees of the Public Library 1880*. City of Boston, City Document No. 94, 1880.

"Appendixes to the Librarian's Report." *Thirtieth Annual Report of the Trustees of the Public Library 1882*. City of Boston, City Document No. 92, 1880.

"Are the Classics Read?" *Library Journal* 38, no. 3 (1912): 145–146.

Arnold, Martin. "Placed Products, and Their Cost." *New York Times*, 13 September 2001, sec. E, p. 3.

Asheim, Lester. "Response to the Great Issues Program." *ALA Bulletin* 44, no. 7 (1950): 285–289.

_____. *Training Needs of Librarians Doing Adult Education Work: A Report of the Allerton Park Conference, November 14–16, 1954*. Chicago: American Library Association, 1955.

Associated Press. "St. Louis Library Clerk Leaves $350,000." *New York Times* [online], 9 May 2005. (Accessed May 10, 2005).

Baillargeon, Stéphane. "La Fièvre de l'Hyperfestif." *Le Devoir*, 25 June 2005, sec. A, pp. 1, 10.

Baker, Sharon L. "What Patrons Read and Why: The Link between Personality and Reading." In *Research Issues in Public Librarianship: Trends for the Future*. Edited by Joy M. Greiner, 131–147. Westport, CT: Greenwood Press, 1994.

_____. "Will Fiction Classification Schemes Increase Use?" *RQ* 27, no. 3 (1988): 366–376.

Baker, Sharon L., and Gay W. Shepherd. "Fiction Classification Schemes: The Principles behind Them and Their Success." *RQ* 27, no. 2 (1987): 245–251.

Baker, Sharon L., and Karen L. Wallace. *The Responsive Public Library: How to Develop and Market a Winning Collection*. 2nd ed. Englewood, CO: Libraries Unlimited, 2002.

Balcom, Ted. "The Adult Reading Round Table: Chicken Soup for Readers' Advisors." *Reference & User Services Quarterly* 41, no. 3 (2002): 238–243.

_____. "Rediscovering Readers' Advisory—and Its Rewards." *Illinois Libraries* 70, no. 9 (1988): 583–586.

Baldick, Christopher. *The Concise Oxford Dictionary of Literary Terms*. Oxford University Press, 1996. *Oxford Reference Online*. Oxford University Press. University of Toronto Libraries. Available at http://www.oxfordreference.com.myaccess.library.utoronto.ca (accessed August 21, 2004).

Baltimore County Public Library's Blue Ribbon Committee. *Give 'Em What They Want: Managing the Public's Library*. Chicago: American Library Association, 1992.

Barden, John P. "The Great Books and the Good Life." *Wilson Library Bulletin* 22, no. 4 (1947): 313–316.

Barnes, Fred. "The Truth about Vietnam; It Was a Just

War and We Had It Won." *The Weekly Standard* 5, no. 1 (September 20, 1999): 31–34.

Bates, Marston. *Expanding Population in a Shrinking World.* Chicago: American Library Association, 1963.

Baudry, Leo. *Frenzy of Renown: Fame and Its History.* New York: Oxford University Press, 1986.

Beck, John C., and Mitchell Wade. *Got Game: How the Gamer Generation is Reshaping Business Forever.* Boston: Harvard Business School Press, 2004.

Beinart, Peter. "Failing Grade." *The New Republic* 234, no. 8 (March 6, 2006): 6.

Berelson, Bernard. "Reply to the Discussants." In *A Forum on the Public Library Inquiry: The Conference at the University of Chicago Graduate Library School, August 8–13, 1949.* Edited by Lester Asheim, 60–65. New York: Columbia University Press, 1950.

Berelson, Bernard, and Lester Asheim. *The Library's Public.* New York: Columbia University Press, 1949.

Bernardin, Susan. "The Authenticity Game: 'Getting Real' in Contemporary American Literature." In *True West: Authenticity and the American West.* Edited by William R. Handley and Nathaniel Lewis, 155–175. Lincoln: University of Nebraska Press, 2004.

Bernstein, Viv. "Eau de Nascar: Licensing and the Smell of Money." *New York Times,* 12 March 2006, sec. 8, p. 5.

Birge, E. A. "The Effect of the 'Two-Book System' on Circulation." *Library Journal* 23, no. 3 (1898): 93–101.

Birge, Lynn E. *Serving Adult Learners: A Public Library Tradition.* Chicago: American Library Association, 1981.

Blackshear, Orrilla T. "A Bibliotherapy Workshop." *Wisconsin Library Bulletin* 60, no. 5 (1964): 296–298.

Block, Marylaine. "How to Become a Great Public Space." *American Libraries* 34, no. 4 (2003): 72–74.

Bloom, Alan. *The Closing of the American Mind.* New York: Simon and Schuster, 1987.

Bob, Murray C. "The Case for Quality Book Selection." *Library Journal* 107, no. 16 (1982): 1707–1710.

Bobinski, George S. *Carnegie Libraries: Their History and Impact on American Public Library Development.* Chicago: American Library Association, 1969.

Bolton, C. Knowles. "Better Circulation in Small Libraries—The 'Two-Book' System." *Library Journal* 19, no. 5 (1894): 161–162.

Booton, Mabel. "A Close View of Advisory Service: In a Large Library." In *Helping Adults to Learn: The Library in Action.* Edited by John Chancellor, 9–26. Chicago: American Library Association, 1939.

Borden, William Alanson. "On Classifying Fiction." *Library Journal* 34, no. 6 (1909): 264–265.

Bordin, Ruth. *Woman and Temperance: The Quest for Power and Liberty, 1873–1900.* Philadelphia, PA: Temple University Press, 1981.

Bosman, Julie. "A Match Made in Product Placement Heaven." *New York Times,* 31 May 2006, sec. C, p. 3.

Bostwick, Arthur E. "The Purchase of Current Fiction." *Library Journal* 28, no. 7 (1903): C31–C33.

Bourdieu, Pierre. *Distinction: A Social Critique of the Judgement of Taste.* Translated by Richard Nice. Cambridge, MA: Harvard University Press, 1984.

_____. "The Market of Symbolic Goods." In *The Field of Cultural Production: Essays on Art and Literature.* Edited and introduced by Randal Johnson, 112–141. Cambridge, UK: Polity Press, 1993.

_____. "The Production of Belief: Contribution to an Economy of Symbolic Goods." In *The Field of Cultural Production: Essays on Art and Literature.* Edited by Randal Johnson, 74–111. Cambridge, UK: Polity Press, 1993.

_____. *The Rules of Art: Genesis and Structure of the Literary Field.* Translated by Susan Emanuel. Cambridge, UK: Polity Press, 1996.

Bourdieu, Pierre, and Loïc J. D. Wacquant. *An Invitation to Reflexive Sociology.* Chicago: University of Chicago Press, 1992.

Bouricius, Ann. *The Romance Readers' Advisory: The Librarian's Guide to Love in the Stacks.* Chicago: American Library Association, 2000.

Bouton, Terry. "Whose Original Intent? Expanding the Concept of the Founders." *Law and History Review* 19, no. 3 (2001): 661–71.

Bowerman, George F. "The Public Library of the District of Columbia as an Organ of Social Advance." *Charities and the Commons* 16, no. 2 (1906): 105–110.

Boxer, Sarah. "Literary Sport: The Roar of the Crowd, the Review of the Books." *New York Times,* 17 February 2005, sec. E, pp. 1, 5.

Brethour, Patrick. "Sorry, Your Coefficients Aren't Right for the Job." *The Globe and Mail,* 7 March 2006, sec. B, p. 1, 3.

Brooks, David. *Bobos in Paradise: The New Upper Class and How They Got There.* New York: Simon & Schuster, 2000.

_____. "The Education Gap." *New York Times,* 25 September 2005, sec. 4, p. 11.

_____. "Harvard-Bound? Chin Up." *New York Times.* 2 March 2006, sec. A, p. 27.

_____. "Joe Strauss to Joe Six-Pack." *New York Times,* 16 June 2005, sec. A, p. 27.

Brooks, Richard. "Biographies See Churchill as Far Less Than Saintly: One Calls Him a Racist, the Other an Appeaser." *State Journal Register,* 20 March 1994, p. 51.

Brooks, Robert C. *Russia: The Soviet Way.* Chicago: American Library Association, 1933.

Brown, Eleanor Frances. *Bibliotherapy and Its Widening Applications.* Metuchen, NJ: Scarecrow Press, 1975.

Brubeck, Viarda Clark. "A Close View of Advisory Service: In a Small Public Library." In *Helping Adults to Learn: The Library in Action.* Edited by John Chancellor, 3–9. Chicago: American Library Association, 1939.

Bryan, Alice I. "Can There Be a Science of Bibliotherapy?" *Library Journal* 64, no. 18 (1939): 773–776.

_____. "Leigh, Robert Devore" (1890–1961)." In *Dictionary of American Library Biography.* Edited by Bohdan S. Wynar, 310–313. Littleton, CO: Libraries Unlimited, 1978.

_____. "Personality Adjustment through Reading." *Library Journal* 64, no. 14 (1939): 573–576.

_____. "The Psychology of the Reader." *Library Journal* 64, no. 1 (1939): 7–12.

_____. "The Reader as a Person." *Library Journal* 65, no. 4 (1940): 137–141.

Burgin, Robert. ed. *Nonfiction Readers' Advisory.* Westport, CT: Libraries Unlimited, 2004.

Butler, Helen L. "An Inquiry into the Statement of Motives by Readers." *Library Quarterly* 10, no. 1 (1940): 1–49.

Caldwell, Rebecca. "CBC Fishes 1928 Novel out of

Obscurity." *The Globe and Mail*, 26 February 2005, sec. R, p. 11.

Cannell, Jeffrey, and Eileen McCluskey. "Generefication: Fiction Classification and Increased Circulation." In *Guiding the Reader to the Next Book*. Edited by Kenneth D. Shearer, 159–165. New York: Neal-Schuman, 1996.

Carlton, W. N. C. *English Literature*. Chicago: American Library Association, 1925.

Carnegie, Andrew. *Autobiography of Andrew Carnegie*. Boston: Houghton Mifflin, 1920.

Carnegie Corporation of New York. *Report of the President & of the Treasurer*. New York: Carnegie Corporation, 1929.

Carnovsky, Leon. "Community Studies in Reading: II. Hinsdale, A Suburb of Chicago." *Library Quarterly* 5, no. 1 (1935): 1–30.

Carr, Nancy. "Indigo Sees Itself as Purveyor of Lifestyle." *Toronto Star*, 15 September 2004, sec. E, p. 2.

Carrier, Esther Jane. *Fiction in Public Libraries, 1876–1900*. New York: Scarecrow Press, 1965.

_____. *Fiction in Public Libraries, 1900–1950*. Littleton, CO: Libraries Unlimited, 1985.

Carvajal, Doreen. "Amazon.com Plans to Revise Its Ad Program." *New York Times*, 10 February 1999, sec. C, p. 1.

_____. "For Sale: On-Line Bookstore's Recommendations." *New York Times*, 8 February 1999, sec. A, pp. 1, 21.

Cawelti, John G. *Adventure, Mystery, and Romance: Formula Stories as Art and Popular Culture*. Chicago: University of Chicago Press, 1976.

Chambers, John Whiteclay, II. *The Tyranny of Change: America in the Progressive Era, 1890–1920*, 2nd ed. New York: St. Martin's Press, 2000.

Chan, Jeffrey Paul, Frank Chin, Lawson Fusao Inada, and Shawn Wong. "Introduction." In *The Big Aiiieeeee! An Anthology of Chinese American and Japanese American Literature*. Edited by Jeffrey Paul Chan, Frank Chin, Lawson Fusao Inada, and Shawn Wong, xi–xvi. New York: Meridian, 1991.

Chancellor, John. "The Smaller Library and Adult Education." In *Helping Adults to Learn: The Library in Action*. Edited by John Chancellor, 197–205. Chicago: American Library Association, 1939.

Charles, Ron. "Tune In, Drop Out: Trying to Make a Perfect Society Can Be Such a Drag, Man." *Christian Science Monitor*, 3 March 2003, p. 15.

Charmley, John. *Churchill: The End of Glory*. London: Hodder & Stoughton, 1993.

Chelton, Mary K., ed. "Readers' Advisory." *Reference & User Services Quarterly* 40, no. 2 (2000): 135.

Chiles, Nick. "Their Eyes Were Reading Smut." *New York Times*, 4 January 2006, sec. A, p. 21.

Chin, Frank. "Come All Ye Asian American Writers of the Real and the Fake." In *The Big Aiiieeeee! An Anthology of Chinese American and Japanese American Literature*. Edited by Jeffrey Paul Chan, Frank Chin, Lawson Fusao Inada, and Shawn Wong, 1–92. New York: Meridian, 1991.

Cohen, Max. "The Librarian an Educator, and not a Cheap-John." *Library Journal* 13, no. 12 (1888): 366–367.

Commission on Non-Traditional Study. *Diversity by Design*. San Francisco, CA: Jossey-Bass, 1973.

Commission on the Library and Adult Education.

Libraries and Adult Education: Report of a Study Made by the American Library Association. Chicago: American Library Association, 1926.

Compton, Charles H. "The Outlook for Adult Education in the Library." *Adult Education and the Library* 3, no. 3 (1928): 59–71.

_____. *Who Reads What? Essays on the Readers of Mark Twain, Hardy, Sandburg, Shaw, William James, the Greek Classics*. New York: H. W. Wilson Company, 1934.

Cook-Lynn, Elizabeth. "The American Indian Fiction Writers: Cosmopolitanism, Nationalism, the Third World, and First Nation Sovereignty." In *Why I Can't Read Wallace Stegner and Other Essays: A Tribal Voice*, 78–96. Madison: University of Wisconsin Press, 1996.

_____. "American Indian Intellectualism and the New Indian Story." *American Indian Quarterly* 20, no. 1 (1996): 57–76.

Cords, Sarah Stanz, and Robert Burgin. *The Real Story: A Guide to Nonfiction Reading Interests*. Westport, CT: Libraries Unlimited, 2006.

Crowley, Bill. "A History of Readers' Advisory Service in the Public Library." In *Nonfiction Readers' Advisory*. Edited by Robert Burgin, 3–29. Westport, CT: Libraries Unlimited, 2004.

_____. "Rediscovering the History of Readers Advisory Service." *Public Libraries* 44, no. 1 (2005): 37–41.

Crunden, Frederick M. "How Things Are Done in One American Library: Board and Staff Organization and Finances." *The Library* 1 (2nd. series, 1900): 147–152.

_____. "How Things Are Done in One American Library: Juvenile Department, [etc.]." *The Library* 2 (2nd. series, 1900): 20–43.

_____. "How Things Are Done in One American Library: Registration and Circulation." *The Library* 1 (2nd. series, 1900): 384–406.

_____. "How Things Are Done in One American Library: Selection, Purchase, and Cataloguing of Books." *The Library* 1 (2nd. series, 1900): 290–298.

_____. "How Things Are Done in One American Library: The New Novel Problem and Its Solution." *The Library* 1 (2nd. series, 1900): 92–100.

_____. "The Library as a Factor in the Intellectual Life of St. Louis." *Library Journal* 15, no. 5 (1890): 138–139.

_____. "The Most Popular Books." *Library Journal* 16, no. 9 (1891): 277–278.

_____. "Report on Aids and Guides, August, '83, to June, '85." *Library Journal* 11, no. 8/9 (1886): 309–330.

Currier, Joel. "Library Gets $351,000 Bequest: Longtime Clerk's Gift Is Probably the Largest Ever by a Former Employee, Officials Say." *St. Louis Post-Dispatch*, 5 May 2005, sec. B, p. 1

Cutter, Charles A. "Common Sense in Libraries." *Library Journal* 14, no. 5/6 (1889): 147–154.

_____. "Should Libraries Buy Only the Best Books or the Best Books that People Will Read?" *Library Journal* 26, no. 2 (1901): 70–72.

Davies, D. W. "Libraries as Social & Entertainment Centers." In *Public Librarianship: A Reader*. Edited by Jane Robbins-Carter, 109–127. Littleton, CO: Libraries Unlimited, 1982.

Debord, Guy. *Society of the Spectacle*. Detroit, MI: Black and Red, 1983.

Degroot, Gerard. "Review of *Man of the Century: Winston Churchill and his Legend since 1945*: Legend of His Own Making." *Scotland on Sunday*, 24 November 2002, 6.

Dewey, Melvil. "Advice to a Librarian." *Public Libraries* 2, no. 6 (1897): 266–267.

Dilevko, Juris, and Keren Dali. "Electronic Databases for Readers' Advisory Services and Intellectual Access to Translated Fiction Not Originally Written in English." *Library Resources & Technical Services* 47, no. 3 (2003): 80–95.

Dilevko, Juris, and Lisa Gottlieb. *The Evolution of Library and Museum Partnerships: Historical Antecedents, Contemporary Manifestations, and Future Directions.* Westport, CT: Libraries Unlimited, 2004.

_____ and _____. "The Politics of Standard Selection Guides: The Case of the *Public Library Catalog*." *Library Quarterly* 73, no. 3 (2003): 289–337.

Dillon, Sam. "Literacy Falls for Graduates from College, Testing Finds." *New York Times*, 16 December 2005, sec. A, p. 34.

Ditzion, Sidney. *Arsenals of a Democratic Culture: A Social History of the American Public Library Movement in New England and the Middle States from 1850 to 1900.* Chicago: American Library Association, 1947.

Donadio, Rachel. "Promotional Intelligence." *New York Times Book Review*, 21 May 2006, sec. 7, p. 31.

_____. "She'd Be Great on TV." *New York Times Book Review*, 26 June 2005, sec 7, p. 27.

Doud, Margery. "The Readers' Advisory Service of the St. Louis Public Library." In *St. Louis Public Library Annual Report 1928–1929*. St. Louis, MO: 1929.

_____. "The Veteran via the Public Library: A Symposium: Readers' Advisory Service." *Catholic Library World* 18, no. 5 (1947): 139–141.

Douglas, William O. *Freedom of the Mind.* Chicago: American Library Association, 1962.

Doyle, Robert C. "Review of *Stolen Valor: How the Vietnam Generation Was Robbed of Its Heroes and Its History*." *H-Net Reviews in the Humanities & Social Sciences* (May 1999). Available at http://www.h-net.org/reviews/showpdf.cgi?path=6326927655094 (accessed April 23, 2006).

Drury, F. K. W. "Six Years' Activity in Adult Education." *ALA Bulletin* 25, no. 1 (1931): 31–37.

Du Mont, Rosemary Ruhig. *Reform and Reaction: The Big City Public Library in American Life.* Westport, CT: Greenwood Press, 1977.

Egan, Margaret. "An Experiment in Advisory Service and Graded Reading in the C.C.C. Camps." *Library Quarterly* 7, no. 4 (1937): 471–491.

English, James F. *The Economy of Prestige: Prizes, Awards, and the Circulation of Value.* Cambridge, MA: Harvard University Press, 2005.

Epstein, Joseph. "Is Reading Really at Risk?" *The Weekly Standard* 9, no. 46 (August 16–23, 2004): 19–23.

Fallows, James. "In Defense of an Offensive War." *New York Times Book Review*, 28 March 1982, sec. 7, p. 7.

Farquhar, Alice M. "The Organization Plan for Adult Education in a Public Library." In *Helping Adults to Learn: The Library in Action*. Edited by John Chancellor, 182–187. Chicago: American Library Association, 1939.

Fawcett, Brian. "Dooney's Café." *Books in Canada* 35, no. 2 (2006): 10.

"Fiction at the Boston Public Library." [reprint]. *Library Journal* 6, no. 7 (1881): 204–205.

Finkelstein, Norman G. "Abba Eban with Footnotes." *Journal of Palestine Studies* 32, no. 3 (2003): 74–89.

Fiske, John. *Understanding Popular Culture.* Boston, MA: Unwin Hyman, 1989.

Fister, Barbara. "'Reading as a Contact Sport': Online Book Groups and the Social Dimension of Reading." *Reference & User Services Quarterly* 44, no. 4 (2005): 303–309.

Flavelle, Dana. "Next Chapter for Indigo: More Gifts." *Toronto Star*, 9 June 2004, sec. E, p. 1.

Flexner, Abraham. *Universities: American, English, German.* New York: Oxford University Press, 1930.

Flexner, Jennie M., and Sigrid A. Edge. *A Readers' Advisory Service.* New York: American Association for Adult Education, 1934.

Flexner, Jennie M., and Byron C. Hopkins. *Readers' Advisers at Work: A Survey of Development in the New York Public Library.* New York: American Association for Adult Education, 1941.

Flynn, Laurie J. "Like This? You'll Hate That. (Not All Web Recommendations are Welcome.)." *New York Times*, 23 January 2006, sec. C, p. 1, 4.

Fonseca, Anthony J., and June Michele Pulliam. *Hooked on Horror: A Guide to Reading Interests in Horror Fiction*, 2nd ed. Westport, CT: Libraries Unlimited, 2002.

Foster, Jeannette Howard. "An Approach to Fiction through the Characteristics of Its Readers." *Library Quarterly* 6, no. 2 (1936): 124–174.

Foster, W. E. "Methods of Securing the Interest of a Community." *Library Journal* 5, no. 9/10 (1880): 245–247.

_____. "On Aimless Reading and Its Correction." *Library Journal* 4, no. 3 (1879): 78–80.

_____. "Report on Aids and Guides to Readers: 1883." *Library Journal* 8, no. 9/10 (1883): 233–247.

_____. "The School and the Library: Their Mutual Relation." *Library Journal* 4, no. 9/10 (1879): 319–325.

Frank, Robert H., and Philip J. Cook. *The Winner-Take-All Society: How More and More Americans Compete for Ever Fewer and Bigger Prizes, Encouraging Economic Waste, Income Inequality, and an Impoverished Cultural Life.* New York: Free Press, 1995.

Frank, Thomas. "It's Globalicious! Two Servings, Half-baked, of the New Economy." *Harper's Magazine* 299, no. 1793 (October 1999): 72–75

Freedman, Samuel G. "The Achievement Gap in Elite Schools." *New York Times*, 28 September 2005, sec. C, p. 21.

Friedman, Thomas L. *The World Is Flat: A Brief History of the Twenty-first Century* (updated and expanded edition). New York: Farrar, Straus and Giroux, 2006.

Friend, Tad. "The Parachute Artist." *The New Yorker* 81, no. 9 (April 18, 2005): 78–91.

Frykholm, Amy Johnson. *Rapture Culture: Left Behind in Evangelical America.* New York: Oxford University Press, 2004.

Gannon, Michael B. *Blood, Bedlam, Bullets, and Badguys: A Reader's Guide to Adventure/Suspense Fiction.* Westport, CT: Libraries Unlimited, 2004.

Gans, Herbert J. *Popular Culture and High Culture: An Analysis and Evaluation of Taste.* New York: Basic Books, 1974.

Garland, Hamlin. *The Westward March of American Settlement.* Chicago: American Library Association, 1927.

Garrett, George. "'Once More unto the Breach, Dear Friends, Once More': The Publishing Scene and American Literary Art." *Review of Contemporary Fiction* 8, no. 3 (1988): 97–106.

Garrison, Dee. *Apostles of Culture: The Public Librarian and American Society, 1876–1920.* New York: Free Press, 1979.

_____. "The Tender Technicians: The Feminization of Public Librarianship, 1876–1905." *Journal of Social History* 6, no. 2 (1972/1973): 131–159.

Geertz, Clifford. *Available Light: Anthropological Reflections on Philosophical Topics.* Princeton, NJ: Princeton University Press, 2001.

_____. "Thick Description: Toward an Interpretive Theory of Culture." In *The Interpretation of Cultures: Selected Essays,* 3–30. New York: Basic Books, 1973.

Gewen, Barry. "Forget the Founding Fathers." *New York Times Book Review,* 5 March 2005, sec. 7, pp. 30–33.

Gillmor, Don. "Anatomy of a Bestseller." *Toronto Life* 37, no. 9 (2003): 86–92.

Gladwell, Malcolm. "How the Information Age Could Blow away the Blockbuster." *The New Yorker* 75, no. 29 (October 4, 1999): 48–55.

Glatzer, Jenna. "Book Packaging: Under-explored Terrain for Freelancers." Available at http://www.absolutewrite.com/site/book_packaging.htm (accessed March 12, 2006).

Graeff, Virginia E. "The Gentle Librarian: A Transcript from Experience." *Library Journal* 30, no. 12 (1905): 922–923.

Gray, William S., and Ruth Munroe. *The Reading Interests and Habits of Adults: A Preliminary Report.* New York: The Macmillan Company, 1930.

Green, Samuel S. "Aids and Guides for Readers." *Library Journal* 7, no. 7/8 (1882): 139–147.

_____. "Personal Relations between Librarians and Readers." *Library Journal* 1, no. 2 (1876): 74–81.

_____. "Second Session: Novel-Reading." *Library Journal* 1, no. 2 (1876): 99.

_____. "Sensational Fiction in Public Libraries." *Library Journal* 4, no. 9/10 (1879): 345–355.

Grenfell, Wilfred T. *Religion in Everyday Life.* Chicago: American Library Association, 1926.

Gross, Robert. "Origins of the American Revolution." *Virginia Quarterly Review* 77, no. 1 (2001): 149–159.

Haines, Helen E. *Living with Books: The Art of Book Selection.* New York: Columbia University Press, 1935.

_____. "Technics or Humanization in Librarianship?" *Library Journal* 63, no. 15 (1938): 619–627.

Hakim, Danny. "Would You Base the Purchase of a Car on the Prose of a Chick-lit Novelist? Ford Hopes So." *New York Times,* 23 March 2004, sec. C, p. 1.

Hall, Stuart. "Notes on Deconstructing 'the Popular.'" In *Cultural Theory and Popular Culture: A Reader.* Edited by John Storey, 465–466. New York: Harvester Wheatsheaf, 1994.

Hannigan, Margaret C. "Counseling and Bibliotherapy for the General Reader." In *Reading Guidance Institute June 29–July 2, 1965,* 59–65. Madison: The University of Wisconsin Library School and University Extension Division, Department of Library Science.

Hansen, Andrew M. "RASD: Serving Those Who Serve the Public." Available at http://www.ala.org/ala/rusa/rusapubs/rusq/specialfeatures/rasdhistory/rasdhistory1.htm (accessed February 8, 2006).

Harig, Katherine J. *Libraries, the Military, & Civilian Life.* Hamden, CT: Library Professional Publications, 1989.

Harrell, Gail. "Use of Fiction Categories in Major American Public Libraries." In *Guiding the Reader to the Next Book.* Edited by Kenneth D. Shearer, 149–157. New York: Neal-Schuman, 1996.

Harris, Michael H. "The Purpose of the American Public Library: A Revisionist Interpretation of History." *Library Journal* 98, no. 16 (1973): 2509–2514.

_____. "State, Class, and Cultural Reproduction: Toward a Theory of Library Service in the United States." *Advances in Librarianship* 14 (1986): 211–252.

Harris, Michael H., and Gerard Spiegler. "Everett, Ticknor and the Common Man: The Fear of Societal Instability as the Motivation for the Founding of the Boston Public Library." *Libri* 24, no. 4 (1974): 249–275.

Harris, Roma M., and Victoria Marshall. "Reorganizing Canadian Libraries: A Giant Step Back from the Front." *Library Trends* 46, no. 3 (1998): 564–580.

Harwell, Richard, and Roger Michener. "As Public as the Town Pump." *Library Journal* 99, no. 7 (1974): 959–963.

Hawes, Marion E. "The Role of the Large Public Library in Adult Education." *Library Trends* 8, no. 1 (1959): 15–40.

Hayes, Bartlett H., Jr. *The Contemporary Arts.* Chicago: American Library Association, 1962.

Hayward, Almira L. "The Training of a Librarian." *Library Journal* 17, no. 12 (1892): 478–480.

Heilbroner, Robert L. *The World of Economics.* Chicago: American Library Association, 1963.

Henderson, Maude R. "The Librarian as a Host." *Public Libraries* 1, no. 5 (1896): 187–189.

Herald, Diana Tixier. *Fluent in Fantasy: A Guide to Reading Interests.* Englewood, CO: Libraries Unlimited, 1999.

_____. *Genreflecting: A Guide to Popular Reading Interests.* Edited by Wayne A. Wiegand. 6th ed. Westport, CT: Libraries Unlimited, 2006.

_____. *Genreflecting: A Guide to Reading Interests in Genre Fiction.* 5th ed. Englewood, CO: Libraries Unlimited, 2000.

Herald, Diana Tixier, and Bonnie Kunzel. *Strictly Science Fiction: A Guide to Reading Interests.* Westport, CT: Libraries Unlimited, 2002.

Hill, Agnes. "The Public Library and the People." *Library Journal* 27, no. 1 (1902): 11–15.

Hill, Frank P. "Fiction in Libraries." *Library Journal* 15, no. 11 (1890): 325.

Hodgson, Godfrey. *The World Turned Right Side Up: A History of the Conservative Ascendancy in America.* Boston: Houghton Mifflin, 1996.

Hoffman, Frank W. *Popular Culture and Libraries.* Hamden, CT: Shoe String Press, 1984.

Holt, Pat. "That Bookstore in Blytheville: A Talk with Mary Gay Shipley—Part I." Available at http://www.holtuncensored.com/members/column321.html (accessed November 21, 2003).

Holton, Woody. *Forced Founders: Indians, Debtors, Slaves, and the Making of the American Revolution in Virginia.* Chapel Hill: University of North Carolina, 1999.

Hopkins, Michael F. "Churchill and the Making of His Legend." *Contemporary Review* 283, no. 1650 (2003): 47–48.

Houle, Cyril O. "Chicago Public Library Staff Studies Adult Education." *Library Journal* 71, no. 1 (1946): 23–27, 47.

Houser, L., and Alvin M. Schrader. *The Search for a Scientific Profession: Library Science Education in the U.S. and Canada.* Metuchen, NJ: Scarecrow Press, 1978.

Hubbard, James M. "How to Use a Public Library." *Library Journal* 9, no. 2 (1884): 25–29.

Hutchins, Robert M. "The Public Library: Its Place in Education." *Library Quarterly* 20, no. 3 (1950): 180–186.

"Individualizing Library Service." *Libraries (A Continuation of Public Libraries)* 33, no. 6 (1928): 279–301.

Isom, Mary Frances. "The Library a Civic Center." *Public Libraries* 19, no. 2 (1914): 93–96.

Jackson, Evalene P. "Bibliotherapy and Reading Guidance: A Tentative Approach to Theory." *Library Trends* 11, no. 2 (1962): 118–126.

Jauss, Hans Robert. "Theory of Genres and Medieval Literature." In *Toward an Aesthetic of Reception.* Translated by Timothy Bahti, 76–109. Minneapolis: University of Minnesota Press, 1982.

Jennings, Judson T. "Sticking to Our Last." *Library Journal* 49, no. 13 (1924): 613–618.

Joeckel, Carleton Bruns, and Leon Carnovsky. *A Metropolitan Library in Action: A Survey of the Chicago Public Library.* Chicago: University of Chicago Press, 1940.

Joeckel, Carleton Bruns, and Amy Winslow. *A National Plan for Public Library Service: Prepared for the Committee on Postwar Planning of the American Library Association.* Chicago: American Library Association, 1948.

Johansen, Bruce E. *Forgotten Founders: How the American Indian Helped Shape Democracy.* Boston: The Harvard Common Press, 1982.

Johnson, Alvin S. *The Public Library—A People's University.* New York: American Association for Adult Education, 1938.

_____. *A Report to Carnegie Corporation of New York on the Policy of Donations to Free Public Libraries.* New York: Carnegie Corporation, 1915.

Johnson, Roberta. "Origins of Fiction_L." *Reference & User Services Quarterly* 42, no. 1 (2002): 30–33.

Johnson, Sarah L. *Historical Fiction: A Guide to the Genre.* Westport, CT: Libraries Unlimited, 2005.

Johnson, Steven. *Everything Bad is Good for You: How Today's Popular Culture is Actually Making us Smarter.* New York: Riverhead Books, 2005.

Kakutani, Michiko. "Bending the Truth in a Million Little Ways." *New York Times,* 17 January 2006, sec. E, p. 1.

_____. "Review of *The Last Lion: Winston Spencer Churchill: Visions of Glory.*" *New York Times,* 25 May 1983, sec. C, p. 26.

_____. "Taking on Wildness in Nature or People." *New York Times,* 17 February 2003, sec. E, pp. 1, 12.

Karetzky, Stephen. *Reading Research and Librarianship: A History and Analysis.* Westport, CT: Greenwood Press, 1976.

Kellogg, Vernon *Biology.* Chicago: American Library Association, 1925.

Kelso, Tessa L. "Some Economical Features of Public Libraries." *The Arena* 7, no. 6 (1893): 709–713.

Kennedy, Randy. "Cash Up Front." *New York Times Book Review,* 5 June 2005, sec. 7, pp. 14–15.

Kilgannon, Corey. "Street Lit with Publishing Cred: Relentless Aaron's Journey from Prison to Four-Book Deal." *New York Times,* 14 February 2006, sec. E. pp. 1, 7.

Kimball, Melanie A. "A Brief History of Readers' Advisory." In Diana Tixier Herald, *Genreflecting: A Guide to Popular Reading Interests.* Edited by Wayne A. Wiegand. 6th ed., 15–23. Westport, CT: Libraries Unlimited, 2006.

Kite, William. "Fiction in Public Libraries." *Library Journal* 1, no. 8 (1877): 277–279.

Klatch, Rebecca E. *A Generation Divided: The New Left, The New Right, and the 1960s.* Berkeley: University of California Press, 1999.

Koch, Theodore Wesley. *Books in the War: The Romance of Library War Service.* Boston: Houghton Mifflin Company, 1919.

_____. *War Service of the American Library Association.* Washington, DC: American Library Association War Service, Library of Congress, 1918.

Korten, David C. "We Are the Capitalists. You Will Be Assimilated. Resistance Is Futile." *Tikkun* 14, no. 4 (July/August 1999): 71–76.

Krieg, Laurel. "Community Studies in Reading: IV. A Middle-Western Manufacturing Community." *Library Quarterly* 9, no. 1 (1939): 72–86.

Kroeger, Alice B. "The Encouragement of Serious Reading: Survey of the Field." *Library Journal* 28, no. 5 (1903): 222–225.

Kuhlthau, Carol Collier. *Seeking Meaning: A Process Approach to Library and Information Services.* Norwood, NJ: Ablex, 1993.

Larsen, Hanna Astrup. *Scandinavian Literature.* Chicago: American Library Association, 1930.

Lasch, Christopher. *The Culture of Narcissism: American Life in an Age of Diminishing Expectations.* New York: W. W. Norton, 1979.

Learned, William S. *The American Public Library and the Diffusion of Knowledge.* New York: Harcourt, Brace and Company, 1924.

Lears, Jackson. "The Magicians of Money." *The New Republic* 232, no. 23 (June 20, 2005): 35–44.

Lee, Robert Ellis. *Continuing Education for Adults through the American Public Library, 1833–1964.* Chicago: American Library Association, 1966.

Leigh, Robert D. *The Public Library in the United States: The General Report of the Public Library Inquiry.* New York: Columbia University Press, 1950.

Leitch, Vincent B. *American Literary Criticism from the Thirties to the Eighties.* New York: Columbia University Press, 1988.

"Librarian's Report." *Twenty-eighth Annual Report of the Trustees of the Public Library 1880.* City of Boston, City Document No. 94, 1880.

"Librarian's Report." *Twenty-ninth Annual Report of the Trustees of the Public Library 1881.* City of Boston, City Document No. 97, 1881.

"Librarian's Report." *Thirtieth Annual Report of the Trustees of the Public Library 1882.* City of Boston, City Document No. 92, 1880.

Locke, Alain. *The Negro in America.* Chicago: American Library Association, 1933.

Locke, George. *English History.* Chicago: American Library Association, 1930.

Lorenzen, Michael. "Deconstructing the Philanthropic Library: The Sociological Reasons behind Andrew Carnegie's Millions to Libraries." Available at http://michaellorenzen.com/carnegie.html (accessed November 2, 2005).

Lupton, A. W. "Social Activities of the Library." *Library Journal* 39, no. 6 (1914): 441–443.

Luyt, Brendan. "Regulating Readers: The Social Origins of the Readers' Advisor in the United States." *Library Quarterly* 71, no. 4 (2001): 443–466.

Lyman, Helen Hugenor. "The Art of Reading Guidance." In *Reading Guidance Institute June 29–July 2, 1965*, 67–81. Madison: The University of Wisconsin Library School and University Extension Division, Department of Library Science.

_____. "Discussion Groups and World Understanding." *ALA Bulletin* 46, no. 2 (1952): 43–44.

_____. *Reader's Guidance Service in a Small Public Library*. Chicago: American Library Association, 1962.

Lynd, Robert S., and Helen Merrell Lynd. *Middletown: A Study in American Culture*. New York: Harcourt, Brace and Company, 1929.

Lytle, Mark Hamilton. *America's Uncivil Wars: The Sixties Era from Elvis to the Fall of Richard Nixon*. New York: Oxford University Press, 2006.

Maack, Mary Niles. "Bryan, Alice I. (1902–1992)." In *Dictionary of American Library Biography, Second Supplement*. Edited by Donald G. Davis, Jr., 43–47. Westport, CT: Libraries Unlimited, 2003.

Manley, Will. "Book Lust: A Celebration of the Written Word." *American Libraries* 35, no. 2 (2004): 72.

Manly, Lorne. "The Goat at Saks and Other Marketing Tales." *New York Times*, sec. C, pp. 1, 4.

Marchese, Theodore J. "U.S. Higher Education in the Postwar Era: Expansion and Growth." *U.S. Society & Values* 2, no. 4 (1997). Available at http://usinfo.state.gov/journals/itsv/1297/ijse/marchese.htm (accessed February 23, 2006).

Martin, Lowell. "The American Public Library as a Social Institution." In Barbara McCrimmon (selector and introducer), *American Library Philosophy: An Anthology*, 88–105. Hamden, CT: Shoe String Press, 1975.

_____. "Guided Group Reading as a Library Service: The Chicago Project." *Library Journal* 71, no. 10 (1946): 734–739.

Matthews, Mildred V. D. "Readers' Services: Role as Adult Educators." *Library Journal* 79, no. 3 (1954): 170–176.

May, Anne K., Elizabeth Olesh, Anne Weinlich Miltenberg, and Catherine Patricia Lackner. "A Look at Reader's Advisory Services." *Library Journal* 125, no. 15 (2000): 40–43.

McCallum, Judi, and Debbie Walker. ""A 'Wow!' Library": FIS Grads Plan Markham's Library for the 21st Century." *Informed* 57 (December 2005): 9.

McConville, Brendan. *These Daring Disturbers of the Public Peace: The Struggle for Property and Power in Early New Jersey*. Ithaca, NY: Cornell University Press, 1999.

McCook, Kathleen de la Peña, and Gary O. Rolstad, eds. *Developing Readers' Advisory Services: Concepts and Commitments*. New York: Neal-Schuman, 1993.

McHenry, Elizabeth. *Forgotten Readers: Recovering the Lost History of African American Literary Societies*. Durham, NC: Duke University Press, 2002.

McNett, Gavin. "Reaching to the Converted: Oprah's Book Club Introduces Readers to People They Already Know—Themselves." *Salon*, 12 November 1999. Available at http://www.salon.com/books/feature/1999/11/12/oprahcon/index.html (accessed May 8, 2005).

McPheron, Judith. "A Critique of the Progressive Public Library Movement in America." In *Library Lit. 8–The Best of 1977*. Edited by Bill Katz, 285–293. Metuchen, NJ: Scarecrow Press, 1978.

McWhirter, William A. "Blinkers On: A Journalist Looks at Global Changes in Technology and Finance but Doesn't See the Whole Picture." *Chicago Tribune*, 18 April 1989, p. 3.

Medway, Hazel I. "Understanding the Reader." In *Helping the Reader toward Self-Education*. Edited by John Chancellor, Miriam D. Tompkins, and Hazel I. Medway, 55–70. Chicago: American Library Association, 1938.

Meiklejohn, Alexander. *Philosophy*. Chicago: American Library Association, 1926.

Mickelson, Peter. "American Society and the Public Library in the Thought of Andrew Carnegie." *The Journal of Library History* 10, no. 2 (1975): 117–138.

Mihm, Stephen. "McProfiling." *The New York Times Magazine*, 12 December 2004, p. 83.

Miksa, Francis. "The Interpretation of American Public Library History." In *Public Librarianship: A Reader*. Edited by Jane Robbins-Carter, 73–90. Littleton, CO: Libraries Unlimited, 1982.

Miller, Laura. "A Change in the Weather." *New York Times Book Review*, 30 November 2003, sec. 7, p. 31.

Miller, Laura J. *Reluctant Capitalists: Bookselling and the Culture of Consumption*. Chicago: University of Chicago Press, 2006.

Mohl, Raymond A. "Review of *The Urban Crucible: Social Change, Political Consciousness, and the Origins of the American Revolution*." *The Journal of American History* 67, no. 2 (1980): 390–391.

Monroe, Margaret E. "Flexner, Jennie Maas (1882–1944)." In *Dictionary of American Library Biography*. Edited by Bohdan S. Wynar, 179–182. Littleton, CO: Libraries Unlimited, 1978.

_____. *Library Adult Education: The Biography of an Idea*. New York: Scarecrow Press, 1963.

_____. "Reading Guidance as a Fundamental Library Service." In *Reading Guidance Institute June 29–July 2, 1965*, 19–27. Madison: The University of Wisconsin Library School and University Extension Division, Department of Library Science.

Montopoli, Brian. "A Publisher Borrows a Page from the Movies." *New York Times*, 27 June 2005, sec. C, p. 4.

Moran, Joe. *Star Authors: Literary Celebrity in America*. London: Pluto Press, 2000.

Mort, John. *Christian Fiction: A Guide to the Genre*. Westport, CT: Libraries Unlimited, 2002.

Moser, Kate. "How They Know What You Like Before You Do." *The Christian Science Monitor*, 16 February 2006, p. 13.

Mumford, Lewis. *Architecture*. Chicago: American Library Association, 1926.

Munson, Edward L. "Libraries and Reading as an Aid to Morale." *ALA Bulletin* 13, no. 3 (1919): 184–187.

Nadel, Alan. *Containment Culture: American Narratives,*

Postmodernism, and the Atomic Age. Durham, NC: Duke University Press, 1995.

Nafisi, Azar. *Reading Lolita in Tehran: A Memoir in Books.* New York: Random House, 2003.

Nash, Gary B. *Race, Class, and Politics: Essays on American Colonial and Revolutionary Society.* Urbana: University of Illinois Press, 1986.

____. *The Urban Crucible: Social Change, Political Consciousness, and the Origins of the American Revolution.* Cambridge, MA: Harvard University Press, 1979.

Newman, Andrew Adam. "Placing Products, Advertisers Find Room at the Inn." *New York Times,* 5 September 2005, sec. C, p. 5.

Newsinger, John. "Churchill: Myth and Imperialist History." *Monthly Review* 46, no. 8 (1995): 56–64.

Niebuhr, Gary Warren. *Make Mine a Mystery: A Reader's Guide to Mystery and Detective Fiction.* Westport, CT: Libraries Unlimited, 2003.

Nolen, John. "Aid from University Extension Methods." *Library Journal* 28, no. 5 (1903): 225–227.

Novak, Robert D. "What Happens When Reporters Make War." *The Weekly Standard* 1, no. 18 (January 15, 1996): 36.

Olasky, Marvin. *The Tragedy of American Compassion.* Washington, DC: Regnery Publishing, 1992.

O'Meara, Bridget. "The Ecological Politics of Leslie Silko's *Almanac of the Dead.*" *Wicazo Sa Review: A Journal of Native American Studies* 15, no. 2 (2000): 63–73.

Osburn, Charles B. *Academic Research and Library Resources: Changing Patterns in America.* Westport, CT: Greenwood Press, 1979.

Paglia, Camille. "The Nursery-School Campus: The Corrupting of the Humanities in the U.S." In *Vamps & Tramps: New Essays,* 97–102. New York: Vintage Books, 1994.

____. "An Open Letter to the Students at Harvard." In *Vamps & Tramps: New Essays,* 117–121. New York: Vintage Books, 1994.

Paine, Paul M. "The Library's Task in Reconstruction." *ALA Bulletin* 13, no. 3 (1919): 117–120.

Pal, Amitabh. "The Pooh Bah of Capitalism." *The Progressive* 63, no. 7 (July 1999): 41–43.

Parker, Alison M. *Purifying America: Women, Cultural Reform, and Pro-Censorship Activism, 1873-1933.* Urbana: University of Illinois Press, 1997.

Parker, Ian. "Absolute Powerpoint: Can a Software Package Edit Our Thoughts." *The New Yorker* 77, no. 13 (May 28, 2001): 76–87.

Pawley, Christine. *Reading on the Middle Border: The Culture of Print in Late-Nineteenth-Century Osage, Iowa.* Amherst: University of Massachusetts Press, 2001.

Pearl, Nancy. *Book Lust: Recommended Reading for Every Mood, Moment, and Reason.* Seattle, WA: Sasquatch Books, 2003.

____. "Gave 'Em What They Wanted." *Library Journal* 121, no. 14 (1996): 136–138.

____. *More Book Lust: Recommended Reading for Every Mood, Moment, and Reason.* Seattle, WA: Sasquatch Books, 2005.

____. *Now Read This: A Guide to Mainstream Fiction, 1978-1998.* Englewood, CO: Libraries Unlimited, 1999.

____. *Now Read This II: A Guide to Mainstream Fiction, 1990-2001.* Englewood, CO: Libraries Unlimited, 2002.

Pearl, Nancy, and Craig Buthod. "Upgrading the 'McLibrary.'" *Library Journal* 117, no. 17 (1992): 37–39.

Peck, A. L. "What May a Librarian Do to Influence the Reading of a Community?" *Library Journal* 22, no. 2 (1897): 77–80.

____. "Workingmen's Clubs and the Public Library." *Library Journal* 23, no. 11 (1898): 612–614.

Pejtersen, Annelise Mark. "Fiction and Library Classification." *Scandinavian Public Library Quarterly* 11, no. 1 (1978): 5–12.

Pejtersen, Annelise Mark, and Jutta Austin. "Fiction Retrieval: Experimental Design and Evaluation of a Search System Based on Users' Value Criteria (Part 1)." *Journal of Documentation* 39, no. 4 (1983): 230–246.

____ and ____. "Fiction Retrieval: Experimental Design and Evaluation of a Search System Based on Users' Value Criteria (Part 2)." *Journal of Documentation* 40, no. 1 (1984): 25–35.

Pestana, Carla Gardina, and Sharon V. Salinger. "Introduction: Inequality in Early America." In *Inequality in Early America.* Edited by Carla Gardina Pestana and Sharon V. Salinger, 1–22. Hanover, NH: University Press of New England, 1999.

Piereson, James. "The Left University." *The Weekly Standard* 11, no. 3 (October 3, 2005): 21–30.

Poe, Clarence. *Farm Life: Problems and Opportunities.* Chicago: American Library Association, 1931.

Ponting, Clive. *Churchill.* London: Sinclair-Stevenson, 1994.

Porter, Noah. *Books and Reading, or What Books Shall I Read and How Shall I Read Them?* Freeport, NY: Books For Libraries Press, 1972 [reprint of the 1881 ed.].

Postman, Neil. *Amusing Ourselves to Death: Public Discourse in the Age of Show Business.* New York: Viking, 1985.

Powell, John. "One Step Nearer Leadership: Guided Group Reading as a Library Service." *Library Journal* 71, no. 7 (1946): 443–449.

"Preliminary Report of Committee on Enlarged Program for American Library Service." *Library Journal* 44, no. 10 (1919): 645–653.

Price, Paxton P. "Compton, Charles Herrick (1880–1966)." In *Dictionary of American Library Biography.* Edited by Bohdan S. Wynar, 91–94. Littleton, CO: Libraries Unlimited, 1978.

Quincy, J. P. "Free Libraries." In *Public Libraries in the United States of America: Their History, Condition, and Management: Part I,* 389–402. Washington, DC: Government Printing Office; reprinted by the University of Illinois Graduate School of Library Science Monograph Series Number 4.

Radway, Janice A. *Reading the Romance: Women, Patriarchy, and Popular Literature.* Chapel Hill: University of North Carolina Press, 1984.

Ramsden, John. *Man of the Century: Winston Churchill and His Legend since 1945.* London: HarperCollins, 2002.

Ranck, Samuel H. "The Relation of the Public Library to Technical Education." *Library Journal* 36, no. 6 (1911): 278–285.

Rathbone, Frances L. "A Successful Experiment in Directing the Reading of Fiction." *Library Journal* 32, no. 9 (1907): 406–408.

Rathbone, Josephine Adams. "The Classification of Fiction." *Library Journal* 27, no. 3 (1902): 121–124.

Rawlinson, Nora. "Give 'Em What They Want!" *Library Journal* 106, no. 20 (1981): 2188–2196.

Regan, Lee. "Status of Reader's Advisory Service." *RQ* 12, no. 3 (1973): 227–233.

Reilly, Jane A. *The Public Librarian as Adult Learners' Advisor: An Innovation in Human Services.* Westport, CT: Greenwood Press, 1981.

Reitz, Joan M. *Dictionary for Library and Information Science.* Westport, CT: Libraries Unlimited, 2004.

_____. *Online Dictionary for Library and Information Science.* Westport, CT: Libraries Unlimited, 2004. Available at http://lu.com.odlis (accessed December 31, 2005).

"Report of the Examining Committee." *Fifteenth Annual Report of the Trustees of the Public Library 1867.* City of Boston, City Document No. 114, 1867.

"Report of the Examining Committee." *Twenty-sixth Annual Report of the Trustees of the Public Library 1878.* City of Boston, City Document No. 61, 1878.

"Report of the Examining Committee." *Twenty-ninth Annual Report of the Trustees of the Public Library 1881.* City of Boston, City Document No. 97, 1881.

"Review of *A Portrait of Egypt: A Journey through the World of Militant Islam.*" *Virginia Quarterly Review* 75, no. 3 (1999): 99–101.

Rhoades, Rachel. "The Work of a Library Information Desk." *Library Journal* 39, no. 5 (1914): 350–353.

Rich, Motoko. "Product Placement Deals Make Leap from Film to Books." *New York Times,* 12 June 2006, sec. C, pp. 1, 5.

Rich, Motoko, and Dinita Smith. "First, Plot and Character. Then, Find an Author." *New York Times,* 27 April 2006, sec. A, p. 1.

Richardson, John V., Jr. *The Gospel of Scholarship: Pierce Butler and a Critique of American Librarianship.* Metuchen, NJ: Scarecrow Press, 1992.

_____. *The Spirit of Inquiry: The Graduate Library School at Chicago, 1921–51.* Chicago: American Library Association, 1982.

Ridgway, Helen A. "Community Studies in Reading: III. Reading Habits of Adult Non-Users of the Public Library." *Library Quarterly* 6, no. 1 (1936): 1–33.

Riding, Alan. "Pierre Bourdieu, 71, French Thinker and Globalization Critic [Obituary]." *New York Times,* 25 January 2002, sec. A, p. 21.

Roemer, Kenneth M. "Silko's Arroyos as Mainstream: Processes and Implications of Canonical Identity." *Modern Fiction Studies* 45, no. 1 (1999): 10–37.

Rose, Jonathan. *The Intellectual Life of the British Working Classes.* New Haven, CT: Yale University Press, 2001.

Rosenberg, Betty. *Genreflecting: A Guide to Reading Interests in Genre Fiction.* Littleton, CO: Libraries Unlimited, 1982.

Rosenberg, Betty, and Diane Tixier Herald. *Genreflecting: A Guide to Reading Interests in Genre Fiction,* 3rd ed. Englewood, CO: Libraries Unlimited, 1991.

Rosenberg, Ida. "Directing the Taste of Casual Readers." *Public Libraries* 13, no. 7 (1908): 295–299.

Ross, Catherine Sheldrick. "Finding without Seeking: The Information Encounter in the Context of Reading for Pleasure." *Information Processing and Management* 35, no. 6 (1999): 783–799.

_____. "'If They Read Nancy Drew, So What?' Series Book Readers Talk Back." *Library & Information Science Research* 17, no. 3 (1995): 201–236.

_____. "Making Choices: What Readers Say About Choosing Books to Read for Pleasure." *The Acquisitions Librarian* 25 (2001): 5–21.

_____. "Readers' Advisory Service: New Directions." *RQ* 30, no. 4 (1991): 503–518.

_____. "What We Know from Readers about the Experience of Reading." In *The Readers' Advisor's Companion.* Edited by Kenneth D. Shearer and Robert Burgin, 77–95. Englewood, CO: Libraries Unlimited, 2001.

Ross, Catherine Sheldrick, and Mary K. Chelton. "Reader's Advisory: Matching Mood and Material." *Library Journal* 126, no. 3 (2001): 52–55.

Ross, Catherine Sheldrick, Lynne (E. F.) McKechnie, and Paulette M. Rothbauer. *Reading Matters: What the Research Reveals about Reading, Libraries, and Community.* Westport, CT: Libraries Unlimited, 2005.

Rothrock, Mary U. "On Some Library Questions of Our Time." *ALA Bulletin* 41, no. 7 (1947): 241–246.

Rothstein, Edward. "Strumming the Mystic Chords of Memory." *New York Times,* 19 April 2005, sec. E., pp. 1, 7.

Rubin, Louis D., Jr. "Did Churchill Ruin 'the Great Work of Time'? Thoughts on the New British Revisionism." *Virginia Quarterly Review* 70, no. 1 (1994): 59–78.

Rubin, Rhea Joyce, ed. *Bibliotherapy Sourcebook.* Phoenix, AZ: Oryx Press, 1978.

_____. *Using Bibliotherapy: A Guide to Theory and Practice.* Phoenix, AZ: Oryx Press, 1978.

Russell, William F. *American Education.* Chicago: American Library Association, 1926.

Rutzen, A. Ruth. "The Marshall Plan—Pro and Con." *ALA Bulletin* 42, no. 1 (1948): 10–14.

_____. "The Readers' Advisory Corps in the Large City Public Library: In a Large Open-Shelf Room." In *Helping Adults to Learn: The Library in Action.* Edited by John Chancellor, 27–32. Chicago: American Library Association, 1939.

Said, Edward. "Impossible Histories: Why the Many Islams Cannot Be Simplified." *Harper's Magazine* 305, no. 1826 (July 2002): 69–74.

_____. *Orientalism* [Twenty-fifth anniversary edition]. New York: Vintage Books, 2003.

Sanderson, Lucia H. "A Many-sided Adult Education Program: In a Large Library." In *Helping Adults to Learn: The Library in Action.* Edited by John Chancellor, 155–163. Chicago: American Library Association, 1939.

Saricks, Joyce G. *The Readers' Advisory Guide to Genre Fiction.* Chicago: American Library Association, 2001.

_____. *Readers' Advisory Service in the Public Library.* 3rd ed. Chicago: American Library Association, 2005.

Saricks, Joyce G., and Nancy Brown. *Readers' Advisory Service in the Public Library.* Chicago: American Library Association, 1989.

_____ and _____. *Readers' Advisory Service in the Public Library.* 2nd ed. Chicago: American Library Association, 1997.

Schiffrin, André. *The Business of Books: How International Conglomerates Took over Publishing and Changed the Way We Read.* London: Verso, 2000.

Schull, Diantha. "The Civic Library: A Model for 21st Century Participation." *Advances in Librarianship* 28 (2004): 55–81.

Scialabba, George. "Zippie World!" *The Nation* 280, no. 23 (June 13, 2005): 37–40.

Sharkey, Joe. "Honorable Soldiers; Debunking the Myth of the Vietnam Vet." *The Weekly Standard* 3, no. 49 (September 7, 1998): 36–38.

Shearer, Kenneth D., ed. *Guiding the Reader to the Next Book*. New York: Neal-Schuman, 1996.

Shearer, Kenneth. D., and Robert Burgin, eds. *The Readers' Advisor's Companion*. Englewood, CO: Libraries Unlimited, 2001.

Shera, Jesse H. *The Foundations of Education for Librarianship*. New York: Becker and Hayes, 1972.

_____. *Foundations of the Public Library: The Origins of the Public Library Movement in New England 1629–1855*. Hamden, CT: Shoe String Press, 1965.

Shields, Gerald R. "Another Hornblowing Bandwagon." *Library Journal* 100, no. 10 (1975): 927.

Shortt, May. "Advisers Anonymous, Arise!" *Ontario Library Review* 49, no. 2 (1965): 81–83.

Sifry, Micah L. "Sermon from the Mount." *The Nation* 249, no. 17 (November 20, 1989): 605–607.

Silverman, Oscar A. "Why Read the Great Books?" *Wilson Library Bulletin* 22, no. 4 (1947): 317–330.

Slater, Jerome. "Review of *Six Days of War: June 1967 and the Making of the Modern Middle East*." *Political Science Quarterly* 118, no. 2 (2003): 363.

Slosson, Edwin E. "How the Public Library Looks to a Journalist." *Library Journal* 40, no. 11 (1915): 786–790.

Smith, Duncan. "Reinventing Readers' Advisory." In *The Readers' Advisor's Companion*. Edited by Kenneth D. Shearer and Robert Burgin, 59–76. Englewood, CO: Libraries Unlimited, 2001.

_____. "Talking with Readers: A Competency Based Approach to Readers' Advisory Service." *Reference & User Services Quarterly* 40, no. 2 (2000): 135–142.

Smith, Helen Lyman. *Adult Education Activities in Public Libraries*. Chicago: American Library Association, 1954.

Smith, J. Russell. *Geography and Our Need of It*. Chicago: American Library Association, 1928.

Spratford, Becky Siegel, and Tammy Hennigh Clausen. *The Horror Readers' Advisory: The Librarian's Guide to Vampires, Killer Tomatoes, and Haunted Houses*. Chicago: American Library Association, 2004.

Stansky, Peter. "Failure, Success, Failure." *New York Times Book Review*, 13 June 1982, sec. 7, p. 12.

Stellin, Susan. "Library Science, Home Depot Style." *New York Times*, 4 November 2004, sec. F, p. 10.

Stevens, E. F. "Adult Erudition." *Libraries (A Continuation of Public Libraries)* 34, no. 6 (1934): 250–254.

Stevenson, Gordon. "Popular Culture and the Public Library." *Advances in Librarianship* 7 (1977): 177–229.

Stevenson, Grace Thomas. "ALA's New Project." *ALA Bulletin* 45, no. 9 (1951): 301–303.

_____. "Recent Developments in the Methods by which People are Encouraged to Use Public Libraries and Improve their Personal Interests through Books in the United States of America." *Libri* 13, no. 3/4 (1963): 285–296.

_____. "The Role of the Public Library in Adult Reading." In *Adult Reading: The Fifty-fifth Yearbook of the National Society for the Study of Education Part II*. Edited by Nelson B. Henry, 114–135. Chicago: University of Chicago Press, 1956.

Stewart, Cora. "Libraries in Relation to Settlement Work." *Library Journal* 31, no. 8 (1906): C82-C85.

Stotler, Mary Frances. "Forgotten Founders." Available at http://web.syr.edu/~mfstotle/johansen.html (accessed March 11, 2006).

Swift, Lindsay. "Paternalism in Public Libraries." *Library Journal* 24, no. 11 (1899): 609–618.

Synder, Terri L. "Review of *Forced Founders: Indians, Debtors, Slaves, and the Making of the American Revolution in Virginia*." *The Virginia Magazine of History and Biography* 108, no. 3 (2000): 310–312.

Taylor, Frederick Winslow. *The Principles of Scientific Management*. New York: Harper & Brothers, 1911.

Tews, Ruth M. ed. *Bibliotherapy*. Special Issue of *Library Trends* 11, no. 2 (1962).

"The American Heritage Project at Work." *Wilson Library Bulletin* 27, no. 6 (1953): 436–450.

"The Library as a Social Center." *Public Libraries* 21, no. 7 (1916): 315–316.

"The Predominance of Fiction in Public Libraries." *Library Journal* 30, no. 8 (1905): 473–474.

"The Public Library and Allied Agencies." *Library Journal* 30, no. 8 (1905): 459–472.

Thomas, Scarlett. "The Great Chick Lit Conspiracy." *Independent on Sunday* (London), 4 August 2002, pp. 1, 2.

Thompson, C. Seymour. "Comment on the Reply." *Library Journal* 56, no. 16 (1931): 746–747.

_____. "Do We Want a Library Science?" *Library Journal* 56, no. 13 (1931): 581–587.

Thompson, Clive. "Meet the Life Hackers." *New York Times Magazine*, 16 October 2005, pp. 40–45.

"Those Who Follow Reading Courses." *Adult Education and the Library* 3, no. 2 (1928): 35–43.

"'Topic Blanks' at Cincinnati Public Library." *Library Journal* 28, no. 5 (1903): 239.

Trott, Barry. "Advising Readers Online: A Look at Internet-Based Reading Recommendation Services." *Reference & User Services Quarterly* 44, no. 3 (2005): 210–215.

Ulveling, Ralph A. "The Public Library—An Educational Institution?" *Library Resources & Technical Services* 3, no. 1 (1959): 12–20.

Van Slyck, Abigail A. *Free to All: Carnegie Libraries & American Culture, 1890–1920*. Chicago: University of Chicago Press, 1995.

Vann, Sarah K. *Training for Librarianship before 1923: Education for Librarianship Prior to the Publication of Williamson's Report on Training for Library Service*. Chicago: American Library Association, 1961.

Veblen, Thorstein. *The Higher Learning in America: A Memorandum on the Conduct of Universities by Business Men*. New York: Hill and Wang, 1967.

Von Drehle, David. "Fighting Words." *The Washington Post Magazine*, 17 July 2005, sec. W, pp. 12–19.

Walker, Rob. "Stranger than Fiction." *New York Times Magazine*, 1 May 2005, sec. 6, p. 30.

Waples, Douglas. "Community Studies in Reading: I. Reading in the Lower East Side." *Library Quarterly* 3, no. 1 (1933): 1–20.

_____. "Do We Want a Library Science? A Reply." *Library Journal* 56, no. 16 (1931): 743–746.

_____. "The Graduate Library School at Chicago." *Library Quarterly* 1, no. 1 (1931): 26–36.

_____. "People and Libraries." In *Current Issues in Library Administration: Papers Presented before The Library Institute at the University of Chicago, August 1–12, 1938*. Edited by Carleton Bruns Joeckel, 355–370. Chicago: University of Chicago Press, 1939.

_____. *People and Print: Social Aspects of Reading in the Depression*. Chicago: University of Chicago Press, 1937.

_____. "Propaganda and Leisure Reading: A Method by Which to Identify and Offset Propaganda in Students' Leisure Reading." *Journal of Higher Education* 1, no. 2 (1930): 73–77.

_____. "The Relation of Subject Interests to Actual Reading." *Library Quarterly* 2, no. 1 (1932): 42–70.

Waples, Douglas, and Ralph W. Tyler. *What People Want to Read About: A Study of Groups Interests and A Survey of Problems in Adult Reading*. Chicago: American Library Association and the University of Chicago Press, 1932.

Warren, Althea. "Foreword." In Helen E. Haines *Living with Books: The Art of Book Selection*, 2nd ed., vii–x. New York: Columbia University Press, 1950.

Waters, Richard. "Screened Out: Life Online is Widening Choice but Risks a Surrender of Serendipity." *Financial Times* (London, England), 29 December 2005, p. 13.

Waxman, Sharon. "A Small Step at Starbucks from Mocha to Movies." *New York Times*, 1 May 2006, sec. C., p. 1, 2.

Weisman, Steven R. "On Trip to South, Rice Uses an Atypical Topic: Herself." *New York Times*, 24 October 2005, sec. A, p. 15.

Wellard, James Howard. *Book Selection: Its Principles and Practice*. London, England: Grafton & Co., 1937.

Wellman, Hiller C. "President's Address." *Library Journal* 40, no. 7 (1915): 467–471.

Wernick, Andrew. *Promotional Culture: Advertising, Ideology and Symbolic Expression*. London: Sage, 1991.

White, Carl M. *A Historical Introduction to Library Education: Problems and Progress to 1951*. Metuchen, NJ: Scarecrow Press, 1976.

Whitehill, Walter Muir. *Boston Public Library: A Centennial History*. Cambridge, MA: Harvard University Press, 1956.

Wiegand, Wayne A. *The Politics of an Emerging Profession: The American Library Association, 1876–1917*. New York: Greenwood Press, 1986.

_____. "Tunnel Vision and Blind Spots: What the Past Tells Us about the Present: Reflections on the Twentieth-century History of American Librarianship." *Library Quarterly* 69, no. 1 (1999): 1–32.

_____. "Where Stories Aren't Important: An Alternative Perspective on Library and Information Science Education." In *Alternative Library Literature, 2000/2001: A Biennial Anthology*. Edited by Sanford Berman and James P. Danky, 153–156. Jefferson, NC: McFarland, 2002.

Williamson, C. C. "The Place of Research in Library Service." *Library Quarterly* 1, no. 1 (1931): 1–17.

Wilson, Louis R. *The Geography of Reading: A Study of the Distribution and Status of Libraries in the United States*. Chicago: University of Chicago Press, 1938.

Winser, Beatrice. "Encouragement of Serious Reading by Public Libraries." *Library Journal* 28, no. 5 (1903): 237–238.

Winsor, Justin. "Reading in Popular Libraries." In *Public Libraries in the United States of America: Part I: 1876 Report*. Edited by S. R. Warren and S. N. Clark, 431–433. Reprinted by the University of Illinois Graduate School of Library Science, 1966.

Wolf, Naomi. "Wild Things." *New York Times Book Review*, 12 March 2006, sec. 7, p. 22.

Won, Shirley. "Indigo Targets Kids with 'Edutainment.'" *The Globe and Mail*, 30 September 2005, sec. B, p. 3.

Wyatt, Edward. "Attention, Shoppers: Sale on Fresh Books in Aisle 3." *New York Times*, 28 April 2005, sec. E, pp. 1, 10.

_____. "For This Author, Writing is Only the Beginning." *New York Times*, 22 June 2005, sec. E, pp. 1, 10.

_____. "Michael Crichton? He's Just the Author." *New York Times*, 6 February 2005, sec. 3, pp. 1, 4.

Wyer, James I. *Reference Work: A Textbook for Students of Library Work*. Chicago: American Library Association, 1930.

Yarmolinsky, Avrahm. *Russian Literature*. Chicago: American Library Association, 1931.

Young, Arthur P. "Aftermath of a Crusade: World War I and the Enlarged Program of the American Library Association." In *Library Lit. 11—The Best of 1980*. Edited by Bill Katz, 70–84. Metuchen, NJ: Scarecrow Press, 1981.

Youtz, Philip N. *American Life in Architecture*. Chicago: American Library Association, 1932.

Zeitchik, Steven, and Jim Milliot. "The Strangest Program You've Never Heard of." *Publishers Weekly* 252, no. 14 (April 4, 2005): 5–6.

Index